Certified Software Technician

Student Edition

30 Bird Media
510 Clinton Square
Rochester NY 14604
www.30Bird.com

Certified Software Technician

Student Edition

CEO, 30 Bird Media: Adam A. Wilcox

Series designed by: Clifford J. Coryea, Donald P. Tremblay, and Adam A. Wilcox

Managing Editor: Donald P. Tremblay

Instructional Design Lead: Clifford J. Coryea

Instructional Designer: Robert S. Kulik

Keytester: Kurt J. Specht

CST1002-R10-SCB

Table of Contents

Introduction

Welcome to *Computer Software Technician*. This course provides the basic knowledge needed to be a general computer software technician in a vendor-neutral format. The material covers installing, maintaining, and troubleshooting operating systems, software, security, and operational procedures. This course maps to the CompTIA A+ 220-1002 certification exam. Objective coverage is marked throughout the course. You can download an objective map for the series from http://www.30bird.com.

You will benefit most from this if you wish to further your knowledge as a computer technician.

This course assumes that you have PC technical knowledge and operating system familiarity, equivalent to having been a PC technician for at least few months.

After completing this course, you will know how to:

- Identify client operating system features, install Windows and application software, and work with scripts

- Manage and troubleshoot operating systems using built-in administrative tools, such as the Windows Control Panel and command-line utilities

- Configure and troubleshoot problems with Windows resource sharing and network connections

- Recognize common cybersecurity threats, and the security controls which are used to reduce risk

- Identify and use security features built into operating systems, as well as security hardware and software used on workstations and networks

- Secure workstations and mobile devices against security risks, and troubleshoot common security issues such as malware infection

- Apply best practices in IT operations, including policies, documentation, incident response, and data backups and recovery.

- Maintain an appropriate workplace environment via appropriate safety procedures, environmental maintenance, and professional behavior

Course setup

To complete this course, each student and instructor will need to have a computer running Windows 10. Optionally, they may begin with an unformatted computer or components capable of running Windows 10, then assemble and install it in class. Setup instructions and activities are written assuming computers are newly installed with the Windows 10 October 2018 feature update, also known as version 1809. Future feature updates may change the applicability of some exercises and course elements: This is an unavoidable side effect of the Windows 10 update structure.

Hardware requirements for the Windows 10 computer include:

- 64-bit multi-core processor with support for virtualization extensions (for the "Creating a Virtual Machine" exercise)

- 4 GB RAM (for the "Creating a Virtual Machine" exercise)

- 25 GB total primary drive space (50 GB or more recommended)

- Unformatted hard disk space on the primary drive, or a secondary drive (which students may physically install)

- DirectX 9 video card or integrated graphics, with a minimum of 128 MB of graphics memory

- A monitor with 1024x768 or higher resolution (1280x800 or higher recommended)

- Wi-Fi or Ethernet adapter

- A USB storage device, such as a flash drive, containing the student data files. The data files themselves are available at http://www.30bird.com. If USB storage devices aren't available for all students, they can also be instructed to access the data files on any other storage media, but exercises related to USB devices will not work as published.

Software requirements include:

- Windows 10 with October 2018 Update (Version 1809). If performing the "Installing and upgrading Windows" exercise, you will need it on installable media in the class.

- Python 3.7.1 or later (downloaded and installed by students)

Network requirements include:

- Internet access, used to access websites, download software, and use cloud storage

- A free Microsoft account for each student. Microsoft accounts must be associated with email accounts, but you can use a free email account such as Outlook.com or Gmail

For hands-on labs and instructor demonstrations, you should gather some or all of the following hardware:

- Computers with other operating systems, such as different Windows versions, MacOS, or Linux

- A computer with some sort of solvable network connection issue

- An uninterruptible power supply and driver software

Because this course involves setting up accounts and altering Windows settings, it's recommended that each course begin with a new installation of Windows 10 and a new Microsoft account. If the same installation has been used for a previous class, some exercises won't work as written.

1. On each student workstation, perform an installation of Windows 10.

   You can also wait until the "Operating systems" chapter so that students install Windows themselves, but students will not be able to complete earlier exercises using Windows on the same computer

   • Use a Microsoft account as the primary user

   • Enable OneDrive and Cortana

   • Configure a device PIN

2. Download the *Computer Software Technician* data files from http://www.30bird.com/

   If you're performing the "Creating a virtual machine" optional exercise, you also need to download the Linux Mint VM. Since it is much larger than the other data files, it is a separate download.

3. Extract the data files to the USB flash drive.

Software technician skills inventory

If you're taking this course to prepare for a certification exam, odds are that it has some topics you'll need to study in depth, and others you just need a quick refresher on. Maybe there are some you know so well you can move right past them. To make the best use of your time, start this course with a quick skills inventory. This isn't a test itself: it's just a self-evaluation of how confident you are in your own knowledge of the course material.

List your skills and/or knowledge for each of the following topics. Use a 1-10 scale, with 1 representing no knowledge and 10 representing expertise. You can then use it as a guideline of which portions of the course you might need to spend more time studying. If you know very little about any of the topics, you might want to consider beginning with a more introductory course first. On the other hand, if you know all of these topics very well, you might be better suited seeking a more advanced course in computer networking or security.

Chapter	Module	Skill	Skill Level
1	A	Identifying features found in different Windows versions	
1	B	Identifying features of non-Windows operating systems	
1	C	Installing and upgrading Windows	
1	D	Planning and performing application installations	
1	D	Identifying script formats and elements	
2	A	Using Windows system utilities	
2	B	Using the Windows Control Panel	
2	C	Using command-line utilities	
2	D	Troubleshooting operating system and application problems	
3	A	Configuring folder and printer sharing in Windows	
3	A	Joining a computer to an Active Directory domain	
3	B	Creating and configuring network connections in Windows	
3	B	Using remote access programs	
3	C	Troubleshooting network connections using command line and GUI tools	
4	A	Recognizing common cybersecurity threats and vulnerabilities	
4	B	Choosing logical security controls such as encryption, authentication, and access control	

Chapter	Module	Skill	Skill Level
4	B	Choosing physical security controls to protect IT resources	
5	A	Managing access permissions for local and shared files	
5	A	Using Windows security policies in local and Active Directory environments	
5	B	Configuring Windows firewall	
5	B	Identifying network-based security appliances	
6	A	Securing workstations	
6	A	Managing Windows accounts	
6	A	Protecting data with storage encryption and secure disposal	
6	B	Configuring security options on mobile devices	
6	C	Securing network hosts and devices	
6	D	Troubleshooting security problems	
6	D	Removing malware	
7	A	Complying with and enforcing organizational policies	
7	A	Using and maintaining IT documentation	
7	B	Responding to security incidents	
7	C	Planning and performing data backups	
8	A	Following component, personal, and materials safety procedures	
8	B	Identifying hazardous materials and environmental conditions in the workplace	
8	B	Installing surge protectors and uninterruptible power supplies	
8	C	Behaving professionally with customers and non-technical users	

Chapter 1: Operating systems

You will:

- Compare and contrast the features and requirements of various Microsoft operating systems.
- Learn how to install a Windows operating system.
- Identify common features and functionality of the Mac OS and Linux operating systems.

Module A: Windows versions and features

Microsoft has released almost a dozen versions of Windows over the past 20 years, and each version has its own set of features.

You will learn:

- The different versions of Windows currently in use that are tested on the A+ exam.

- The features that set each operating system apart from the other and which features they have in common.

About operating systems

In general, an operating system is the central piece of system software on a computer, especially powerful and complex computers like PCs. It manages the hardware resources of the computer and uses them to provide *services* that can be utilized by programs, like user applications, which run on the computer. For example, on a desktop PC, the operating system performs task management for running multiple applications at once, and provides services to those applications such as file management, network access, and a user interface for input and output. In addition to a user interface and management tools, operating systems frequently include a variety of bundled user applications, as well as the ability to install and run third-party software.

In the typical enterprise environment, you're likely to run into four main OS categories:

Workstation   Used for desktop and laptop computers. Workstations may support multiple users but are generally only used by a single person at a time; their design prioritizes user interfaces including input, output, and application support. Common workstation operating systems include Windows, macOS, and Linux.

Server   Used for computers that primarily provide services for other computers over the network; examples include web servers, email servers, and application servers. Servers tend to support multiple concurrent users, but are usually accessed through the network. Servers also tend to use Windows, macOS, or Linux and other UNIX-like operating systems; however, they usually use server editions with more focus on network services and less on local user applications.

Mobile   Used for mobile devices such as smartphones and tablets which can perform general computing capabilities. Mobile operating systems are similar to those on workstations but are specialized for mobile hardware and networks; they also tend to be more restrictive and tightly integrated. Common mobile operating systems include iOS, Android, and ChromeOS.

Embedded   Used for specialized devices that don't perform general computing tasks, ranging from consumer devices like TVs and game consoles to network devices like printers and routers. Embedded operating systems usually provide limited services and interface features, and don't allow users to load and run arbitrary applications. Instead, they're focused on the core functions of the device. Some embedded operating systems are more limited versions of a server or mobile OS.

OS compatibility

Choosing an operating system is more than finding one with a set of bundled features that you like. It must also be compatible with the hardware you need to install it on, and with the software you want to use with it. In networked environments, you even need to consider its compatibility with other computers it needs to communicate with.

 Exam Objective(s): 220-1002 1.1.1, 1.1.5

Since the operating system allocates hardware resources, it must interface closely with hardware devices. An embedded OS might be built for very specific hardware, but in general an OS includes a variety of *drivers* for hardware devices it supports. Hardware manufacturers can also create drivers for their own devices, but a given device needs a different driver for each operating system version the manufacturer wants to support.

In turn, installed applications and other software must be compatible with the OS. In general, executable programs must be designed for a specific OS, such as Windows or Linux, so you need to have a version that's compatible with yours. They might also work only with specific versions of a given OS, so read the system requirements for any software you want to use.

Both the OS and installed applications must be compatible with the CPU architecture of the computer, such as Intel x86 used by desktop PCs or ARM used by most mobile devices. Both x86 and ARM are also available in 32-bit and 64-bit variants.

Note: "x64" hardware and software generally means 64-bit x86, while "x86" often refers specifically 32-bit systems.

- If your CPU is 32-bit, your OS, drivers, and apps must be 32-bit.
- If your CPU is 64-bit, you can install both 32-bit and 64-bit operating systems and applications.

  - A 32-bit OS can only run 32-bit applications.
  - A 64-bit OS can run 64-bit applications. Most also provide support for 32-bit applications.

One of the main reasons 64-bit operating systems have become popular is because 32-bit computers cannot address more than 4 GB of system RAM. In fact, for technical reasons it's usually even less. To use 4GB of RAM or more both your CPU and OS must be 64-bit. Fortunately, modern operating systems all feature 64-bit support, but you might need to make sure you're installing the right edition.

OS updates and support

Just like with any other software, operating system vendors vary in how they provide updates and technical support for their products, and spell them out in the license agreement. In general, vendors will provide free downloadable bugfixes and security patches on a regular basis, which can be installed manually or automatically. These free updates may include other updates such as drivers or even entirely new features. On embedded devices with a firmware-based OS an update might require you to download and install a whole new firmware. Technical support, especially via live technician, may be included or require an additional fee depending on the license.

Exam Objective(s): 220-1002 1.1.4

Larger updates such as new operating system versions or major feature changes might be another matter.

- Some vendors provide free upgrades, while others require you to purchase or install an entirely new product.
- Installing a major update may be a more complicated process than applying security patches, and might require you to completely reinstall the operating system or applications.
- The new version might even have different hardware requirements and drivers; if it's not compatible with your existing hardware, you won't be able to upgrade without hardware changes.
- OS upgrades can introduce compatibility issues with existing applications, so enterprise customers in particular tend to upgrade operating systems only after a careful testing process.

Vendors may also specify the *end-of-life* (*EOL*) of a given OS version. Once the software reaches EOL, further updates and support will not be provided. If bugs or security problems crop up at that point, users must address the problems themselves, or else upgrade to a newer software version. Sometimes enterprise users will keep *legacy systems* far beyond the operating system EOL, especially if they rely on specialized hardware and software not supported by newer systems.

Windows versions

Microsoft has been releasing Windows operating systems since the 1980s, but the Windows look that we know today has been around since 1995. Windows is the dominant operating system in the world, installed on more PCs in far greater number than any other operating system. Most computer users have encountered Windows at one time or another, from Windows 95, through Windows XP, and up to the current version, Windows 10. Even if you've used a computer just to browse the Internet or send and receive email, chances are you've done it on a PC with a Windows operating system.

Exam Objective(s): 220-1002 1.1.2.1, 1.2.1, 1.2.2, 1.2.3, 1.2.4

Windows is used for both client workstations and servers. The following table lists each Windows client operating system released since 2001.

Windows release dates

Year	Windows version	Notes
2001	Windows XP	First NT-based Windows marketed to both home and business users. Oldest Windows version still found in common use.
2006	Windows Vista	Major changes in security and functionality. First Windows version with widespread 64-bit support.
2009	Windows 7	A refinement of Windows Vista, which quickly replaced earlier versions. Still very common, especially in enterprise environments.
2012	Windows 8	Major changes in interface and online functionality. First version to support Windows Store apps.
2013	Windows 8.1	A free upgrade to Windows 8 intended to refine shortcomings and unpopular features.
2015	Windows 10	Uses a "rolling release" schedule with regular free feature updates that add new features but don't change the version number.

Each version of Windows has multiple editions, tailored toward different audiences. Some editions are for the home user and have features that are optimized for browsing the web, gaming, and storing and playing multimedia files, such as music and movies. Other editions are more for the business user and have the ability to join and participate in Windows security groups, called domains, where they can share networked resources, such as Internet connections, file servers and printers.

Starting with Windows XP, each Windows version has been available both in 32-bit (x86) and 64-bit (x64) editions. This does actually affect your hardware and applications:

- 32-bit and 64-bit editions use separate device drivers.

- In practice, 32-bit Windows editions can't address more then 2.5-3 GB of system RAM.

- Only 64-bit Windows editions can run 64-bit applications or use certain 64-bit processor features, while 32-bit Windows editions are more compatible with some very old software.

The following table lists the Windows versions you need to know for the A+ exam, and the editions offered within each version. Unless otherwise noted, each is available in both 32-bit and 64-bit variants.

Windows versions

Windows version	Editions
Windows 7	• Windows 7 Starter (32-bit only) • Windows 7 Home Basic • Windows 7 Home Premium • Windows 7 Professional • Windows 7 Ultimate • Windows 7 Enterprise
Windows 8	• Windows 8 • Windows 8 Pro • Windows 8 Enterprise
Windows 8.1	• Windows 8.1 • Windows 8.1 Pro • Windows 8.1 Enterprise
Windows 10	• Windows 10 Home • Windows 10 Pro • Windows 10 Education • Windows 10 Enterprise

In addition to the client versions of Windows discussed above, there are multiple versions of *Windows Server*, designed for network servers. While the core of the operating system is the same, Windows Server includes a number of network services you wouldn't normally need on a desktop PC, and can even support additional hardware such as multiple processors and more RAM than a typical desktop can use. Windows Server generally has a name corresponding to its year of release, such as Windows Server 2016, and it has an interface and features based off the client edition of Windows that's current when it was released.

There are other specialty versions of Windows you might encounter, intended for other devices than general-purpose PCs.

- *Windows Mobile* (previously Windows Phone) is for use on smartphones running on ARM processors. It is no longer being developed, but still is supported with security fixes. Its numbering generally corresponds to that of client versions with similar features, such as Windows 10 Mobile or Windows Phone 8.1.

- *Windows IoT* (formerly Windows Embedded) is for use on specialized embedded devices. Windows 10 IoT supports x86, x64, and ARM processors, but some older versions also supported other architectures.

Windows interface styles

As computer hardware and uses have evolved over the years, so has the Windows interface. With a little practice, you can learn what Windows edition you're looking at from a glance at the desktop or an open window. Even most third-party apps take on appearance elements from the Windows version you're currently using.

Exam Objective(s): 220-1002 1.2.5

Windows 7 uses the *Windows Aero* interface with glassy-looking windows, highly detailed icons, and a lot of flashy visual effects. Aero was introduced with Windows Vista, but was an evolutionary improvement over long-term trends of colorful, complex icons and soft, detailed windows. Some Windows 7 components use a *Ribbon* interface similar to that of Microsoft Office, while others use a combination of text menus and graphical toolbars like older Windows applications. Third-party apps designed for Windows 7 and earlier use similar interfaces.

The Windows 7 Start menu and an application window.

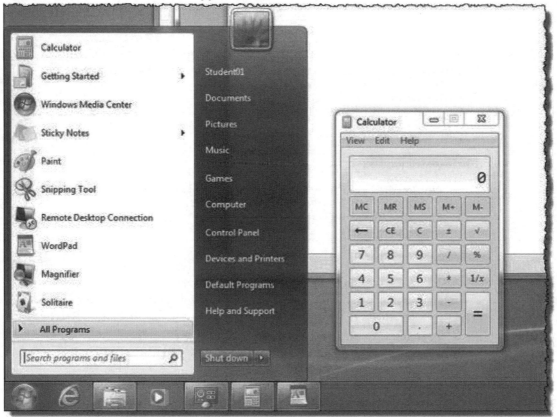

Windows 8 introduced the markedly different **Modern UI**. In a departure from Aero, Modern uses bold, solid colors backing larger text and simply colored icons. Modern windows have sharper corners and less ornamentation. Instead of tiny detailed icons and text, information such as application lists are shown as large and clear *tiles*. Applications designed for the Modern UI have more streamlined interfaces as well, with larger menu options and other controls. Compared to Aero, these changes make the Modern UI easier to navigate on touchscreens, mobile devices, and under changing lighting conditions.

The Start menu in Windows 10

Core Windows features

Each version of Windows introduces new features, and retires or replaces old ones. but most core features even in Windows 10 today were included in Windows 7, Windows Vista, or earlier. The names and details change over the years of course, but if you learn to use one version of Windows, you'll have knowledge to help you with others. Even entirely different operating systems still need to perform most of the same tasks, so they'll have corresponding features.

Action Center in Windows 7

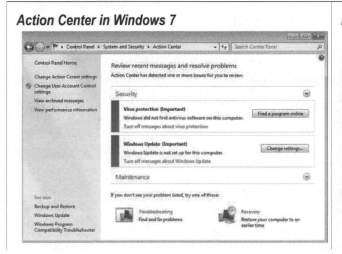

PowerShell

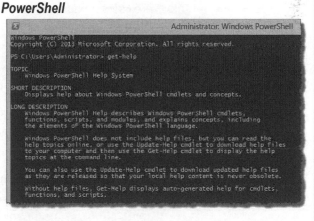

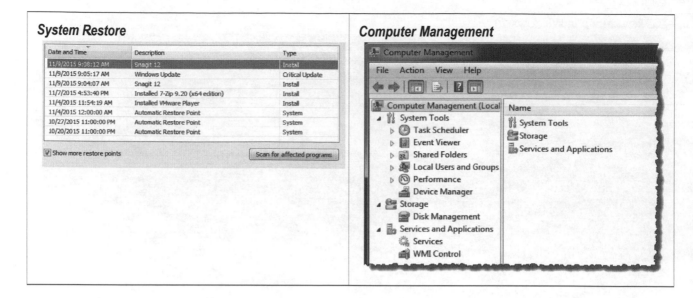

Windows Explorer / File Explorer	The *Windows shell*, or the primary application used to interact with Windows. It includes both an interface to navigate the folders and other locations on your computer and the network, and the *taskbar* that displays running applications on your desktop.
Start Menu	A menu located on the Windows taskbar, which allows you to access all installed applications and many other Windows features. In Windows 8 it was replaced by the slightly different **Start screen**, but in Windows 10 a new Start menu combines the features of both.
Command Prompt	A text-based interface, similar to that used on the oldest PCs. It provides an alternative route for advanced users to perform many operating system tasks. It can also run command-line applications that don't use the graphical Windows environment.
PowerShell	A more advanced command prompt included with Windows 7 and later. It provides a wider variety of commands and features than the original Command Prompt, and also provides a scripting language that power users can use for task automation.
Search / Cortana	Windows always had some features to help you search for files and programs on your computer, but in Windows Vista and later it became more robust and easier to use. Later versions expanded this to include online search results, and in Windows 10 the *Cortana* personal assistant also allows you to perform voice searches and arrange your schedule.
Control Panel/Settings	A utility providing central access to Windows settings. Control Panel is included in all versions of Windows, while the complementary Settings app was introduced in Windows 8. You can use both to change system or hardware settings, uninstall applications, configure networking features, manage user accounts, and personalize the appearance and behavior of Windows.
Network and Sharing Center	An interface to manage your computer's network controllers and connections, both to the internet and to local networks.
Action Center / Security Center	An interface to manage built-in utilities to secure and protect your computer. These include Windows Firewall, Windows Defender, and troubleshooting and recovery tools. In Windows 10 the "Action Center" refers to a separate feature that displays system notifications and quick access features.

Computer Management	A software console allowing direct access to a number of system administration tools. You can use it to schedule automated tasks, partition hard drives, view logged system events, and manage Windows services and hardware devices.
Event Viewer	A logging tool that records errors, warnings, and routine events generated by Windows and its installed applications. You can use it to troubleshoot hardware and software problems or security issues.
System Restore	A feature that automatically saves configuration settings periodically or before system changes. If you encounter system problems, you may be able to fix them by reverting to a restore point.
Windows Accessories	User applications included with Windows. Some include Notepad, WordPad, Paint, Calculator, Internet Explorer, and Windows Media Player.

New Windows 8 features

In addition to the Metro UI, Windows 8 added several important Windows features and dramatically changed some existing ones. You may not encounter Windows 8 or 8.1 PCs in many workplaces, since they didn't entirely replace Windows 7 and many Windows 8 users took advantage of a free upgrade to Windows 10. However, most new features in Windows 8 and 8.1 are also in Windows 10, so you should know them in order to support newer editions too.

One of the most dramatic changes in Windows 8 is its integration with Microsoft's online services by linking your user profile with an online *Microsoft account*. You can even use a Microsoft account as your local user account. By linking to your online account, you can access online services like email and calendar, and share your user data and settings across multiple devices. Windows 8.1 adds the *OneDrive* cloud storage app, which allows you to synchronize user files between multiple PCs.

Another big change is the *Windows Store* (*Microsoft Store* in Windows 10.) It's an app store similar to those found on mobile operating systems like Android and iOS. By signing in with your Microsoft account you can download free or paid applications and games designed for Windows 8 and later; you can also download media files such as movies, TV shows, and e-books. Both free and paid content is linked to your Microsoft account, meaning that you can install it on multiple devices provided you link that device to the same account.

Beyond these changes, Windows 8 added a number of new integrated apps and accessories, and updated existing ones. Important changes from an administration and support perspective include:

- A Settings app which allows easier access to many features previously in Control Panel.

- An updated version of Windows Defender which includes real-time antivirus scanning.

- Improved backup and restore capability using the File History feature.

- Improved support for hardware such as touchscreens, multiple displays, UEFI firmware, and USB 3.0 controllers.

Windows 8.1 was a free upgrade release for Windows 8, containing primarily refinements and updates of existing features. Some important changes include:

- The *OneDrive* cloud storage app, which enables you to synchronize user files between multiple PCs via your Microsoft account. It was available as a separate download previously.

- A new *Task View* task switcher, with support for multiple virtual desktops.

- Ability to boot directly to the Windows desktop, like Windows 7 but unlike Windows 8.

New Windows 10 features

The most dramatic change to Windows 10 isn't its interface or bundled apps, but rather how it is distributed and updated. While older versions of Windows distributed regular security and stability updates, when a new version of Windows came out, you'd only get it if you purchased an upgrade license or a new computer. By contrast, Windows 10 was released with what Microsoft calls an "operating system as a service" model, and what some other sources call a "rolling release".

Microsoft still releases regular security and stability updates for Windows 10, but every six months or so comes a *feature update* that adds or changes Windows features. Each update has an internal build number and possibly a catchy name such as "Anniversary Update" or "Fall Creators Update", but no matter how much changes over time they're still all under the same Windows 10 product rather than being "Windows 11." Whenever a new version comes out, it will be freely available to all Windows 10 users—this way, all of your devices will be using the same version of Windows. In theory, this isn't just convenient for users, but it means that Microsoft doesn't have to support several versions of Windows all at once.

One drawback of this system is that enterprise users in particular might experience compatibility or stability issues with new updates. For this reason, business users of Windows 10 can join release channels that delay feature updates until they are more thoroughly tested.

As of the October 2018 feature update, some of the big changes from Windows 8.1 include:

- A new Start menu that combines features of the Windows 7 Start menu and Windows 8 Start screen
- Windows Store apps that operate in windowed mode, rather than full screen as in Windows 8
- *Cortana*, a digital assistant and search tool which responds to both keyboard and voice requests
- *Edge*, a newly designed web browser replacing the deprecated Internet Explorer
- The Microsoft Defender Security Center, replacing the security-themed Action Center
- A new Action Center on the taskbar, used for quick settings and centralized notifications
- Improved integration with phones and mobile devices

Deprecated Windows features

New versions of Windows sometimes deprecate existing features, or remove them entirely. Sometimes they're just moved around or replaced. For example, since Windows 7 configuration settings have gradually been moved from the Control Panel utility to the Settings app, and the old Photo Viewer application has been replaced with a Photos app having similar features and a much different interface. In other cases, features are replaced by much different ones, or removed entirely, often because they weren't widely used. In those cases, after a Windows upgrade, you might need to find a third-party tool with similar features.

The following features were once popular, but have been deprecated or removed since Windows 7:

- *Gadgets* featured in Windows Vista and Windows 7 proved to be a security risk and were disabled by Windows 7 updates. They are not available in later versions.
- Beginning with Windows 8, File History has replaced Backup and Restore. The old utility is still available as "Backup and Restore (Windows 7)". Its related *Shadow Copies* function was limited in Windows 8, but restored in Windows 10.
- In Windows 8 and later, Windows Media Center and DVD video playback are no longer included.
- In Windows 10, Edge has replaced Internet Explorer as the default browser, but IE remains available for compatibility reasons.
- The April 2018 Update for Windows 10 removed the Homegroup resource sharing feature introduced in Windows 7.

Corporate and enterprise features

In the past, business and home editions of Windows could be very different, even to the point of different kernels and compatibility with third party software. On any modern version of Windows, however, the only significant difference is that Pro, Enterprise, Education, and Ultimate editions have some built-in features that Home editions do not. Most of these have to do with centralized management and security features that are common in enterprise networks but not often used by home users.

Exam Objective(s): 220-1002 1.2.5

The following features are found in any Enterprise, Education, or Ultimate edition of Windows 7 and later, but not in Home editions. Most of them will also be found in Pro editions, but the details vary by version, so double-check before you choose an edition to install.

Hardware support   While all versions of Windows support the same hardware devices, 64-bit Professional and Enterprise editions can generally support more physical RAM and CPUs than Home editions. Unless you're using a very limited edition such as Windows 7 Starter, it is unlikely to be a limitation on all but the most powerful workstations.

Domain access   Allows the computer to join an Active Directory domain managed by a Windows server. Domains allow central management of user accounts and network resources, as well as *Group Policies* that can enforce system and user settings throughout the domain.

RDP host   Allows the computer to serve as a host for remote desktop connections. Home editions can still run the RDP client application, but cannot serve as hosts.

EFS   Allows users to protect specific files and folders from unauthorized access with *Encrypting File System* encryption.

BitLocker   When enabled, protects entire drives and volumes with full disk encryption. Not available in Windows 7 Professional, but available in Windows 8/8.1/10 Pro.

BranchCache   Optimizes network performance on wide area networks by letting computers cache and share downloaded files with other local computers. Not available in Pro editions, A similar principle is used by all Windows 10 editions for distributing updates, but it is more limited than the enterprise feature.

Not all features found only in some editions are business-oriented. Some other examples include:

- Windows Media Center is not included in Windows 7 Starter or Home Basic, and has been discontinued for Windows 10. It is included in Windows 8 and 8.1, but on Pro editions it must be installed as an add-on.

- Some entertainment features such as games may not be installed by default in Pro and Enterprise editions.

- In Europe and South Korea each Windows edition has a corresponding N or KN edition which removes Windows Media Player and other bundled media features to comply with anti-trust regulation. If you want those features, you can download them as a separate "Media Feature Pack"

Exercise: Identifying Windows versions and features

Microsoft evolved the Windows operating system with each new product line. The included features vary between product line and versions within the product line. As a PC technician, you must be able to identify the features included in the version you are going to implement and support within your organization.

Do This	How & Why
1. Open an internet browser.	
2. Use your search engine to find articles comparing Windows 7, Windows 8, and Windows 10.	
3. Based on your findings, which Windows versions and editions would best suit the needs of your company? Why?	
4. What older versions of Windows are at use at your company? Why haven't they been upgraded yet?	
5. Based on your findings, what versions of Windows would meet your needs for a personal computer? Why?	
6. Under what conditions would you foresee upgrading your personal computer to Windows 10? If you already upgraded, why?	

Assessment: Windows versions and features

1. Which of the following is true about 64-bit support in Windows? Choose the best response.

   - 32-bit support was removed beginning with Windows 8.1,
   - 64-bit support was first introduced in Windows 7.
   - All workstation product lines from Windows Vista through Windows 10 come in both 32-bit and 64-bit editions.
   - Home editions are 32-bit while professional editions are 64-bit.

2. At most, how much memory can the 32-bit versions of Windows address? Choose the best response.

   - 2 GB
   - 4 GB
   - 16 GB
   - 32 GB

3. With which Windows product line did Microsoft cut back the number of audience-targeted versions from five to three? Choose the best response.

   - Windows 7
   - Windows 8
   - Windows 8.1
   - Windows 10

4. The Windows user interface feature "Aero" was included in which Windows product lines? Choose the best response.

   - Windows Vista
   - Windows 7
   - Windows 8
   - Windows 10

5. Which Windows features were not included in Windows 7?

   - Action Center
   - Cortana
   - Event Viewer
   - Real-time antivirus scanning in Windows Defender
   - System Restore
   - Windows PowerShell

6. The Windows Store was introduced with which product line? Choose the best response.

   - Windows Vista
   - Windows 7
   - Windows 8
   - Windows 8.1

7. What features were available in the initial version of Windows 7, but not in the latest version of Windows 10? Choose all that apply.

   - Backup and Restore
   - Computer Management
   - Desktop Gadgets
   - Homegroups
   - Shadow Copies

Module B: Non-Windows operating systems

While Windows is the dominant client operating system, there are two others you'll likely encounter while providing technical support: Apple Mac OS and Linux.

In this module, you'll learn:

- Common features and functionality of the Mac OS.
- Common features and functionality of the Linux operating system.
- Basic Linux commands.

Mac OS

Mac OS is the operating system for Macintosh computers produced by Apple. Like Windows and Linux, Mac OS has had multiple iterations throughout the years, with Mac OS X versions being the latest releases beginning in 2001. In addition to version numbers, Mac OS X releases are also known by their codenames. Some notable releases are described in the following table.

Exam Objective(s): 220-1002 1.1.2.2

Mac OS X selected releases

Mac OS X version and codename	Year	Introduced
10.3 Panther	2003	Fast User Switching, an updated Finder, and the new browser Safari. It also included built-in support for Microsoft Active Directory.
10.4 Tiger	2005	Support for Intel x86 architecture in version 10.4.4. It also introduced Spotlight and new versions of Mail and Safari.
10.7 Lion	2011	AirDrop file sharing, emoji support, and Recovery Partition. It also bundled FaceTime with the operating system.
10.8 Mountain Lion	2012	Notification Center, some iOS features, such as Game Center, and OS X updates through the App Store.
10.11 El Capitan	2015	Support for snapping side-by-side windows, San Francisco system typeface, a Notes overhaul, and the System Integrity Protection security feature.
10.12 Sierra	2016	Siri digital assistant, improved iCloud Drive functions, tabbed apps, improved Photos app, and shared clipboard with iPhone.
10.13 High Sierra	2017	APFS file system, browser and media improvements, and refinements to other bundled apps.
10.14 Mojave	2018	New App Store, Dark Mode to reduce eyestrain, Continuity Camera, Quick Look, and security improvements.

Mac OS features and tools

The Mac OS has plenty of features that make it the favorite of many computer users over the more widely used Windows operating system. The table below highlights some important Mac OS features. Many of them correspond closely to similar Windows features, but the specific details for each will differ.

Exam Objective(s): 220-1002 1.9.2, 1.9.3

Mac OS features

Mac OS feature	Use it when you want to...
Mission Control	Get a look at all your open windows, and create or switch between multiple desktops. It provides an easy way to navigate among the resources you're using at any given time. Similar to Task View in Windows.
Keychain	Store and manage passwords for applications, web sites, and network shares. In addition to passwords, Keychain stores private keys and certificates.
Spotlight	Search your Mac for all kinds of files, including documents, music, photos, emails, and contacts. It also provides suggestions for Internet resources.
iCloud	Store your files in the cloud for access from any location in the world using the internet and your Mac, Windows PC, or mobile device. Analogous to OneDrive in Windows 10.
Gestures	Perform just about any action on a Mac with a touchscreen. You can swipe with one or more fingers, tap, pinch, rotate, swipe, and drag to open and close apps and operating system features, such as Mission Control and Notification Center.
Finder	Organize and navigate your files and folders. It's similar to File Explorer in Windows.
Remote Disc	Access files on a CD or DVD on another computer. This feature can't be used to access music, movies, or copy protected software discs.
Dock	Access your favorite apps with just a click. You can configure the Dock to hold shortcuts to your most-used apps so they're only a click away. It's similar to pinning apps to the taskbar in Windows.
Boot Camp	Install Windows on your Mac by repartitioning your hard drive. After the installation, you can switch between Mac OS X and Windows, a convenient feature for those who need to work with both Mac and Windows operating systems and applications.

The table below describes some common tools that you can use when working with the Mac OS and while you're troubleshooting problems users might be having.

Mac OS tools

Tool	Use it when you want to...
Time Machine	Back up your data or schedule regular backups to an external hard drive, Apple's Time Capsule storage unit, or a hard drive connected to an AirPort Extreme base station. You can also use Time Machine to restore data from backup.
Snapshot/Restore	Create a snapshot of an APFS file system representing system files and settings at that time, or restore from that backup. Snapshots are available in High Sierra and later, and have some similarities to Windows restore points.
Terminal	Access the operating system through a command-line shell. You can use Terminal to execute a wide variety of commands, including configuring Time Machine backup intervals, showing hidden files in Finder, and accessing your Mac remotely. Since modern macOS is related to Unix, it's very similar to a Linux shell.
Force Quit	Force an unresponsive app to close. You can use this feature when you're trying to troubleshoot app and system issues.
Screen sharing	Troubleshoot problems or coach a user on a remote computer. This feature is especially useful when the user or computer you're working with isn't anywhere near your location. But it can be just as useful when you're working with someone in the office next to yours.
Disk Utility	Perform setup or maintenance on hard disks. You can use the Disk Utility to create and format partitions, or to check for disk errors and file system problems. You can also use it to create disk images, or recover a disk from a backup image.

Mac OS best practices

As with any operating system, there are some best practices in the Mac OS that you can follow to ensure optimal performance of your Macs for you and your users. The table below lists some basic administrative tasks you can perform to support your Mac users.

 Exam Objective(s): 220-1002 1.9.1

Mac OS best practices

Best practice	Why it's important
Scheduled backups	To protect against data loss. Regular backups to a removable media or to an offsite location can help prevent data loss due to system problems and physical damage and theft. You can configure regular backups in Time Machine. iCloud functions provide some cloud backup capabilities.
Scheduled disk maintenance	To prevent data loss from corrupt hard disk sectors and to improve read/write time. Use Disk Utility to manage your hard disks.

Best practice	Why it's important
System updates/App store	To keep the system up-to-date to fix bugs and patch security flaws in the operating system and installed applications. You can update Mac OS X using the Mac App Store.
Patch management	To keep up with operating system fixes and patches for security flaws.
Driver/firmware updates	To ensure devices work properly.
Anti-virus and anti-malware updates	To protect against hackers and threats of data destruction or theft.

Linux

Linux is an operating system in the Unix family that is used to run personal computers, servers, tablets, and smartphones. Linux is an open source software, meaning its source code maybe be modified and distributed both commercially and non-commercially, unlike both Windows and Mac OS. Linux is typically packaged as a distribution, which include the operating system and bundled applications. Some of the popular distributions include Debian, Ubuntu, Fedora, and Gentoo. Commercial distributions include Red Hat Linux and SUSE Linux Server. The figure below shows an installation of Ubuntu.

Exam Objective(s): 220-1002 1.1.2.3

Ubuntu with System Settings displayed

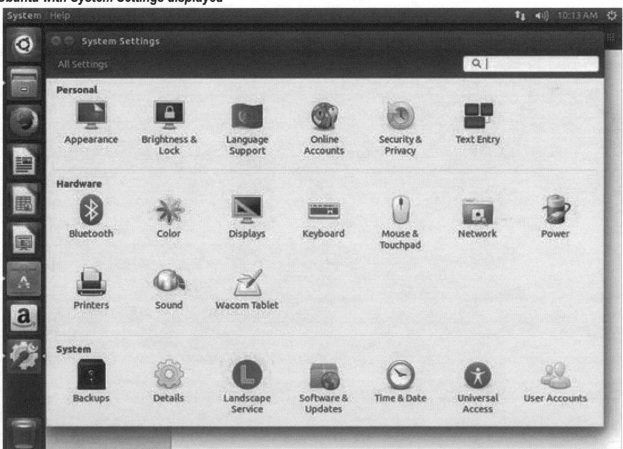

Linux features

Linux feature	Use it when you want to...
Workspaces (multiple desktops)	Organize your open windows into groups. You can create workspaces for different functions, such as separating work-related projects or creating a separate space for personal use.
Gestures	Use finger motions on a touchscreen to manipulate the operating system, providing the same functionality as gestures on Windows or Mac OS touchscreen devices.

Basic Linux commands

Like Windows and Mac, Linux offers a flexible command-line interface called Terminal, which you can see in the following figure. You can use Terminal to configure settings on your Linux computer and help troubleshoot any issues you might be having. The table below lists many useful commands that you can use to manage the operating system from day to day. To get help with a specific command, enter the command with *-h* or *-help*.

 Exam Objective(s): 220-1002 1.9.4

Basic Linux commands

Linux command	Use it when you want to...
`ls`	View a list of directories on the computer.
`grep`	Search for a pattern of text in files and display the results. This command helps you find files with specific words or phrases.
`pwd`	Show the directory you're currently in (the working directory). Not to be confused with `passwd`.
`cd`	Change from one directory to another.
`mv`	Move a file to a specific directory.
`cp`	Copy a file.
`rm`	Delete (remove) a file or directory.
`chown`	Change the owner of a particular file or directory.
`chmod`	Modify file permissions.
`shutdown`	Shut down the system.
`passwd`	Change the password for a user account.
`iwconfig`	Display information about your wireless network adapters and addressing configuration.
`ifconfig`	Display information about your wired network adapters and addressing configuration.

Linux command	Use it when you want to...
`ps`	Display the running system processes. You can use this to troubleshoot system problems.
`kill`	Send a signal to end a process or modify its behavior. You can use this to stop malfunctioning programs, or restart system daemons.
`su`	Login as a superuser from your current login.
`sudo`	Execute a command as another user. You can use `sudo` to execute a command as a user with higher privileges, such as the root user.
`Apt -get`	Updating, upgrading, or installing packages.
`vi`	Edit text files.
`dd`	Convert and copy a file.
`clear`	Clear the Terminal screen.

Executing basic Linux commands

You enter a command at the prompt in Terminal. For more information about a specific command's syntax, use the help system in Terminal.

1. Open Terminal.
2. Type the command name, adding any options, using this syntax: **command** *-option* or **command** *argument*. The figure below shows an example.

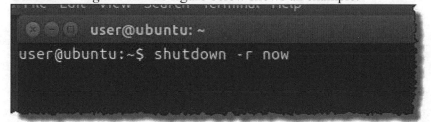

3. Press **Enter**.

Mobile device operating systems

Laptop computers typically run the same workstation operating systems as desktops, but there are several popular operating systems for smaller devices.

Exam Objective(s): 220-1002 1.1.3

Android	Developed by Google. Android is an open source operating system, which means that application developers have access to the operating system's framework for creating applications. It is based on the Linux kernel, but much of the rest of the operating system is very different from desktop Linux distributions. Android is found on a wide variety of smartphones, tablets, and IoT devices.
iOS	A vendor-specific operating system developed by Apple, meaning developers must register as Apple application developers and use Apple's software development kit (SDK). It is used exclusively by Apple mobile devices.
Chrome OS	Also designed by Google, but originally designed for inexpensive laptops known as *Chromebooks* rather than smartphones. Chrome OS uses the Chrome web browser as its primary interface, but can also run *Chrome Apps*. Some devices can run Android or Linux apps as well. Chrome OS itself is only available pre-installed on devices from Google's hardware partners, but the related *Chromium OS* is open-source. Chromebooks are especially popular in K-12 educational environments, and there are now Chrome based desktops and tablets. found in a variety of other environments.
Windows	The same closed-source, proprietary operating system Microsoft markets for workstations and servers now has features specifically meant for mobile hardware and usage patterns. Currently, Microsoft is phasing out the Windows 10 Mobile brand designed for ARM-based smartphones and tablets, but Windows 10 itself is popular for x86 tablets and 2-in-1 laptops. The Windows 10 IoT family is intended for embedded IoT devices.

In addition to Apple's SDK, there are other SDKs and application development kits (ADKs) for developing apps for the various operating systems. App development and availability drives device sales as users choose devices that have the apps they want.

Mobile OS features

Each operating system offers a variety of features, some unique, most similar in some form or another. The table below lists some of the more prominent features of each operating system and the devices they run.

Operating system features

Feature	Description
App source	All the software vendors offer a place to obtain free and paid apps. • Android and Chrome: Google Play • iOS: Apple App store • Windows: Microsoft Store
Screen orientation (accelerometer/gyroscope)	Tablets and smartphones use accelerometers and gyroscopes to determine which way the devices is being held and detect how they are being moved. This enables automatic screen rotation, exercise step counters, and other app features that rely on movement of the device itself.

Feature	Description
Screen calibration	Some laptops and nearly all smaller devices have touchscreens. Modern capacitive touchscreens seldom need to be recalibrated, but it's a regular part of maintenance for older resistive touchscreens. If you need to test or change screen calibration, check its documentation for a built-in utility, or seek one on its app store.
GPS and geotracking	Mobile devices use satellites, cellular towers, and Wi-Fi towers to determine your location, which can be helpful when you're looking for a local business or trying to figure out where you are on a map, but can be a privacy concern if it's reported to an app or service you don't want to tell your location. Geotracking features also keep a record of your location over time.
Wi-Fi calling	Some devices all you to make calls over a Wi-Fi network to help improve performance in locations with poor cell reception and to help save you from using your voice plan. You'll need to verify that a specific device has this feature.
Launcher/GUI	A launcher is a graphical user interface (GUI) utility from which you can open programs and apps. Android uses launchers for the home screen, among other components. You can use the default Google launcher or download a free or paid launcher to customize your device.
Virtual assistant	Each operating system has its own virtual assistant. You can also download apps to act as virtual assistants. The default virtual assistants are: • Android: Google Assistant • iOS: Siri • Windows: Cortana
Emergency notification	Emergency notifications are sent to mobile carriers, which pass them on to users' devices. Some of the messages include: • Weather emergencies • AMBER Alerts • Local and national emergencies
Mobile payment service	Some operating systems and devices allow you to store credit card information and use it to pay with your mobile device by holding it close proximity to a device that accepts payments at a store or restaurant. So far, the most prominent mobile payment services are: • Google Pay, for Android devices • Apple Pay, for iOS devices • Samsung Pay, for Samsung-made Android devices.

Embedded systems

Since we often use "computer" to refer specifically to powerful general-purpose workstations and servers, and maybe smartphones or tables, it's easy to forget that more limited and specialized computers have their own operating systems. Computers are found in network devices, home appliances, vehicles, televisions and game consoles, streetlights, and digital clocks. Broadly speaking, they're called *embedded systems*, especially when they're built into a larger device meant to do tasks beyond computing. The vast majority of the world's microprocessors are used in embedded systems.

Exam Objective(s): 220-1001 2.5.3

The simplest embedded systems might only ever run a single program with little direct user interaction, and require very little in the way of system resources. Others might have high performance hardware and run multiple complex tasks, but they're still more limited than a general-purpose operating system. A network router or inexpensive *feature phone* might have robust computing power and perform multiple foreground and background tasks, but it doesn't provide the full range of services a workstation or smartphone does. Most importantly, embedded systems don't generally let users install or run arbitrary applications. All available software is in a single monolithic piece of "firmware"; users can only add functionality to the system by seeking firmware updates, if they can at all.

Important embedded system categories that are important in home and enterprise networks include:

Network appliances   Network hardware such as routers, switches, firewalls, broadband modems, and wireless access points.

Network-enabled devices   Limited network devices such as network printers, network-attached storage (NAS) appliances, voice-over-IP (VOIP) phones, kiosks, and point-of-sale systems.

Media devices   TVs, game consoles, projectors, DVD/Blu-ray players, DVRs, and streaming devices.

IoT   The *Internet of Things* is a catch-all term for appliances, devices, and equipment which connect to each other or to general purpose computers. These include smart appliances, lighting or HVAC controls, security cameras, door locks, medical equipment, and any other sort of home or industrial automation system.

Vehicles   Modern vehicles use computing systems for GPS and navigation, engine controls, security systems, and even emerging self-driving or remote-control technologies. Even when different functions are controlled by multiple computers, they are becoming increasingly networked and centrally controlled.

Embedded device operating systems vary greatly. A microwave oven needs a much simpler operating system than a network printer, for example. Many embedded devices that interact with the physical world need *real-time operating systems* which can be guaranteed to respond to outside input in strict time limits, such as an industrial device which must promptly respond to sensor or control input regardless of what it was doing already.

Many embedded operating systems are stripped-down versions of those used in general-purpose computers. Many use Linux or BSD kernels, while Apple or Microsoft embedded devices are likely to use iOS or Windows kernels. That doesn't mean they use the whole operating system, since only the functions needed for the device are included. For instance, a home router or network printer won't even have a desktop or command line interface available, only the web interface you can access through a browser on a different computer.

Embedded operating systems have some advantages over general-purpose ones, even on powerful hardware which could just run Windows or Linux. Not only is an embedded operating system more efficient in its specialized area, the monolithic nature makes support simpler and the limited feature set can reduce security risks.

Thin clients

One type of embedded computer used in enterprise is the *thin client*, a stripped-down computer which is designed primarily to connect to remote computers such as servers, workstations, or remote desktops. Thin clients are the modern equivalent of remote terminals used to connect to early mainframes and servers - the remote system does all the actual computing, while the client just serves as a display and input interface. By contrast, a *thick client* is a fully featured workstation which runs client software to connect to remote computers.

On the surface, a typical thin client looks and acts like a streamlined desktop or laptop PC. It has a keyboard, monitor, mouse, and network connection. It may support other USB peripherals as well. Internally, it's an inexpensive, low-power computer on tightly integrated hardware, with only flash-based firmware rather than local storage. Thin client operating systems are limited to the functions needed for connecting to remote systems, such as network setup utilities and the remote access protocols used by compatible servers. Some are embedded versions of Linux or Windows while others use vendor-specific proprietary systems. Other thin client variants include *zero clients* which have even more minimal local capabilities, and *web clients* which only run a web browser which can in turn be used to connect to remote systems.

Thin clients were developed as a way for the enterprise to save money both in endpoint hardware and in IT administration costs. The first has become less of a factor due to sharp drops in workstation computer prices compared to that of thin clients, but the second is still valuable. Embedded thin clients are easier to secure and maintain than thick clients or workstations, and the systems doing actual computing tasks can be centralized and virtualized to reduce administrative overhead.

One drawback of thin (and thick) clients is that they can consume more network bandwidth than simply performing computing tasks locally. Another is that they may not be well-suited to graphically intensive tasks like 3D modeling or video editing.

Configuring thin clients

Thin clients are generally specialized embedded devices, but you can also install a thin client OS onto a cheap or obsolete PC. The important thing is a read-only local operating system that doesn't have local applications or storage to complicate support. Since the OS is simpler, it's easier to configure than a workstation.

Exam Objective(s): 220-1001 3.9.1.1, 3.9.1.2

Note: Configuring a thick client is the same process, except that you're installing a client application onto a computer that can also run local applications.

1. Ensure that the thin client is compatible with your server architecture.
   The server must have a remote access service, and user accounts for the client to access.

2. Install the hardware and connect it to the network.
   If it's using custom hardware, install the thin client operating system.

3. Using the administrative interface, connect the thin client to the network.
   Depending on your LAN environment this may be as simple as plugging it in, or it may require custom network settings.

4. Create a connection to a compatible server or other system.
   You will need to specify both the address of the server, and the remote access protocol it accepts. Protocols may include options such as Citrix, RDP, or VNC.

5. Configure options for the specific protocol.
   Depending on the protocol you might be able to control graphics settings, audio and visual quality, or use of local resources like printers and removable storage.

Exercise: Identifying the features of non-Windows operating systems

While most client computers in the business environment are Windows-based, you might encounter and need to support Apple Macintosh or Linux-based clients. Each has its own unique features you'll need to be familiar with.

Do This	How & Why
1. Open an Internet browser.	
2. Use your search engine to find articles comparing Windows, Macintosh, and Linux operating systems.	
3. Based on your findings, which do you feel is the best fit right now for your company? Why?	
4. Are there any areas that would benefit from using a different operating system from your company's standard?	
5. Based on your findings, which do you feel is the best fit right now for your personal computer? Why?	
6. Are there any areas that would benefit from using a different operating system on your personal computer?	

Assessment: Non-windows operating systems

1. In which Macintosh OS X version was the Siri digital assistant introduced? Choose the best response.

   - 10.7 Lion
   - 10.11 El Capitan
   - 10.12 Sierra
   - 10.14 Mojave

2. Which Mac OS feature stores and manages passwords for applications, web sites, and network shares? Choose the best response.

   - Finder
   - iCloud
   - Keychain
   - Mission Control

3. Which of the following is true about Linux? Choose all that apply.

   - It can be distributed both commercially and non-commercially
   - It is only distributed non-commercially
   - It is used only for desktops and servers
   - It is used on mobile and embedded devices as well as desktops and servers
   - It usually only has a command line interface

4. Linux is an operating system that runs on only desktop and laptop computers. True or false?

   - True
   - False

5. Which Linux command would you use to show the directory you're currently in (the working directory)? Choose the best response.

   - cd
   - ls
   - mw
   - pwd

6. What advantages does an embedded operating system have over a workstation operating system? Choose all that apply.

   - Better for connecting to remote computers
   - Broader compatibility with user-installed applications
   - Can run on less powerful hardware
   - Easier to support
   - More built-in services

Module C: Operating system installation and upgrades

New versions of Windows and many other operating systems are rather easy to install, requiring little input from a user. However, there are things you need to consider before and after the installation process in order to make it as easy and error-free as possible.

In this module, you'll learn:

- About operating system installation types

- How to partition and format drives for installation

- How to perform a clean installation of Windows

- How to upgrade from one version of Windows to another

Boot methods

Installing an operating system isn't just like installing any other application, especially when you need to put it on a computer that doesn't have an operating system already. Fortunately, the firmware of the computer is like a very limited operating system which can search in various places for an executable installer and run it for you.

 Exam Objective(s): 220-1002 1.3.1

Traditionally PC operating systems were distributed on removable media like DVD, CD-ROM, or originally floppy disk. Today, you're just as likely to download the file and put it on appropriate media. Popular options include:

External   The easiest way to locally install an OS on a computer without one is by using install files on bootable external media. For commercially distributed software this will usually be a CD-ROM or DVD, but you can also put the installer onto other removable media such as a USB flash drive, hard drive, or SSD. You can even use a USB optical drive to perform a DVD installation on a computer without an internal optical drive.

Internal   You can also install an operating system from files right on its internal hard drive. This method is useful when you have an operating system which will boot successfully but which you want to upgrade or repair. Some drives also have separate recovery partitions you can boot from when the normal operating system installation doesn't work.

Network   Enterprise environments frequently boot computers from a disk image stored on the network. The image may be a fully functional operating system, or else an installer which can install and configure a local operating system on a new computer. Network booting requires a compatible network card on the local computer, and a network server configured to provide boot images. There are two common standards for network booting:

- *Preboot eXecution Environment* (*PXE*) is used by Windows and Linux systems.

- *NetBoot* is used by MacOS systems.

There are several methods that you can use to access source files for a Windows installation. These are the files that form the basis of the operating system. They're traditionally provided on a DVD, but the following table shows you some of the ways you can boot the computer to start the installation process.

Types of installations

There are several methods for installing on operating system on a computer, each with a different type of outcome. The exact options and terms vary by operating system version, but some of the most common are as follows:

Exam Objective(s): 220-1002 1.3.2

Clean	Installs an operating system on the computer without saving any existing files or settings, just like if it were a new computer. A clean install is a good choice when you don't care about preserving anything on the computer.
Upgrade	Installs a newer operating system version while preserving current settings, applications, and user files. In-place upgrade installs are useful when you want to upgrade but want to save time on configuration and restoring backup data.
Repair	Resolves operating system errors that are preventing it from operating normally, if at all. Usually a repair installation requires installation media or a recovery environment, but won't erase any existing applications or user files. It may change settings which have rendered the computer inoperable.
Refresh/Restore	Resets system settings, removes applications, and repairs damaged operating system files. Depending on the specific options, user files may or may not be preserved. Some restore options are meant to return the operating system to a clean factory state, and are similar to clean or repair installs. Others return the system to an earlier saved configuration or system backup file, and are useful when software changes cause system problems.
Recovery partition	Boots the computer to a recovery partition on the hard drive, which can restore the computer to its factory condition, similar to a clean install.
Unattended	Installs an operating system without user input. You can create a file that provides the information the operating system setup needs to complete the installation, and then point the setup wizard to that file, which it would use to answer any prompts it might normally display for a user to contribute specific information during setup, such as locale information and user accounts.
Image deployment	Deploys identical operating system installations to multiple computers. You can create a system image that contains the operating system and exact settings that you want to deploy, along with any other software and data you wish to be installed, then install that image on a different computer with a similar hardware configuration. It's an easy way to deploy custom installations to a large number of computers.
Remote network	Installs an operating system from an image on a network server using PXE or NetBoot.
Multiboot	Deploys multiple operating systems to the same computer. Users will then have the option of booting to one operating system or another when they start their computer.

Partitioning

Before a hard drive can be formatted, it must be laid out into one or more *partitions*, volumes which can hold their own separate data in individual file systems. When you purchase a preconfigured computer or perform a default operating system installation, its system disk will be automatically partitioned; if you don't like the default configuration, you have many choices for creating and managing partitions both during and after installation.

Exam Objective(s): 220-1002 1.3.3, 1.3.9

On a default Windows installation, the C:/ drive is the system partition which holds all system, application, and user data files. Depending on how you've obtained your computer, you might also see a factory recovery partition on the hard disk, which you can use to boot into Windows setup to recover or repair a Windows installation. You can see an example of the recovery partition in Disk Management in the figure below. Since you're not intended to access it directly from Windows, it isn't assigned a drive letter.

In addition to a factory recovery partition, Windows 7 and later usually create a *System Reserved* partition during installation onto a new disk. Located just before the system partition, this partition isn't assigned a drive letter; it usually takes up 100 MB on Windows 7, 350 MB on Windows 8, and 500 MB on Windows 10. It contains the Boot Manager and configuration data. Since it contains files used for BitLocker drive encryption, you also need the partition if you want to use BitLocker.

A System Reserved and a Recovery Partition

There are many types of partitions, and which you can create depends on your operating system and how you configure your disk. Windows recognizes two disk types.

Basic   The original and default partitioning style used by Windows and DOS since the 1980s. Partitions are defined by a *partition table* stored on the disk. Each partition represents a single contiguous portion of the disk. Basic disks can be formatted with any file system and accessed by any operating system, so they're usually the safest kind to use.

Dynamic   Uses *logical volume management* technology to arrange data more flexibly on the disk. Dynamic disk partitions can span non-contiguous disk segments or even multiple physical drives. However, they are incompatible with older versions of Windows and with other operating systems. While dynamic disks are still supported in Windows 10, they've been deprecated in favor of the new Storage Spaces feature.

On a basic disk, the partition table contains information such as where each partition begins and ends, and what kind of partition it is. That allows the operating system to know where it can read and write data. There are two partition table formats used on PCs.

MBR   *Master Boot Record* partition tables are an older standard compatible with nearly all operating systems, which stores partition info on a *boot sector* at the beginning of the disk. It supports up to four defined partitions, and the entire drive must be 2 TB or smaller.

GPT   *GUID Partition table* is a new standard supported by modern operating systems. It can be used with disks of any size, and allows an almost unlimited number of partitions (128 in Microsoft's implementation). Since partition information is stored in multiple areas of the disk, it's also less susceptible to errors from a corrupt boot sector. One drawback is that in Windows and some other operating systems, you can only use GPT for boot drives if your computer has UEFI firmware.

Partitions themselves can be categorized three ways, but the options depend on your partition table format and firmware.

Primary   A storage area containing a single file system. In GPT all partitions are primary, but MBR disks can have only four primary partitions. One primary partition can be marked *active*, which means the computer uses it as the boot volume for that disk.

Extended   A special partition on an MBR disk which serves as a container for any number logical partitions. There can be only one extended partition per disk, and it takes the place of one primary partition.

Logical   A partition defined within the extended partition of an MBR disk. It can be formatted and used just like a primary partition, but cannot be a boot volume.

File systems

A partition is just a reserved space, so before it can hold data it must be *formatted* with a specific file system. The file system is what actually defines how files are stored on the drive and accessed by the operating system. Different formats store data in different ways and provide different features.

Exam Objective(s): 220-1002 1.3.4

There are a number of drive formats used by popular operating systems. You only really have to worry about them when formatting or installing a drive. A newly purchased external drive may be formatted already.

FAT   *File Allocation Table* is the file system Microsoft originally developed for formatting floppy disks in DOS and early versions of Windows. While the original FAT only supported short file names and small volumes, it's been extended over the years into more sophisticated variants. While even the newest ones are obsolete for internal Windows drives, FAT partitions can be read by almost any operating system so they're still useful for removable drives.

- FAT32 was introduced in Windows 95. It supports much larger drive sizes and longer file names, but it doesn't support modern drive security and performance features. It also has a maximum file size of 4 GB. FAT32 is widely supported by non-Windows computers, so it's commonly used for removable storage such as flash drives and SD cards.

- *Extended FAT*, or *ExFAT* was introduced in Windows Vista Service Pack 1, and is designed for use in very large SD cards and other removable devices. It supports much larger file sizes and has other improvements over FAT32. Since it's less widely supported, it's best used on drives that actually need it.

NTFS   *NT File System* was introduced with Windows NT. It supports very large drives and files, and has a lot of other improvements over FAT for performance, reliability, and security. It's the default file system for internal hard drives in all modern versions of Windows, and you should always use it for the system volume. Since NTFS isn't well-supported by non-Windows operating systems, you shouldn't use it on a volume that might be accessed by non-Windows computers.

HFS   *Hierarchical File System* is the family of file systems used by Mac OS and iOS. The original HFS was used in very old Macs, while newer Apple products use refined versions like *HFS+* and *APFS*. Windows can't usually read or write to HFS drives, so Apples also should use FAT32 or ExFAT for removable storage.

ext   *Extended file system* was designed for Linux. It's also a family: *ext4* is the newest version while *ext2* and *ext3* are older. Mac OS and Android can also read and write ext4 partitions, but Windows needs third party software to do so.

Swap A partition used to store *virtual memory* which the operating system writes to disk in order to free physical RAM. Some operating systems, like Linux, use dedicated swap partitions which have no other files. By contrast, Windows uses a *page file* within an existing file system; it usually is stored on the system partition rather than separately.

CDFS *Compact Disc File System* is used for data and audio CD-ROMs, based on the ISO 9960 standard.

UDF *Universal Disk Format* is an open vendor-neutral file system which can be used for a variety of purposes, but in practice is usually used for DVDs and writeable optical discs.

Formatting

When you format a disk, you remove the file system structure from the disk and install a new structure. There are two options for formatting a hard disk during Windows installation:

Full format Checks for bad sectors on the physical disk before installing the file system structure. It can be very slow, especially on large hard drives.

Quick Format Skips the disk check and just installs a new file system structure. It's much quicker, but you should only use it on a disk you're sure has no bad sectors. Usually with a new disk this won't be a problem.

Other installation considerations

In addition to boot methods, partitions, and file systems, there are a few other considerations you need to keep in mind during an installation. Some of these are decisions you need to make ahead of time, while others are input you will need to provide during the installation either manually or as part of an answer file during an unattended installation. Since many of these factors can increase the time needed for installation, you might want to investigate unattended or image-based installations if you need to install new operating systems regularly. For Windows, the following may be important.

 **Exam Objective(s):** 220-1002 1.3.5, 1.3.6, 1.3.7, 1.3.8, 1.3.10

Other installation considerations

Consideration	Why it's important
Partitioning	If you need a different partition setup than the default, a properly formatted boot drive with correct partitions will save you work during installation.
Drivers	Windows includes drivers for common hardware, but if you have unusual or just very new hardware make sure you have drivers for it to install after setup. For critical hardware like displays, disk controllers, and network interface cards, you may need to select an option to install alternate third-party drivers during setup. You will need to have those ready, or integrate them into your installation package.
Updates	You should update Windows immediately after installation, but you can save time by making sure you have the newest version of the install media. If you have network access you can also choose to download Windows updates at the beginning of the installation.
Software	Keep important third-party software at hand and ready to install after installation. Make sure it also is up to date.

Consideration	Why it's important
Network/account	The setup process will vary depending on your account type and the network model you're using. • You can create a local account by any name you like, and join a workgroup of your choice during setup. • If you are installing Windows 8 or later using a Microsoft account, you will need internet access. • If you are joining the computer to an Active Directory domain, you will need a username and password authorized to join the computer to the domain. You can then log on as any valid domain user.
Time/location	Your time and date might or might not be set properly in the system BIOS, but Windows still requires you to choose your time zone, region, and language.

Preparing for operating system installation

If you have a freshly assembled computer and a Windows DVD you probably just need to put it in and start it up, but otherwise you might need to make other preparations.

 Exam Objective(s): 220-1002 1.3.11, 1.3.12

- If you're upgrading or installing a new OS onto a computer that already has valuable data, make sure to back it up in case something goes wrong.
- Make sure that you're choosing an operating system and edition that suits your needs.
  - Check installation requirements and compatibility with system hardware.
  - Make sure that all applications you want to use are compatible with the new operating system. If not, examine application upgrades or alternatives.
  - Different editions may use different installation media. Make sure the specific edition you're installing supports features you need such as 64-bit architecture or Active Directory domains.
  - Check licensing requirements to make sure you are authorized to install the specific version and edition.
- When installing from external media, make sure the media is installed in a bootable format compatible with your computer. You may need to create install media from a working computer.
  - Disc burning programs accept ISO disk image files as input.
  - Various ISO-to-USB tools can allow you to create a bootable USB flash or hard drive from an ISO.
  - Some distributions have specific tools. For example, Microsoft's Media Creation Tool will automatically download a current Windows install image from the internet and place it on a blank DVD or USB drive.
- The process for installing from an internal drive depends both on what your current OS is and what kind of installation you want to perform.
  - Operating system upgrades often work like other application installers, but may need internet access during the installation process.
  - Upgrade and restore settings are typically available in system settings or in initial boot options. In Windows 10 you can find them in **Settings** > **Update & Security** > **Recovery**, or in the Advanced Startup menu during boot.

- Make sure the computer is configured to boot from your chosen medium.
  - In BIOS/UEFI settings, look for **Boot Order** options to choose what devices the computer checks first.
  - PXE settings may also be called **Network Boot ROM** or **Boot to Network.**

Installing Windows

While much of the installation process is waiting for the Windows installer to copy and extract files, you'll need to make some decisions along the way. The process generally follows these steps.

1. Boot the computer to your preferred installation method or insert an optical disc with the installation files and wait for the setup wizard to start.

2. Accept license terms.

3. Choose whether to get important Windows updates for the installation.

4. Choose an installation type.

   - Install a new copy of Windows.

   - Perform a custom installation if you want to choose or create a partition and format it.

5. Complete the installation wizard, supplying any requested information to complete the installation, including language and region options, a computer name, and an initial user account.

   - For RAID controllers or other specialized devices, you may need to load third-party drivers during setup. Have driver install media handy.

   - To join a domain or create a Microsoft account, you will need to configure network access.

6. Verify that all devices are working in Device Manager, and update or replace drivers as necessary.

Upgrade paths

You can perform a clean installation on a computer that already has an operating system, but you'll need to reinstall your applications, reconfigure settings, and restore important user files from backup. It's often more tempting to perform an *in-place upgrade*; that method installs the newer version while preserving the existing user files, such as documents and photos, and most (if not all) of the current system settings, including applications, networking settings, hard disk configuration, and device settings. In-place upgrades can also sometimes carry over configuration problems or performance issues from an old installation, so sometimes it's better to upgrade by performing a clean install with the new version.

Exam Objective(s): 220-1002 1.3.13

While there might be a temptation to upgrade an older computer to the newest version of Windows (or whatever operating system it has), you need to consider the computer's hardware capabilities and whether they can support the requirements of the newer operating system. The new version may also remove features you use, or have compatibility issues with third-party applications you need. You'll also need a valid license for the new operating system; while some upgrades are free, others must be purchased.

In addition, vendors support only specific types of in-place upgrades, called *upgrade paths*, from one version to another. While you can attempt a Windows upgrade outside the supported upgrade paths, it might not work properly, and you won't get any technical support from Microsoft if the upgrade fails.

For any operating system you need to read documentation to see what upgrades are possible, and often read it very closely. With Windows operating systems, you can perform in-place upgrades along the following paths:

- Windows 7 to Windows 8
- Windows 7 to Windows 10
- Windows 8 to Windows 8.1
- Windows 8.1 to Windows 10

Notice that you can't move directly from Windows 8 to Windows 10 without installing 8.1 first. While you can upgrade from Windows 7 directly to Windows 8.1, the process will remove all your third-party apps, requiring you to reinstall them.

Keep in mind that just because Microsoft supports an upgrade from one Windows version to another, the specific version you're using of each is very important. You might not be able to upgrade from Windows 7 Home to Windows 10 Pro, or switch from a 32-bit Windows edition to a 64-bit edition. You'll need to check which edition of Windows you're trying to upgrade and then verify which editions you can upgrade to in the newer Windows version.

Windows Upgrade Advisor

Microsoft has created a downloadable application called the Upgrade Advisor or Upgrade Assistant that you can use to scan your computer to determine if the operating system, applications, and connected devices are compatible with the newer version of Windows to which you're considering an upgrade. To find the Upgrade Advisor or Assistant for the newer operating system to which you want to upgrade, search Microsoft's site or perform a general web search. You can then find the utility, as well as other compatibility tools, that you can use to help plan your upgrade.

Upgrading Windows

While the process might differ slightly based on the operating system you're upgrading from and the operating system you're upgrading to, it generally follows these steps.

1. Ensure that your computer will support the upgrade, including the operating system version, the installed applications, and the connected devices.
2. Insert the DVD or flash drive containing the new operating system. Restart the computer and boot to the install media.
3. Follow the steps in the wizard, choosing to upgrade and keep all the files, settings, and applications. Note: If this option isn't available, you'll need to determine if the upgrade you're attempting is supported as an in-place upgrade.
4. Complete the wizard. The computer will likely restart at least once.
5. Log on to the computer using the same credentials that you used in the earlier version of Windows.
6. Verify that the settings have been retained and all the applications and devices work correctly. You can try to start and use the applications, while a quick check in Device Manager will show you any device problems.

Exercise: Installing and upgrading Windows

To complete this exercise as written, you'll need to have network access and a Microsoft account. If you do not have these you can continue with another type of account, but it will change both the exercise and the rest of the course. This exercise was written using the latest feature update of Windows 10 as of Fall 2018 (Version 1809). Setup steps may differ using any other version.

If you have a desktop or laptop computer with an older Windows version installed, perform an upgrade installation to Windows 10. If you have a computer without an operating system, install Windows 10 as follows:

Do This	How & Why
1. Insert the Windows 10 installation media.	Your BIOS must be configured to boot from the type of media you've selected.
2. Turn on or restart the computer.	If necessary, press any key to boot from installation media when prompted.
3. Configure initial setup options, then accept the license terms.	You will be asked to choose settings including Windows edition, language, and product key. If you don't have a product key, you can skip it and enter one later.
4. Choose an installation type and location.	
a) Click **Custom: Install Windows only (advanced)**.	If you were installing Windows 10 onto a computer that already had an earlier edition, you could click **Upgrade** to keep your files and applications.
b) Select an available hard disk partition or unallocated space, and click **Next**.	You can use other options if you need to change your hard disk partitions. Windows will take a while to copy files to your hard drive.
5. Click appropriate options to choose your installation region, then your keyboard layout.	When you first set up Windows on a new computer, you will be prompted to choose setup options, such as the country you're in.
6. When the How would you like to setup? screen appears, experiment with account options.	Windows 10 Pro and Enterprise allow you to create both personal and enterprise accounts. If you're using Windows 10 Home, this screen won't appear, so you can skip this step.
a) Click **Set up for an organization**, then click **Next**.	To explore Active Directory account options. First, you're prompted to set up with a Microsoft Azure account.
b) Click **Domain join instead**.	You're asked to enter a username for a local Active Directory domain.
c) Click **Or, even better, use an online account**.	Since you don't have an Active Directory account, you'll create a personal account.
d) Click **Set up for personal use**, then click **Next**.	You're asked to enter credentials for your Microsoft account. First, you'll look at local account options.

Do This	How & Why
e) Click **Offline account**.	To begin creating a local account. On second thought, you'll sign in with a Microsoft account.
f) Click **Yes**.	To take Windows' recommendation.
7. Sign into Windows with a Microsoft account.	
a) Click **I own it**, then click **Next**.	This time you'll sign in using your Microsoft account. You can use this screen to sign up for a Microsoft account, request a password reset, or make a local account instead.
b) Sign in with your user name and password.	chris.marhall@javatucana.com ☒ Create account If you don't have your own Microsoft account, it should be an email address supplied by your instructor. While you can log into the computer with your Microsoft account password, Windows prompts you to set up a device-specific PIN.
c) Enter the same PIN of your choice in both fields.	The PIN can be 4-7 digits, and you can check **Include letters and symbols** for added security.
8. Choose Windows cloud and privacy options.	Windows 10 includes a variety of cloud synchronization and data sharing functions which you can configure to your liking before completing setup.
a) At the Link your phone and PC screen, click **Do it later**.	Linking is a useful feature, but not required for this course.
b) At the Protect your files with OneDrive screen, click **Next**.	To save documents on the cloud.
c) At the Meet Cortana screen, click **Accept**.	Without the Cortana digital assistant, you can only use Windows 10's more basic search features. You're asked whether you want to use activity history to sync activities across multiple devices.
d) Don't enable activity history.	This option is useful if you have multiple devices, but you won't use it.
e) Read the available privacy settings, then click **Accept.**	Windows allows you to choose what information it shares with Microsoft. You can always change them later. Windows will take a few minutes to complete setup, then the Windows 10 desktop appears.

Assessment: Operating system installation and upgrades

1. You have a computer with Windows 7 on it. You need to upgrade it to Windows 8.1 and deploy it to a new employee. Which is the best upgrade type for this situation? Choose the best response.

   - Clean installation
   - In-place upgrade
   - Either, depending on user account type
   - Either, depending on whether you're booting locally or from the network.

2. There is no way to upgrade from Windows 7 to Windows 8.1 and preserve the existing user files, such as documents and photos, and most (if not all) of the current system settings, including applications, networking settings, hard disk configuration, and device settings. True or false?

   - True.
   - False

3. Which of the following boot methods can be used to install Mac OS from a network location? Choose the best response.

   - Netboot
   - Netexe
   - PXE
   - USB device

4. Which installation type can be used for identical operating system installations to multiple computers? Choose the best response.

   - Clean
   - Image deployment
   - Multiboot
   - Remote network
   - Unattended

5. Master Boot Record Partitions can't support hard disks that are larger than what size? Choose the best response.

   - 2 MB
   - 2 GB
   - 2 TB
   - 2 PB

6. How many primary partitions are supported by MBR? Choose the best response.

- 2
- 4
- 8
- unlimited

7. Which file system is used on Linux? Choose the best response.

- ext4
- exFAT
- FAT32
- NTFS
- UDF

Module D: Applications and scripting

Modern operating systems contain a wide variety of programs, utilities, and configuration interfaces you can use to perform tasks, but you're likely to want to expand upon them. It's easy to install applications that add whatever functionality you like, provided they're compatible with your other software and hardware. You can also make use of scripts to automate functions either at the command line or to control other software.

You will learn:

- How to install and configure applications
- About scripts and scripting languages

Application sources

Before you can install a program you need to have access to it. You can get programs in a variety of ways. It's simplest for web apps: you just need to navigate to them in a browser and possibly supply user credentials. For some you might have to install a browser add-in, such as Java or Flash, but increasingly web apps work only on standards built into browsers themselves.

Exam Objective(s): 220-1002 1.7.3

Otherwise, you're going to need some way to put the application on your computer. There are multiple ways to do this, and which you can use depends on the software and your operating system.

Physical media   If the application is on a printed CD or USB drive, you can generally just run its installer. If it's a *portable application* you don't even need to install it - you can run its executable directly.

Internet   Many applications have installers you can download from the internet.

- *Standalone installers* are complete application installers. You need a network connection to download them, but once it's downloaded you have all the files you need.

- *Online installers* are small files which connect to the internet and download the application when you install it. They can make sure to install the latest software version, but they won't work if you don't have a network connection during installation.

- *Source code* doesn't use an installer, but instead is program code you must turn into executable format using a *compiler* application. Source code distribution is most common for Linux applications, but there are compilers for other operating systems.

Local network   Applications can be hosted on file servers on the enterprise network. They might be installers hosted on a file share, or centrally deployed to workstations using a deployment service or other remote management tool. On a Windows domain, necessary software might be configured to automatically install when a user logs in.

App store   Apps can be downloaded from a central app store, whether it's included with the operating system or is a third-party application on its own. Common app stores include the Apple App Store for MacOS and iOS, Google Play Store for Android, and Microsoft Store for Windows.

WARNING: Malware is always a risk when you install an application. Before you install software, you need to make sure not only that it is genuine, but that it hasn't been altered on the way from the manufacturer to your computer. Apps from a trustworthy store are generally monitored and protected by the store's technicians and security features, and those on commercially pressed optical discs are usually safe as well. The prime risk is apps on flash media or burned discs, and those downloaded from unauthorized websites. Especially if an application comes from a third-party site or a file-sharing service, you should treat it as potentially suspect.

System requirements

To install and run an application, your computer must meet its *system requirements*. You can find the requirements for an app on its packaging or download page. Many have separate minimum requirements and recommended requirements. If you meet the minimum requirements but not the recommended ones you can install the application, but you might have low performance or limited function.

Exam Objective(s): 220-1002 1.7.1, 1.7.2

System requirements for Microsoft Office 2013

For business

Office Standard 2013, Office Professional 2013, and Office Professional Plus 2013   —

COMPONENT	REQUIREMENT
Computer and processor	1 gigahertz (GHz) or faster x86-bit or x64-bit processor with SSE2
Memory	1 GB RAM (32-bit); 2 GB RAM (64-bit)
Hard disk	3.0 GB available disk space
Display	1024 x 768 screen resolution
Graphics	Graphics hardware acceleration requires a DirectX 10 graphics card.
Operating system	Windows 10, Windows 8.1, Windows 8, Windows 7 Service Pack 1, Windows 10 Server, Windows Server 2012 R2, Windows Server 2012, or Windows Server 2008 R2 For the best experience, use the latest version of any operating system.

Requirements can be hardware or software. Common requirements you'll see include:

Drive space   The amount of free disk space on your computer needed to store the application along with required data files. You might need additional space for large data files, depending on the application.

RAM   The amount of memory needed to run the application. You might need more RAM than the requirements if you're simultaneously running more applications; some applications will also use more RAM when handling large or complex workloads.

CPU   The processor architecture and speed needed to run the application acceptably. Some apps might require 64-bit CPUs, multiple cores, specific CPU features, or other details.

Network   Some applications require an internet connection during setup. Others require one during operation, either for core or optional functions. Online-focused applications may also specify minimum network performance. Applications with network components or activation requirements may need to access outside computers, so firewalls or other network security systems must be configured to allow access.

Graphics/Display   Some applications may specify a minimum screen resolution or other graphical settings. Others, especially games and 3D applications, will specify GPU requirements. Particularly demanding apps may even need a modern discrete graphics card for adequate performance.

Other hardware   Any other required hardware will be specified. Common requirements include specific peripherals such as speakers, microphone, or camera.

Operating system   Applications are typically written for a specific operating system, and beyond that may require a specific version of that operating system. Possibilities include the operating system version, service pack, architecture (32/64-bit), and edition.

 Note: While more is usually better for system requirements, apps written for an older operating system may not be compatible with newer ones. While most Windows 7 apps will run under Windows 10, for example, some will not. Others may require you to configure backward compatibility settings when you run them.

Services/drivers   An application may require other software services in order to run. They may be installed automatically with the application, or you might need to configure them separately. These may include:

- Optional operating system services

- Libraries and frameworks such as Microsoft Visual C++ or .NET Framework

- Specific drivers for hardware or virtual hardware devices

- Additional applications which integrate with the one you're installing.

Licensing and permissions

Before you install any software, you need to make sure that you have the legal right to use it. Software publishers can put whatever restrictions they want on their intellectual property. While some applications are free to use, others are only available for a paid license, or can only be used for specific purposes. Unlicensed software may not operate properly, and even if it does it can open you or your organization to legal liability.

 Exam Objective(s): 220-1002 1.7.4, 4.6.2

Software licenses are highly varied, but they fall into two general categories:

Open source   Open source content and software is freely available to all who want to acquire it, and like Unix and Linux, can often be modified and redistributed. Since open source software is still typically governed by copyright law, even an open source license might have restrictions on how the software may be used, and technical support is typically not included.

Commercial license   The software's source code is owned by a private entity like a corporation. While usually associated with paid software, free software can also be distributed under a commercial license. The license itself will specify what support and updates are included, as well as how the software may be used, and how many separate computers it can be installed on.

- Personal licenses are purchased by individual users, or by a company for select users. Some may specify that they are only for non-commercial use.

- Enterprise licensing offers licenses for multiple users, often at a discount over personal licenses. Licenses for commercial organizations may be more expensive than those for personal or non-profit use.

Both commercial and open source software can have licenses and terms of agreement. Commercial software generally includes an *end-user license agreement* (*EULA*) which governs ownership rights and what the purchaser (the end user) may do with the software. Free apps and software will also typically have a EULA, to simply express the rights and responsibilities of the parties involved. It may simply be the open source license agreement used to publish it. You'll almost certainly be asked to read and accept the EULA before installing commercial software.

Any sort of software license might only be good for specific versions of an application. If a major upgrade comes out, you'll need to purchase a new license to install it. Other licenses are subscription-based, so they'll only work for a limited time before you renew it.

Commercially distributed software and media often makes use of *digital rights management* (*DRM*) to enforce copyright restrictions. DRM may be any variety of digitally enforced techniques such as copy protection, online registration and activation, or hardware dongles needed to run an application.

Even if you have the legal right to use an application, you also need to have permissions within the operating system to install it. In Windows you generally need administrative permission to install a desktop application. If the application needs access to system settings, you'll need administrative permission to run it as well. The application itself will need to have permission to access any files or folders it needs in order to operate. On a personal computer all of this probably won't be a problem, but on more tightly secured enterprise workstations software installation is typically restricted to specific personnel. Some apps can be installed so that only a single user has access to them.

On mobile devices you might not have full administrative access even if you own the device. Some apps are intended only for use on a rooted, jailbroken, or otherwise unlocked device.

Installing applications

How you actually install applications depends on how you're deploying them. You should generally follow these steps:

Exam Objective(s): 220-1002 1.7.5

- Before you purchase or download an application, make sure that it suits your needs and that it is compatible with the computer's hardware and software. If necessary, install hardware or software to meet the requirements.

- If necessary, research how the application may affect functionality or security on the system.

  - Potential compatibility issues or conflicts with other software.

  - Software vulnerabilities that can impact device security or stability.

  - Network services and vulnerabilities which may impact network security.

- Make sure you meet licensing requirements, including online activation or license keys.

- Make sure you have necessary network access.

- If necessary, research installation options to ensure the software is configured correctly.

- After installation, perform configuration or activation tasks so that the software is ready to use.

About scripts

Most applications operate as compiled executable programs that run directly on top of the operating system and interface with various services, libraries, and *application programming interfaces* (*APIs*) installed on the computer. By contrast, a *script* is a sort of program that runs in a more limited run-time environment, such as the operating system's command line shell or a scripting engine within some application like an office suite or web browser. Instead of being compiled into executable code, scripts usually remain as human-readable code which is interpreted a line a time as it runs. Even if the script can still access services and APIs, it still is a component that operates within that scripting environment, rather than a standalone executable entity.

Scripts also differ from applications in how they are used. Scripting languages are generally optimized for short, simple programs which users can create quickly and customize to specific needs. Some are *high-level programming languages* designed to perform complex programming tasks while remaining highly abstracted from the underlying hardware, such as the client-side code inside a web application. Others are used more to automate simple, repetitive tasks which a human would otherwise enter into the interface one step at a time, such as a script which configures network shares from the command line when a user logs into Windows.

Script file types

It doesn't really matter what language was used to write a compiled program since the compiler turns it into executable format. Scripts, on the other hand, must be run within a compatible executable environment, so their language is very important. In general, they're text files which you can open in any text editor to examine or modify. Even if you don't know any scripting languages, the file extension of a script can tell you the type of system meant to run it. Common formats you might encounter include:

Exam Objective(s): 220-1002 4.8.1

.bat   A *batch file* is a script that runs in the Windows Command Prompt environment (**CMD.EXE**), or even in its DOS-based predecessors. It can automate any number of actions that would normally be performed from the command prompt into a file that can run with a single click. `.cmd` files are also batch files, but are processed in a slightly different way. The Command Prompt was not designed for complex scripts, so batch files are more limited than scripts written for a real scripting language.

.sh   A *shell script* is designed to run in a Unix style command shell such as bash or csh., so you'll usually find them on Linux systems. They can also run in other operating systems that run these shells, including Windows with the right components installed. A shell script can perform similar functions to a batch file, but using the syntax of the shell it's written for. Since most shells are more powerful than the Command Prompt, shell scripts can often perform more sophisticated tasks than a batch file while requiring fewer lines of code.

.ps1   A script designed to run in the Windows PowerShell environment. Unlike Command Prompt, PowerShell was designed as both a command shell and a scripting language, and can interface directly with Windows .NET and COM+ libraries. This means that PowerShell scripts are much more powerful and flexible than batch files, but they can also be harder for non-programmers to write and interpret.

.vbs   A script written for the *Visual Basic Scripting* environment that's included with Windows. Instead of a command shell it runs through the *Windows Scripting Host* (*WSH*), Internet Explorer, Internet Information Services, or other Windows components. VBS doesn't have the flexibility of PowerShell, but it's been in use longer and can have performance advantages, so you're still likely to see it widely used where batch files aren't enough. Unlike shell scripts VBS can be used for web pages in Internet Explorer or for server-side scripts on Microsoft web servers.

.js   A script written for the *JavaScript* language used by web pages, or else for the related *JScript* language developed by Microsoft. Both are fairly complete programming languages that can support complex programs, and can run through WSH or in a web browser. In modern versions, the main difference between the two is that JScript has special functions for interfacing with Windows, while JavaScript is a platform-independent standard.

.py   A script written for *Python*, a general-purpose interpreted programming language. It is included with most non-Windows operating systems, and Windows implementations are available; it's also used as a scripting language within many local applications and as a server-side language for web applications.

There are more scripting languages, of course, and more complications even with those file types. A given script might be written for specific interpreter versions. Since some scripting environments allow you to call upon separate interpreters, a script written in one language might contain other languages inside of it.

Basic scripting elements

While computer programming is beyond the scope of this topic, basic automation scripts aren't that hard to understand provided you know how to use a command line interface in the first place. A simple script is nothing more than a sequence of commands run one after another automatically. In the case of a batch file, for example, commands might be operations built into **CMD.EXE**, executable programs you can launch from the command line, or even other batch files and scripts. Other scripting languages allow you to connect number of externally defined functions, libraries, or whatever else the language supports.

 Exam Objective(s): 220-1002 4.8.4

A given command or statement is likely to accept various *arguments* that specify exactly what it acts on, and *options* that change exactly what it does. For example, in a batch file the **copy** command requires arguments for both the files you want to copy and the location you want to send it to. You can then add options if you want to specify what happens if the destination file already exists.

A list of commands with their options and arguments is good enough for some scripts, but more powerful programming techniques rely heavily on *variables* which allow the programmer to store some kind of data then refer to or alter it later. For example, you might define a variable as some user name, or file path, number, or whatever else you might want to store. In a later command you can refer to the variable in place of an argument. Scripting languages (and other programming languages) must have syntax to define, alter, and refer to variables.

Many statements require other input, or produce output, so the script needs to supply input and choose how to display output. Some scripts are designed to pause and wait for user input rather than being completely automated. Output might be displayed onscreen, redirected to a file, or just sent to a *null* output that discards it.

Complex scripts and other programs don't simply perform a series of commands in sequence. On any given running of the script, a given statement might be repeated, reused in different contexts, or omitted entirely. Programming languages have *control flow* statements which can be used to alter the flow of the overall program.

Function	A named sequence of commands which can be referred to elsewhere in the script. When a function is called, the script performs it then returns to where it left off.
Conditional statement	A construct that performs different actions depending on whether some condition evaluates as true or false. The simplest example is the if-then-else statement which performs one set of actions if a Boolean condition is true, and a different set (or none at all) if it's false.
Loop	A construct that repeats a sequence of actions one or more times depending on some set of conditions. The simplest loop types are:

- FOR some defined number of iterations
- WHILE a Boolean condition remains true

Variables and data

A variable can represent almost any kind of value such as a number, name, file path, or memory location. When a script calls on a variable, it's very important that the value make sense in context, so it doesn't try to run that loop "cucumber" times. Some scripting languages require the programmer to keep track of valid values for a variable, while others define *types* for variables or their underlying values. Each language has its own list of allowed types, but common categories include:

 Exam Objective(s): 220-1002 4.8.2, 4.8.5

Integer   A whole number. Most integer values have a fixed size in bits, such as 8-bit or 32-bit. A language might have multiple integer types representing different sizes. *Signed* integers can be positive or negative.

Floating-point   A number that can have digits before or after a decimal point. Like integers, a floating point number has a fixed size which determines how large it can be, how many significant digits it can store, and whether it's signed. A language might have multiple floating point values.

String   A sequence of alphanumeric characters. A string typically has a maximum length.

Character   A single alphanumeric character.

Boolean   A true/false value.

Languages can also allow *list* or *array* variables containing an ordered set of values of the same type.

Variables defined within a script are limited to the script itself, though their values can be included in script output. However, you can also make use of *environment variables* that exist within the operating system or scripting environment. From within a script or in the command shell, you can read or set environment variables like any other kind. A script can even define its own to share with child processes. There are many standard environment variables, but some of the most common include:

Windows name	Linux name	Function
%PATH%	$PATH	A list of directories where the operating system will search if you type a command name without specifying its absolute or relative path
%USERPROFILE%	$HOME	The current user's home folder.
%TEMP% or %TMP%	$TEMP	A folder where programs can safely store temporary files.
%CD%	$PWD	The current folder.
%APPDATA%		The current user's application data folder.
%SystemRoot%		The absolute file path of the Windows system folder.

Syntax and comments

Like any other kind of programs, and for that matter the command line instructions they automate, scripts are notoriously picky about exactly how they're typed and formatted. Misspelled commands or arguments are just a start. Missing, misplaced, or extra punctuation can easily cause fatal errors or unexpected behavior. Some languages are fairly forgiving about capitalization, or about *whitespace* characters such as spaces, tabs, and carriage returns; others use capitalization or whitespace as a vital part of script syntax. For these reasons, you should be very careful editing a script unless you know how its language works.

 Exam Objective(s): 220-1002 4.8.3

Scripting languages allow *comments* which will not be parsed as part of the script. A comment might be a note or reminder from a programmer explaining how nearby code operates, for example. You can also "comment out" code you want to disable but not permanently delete, in case you need it later. Comment syntax depends on scripting language, but it's good to know even if you don't know anything else about the language.

- REM In a .bat file, any line beginning with the word "REM" is a comment.

- # In a .sh script, any text on a single line following "#" is a comment.

- <# In a .ps1 script, any text following "# " is a comment, but you can also create multi-line block comments by placing "<#" and "#>" at the beginning and end.

- ' In a .vbs script, a statement can be commented out either with a single quote "'", or with "REM".

- /* In a .js script, single line comments are prefaced by "//", while comment blocks are enclosed by "/*" and "*/" at beginning and end. */

- # In a .py script, comments are prefaced by "#". Make sure to follow the # with a single space, and indent it at the same level as the code it comments. You can also mark multiple lines with triple quotes before and after, but it's not recommended.

Exercise: Exploring a script

In this exercise you'll run and read a program written in Python.

```
*area.py - F:\area.py (3.7.1)*                                    —
File  Edit  Format  Run  Options  Window  Help

import math

def get_area(radius):
    area = math.pi * radius ** 2
    return round(area, 2)

def main():
    quitProgram = False
    while quitProgram == False:
        circleRadius = input("Please enter the radius (Q to quit): ")
        if circleRadius.upper() == "Q":
            quitProgram = True
        else:
            try:
                area = get_area(float(circleRadius))
                print("The area of the circle is " + str(area))
                print()
            except:
                print("That's not a number")
                print()
    print("OK. Bye!")

main()
```

Do This	How & Why
1. Copy `area.py` to your desktop.	This script is a short program, written in Python.

Do This	How & Why
2. Download Python.	Windows doesn't include Python support like some operating systems, but it's easy to install a Python interpreter.
a) In your browser, navigate to `http://www.python.org/downloads/`.	The Python website displays downloads for each version of the software. You want the newest version, but if you had specific compatibility needs you could download an older one.
b) Click the newest release version.	At the time of publishing, it was 3.7.1. The page contains release notes for that version, and a list of downloadable files.
c) View the listed files.	You can download source code, or installers for MacOS and Windows. Windows installers are available in 32-bit and 64-bit versions, and in .zip, standalone installer, and online installer varieties.
d) View the right-hand columns.	Each file has an MD5 hash and GPG digital signature. Both are security measures you could use to verify that the file was not corrupted or altered when you downloaded it.

MD5 Sum	File Size	GPG
99f78ecbfc766ea449c4d9e7eda19e83	22802018	SIG
0a57e9022c07fad3dadb2eef58568edb	16960060	SIG
ac6630338b53b9e5b9dbb1bc2390a21e	34360623	SIG

Do This	How & Why
e) Download the executable installer for your Windows architecture.	It will probably be x86-64.
3. Install Python.	
a) Run the Python installer.	
b) At the setup screen, check **Add Python to PATH**.	Adding Python to your path allows you to use it from the Command Prompt or PowerShell. This makes it more useful as a scripting tool.
c) Click **Install Now**.	Follow all further defaults, including disabling the path length limit.
4. Run `area.py`.	Now that you have Python installed, you can run the program.
a) In File Explorer, double-click `area.py`.	Python opens in a command line interface. You're asked to enter a radius.
b) Enter a number, such as `5` or `2.82`	The program displays the area of a circle with the radius you entered. You're prompted to enter another radius.
c) Enter the word `twelve`.	The program tells you that isn't a number, and asks again.

Do This	How & Why
d) Enter the lette rq.	The window closes. Now you'll view the inner workings of the program.
5. Right-click `area.py` and click **Edit with IDLE > Edit with IDLE**.	You could view or create Python scripts in Notepad, but IDLE is a much easier way to read, edit, and debug them. To view the program in Python's integrated development environment.
6. Examine the contents of the program.	Notice that IDLE color-codes program elements based on how Python will parse them. In a text editor, no colors would be visible.
a) View the red text at the top.	It's a comment explaining the functions of the program. Each line begins with #, marking it as a comment.

```
#This program prompts the user for the radius
#of a circle and then returns the area.
#It checks that the input is a number.
#Entering 'Q' or 'q' will end the program.
```

Do This	How & Why
b) View the first statements of the program.	First, the script imports Python's math library so it can perform mathematical calculations. Then it defines a `get_area` function that calculates the area of a circle. After that, it runs the main program.
c) Identify variables in the function.	Python doesn't require you to declare a variable's type when it's created, so programmers need to keep track of what kinds of value a variable might hold. `get_area` requires a *radius* variable as input, and uses an *area* variable in its calculations.
7. Read the program's main section.	The program asks for user input. If the user inputs "Q" it quits the program. Otherwise it attempts to calculate the area of a circle using the input and the `get_area` function. All green text is in quotes, and includes everything you saw printed onscreen.
a) Identify variables.	*quitProgram* is a Boolean variable which can be set "True" or "False." *area* is used to calculate the circle, and *circleRadius* is accepted from user input.
b) Identify the loop.	The `while` loop repeats as long as *quitProgram* is False, so it won't end until the user types "Q".
c) Identify the conditional statement.	The `if/then` statement checks if the input is "Q". Otherwise, it runs the nested `try/except` statement.
d) Examine the `try/except` statement.	Python attempts to convert *circleRadius* into a floating point value for the `get_area` function. If the user entered a text string instead of a number, it produces an error. In that case, Python sends an error message to the user rather than ending the program.

Do This	How & Why
8. If time allows, try editing the program and running it again.	You could add new comments, change the text displayed to the user, or alter the underlying math, depending on your understanding of the language.
9. Close all open windows.	

Assessment: Applications and scripting

1. You want to install an application on a computer that has no internet connection, but the software is only available as an internet download. You hope you can download it to a USB flash drive from another computer, then put it on the target system. What kind of installer would this NOT work for? Choose the best response.

   - Online installer
   - Portable app
   - Source code
   - Standalone installer

2. What type of software can you modify and redistribute freely? Choose the best response.

   - Commercial license software
   - Open source software
   - Any software
   - No software

3. Which of the following governs software ownership rights and what the purchaser (the end user) may do with what he or she has purchased? Choose the best response.

   - DRM
   - EULA

4. Match the script file formats with their scripting environments.

.bat	Microsoft Visual Basic	
.js	Unix shell	
.ps1	Python interpreter	
,py	Windows Command prompt	
.sh	Windows Command prompt	
.vbs	JavaScript	

5. You're not really familiar with this scripting language, but one variable was defined as a "string" data type. What does that mean? Choose the best response.

    *   It can be any whole number

    *   It can be any fractional number

    *   It can be any combination of alphanumeric characters

    *   It is an ordered set of values, rather than one single value.

    *   It is defined by the operating system or scripting language, rather than by the script itself.

6. You see a # character in a .sh script. What can you guess about the text immediately following it? Choose the best response.

    *   It defines a variable

    *   It is a comment

    *   It is a conditional statement

    *   It is part of a loop

Summary: Operating systems

You should be able to:

- Compare and contrast the features and requirements of the most recent versions of Windows that Microsoft has released over the past 20 years.

- Install a Windows operating system using both clean install and in-place upgrade methods, as well as identify the available in-place upgrade paths.

- Identify common features and functionality of the Mac OS and Linux operating systems and how they differ from the more prevalent Microsoft Windows operating systems.

Chapter 2: Windows management

You will learn to:

- Use appropriate Windows features and tools.
- Use Control Panel utilities.
- Apply appropriate Microsoft command-line tools.
- Troubleshoot PC operating system problems.

Module A: Operating system features and tools

Windows provides a wide variety of tools that you can use to manage the operating system and the computer on which it is running. Most of these are included in the Administrative tools and in the Computer Management tool. You need to know where these tools are and the scenarios in which you'd use them.

You will learn how to:

- Use appropriate Microsoft operating system features and tools.

- Choose the appropriate feature and tool given a specific scenario.

System utilities

Windows has a number of built-in tools that you can use to manage specific aspects of your computer and operating system. The following table lists some helpful tools and the scenarios under which you'd use them.

Exam Objective(s): 220-1002 1.5.5

Windows system utilities

Utility	Use it when you want to...
REGEDIT	Directly edit the Windows Registry, the database containing most Windows settings. In general you should only edit the registry directly when some other tool won't let you change a particular setting.
COMMAND.COM	Use non-graphical tools at the command line or script administrative tasks to automate them. You use Command.com to execute tools such as format, dir, md, rd, xcopy, and chkdsk.
SERVICES.MSC	Open the Services console to configure Windows services on your computer. You can stop, start, and change the startup type for each service. You can also configure how the service accesses your computer by changing its logon credentials.
MMC	Open a blank *Microsoft Management Console*. With the blank console, you can add your own snap-ins to the console tree to create a customized console with frequently used tools.
MSTSC	Open the *Remote Desktop Connection utility* to start a remote connection to another computer. Once you've established a remote desktop connection, you can use the remote computer in the same way you would if you were sitting in front of it, configuring settings, using programs, and even connecting to the Internet. You can use a remote connection to troubleshoot problems a user is having without having to visit the user's location.
Notepad	Open a basic text editor. You can use Notepad to take notes, test printers by print a simple text file, and create HTML code for a web page.
Explorer	Open Windows Explorer, also known as File Explorer. You can browse for files on your computer, or you can connect to the network and look for files on other computers and servers.

Utility	Use it when you want to...
MSINFO32	Open the *System Information utility.* You can use this to help troubleshoot system problems ranging from hardware failures, to problems with software and device drivers.
DXDIAG	Open the *DirectX Diagnostic Tool* to troubleshoot DirectX multimedia technologies. The tool reports driver information for system devices, including display, sound, and input. You can view the information in the tool or save it for future reference.
Disk defragmenter, or DEFRAG	Defragment files your hard drives. You can defragment magnetic hard drives to help improve performance. By default, Task Scheduler runs **defrag** on magnetic disks at regular intervals, so you don't usually need to use this tool manually. Defragmenting SSDs is unnecessary and actually reduces drive lifespan.
System Restore, or **rstrui**	Revert your computer to a previous state, undoing changes made to system and application files and settings, and uninstalling recently installed applications. If your troubleshooting has led you to believe that a recent change has made the system unstable, you can undo those changes by reverting to a state before the change was made by choosing a restore point, a backup of the system made at a s specific point in time in the past. System Restore automatically creates restore points at various times, including before software installations, Windows Update installations, and periodically even if no other changes have been made.
Windows Update, or **wuapp**	Update your operating system or programs, or configure settings related to system updates. Windows Update can automatically check for operating system patches and updates and install them without user input. You can also check for updates and install them manually. Updates often fix bugs that cause problems or create security vulnerabilities.

Running system utilities

You can open all the system utilities using their command names. This can be easier than hunting through the programs list.

1. Type the command.
   - In Windows 7 and Windows 10, click **Start** and type the command name.
   - In Windows 8 and Windows 8.1, type the command name at the Start screen.
2. Press **Enter**.

Administrative Tools

All Windows versions from Windows Vista through Windows 8.1 provide a set of tools that you can use to manage the computer and the operating system. These are collectively known as the Administrative Tools, and you can find them in Control Panel under System and Maintenance (Windows Vista) or System and

Security (Windows 7 and Windows 8/8.1). The following figure shows the Administrative Tools in the Control Panel in Windows 7.

Exam Objective(s): 220-1002 1.5.1.1, 1.5.1.4 – 1.5.1.15

Administrative Tools in Windows 7

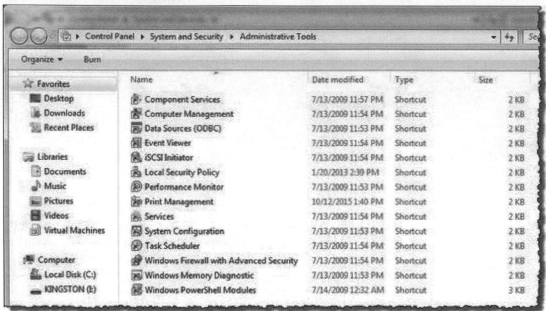

The following table describes some of the Administrative Tools and the scenarios under which you'd use them.

Administrative Tools

Administrative Tool	Use it when you want to...
Component Services	Configure object sharing between applications. Object sharing enables programmers to create applications that share resources, such as databases, on multiple computers across a network, which allows the applications to scale or grow very easily. In day to day work, you probably won't have much use for Component Services unless you're working with a programmer or application support team to fix a faulty application.
Computer Management	Access a variety of management and troubleshooting tools in one place. Computer Management contains several different tools that you can use to manage a computer, including many of the tools listed here, such as Event Viewer, Performance, and Task Scheduler. It also provides Disk Management, which you can use to manage disks and volumes, and Services and Applications, which you can use to stop and start services and programs that might be causing problems on your system.
Data Sources (ODBC)	Manage database drivers and data sources so users can access databases regardless of which application or operating system they're using. Starting in Windows 8, this tool is known as ODBC Data Sources. You're unlikely to use this tool very often unless you're creating and configuring shared databases within your organization.
Event Viewer	Check your computer's health or troubleshoot problems with the operating system or software. Event Viewer captures what are called *events*, which are short notifications of normal operations or errors that are created by the operating system and by applications installed on the computer. Events are logged for a variety of situations on a Windows computer, including software installation and errors, operating system errors and updates, and user logons and logoffs.

Administrative Tool	Use it when you want to...
Local Security Policy	Manage the security policy settings for the computer you're sitting in front of or another computer that you connect to. You can use security policy to configure password requirements, and restrict and allow user access to operating system features. While Group Policy is used at the domain level to apply security settings and countless more settings across an organization that can span a building, a campus, and the world, Local Security Policy allows you to configure only security settings on the local computer.
Performance Monitor	Track and analyze your computer's performance. You add what are called *counters* to Performance Monitor to specify which of your computer's resources you want to monitor, including the processor, memory, page file, TCP/IP connections, and any of the many Windows services that are running at any given time. You can use the data you collect from Performance Monitor to troubleshoot any performance issues you might be having and determine which solutions would have a positive impact on performance.
Print Management	View and manage all the printers that are connected to your computer or that are shared on the network. You can also use it to deploy and manage print servers using the Windows Server operating system.
Services	Display information about all the Windows services that are installed on your computer. Windows services control all aspects of the operating system's interaction with the computer and the network. You can use Services to stop and start services to resolve problems you might be experiencing. You can also configure services to start automatically, and you can configure them to use a specific user account to perform their functions.
System Configuration	Configure and troubleshoot the startup process of the operating system and Windows services.
Task Scheduler	Schedule administrative tasks using an executable program. You can set the program to run at a time interval that you choose. For example, you could run a backup program every day at 6:00 p.m. to back up important files to an external location.
Windows Firewall with Advanced Security	Configure security on your computer's network communications. The firewall filters traffic both entering and leaving your computer to ensure that your computer is safe from hackers and any malware attacks that could steal or destroy private data and communications.
Windows Memory Diagnostic (Memory Diagnostic Tool in Windows Vista)	Troubleshoot computer's memory by detecting errors in your memory chips. The memory test is run during a restart, and you can choose to restart immediately to perform the check, or schedule the check to run the next time you restart your computer. You can use this tool to troubleshoot problems with memory that cause the Blue Screen of Death (BSOD) and spontaneous shutdowns and restarts.

Microsoft Management Console

A Microsoft Management Console (MMC) is tool that you can use to manage a Windows operating system and the computer on which it is running, as well as the network and other computers and services on the network. As you can see in the following figure, an MMC has several components.

A Microsoft Management Console

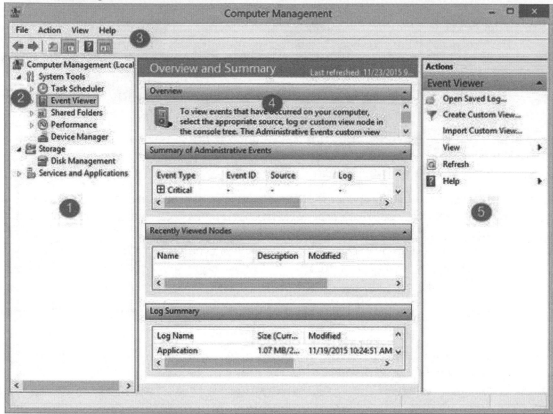

1. The *console tree* contains the name of the tool at the top. The MMC is named for this tool.

2. There is a *snap-in* for each tool in the MMC. As you can see in the figure, there are multiple snap-ins in this MMC.

3. The top of the MMC window has both a menu bar and a toolbar, just like any Windows application.

4. The *details pane* displays any information for the snap-in that's selected in the console tree.

5. The *action pane* displays any actions that you can take based on the snap-in you've selected.

Some Windows utilities, such as Computer Management, are really just MMC instances with a preconfigured assortment of snap-ins. The value of running MMC itself is that you can mix or match snap-ins to suit any combination of management tasks you perform frequently. To do so, start MMC and click **File > Add/Remove Snap-in**

MSCONFIG

MSCONFIG, also known as the System Configuration utility, is used to modify and troubleshoot system startup processes and services. To open the utility, click Start and type `msconfig`. You can also open Control Panel, System and Security, Administrative Tools, and double-click System Configuration.

Exam Objective(s): 220-1002 1.5.2

System Configuration Utility (MSCONFIG)

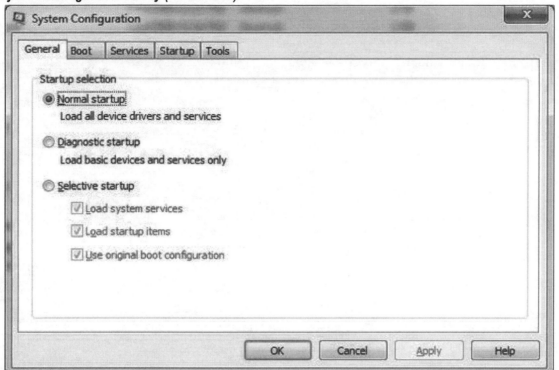

The following table lists the settings you can configure on the tabs in the System Configuration dialog box.

System Configuration settings

Tab	Use it when you want to...
General	Choose the type of startup for the next time you boot the computer to troubleshoot system startup problems. You can select Normal, with all the usual programs and services; Diagnostic, with just the basics; and Selective, with the programs and services that you choose.
Boot	See all the copies of Windows you have installed, set a default operating system, and delete an operating system. You can also set up safe boot options.
Services	Enable or disable Windows services on your computer to troubleshoot system problems.
Startup	Enable or disable startup programs, which can help you troubleshoot a computer that's slow to start. **Note:** In Windows 10 startup programs have been moved to Task Manager.
Tools	Launch a variety of Windows configuration and troubleshooting tools, including Computer Management, Event Viewer, and Performance Monitor.

Exercise: Using administrative tools

Do This	How & Why
1. Explore Administrative Tools.	
a) Click **Start > Windows System > Windows Administrative Tools**.	The **Administrative Tools** screen is also available in Control Panel. It shows a list of links to various system utilities.
b) Double-click **System Information**.	This utility shows information about hardware and software configuration.
c) In Administrative Tools, double-click **Computer Management**.	You can close System Information first if you want. This utility contains a variety of other tools in a console tree. Some are in Administrative Tools too, but some are not.
d) Navigate to **Services and Applications > Services**.	It shows a list of all installed Windows services and their status.
e) Close all open windows.	
2. Use the Microsoft Management Console.	MMC is the same interface as Computer Management, but lets you customize what tools to add. On a network, you can configure many to manage remote computers.
a) In the Start menu, type MMC.	
b) Click **MMC**, then **Yes**.	You need to give Windows permission to run the program. The console opens, but it has no contents.
c) Click **File > Add/Remove Snap-in**.	A list of available snap-ins appears.

d) Select **Device Manager** and click **Add**.

It's added to the selected list.

e) Add some more snap-ins of your choice.	Select them and click **Add**. If you're asked for further options, choose the default.

Do This	How & Why
f) Click **OK** when you're done.	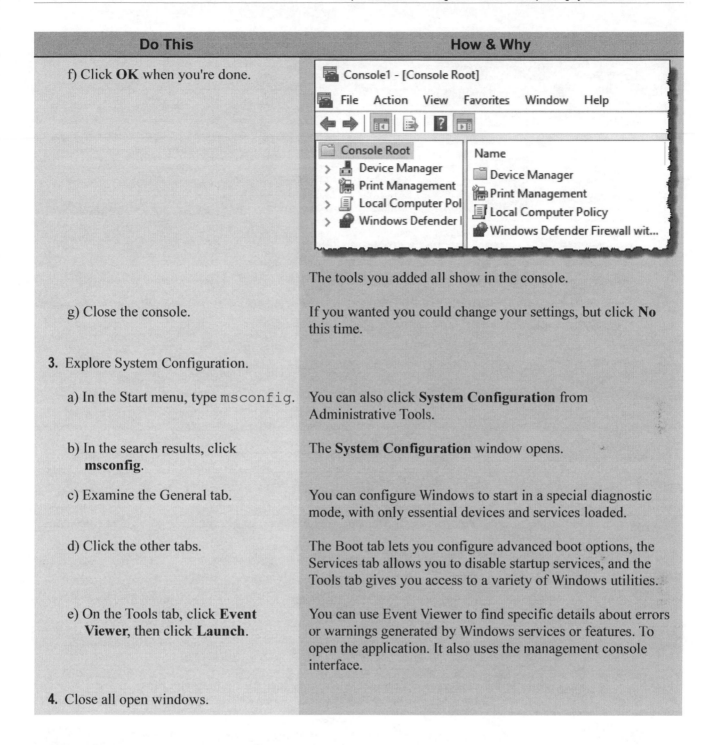
	The tools you added all show in the console.
g) Close the console.	If you wanted you could change your settings, but click **No** this time.
3. Explore System Configuration.	
a) In the Start menu, type `msconfig`.	You can also click **System Configuration** from Administrative Tools.
b) In the search results, click **msconfig**.	The **System Configuration** window opens.
c) Examine the General tab.	You can configure Windows to start in a special diagnostic mode, with only essential devices and services loaded.
d) Click the other tabs.	The Boot tab lets you configure advanced boot options, the Services tab allows you to disable startup services, and the Tools tab gives you access to a variety of Windows utilities.
e) On the Tools tab, click **Event Viewer**, then click **Launch**.	You can use Event Viewer to find specific details about errors or warnings generated by Windows services or features. To open the application. It also uses the management console interface.
4. Close all open windows.	

Task Manager

Task Manager is a tool that's found in every version of Windows that you can use to accomplish a variety of system management and troubleshooting tasks. To open Task Manager:

- Right-click on the taskbar and choose **Task Manager**.
- Press **Ctrl-Shift-Esc**.
- Press **Ctrl-Alt-Del** and click **Task Manager**.

Exam Objective(s): 220-1002 1.5.3

Task Manager in Windows 7

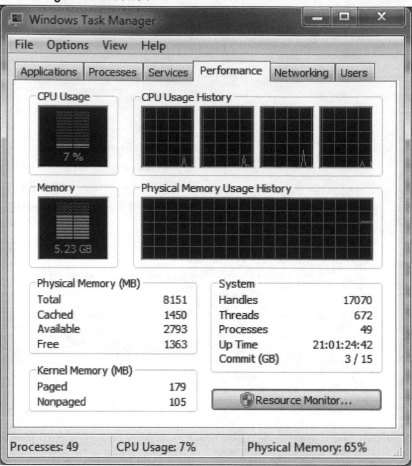

The following table describes how you can use the tabs in Task Manager to configure Windows' performance.

Task Manager settings in Windows Vista and Windows 7

Tab	Use it when you want to...
Applications	Lists all the open applications. You can stop, start, and switch between applications.
Processes	Lists all the processes running on the computer. You can use this to end processes that might be interfering with the computer's operation.
Services	Lists all the services on the computer, both those that are running and those that are stopped. You can start and stop services, and you can open the Services tool from this tab.
Performance	Display performance statistics. You can use this information to troubleshoot system performance by finding performance bottlenecks in the CPU and memory. This tab displays real-time graphical information about system performance. You can also open Resource Monitor from this tab.
Networking	Display networking performance statistics. Like the Performance tab, this tab displays real-time graphical information about your computer's networking performance. You can use this tab to determine whether the network is a performance bottleneck.
Users	Display the users that are currently logged on to the computer. You can use this tab to log yourself off from the computer, and if you have the appropriate administrative rights, you can log off other users or send them a message that they'll see when they log on again.

The first time you open Task Manager in Windows 8 or later, it will show a simplified view with only active applications. To see the rest, you need to click **More Details**. Once you do the interface will look more like Window's 7's, but with different tabs.

Task Manager in Windows 8

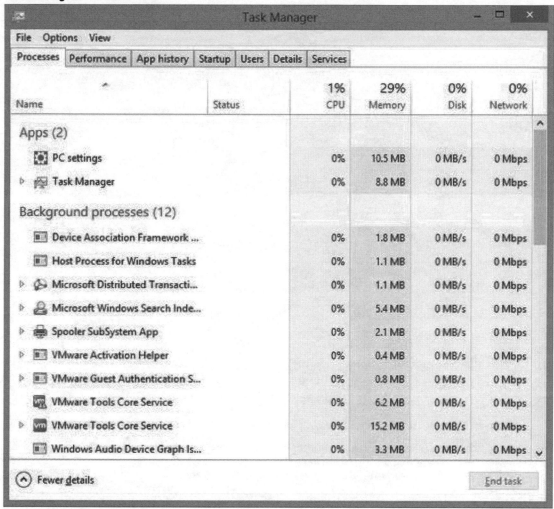

While some of the tabs are the same, there are some differences that are noted in the following table.

Task Manager tabs in Windows 8

Tab	Description
Processes	Lists open apps and running processes.
App History	Displays usage statistics for all the applications installed on the computer, including CPU time and network usage.
Startup	Lists programs that are configured to run at system startup. You can disable programs if you think they're affecting the computer during startup.
Details	Displays a detailed list of processes currently running on the computer.

Exercise: Using Task Manager

Do This	How & Why
1. Open Notepad, Calculator, and Edge.	Before you open Task Manager, you should have some apps running.
2. End a task from Task Manager.	
a) Press **Ctrl+Shift+Esc**.	Task Manager opens, displaying just the three apps you opened.
b) Select **Notepad**.	Normally, you would use Task Manager for closing apps that aren't responding normally, but you can use it on any program.
c) Click **End Task**.	Remember that if you close a program with Task Manager, you'll lose any unsaved information. Notepad closes.
3. View the rest of Task Manager.	
a) Click **More details**.	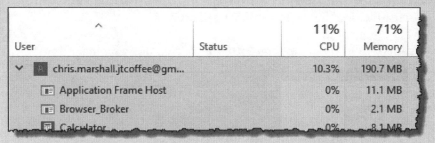
	The full interface of Task Manager opens, showing several tabs. The Processes tab is selected.
b) Scroll through the list of apps and processes.	Not only are running apps displayed, but so are all the background processes running on your computer. Task Manager also displays the CPU, memory, disk access, network use, and power use of each process.
c) Click the **Details** tab.	It shows the same list of processes, but with more details for each.
d) Click **Services**.	To view the full list of Windows services that are installed, whether they're running or not. Some are part of Windows, while others were installed with apps. You could use this tab to enable services that were disabled, or disable those you don't need.
e) Click **Users**.	It looks like the Processes tab, but shows the users logged into the computer. You should be the only one on the list right now.

f) Double-click your user name.

If multiple people are logged on, you can use this tab to sort processes by who is running them.

User	Status	11% CPU	71% Memory
⌄ ▣ chris.marshall.jtcoffee@gm...		10.3%	190.7 MB
▣ Application Frame Host		0%	11.1 MB
▣ Browser_Broker		0%	2.1 MB
▣ Calculator		0%	8.1 MB

Do This	How & Why
g) Click **Startup**.	To view apps that run when you start Windows. If one of them were causing performance issues, you could disable it.
h) Click **App history**.	To view the total CPU and network use for all installed Windows apps over time. Even if an app isn't running right now, you can use this tab to find out if it has consumed unusual amounts of resources.
4. View your computer's performance settings.	
a) Click the **Performance** tab.	To display a graphical chart of your computer's resource usage. The CPU chart is displayed by default, and thumbnails of other elements are on the left. All the charts constantly update to track activity.
b) In the Navigation pane, click **Ethernet**.	Click **Wi-Fi** if your computer is using a wireless connection. To show network use in the main chart.
c) In Edge, open a couple of websites in new tabs.	For best results, choose something with a lot of graphics or other content to display.
d) Switch back to Task Manager.	Network usage sharply increases when Edge loads the page. You can see similar spikes in CPU and disk usage too.
5. Close all open windows.	

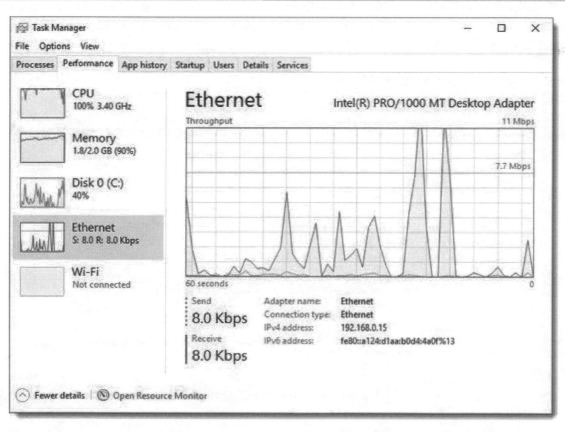

Windows Update

Windows Update is the tool that you use to manage updates and patches to the operating system and select installed applications. You'll typically encounter the following types of updates for your Windows system.

Exam Objective(s): 220-1002 1.5.5.12

Windows updates

Type	This type of update provides...
General update	General fixes and enhancements to the operating system and its features. These updates can fix problems that were introduced by other updates or by known driver or firmware updates from third parties.
Security update	Patches for known security flaws. New security issues are always emerging, and Microsoft tries to keep up with fixes to patch newly found vulnerabilities.
Application update	Updates to Microsoft applications, such as Office, Outlook, or a bundled application, such as Windows Defender.
Service pack	Cumulative updates of all types, wrapped into one update. Service packs are typically considered significant operating system upgrades.
Feature update	In Windows 10, a combination of cumulative security updates plus new operating system features and changes. Feature updates serve the purpose of both service packs and version upgrades in earlier Windows editions.

Windows Update looks different in different Windows editions. In Windows 7 it's in the Control Panel, and in Windows 10 it's in Windows Settings. The available options and functionality also vary between Windows versions, but it's not hard to find your way around any version once you know where to look.

Windows Update in Windows 7, and Windows 10

Updating Windows

You can either update Windows manually by downloading and installing updates, or you can configure automatic updates to take care of the process for you.

1. Open Windows Update.

   - In Windows 7, 8, and 8.1, navigate to **Control Panel > System and Security > Windows Update**,
   - In Windows 10, navigate to **Settings > Update and Security > Windows Update**.'

2. Decide how you want to handle updates.

   - Click **Check for updates**, to manually check for updates and install them manually. In Windows 7, 8, and 8.1 you can also choose which updates to install.

   - In Windows 7, 8, and 8.1 you can enable or disable automatic updates, or modify settings for how updates are automatically downloaded and installed.

   - In Windows 10 you can't choose whether to install updates automatically, but you can choose when they are installed.

   - Advanced options allow you to customize updates further. For example, you can also choose to check for updates for other Microsoft applications.

3. Follow the directions to complete Windows Update configuration and the installation of any updates.

4. After the updates are installed, or at any time you want to see which updates have been installed, click `View update history` to see a list of installed updates.

Migration and upgrade tools

Microsoft provides multiple tools intended for users who want to upgrade Windows but aren't sure if their system supports the new version, or who want to migrate their files and settings from one computer to another. Most of them are highly dependent on both the original and destination operating system.

For each new Windows version, Microsoft has included a downloadable tool called either the *Microsoft Upgrade Advisor* or *Upgrade Assistant.* When you run the program, it scans your computer to determine if upgrade is supported from your current Windows version, and if your installed software and devices will work in the new Windows version. You can download these tools if you are using Windows 8.1 or earlier and are considering an upgrade to a newer Windows version.

Since Windows 10 uses feature updates instead of new versions, the Upgrade Advisor has been replaced with the *Update Assistant* which is designed to help you upgrade more quickly from an older Windows 10 installation to the latest version. It's useful if you have had a computer offline for a long time, or have recently installed from an older media version. You can also download the *Media Creation Tool* to create install media for the newest edition.

When you want to migrate user files and settings from one computer to another, a popular enterprise solution is the *User State Migration Tool. USMT* is a command-line utility which can transfer user accounts, files and folders, multimedia files, Windows settings, program files, and internet settings. To migrate to a Windows 7 computer you will need USMT version 4, included in the Windows Automated Installation Kit (WAIK). To migrate to newer versions of Windows, you will need USMT version 5 or later, included in the Windows Assessment and Deployment Kit (ADK).

USMT is a difficult tool to use, and is intended for experienced IT professionals comfortable with scripting languages. For end users Microsoft included *Windows Easy Transfer* with Windows Vista through Windows 8.1. It performs similar functions to USMT but in a friendlier graphical interface. You can transfer files using a network, a removable storage device, or a specialized Easy Transfer Cable.

Windows 10 doesn't support Windows Easy Transfer either as a source or destination operating system. There arc third party tools with similar functionality, but you might not need them. The Microsoft accounts supported by Windows 8 and later allow you to synchronize files and settings between multiple PCs, so you can just set up the new computer with an existing Microsoft account.

Exercise: Configuring Windows update

Unless you have a good reason otherwise, Windows should always be configured to automatically install updates. If you have a Windows 7 or 8 computer, open Windows Update in Control Panel to make Windows automatically downloads and installs updates. In Windows 10 this shouldn't be a problem, but check update settings as follows:

Do This	How & Why
1. In the **Settings** window, click **Update & security**.	You can open Settings by pressing **Windows+I**. Windows Update settings are displayed, along with when your system was last updated.
2. Click **Check for updates**.	If updates are available, Windows will download and install them. You may need to restart.
3. Change when Windows restarts for updates.	
a) In the Windows Update screen, click **Change active hours**.	By default, Windows won't restart for updates between 8 a.m. and 5 p.m.
b) From the End time list, select **7:00 PM** and click ✓	Sometimes you're at work late, and you don't want Windows to restart when you step out for coffee.
c) Click **Save**.	To return to Windows Update.
d) Click **Restart options**, if it's visible.	If you have an update pending, you can schedule it for a time you know you won't need your computer.
e) Return to the Windows Update tab.	Click **Back**, if necessary.
4. Examine further update options.	Even if Windows 10 removes some update options from earlier versions, it adds some new ones as well.
a) Click **Advanced options**.	You can update other Microsoft products, defer feature updates, and sign in automatically after an update.
b) Check **Give me updates for other Microsoft products when I update Windows**.	You don't have any other Microsoft products right now, but if you installed Office, for example, it would now update along with Windows.
c) Click **Delivery optimization**.	By default, Windows 10 computers share updates with each other, increasing overall update speed.
5. Close all open windows.	

Disk Management

Disk Management provides all the tools you need to manage the hard disks installed in your computer. You can access Disk Management in the Computer Management console, as shown in the following figure.

Exam Objective(s): 220-1002 1.5.4

Disk Management in Windows 10

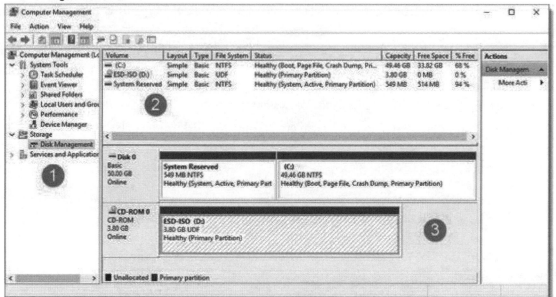

Disk Management contains the following components:

1 You can open Disk Management as an independent tool, or from the console tree in Computer Management. When you select it, it displays information about your disks and volumes in the details pane.

2 The top of the details pane lists the volumes that are configured on your computer. You can see the volume name, the layout, type, file system, and status.

3 The bottom of the details pane displays a graphical representation of your disks and the volumes on each disk. In the figure above, you can see that the volume titled System Reserved doesn't have a drive letter assigned to it. The other volume on that disk is the C drive, which is currently selected.

Creating volumes

You can create multiple types of volumes using Disk Manager. The following table describes the types of volumes you can create.

Types of volumes

Volume	Description
Simple	A volume with space on one physical disk.
Spanned	A volume with space on at least two physical disks.
Striped	A RAID-0 volume where blocks of each file are written across two or more disks to boost performance.

Volume	Description
Mirrored	A RAID-1 volume where the same data is written simultaneously across two disks to boost fault tolerance.
RAID-5	A volume written across at least three disks with parity to provide fault tolerance and prevent data loss.

1. In Disk Management, right-click a block of unallocated space and choose the type of volume you want to create.

   Depending on your disk configuration, not all options will be available. Simple volumes are suitable for most workstation use.

2. Complete the wizard with your specific information, which can include volume size, disks (if creating a volume that spans multiple disks), drive letter, and file system.

3. In Disk Management, verify that the volume has been created and the disk status is Healthy.

Extending volumes

You can increase the size of existing volumes to use unallocated space on a disk. The size of the volume is limited by the size of the disk.

Extending a volume in Windows 8

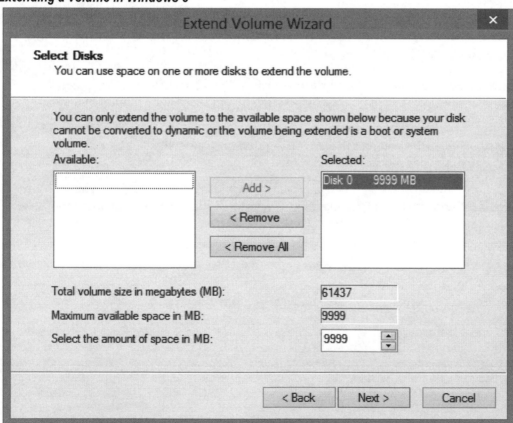

1. In Disk Management, right-click the volume you want to extend and choose **Extend Volume**. Click **Next**.

2. In the Extend Volume Wizard, select the amount of space by which you want to increase the volume. You can only increase the size to the maximum specified in the wizard.

3. Complete the wizard, and in Disk Management, verify that the volume has been extended and the volume status is Healthy.

Shrinking volumes

You can shrink volumes that aren't full to capacity. You can then create additional volumes with the unallocated space you've gained on the disk. This is also known as splitting volumes because you're splitting a single volume into two.

Shrinking a volume

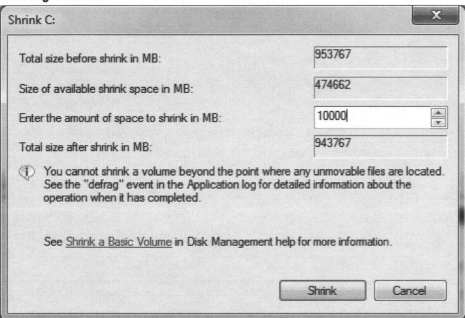

1. In Disk Management, right-click the volume you want to shrink and choose **Shrink Volume** to open Shrink dialog box shown in the figure above.

2. In the Shrink dialog box, enter the amount of space you want to shrink the volume. This is the amount of space you want to gain back.

3. Click **Shrink**. After the operation is complete, you'll see the amount of disk space you created by shrinking the existing volume designated as unallocated space.

Assigning drive letters and paths

You can modify drive letters on the volumes in your computer by using Disk Management. You can also assign a mount-point folder path to a volume so users can access it using the folder path instead of the drive letter.

Changing drive letters and paths

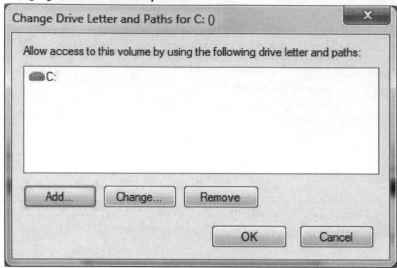

1. In Disk Management, right-click the drive you want to reconfigure and choose **Change Drive Letter and Paths**.

2. In the dialog box, you have three options.

   • Click **Add** to mount the drive in an empty folder.

   • Click **Change** to change the drive letter.

   • Click **Remove** to remove the drive letter.

3. Complete the wizard.

Initializing disks

When you add a new disk to your computer, it may display a status of Not Initialized.

1. To initialize a disk, in Disk Management, right-click the disk and choose **Initialize Disk**.

2. Select the disk you want to initialize, and choose which partition style you want to use.
   If the disk is 2TB or larger, you need to use GPT to utilize all its space.

3. Complete the wizard.

Storage Spaces

While you can use Disk Management in some versions of Windows to implement software RAID, in Windows 8 and later it's generally easier to use the *Storage Spaces* feature. Storage Spaces allows you to create a pool of one or more physical drives, and then allocate virtual drives from within that pool. If there are two or more physical drives, you can enable RAID resiliency features such as mirroring and parity.

To create storage spaces, you need one or more blank drives to create a pool from. Then navigate to **Control Panel > System and Security > Storage spaces**.

Creating a storage space

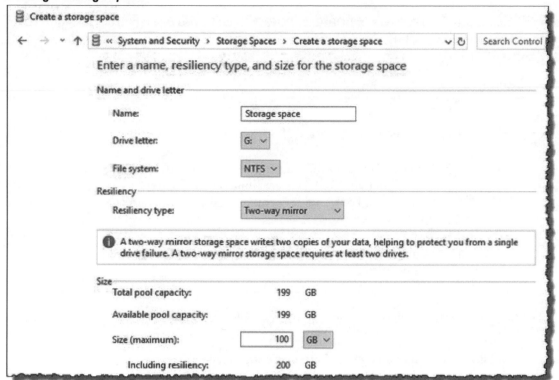

DISKPART

Another program you can use to create and manage disks, partitions, and volumes is **DISKPART**. You run **DISKPART** directly from the command prompt or use it in a script; while it takes some expertise to use effectively, it can do things the Disk Management utility cannot. At the command prompt, type **diskpart** to enter the program. You then use the **LIST** command with **disk**, **partition**, or **volume** to list the hard drives, partitions, or volumes on your computer. To work with a particular disk, partition, or volume, you need to specify it using the **SELECT** command. For example, **SELECT DISK 1**.

Some **DISKPART** commands you can use to manage partitions on a basic disk include:

- **CREATE PARTITION Primary Size=50000**
- **CREATE PARTITION Extended Size=25000**
- **CREATE PARTITION logical Size=25000**
- **DELETE Partition**
- **EXTEND Size=10000**
- **GPT attributes=n** (assign GUID Partition Table attributes)
- **SET id=byte|GUID [override] [noerr]** (Change the partition type)

Additional commands and switches for DISKPART can be found on Microsoft's Website.

FORMAT

Another program you can use to format drives is **FORMAT**. **FORMAT** can be run directly from the command prompt or used in a script. The syntax of the format command is: **FORMAT volume [/FS:file-system] [/V:label] [/Q]**

Format command switches

Switch	Meaning
/FS:file-system	Used to specify a file system. For example: FAT, FAT32, exFAT, NTFS, UDF.
/V:label	Used to specify a label for the volume. A label is not required, but can be useful. FAT and FAT 32 labels are limited to 11 characters. NTFS can have up to 32 characters. UDF supports volumes labels up to 126 characters, but only 32 will show in Windows.
/Q	Forces a quick format. A quick format doesn't run the check for bad sectors on the volume before formatting.

For additional FORMAT command switches, refer to Microsoft's Website.

Note: It can take several hours to format a large hard drive or partition.

Exercise: Managing drives

To complete this activity, you will need an unformatted hard drive partition on your computer. Without one, you will be able to view disk partitions but not create new ones.

Do This	How & Why
1. View your disk partitions.	You can also open Computer Management and navigate to **Storage > Disk Management**
a) In the root of Control Panel, click **System and Security > Create and format hard disk partitions**.	Look under the Administrative Tools section heading. The **Disk Management** window opens. If you have an unformatted hard drive installed, you'll be prompted to initialize it.
b) Click **OK**.	If asked to initialize a disk. You'll keep the default settings.
c) Examine the **Disk Management** window.	Your exact configuration may vary, but at the least you'll have one hard disk containing your NTFS C: partition and likely a small System Reserved partition Windows uses for some repair and diagnostics tools. You'll also see any other hard disks, optical discs, connected USB disks, or card readers on your computer.
d) Right-click the C:\ partition.	You can change an existing volume's drive letter, format it, shrink it, or delete if. Since this is the system partition, it's not a good idea to try those.
e) Look for any unallocated space.	If you have any, it might be on your primary disk, or on a different one.
2. Create and format a disk partition.	If you don't have any unallocated space, you can skip this step.

Do This	How & Why
a) Click the unallocated space.	To select it.
b) Click **Action > All tasks > New simple volume**.	You could also right-click the space and use its context menu. The **New Simple Volume Wizard** window opens.
c) Click **Next**.	By default, Windows will partition the whole space as a single volume, but you could just allocate part of it instead. You could allocate just part of the available space, but you'll use the whole thing.
d) Click **Next**.	You're asked whether to assign the drive a letter, or mount it in an empty folder of an existing drive. By default, Windows chooses the next available letter, and that's fine for your purposes.
e) Click **Next**.	You're asked how to format the partition. By default, it will be an NTFS partition, and it will be quick formatted without scanning for physical errors.
f) In the Volume label field, type `Project Data`.	You'll leave the other defaults as they are.
g) Click **Next**, then **Finish**.	Before Windows completes the task, it shows you a summary of your choices.

h) Click **Finish**.

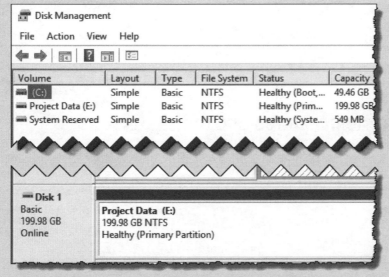

After a few moments, the new drive appears both in the top and bottom panes of the window. An AutoPlay window may also appear for the newly connected disk.

Do This	How & Why

3. In File Explorer, navigate to **This PC**.

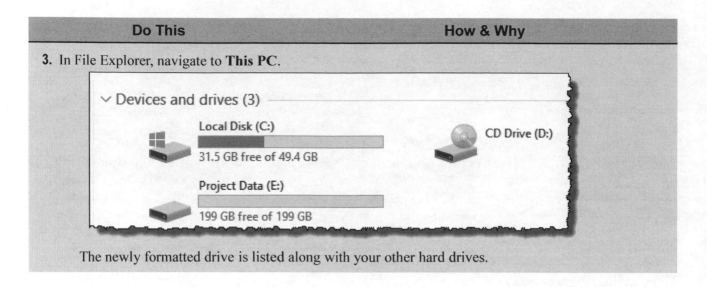

The newly formatted drive is listed along with your other hard drives.

Exercise: Using operating system utilities

Hands-on exercise: Using operating system utilities

If you have a Windows computer available, have students open and explore the following Windows features and tools:

- The Computer Management MMC
- The Administrative Tools folder
- Run MSCONFIG
- Task Manager
- Backup and Restore
- Windows Update
- Registry Editor

Assessment: Operating system features and tools

1. Which Windows utility do you use to access system tools such as Event Viewer and Device Manager?

- Component Services
- Disk Management
- Microsoft Management Console
- Windows Services

2. Which administrative tool can you use to check your computer's health or troubleshoot problems with the operating system or software?

- Component Services
- Disk Management
- Event Viewer
- Performance Monitor

3. Which system utility can you use to troubleshoot a computer that's slow to start by enabling or disabling startup programs?

    *   Disk Management
    *   DXDIAG
    *   MSCONFIG
    *   SERVICES MSC

4. If you have an application that is not responding and you want to force it to shut down, which system utility can you use?

    *   Disk Management
    *   MSCONFIG
    *   Services
    *   Task Manager

5. What RAID types can you implement in software using Windows tools? Choose all correct answers.

    *   RAID 0
    *   RAID 1
    *   RAID 5
    *   RAID 6
    *   RAID 10

6. You want to use Windows Update to update other Microsoft applications such as Office. Which of the following is true? Choose the best response.

    *   No, you must use Office Update instead.
    *   Yes, provided you enable it in Windows Update options.
    *   Yes, provided you have Windows 8.1 or later.
    *   Yes, provided you have Windows 8.1 or earlier.

7. Which switch is used with the FORMAT command to create the label DATA to show up in Windows Explorer? Choose the best Response.

    *   /FS
    *   /N
    *   /Q
    *   /V

Module B: Control Panel utilities

Control Panel is a resource that provides just about every utility you'd need to configure every aspect of a computer. It should be the first place you look when you want to modify system settings or troubleshoot system behavior.

You will learn:

- About the purpose and function of the different Control Panel utilities.

- Under which scenarios to use the various Control Panel utilities.

Control Panel

Control Panel is collection of applets (also called tools, utilities, or apps) that you can use to manage and configure a Windows computer. The applets let you modify just about any option in the Windows operating system, from the way your computer communicates on the network to the way your computer displays images and plays sounds. In Windows 7, you can open Control Panel directly from the Start menu. In Windows 10 you can click **Start > Windows System > Control Panel**. In any edition, you can also open Control Panel by typing its name to search for it, and then clicking on it in the search results.

Control Panel in category view

You can navigate through Control Panel in multiple ways.

- The default *Category view* shows a tree of applets sorted by function. You can click a category name or a link beneath one to navigate to it.

- Click the View By drop-down list then select **Large Icons** or **Small Icons** to view an alphabetical list of individual applets. It doesn't sort by category, but shows some applets which are not easy to find in Category view.

- Type in the **Search Control Panel** box to search for an applet. There are a few applets you actually need search to find.

The Settings app

One new feature in Windows 8 was the *PC Settings* screen, which included an alternate way to access commonly used settings for personalization and account management. By Windows10, the *Settings* window had expanded to include most common settings you might want to change as an ordinary Windows user. In fact, progressive feature updates to Windows 10 have moved settings from Control Panel into Settings, and added entirely new management tools to Settings alone. To manage a Windows 10 computer, you'll need to learn to navigate both Control Panel and Settings.

To open it, click **Settings** on the Start menu, or press **Windows+I**. Each section of the **Settings** window contains a whole list of categories in itself, allowing you to view and adjust all sorts of system options. It also has a search box you can use to find something specific.

User Accounts

User Accounts allows you to create user accounts for multiple users so they can use the same computer. While in large organizations user accounts are controlled by the network or domain administrator and users have the ability to log to the domain from almost anywhere, in smaller organizations different users can share the same computer and have separate settings and private files.

Exam Objective(s): 220-1001 3.9.1.3

User Accounts in Windows 8

In Windows Vista and Windows 7, you can use User Accounts to manage your user account settings such as name, account type, picture, and password. In Windows 8 and later, most of those options are in PC Settings. To access those options, in User Accounts, click **Make changes to my account in PC settings**.

You can use the links in the left column for additional options, depending on your Windows edition:

- Manage your saved Windows and website credentials
- Create a password reset disk
- Manage file encryption certificates
- Manage the properties of the *user profile* which stores your personal settings
- Change the *environment* variables for your account, such as the location of your temporary files.

System

The System utility, pictured in the following figure, provides access to basic system information and links to configurable settings and tools. To open System, navigate to **Control Panel > System and Security > System**.

Exam Objective(s): 220-1002 1.6.5

System in Windows 10

On the main page in System, you can see the following information.

- The Windows edition you have installed, and any service packs that have been applied.

- Basic information about the processor, memory, and system type, either 32-bit or 64-bit.

- The computer name and its membership in a workgroup or domain. You can change that information by clicking the link.

- Windows' activation status.

In the left pane of the window, you also have links to the following tools.

Administrative tools

Link	Use it when you want to...
Device Manager	View, troubleshoot, or update the devices installed in or connected to your computer.
Remote settings	Display the Remote tab in the **System Properties** dialog box. You can use the tab to allow or deny Remote Assistance and Remote Desktop connections to your computer.
System protection	Display the System Protection tab in the System Properties dialog box. You can use the settings on this tab to configure and perform System Restore functions.
Advanced system settings	Display the Advanced tab in the System Properties dialog box. You can use the settings on this tab to optimize Windows' performance, adjust virtual memory options, manage user profiles on the computer, and configure startup and recovery settings.

Device Manager

Device Manager, pictured in the following figure, is a utility that you can use to configure and troubleshoot devices that are connected to your computer. You can access it from the System window, from the Hardware and Sound section of the Control Panel, or just by searching for `Device Manager` at the Start menu.

Exam Objective(s): 220-1002 1.5.1.2, 1.6.16

Device Manager in Windows 8

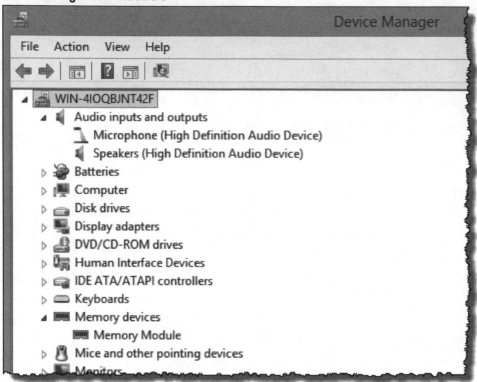

To display information or configure a specific device, double-click that device's category to expand it, and then select the device. You can use Device Manager to perform the following actions on your computer's devices, either by right-clicking the device and choosing from the context menu, or by selecting the device and using the **Action** menu.

- Devices which are disabled or not working properly will have highlighted icons.

- Click **Properties** to view more information about a device.

- Click **Update driver** or **Update driver software** to install a new driver, if you think the current driver is causing problems. You can install a driver from a location on your computer, or let Windows search automatically for one.

- Click **Enable** or **Disable** to toggle the device's active status. Disabling a device is a useful troubleshooting step if you think its operation is interfering with other devices or Windows itself.

- Click **Uninstall** to uninstall the device's current driver. Windows will probably detect the device and reinstall its driver on the next startup if it's still connected, but this can solve some problems.

- Click **Scan for hardware changes** to prompt Windows to see if any devices have recently been added or removed. You can try this if Windows fails to notice a new or removed device automatically.

- Click **Add a legacy device** if you need to add a device which does not support Plug and Play operation. You won't find many of these on a new computer.

Devices and Printers

The Devices and Printers utility displays external devices that are connected to your computer, and you can use it to configure and troubleshoot device settings and add new devices and printers. To open Devices and Printers, navigate to **Control Panel > Hardware and Sound > Devices and Printers**.

Exam Objective(s): 220-1002 1.6.12

Devices and Printers in Windows 7

As you can see in the figure, Devices and Printers doesn't display an exhaustive list of the devices installed inside the computer case. When you open Devices and Printers, you'll see:

- All USB devices that are connected to USB ports on your computer, including flash drives, webcams, keyboards, and mice

- All Bluetooth devices paired with your computer, such as keyboards, mice, speakers, and mobile devices

- Printers, whether connected locally or on the network

- Display devices

- Multimedia devices, such as smartphones, music players, and cameras. This will include devices on the network, and computers which host multimedia capabilities.

You can use Devices and Printers to manage and troubleshoot any device it displays. You can also use it to add devices and printers, whether they're connected directly or over the network.

While Devices and Printers is still available in Windows 10, you can find many of the same functions in **Settings > Devices**. You might find it easier to use for some tasks, but if you know how to use one the other isn't hard to figure out.

Device settings in Windows 10

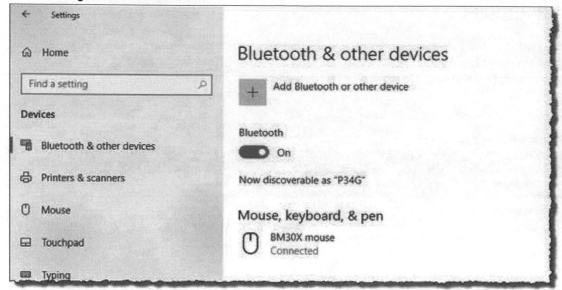

Managing devices and printers

You can use Devices and Printers to view properties of installed devices, add new devices, or troubleshoot problems.

- To view management options for a device, right-click it.
  - Click **Properties** to view general device properties.
  - Click **Remove device** to uninstall the device.
  - Click **Troubleshoot** to run an automated troubleshooter for the device.
  - Other options may be available depending on the device.
- Click **Add a device** to search for available devices to add to the computer.
  For Bluetooth devices in Windows 10, **Settings > Devices > Bluetooth & other devices** has more options.
- Click **Add a printer** to search for available printers to add to the computer.

Network and Sharing Center

Network and Sharing Center provides a central location for managing and troubleshooting a computer's network connection, including the connection not just to the local network but the connection to the Internet as well. You can get real-time information about your network status, and you can use the tools to figure out a solution if you're having problems. You can open it by navigating to **Control Panel > Network and Internet > Network and Sharing Center**. Depending on your Windows version you might also be to right-click your connection icon in the system tray, or click a link in **Settings > Network & Internet**.

Exam Objective(s): 220-1002 1.6.15

Network and Sharing Center in Windows 7

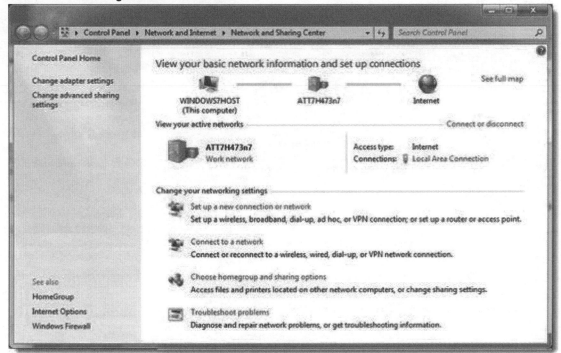

The precise options available in the Network and Sharing Center vary somewhat between Windows versions, but you can generally use it to perform the following tasks related to network configuration and connection troubleshooting:

The **View your basic network information and set up connections** section of the window gives you a visual representation of the network and the ability to see the full network map. You can also see the name and type of network you're connected to.

You can use the links in Network and Sharing Center to configure a wide variety of settings and troubleshoot connection problems.

- Click **Change adapter settings** to display a list of wired and wireless adapters installed in your computer. you can then double-click an adapter to view its status and configure its settings.

- Click **Change advanced sharing settings** to configure settings such as network discovery, sharing of folders and printers, media streaming, and Homegroup connections.

- Click **Set up a new connection or network** to set up network connections. You can configure broadband, wireless, dial-up, or VPN connections.

- Click **Troubleshoot problems** to access troubleshooting wizards that will check your existing network settings and help you fix any potential problems.

- In Windows 7, click **Connect to a network** to connect to a previously configured network.

- In Windows 7, click **Choose homegroup and sharing options** to configure homegroup sharing.

The Network and Sharing Center is still available in Windows 10, but many network settings are more easily accessed through **Settings > Network & Internet**. In practice, you'll probably learn to use both depending on the specific task you want to perform.

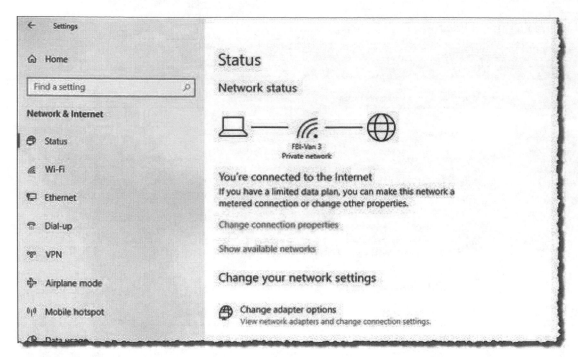

Internet Options

The **Internet Properties** dialog box contains settings relevant to internet connections and the Internet Explorer browser. To open it from Control Panel, click **Network and Internet > Internet Options**. You can also open it directly from Internet Explorer.

Exam Objective(s): 220-1002 1.6.1

Internet Properties dialog box in Windows 7

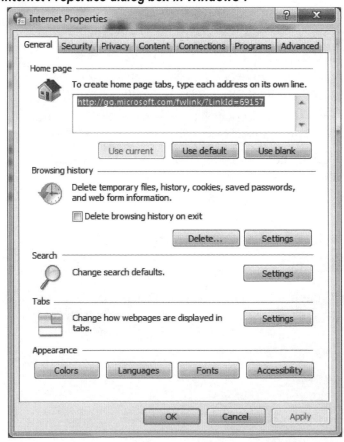

There are several tabs in the Internet Properties dialog box. The table below describes the settings you can configure and how you can use the dialog box to troubleshoot connection issues. Some settings vary depending on your Windows and IE version.

Note: Even if you don't use Internet Explorer, other applications may make use of your Internet Options settings. In particular, browsers and other apps which use web proxies often default to using IE's proxy settings.

- Use the **General** tab to configure IE browsing options such as home page, startup options, search engines, tabbed browsing, browsing history settings, and appearance.

- Click the **Security** tab to configure security settings for different types of websites. You can also add websites to trusted or restricted security zones.

- Click the **Privacy** tab to configure how IE handles cookies and pop-up windows, allows websites to request your physical location, and behaves during InPrivate browsing.

- Click the **Content** tab to configure content-based and parental controls for website access, manage IE's use of security certificates, and set options for AutoComplete and web feeds.

- Click the **Connections** tab to set up internet connections, configure settings for dial-up and VPN connections, set proxy server options, and set options for local area connections. If you don't use IE, this will be the tab you need to access most often.

- Click the **Programs** tab to set options related to program associations. You can configure the default browser, browser add-ons, HTML file editor, Internet program preferences, and general file associations for links you click in IE.

- Click the **Advanced** tab to configure granular options in the areas of accessibility, browsing, multimedia content, and security. If you can't find an option you want, you can look here.

Windows Firewall

Windows Firewall is a built-in firewall product that helps protect your computer by filtering out unwanted or malicious network traffic. You can access Windows Firewall in Control Panel by under **System and Security**. In recent Windows 10 feature updates it has been renamed to **Windows Defender Firewall**, but its underlying functions are the same.

Exam Objective(s): 220-1002 1.6.7

Windows Firewall in Windows 10

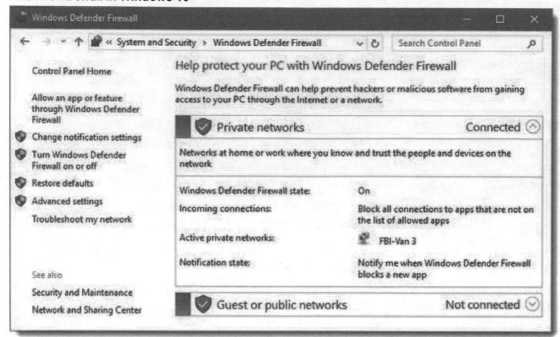

Windows Firewall displays the status of your firewall protection, and the type of network you're connected to. You can configure it separately for public, private, and domain networks. In general, you should only disable it if you use a third-party firewall or need to temporarily turn it off for troubleshooting.

- Use the links on the left to turn Windows Firewall off or on, or change how it notifies you when it blocks a program from accessing the network. You can also access network troubleshooters, but they're the same ones accessible from the Network and Sharing Center.

- Click **Allow a program or feature through Windows Firewall** if Windows Firewall is blocking network access for a particular application or Windows service, or if you've installed a new application which needs network access.

- Click **Advanced settings** to open Windows Firewall with Advanced Security, which allows you to manage firewall rules in more detail.

- Click **Restore defaults** to return all custom firewall settings to the default. This can be useful if you think a change you made is affecting connectivity.

Programs and Features

You can use Programs and Features to uninstall or modify an installed program. You can also use it to view installed Windows update and turn on Windows features. You can open Programs and Features in Control Panel under Programs.

Exam Objective(s): 220-1002 1.6.10

Programs and Features in Windows 7

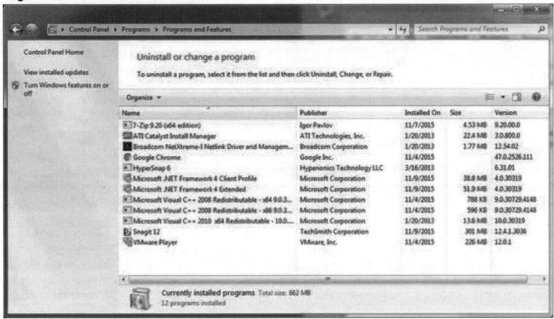

You can use Programs and Features for the following tasks:

- View, uninstall, or repair programs which have been installed on the computer.

- View installed updates to Windows and some other Microsoft components. This allows you to verify that an update has been installed, and troubleshoot performance issues if you think a newly installed update is causing problems.

- Turn optional Windows features on or off, in case you need to use one that isn't installed, or want to disable one that's causing problems. Optional Windows features include interface features like Tablet PC Components in Windows 7, background services like the Indexing Service or Print and Document Services, or network features like SNMP or the Internet Information Services web server.

In Windows 10 you can also manage apps from Windows Settings. To do so navigate to **Apps > Apps & features**. Unlike Programs and Features, Apps & Features allows you to manage Microsoft Store apps,

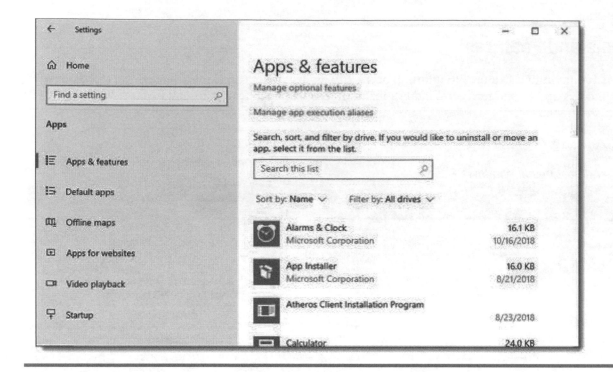

Uninstalling programs

You can uninstall a program in just a few simple steps. In Windows 7, 8, and 8.1, you can use this same procedure to uninstall a Windows update.

1. Navigate to the list of installed programs.
    - In Windows 7 only Programs and Features is available
    - In Windows 10 both are available, but only Apps & Features displays Microsoft Store apps
2. In the list, select the program you want to uninstall.
3. Click Uninstall/Change, and confirm you want to uninstall the program.
4. Complete the wizard.

Folder Options

The Folder Options dialog box (File Explorer Options in Windows 10) lets you configure options for how you interact with folders in Windows Explorer and File Explorer. You can find Folder Options in Control Panel under **Appearance and Personalization**. You can also open Folder Options from within a Windows Explorer or File Explorer window.

Exam Objective(s): 220-1002 1.6.4

Folder Options in Windows 8

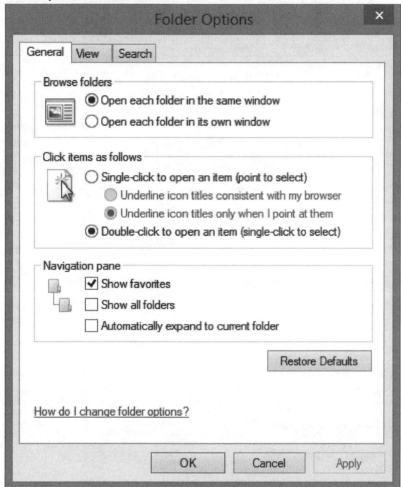

- Use the **General** tab to configure how folders open when you browse them, whether you click or double-click items to open them, and configure the Explorer navigation pane.

- Use the **View** tab to set options for how files and folders are displayed. Important options include whether to display file extensions, hidden files and folders, or protected operating system files. While all three are hidden by default, showing them can be useful for troubleshooting.

- Use the **Search** tab to configure options for file and folder searches.

Each tab has a **Restore Defaults** button in case you need to get yourself out of trouble and set things back to the way they were before you made any configuration changes.

Display

The Display utility in Control Panel lets you configure the options for controlling the computer's output to your display device or devices. You can find Display in Control Panel under **Appearance and Personalization**.

Exam Objective(s): 220-1002 1.6.2

Display in Windows 7

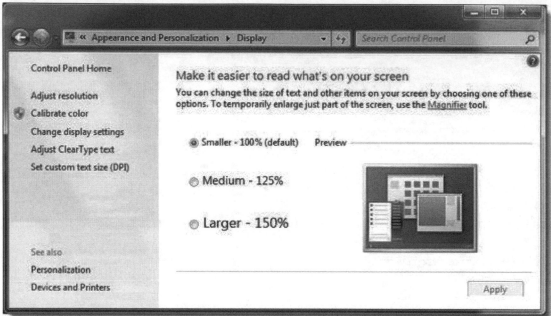

Windows 10 no longer places Display settings in Control Panel. Instead they're in **Settings > System**.

Display in Windows 10

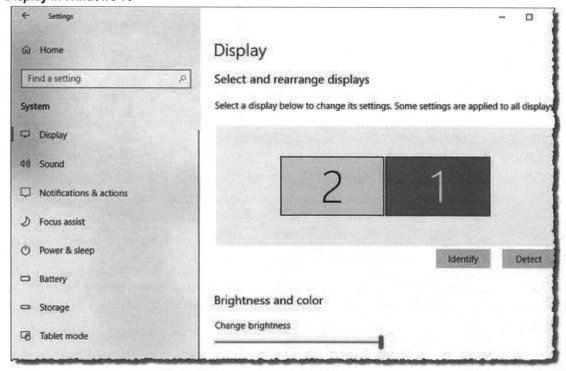

The available settings depend on your Windows version, but some of the more important ones include:

- In Windows 10, settings such as screen resolution and multiple displays are available in the main screen. In Windows 7, click **Adjust resolution** or **Change display settings.**

  - If you have multiple monitors, select one before making any changes. You can also choose whether displays mirror or extend your desktop.

  - Use the **Resolution** list to set screen resolution.

  - Other controls may be available depending on the display.

- You can change the size of text and other items in the main screen of Windows 7 and 8 display or in the Scale and layout section of Windows 10 Settings. Windows 8 and 10 adjust text size more intelligently than Windows 7, in general.

- In Windows 7, click **Adjust ClearType text** to launch a wizard that can make text easier to read on your display. It's less often needed in Windows 10, but you can find it using the Search box.

- In Windows 7, click **Calibrate color** to launch a wizard that can adjust color settings and color depth.

- In Windows 10, turn on Night Light to automatically use warmer color temperatures at night. This can help reduce eye strain.

Sound

The Sound utility is built-in tool for configuring sound properties for your sound output and input devices. You can access it by navigating to **Hardware and Sound > Sound** in Control Panel. In Windows 10 you can still access it through Control Panel, but you can also navigate to **Settings > System > Sound**.

Exam Objective(s): 220-1002 1.6.1

Sound in Windows 7

- The **Playback** tab has settings for audio output devices, including speakers and headphones.

- The **Recording** tab has settings for audio input devices, including standalone microphones and microphones built into headsets.

- The **Sounds** tab has settings for sounds Windows plays during specific events, such as errors or connected and disconnected devices.

- The **Communications** tab has settings for muting or reducing other sounds while you're using your computer to place or receive phone calls.

To manage a playback or recording device, click it and then click an option. One of the most common reasons to adjust sound options beyond the volume control in the notification area is because the wrong device is set as default. Available properties and configuration options vary by device.

Power Options

Power Options give you access to the settings that you can use to configure how your computer uses power. While these options are available for both desktop and mobile devices, you're more likely to get some benefit by carefully selecting power settings on a mobile device than on a desktop computer. You can access power settings in Control Panel under **Hardware and Sound > Power Options**. In Windows 10, some settings are also available in **Settings > System > Power & sleep**.

Exam Objective(s): 220-1002 1.6.8

Power Options in Windows 10

In the main section of the window, you can choose a power plan to manage your computer's power. Power plans combine system and hardware settings to optimize a computer's power consumption. The most visible elements of a power plan are how quickly the computer shuts off the display or goes to sleep, as well as the display brightness on a laptop or tablet. Less visibly, power plans can affect hard drives, processor performance, wireless adapters, and USB devices.

- Depending on your Windows edition and the type of device it's installed on, it may include various settings such as "Balanced", "High performance", and "Power Saver".

- Higher performance settings consume more power, and power-efficient settings will be quicker to shut off displays or hard drives, or put the computer to sleep.

- To change or view plan settings, click **Change plan settings** next to the one you want to change.

  - You can change display, sleep, and brightness settings. On a laptop you can change both settings for when the computer is plugged in, and when it is on battery.

  - Click **Change advanced power settings** to access more detailed options.

  - Click **Restore plan defaults** or **Restore default settings** to undo any changes you've made.

Advanced power settings

- Click **Create a power plan** to design your own custom plan.

- On a laptop you will see additional configuration choices, such as **Choose what the power buttons do** and **Choose what closing the lid does**.

  - *Sleep* or *standby* pauses all processing and places the computer into a low-power state. A sleeping computer still requires some power, but it can power on again very quickly.

  - *Hibernate* saves the contents of your RAM to the hard drive and powers off your computer so it won't use any power. When you turn it on again, it reloads all your open programs, but it takes longer than waking from sleep.

Troubleshooting

The Troubleshooting utility in Control Panel can help you resolve system problems you might be experiencing, such as programs not running correctly, devices not working properly, network connection issues, or general performance and stability problems.

Exam Objective(s): 220-1002 1.6.14

In Windows 7 you can access Troubleshooting in Control Panel under System and Security. Under Action Center, click **Troubleshoot common computer problems**.

Troubleshooting in Windows 7

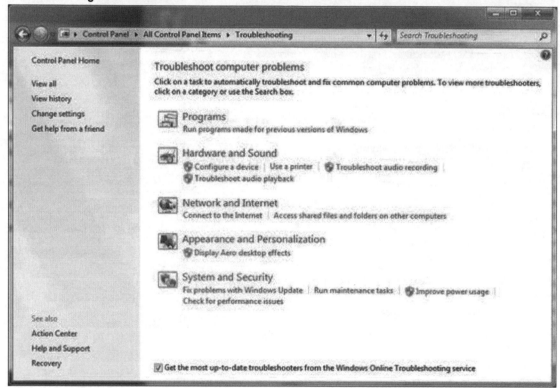

In Windows 10, Troubleshooting is no longer in Control Panel. Instead, navigate to **Settings > Updates & Security > Troubleshooting**.

Exercise: Using Control Panel utilities

Control Panel is a resource that provides just about every utility you'd need to configure every aspect of a computer. You'll use it to modify system settings and troubleshoot system behavior.

Do This	How & Why
1. Explore the Control Panel.	
a) Click **Start > Windows System > Control Panel**.	The **Control Panel** window opens. By default, it shows settings listed by category.
b) From the View by list, select **Large icons**.	
	All Control Panel settings are listed in an alphabetical list.
	Note: You can use either icons view when you can't easily find something in Category view.
c) Return to Category view.	
d) Click **System and Security**.	To view the System and Security category. It contains several subcategories you can explore. The Navigation pane is now visible on the left, showing the other categories.
e) In the Navigation pane, click **Ease of Access**.	To view that section.
f) In the Address bar, click **Control Panel**.	Just like in Windows Explorer, you can use the navigation buttons and breadcrumbs to get around.
2. Examine system settings.	
a) Click **System and Security**.	This section contains a number of subcategories, including the Action Center, Administrative Tools, Power Options, Windows Firewall, Windows Update, and Backup and Restore. Each subcategory also has some direct links to commonly user tasks and settings.
b) Click **System**.	To display your computer's name, organization, and system details. You can also access Device Manager and settings for remote access, system protection, and advanced system configuration.

Do This	How & Why
c) In the content pane, click **Change settings**.	The **System Properties** window opens, with the Computer Name tab active. You can enter a computer description, change the computer name, or join a workgroup or domain.
d) Click the other tabs.	Each gives you access to additional system settings. **Note:** Notice that each of these were visible in the Navigation pane.
e) On the Hardware tab, click **Device Manager**.	You can view and configure hardware devices and drivers here.
f) Close the **Device Manager** and **System Properties** windows.	Control Panel should be open.
3. Examine your power settings.	If you're on a desktop you won't have many useful options, but you should know how to configure power options when you use mobile devices.
a) Navigate to **System and Security > Power Options**.	Use the breadcrumbs or **Back** button if necessary.
b) Click **Power Options**.	Click the **Down** arrow to view more plans if necessary. Your available power plans are displayed in the content pane, while the Navigation pane shows additional options. The details will depend on your PC hardware and manufacturer.
c) Next to the current power plan, click **Change plan settings**.	On a desktop, you're likely to have no options other than how quickly the display turns off. To view available settings for the plan.
d) Click **Change advanced power settings**.	To view advanced power options for the plan.
e) Click **Cancel** twice.	To close the Power Options window and return to Power Options in Control Panel.
4. Navigate to the **Clock and Region** category.	It has two subcategories: Date and Time, and Region. You can use these if you frequently travel or if Windows is displaying an incorrect time. Unlike in earlier versions of Windows, language settings are the Settings app.
5. Navigate to other Control Panel categories.	You can access hardware settings, programs, network settings, and user accounts, among other things. Two important categories from older Windows versions, Display and Troubleshooting, are not visible In Windows 10. They have been moved to the Settings app. Some others can be accessed from Control Panel, but some elements will be links to Settings.
6. Close all open windows.	

Assessment: Control Panel utilities

1. Which Control Panel utility would you use to troubleshoot a printer issue?

   - Device Manager

   - Devices and Printers

   - Printers

   - Programs and Features

2. You would like to set your user's Internet Explorer home page to your company's local intranet. Which Control Panel utility would you use to accomplish this?

   - Device Manager

   - Folder Options

   - Internet Options

   - Network and Sharing Center

   - Programs and Features

3. Which utility is no longer in the Control Panel in Windows 10? Choose the best response.

   - Devices and Printers

   - Display

   - Power options

   - System

4. When configuring laptop power options, what happens when you close the lid is the same as what happens when you press the power button. True or false?

   - True

   - False

5. Which Windows Firewall option is useful when you're troubleshooting network connectivity to determine if a change you made is affecting connectivity? Choose the best response.

   - Allow a program or feature through Windows Firewall

   - Change notification settings

   - Restore defaults

   - Turn Windows Firewall on or off

6. Which tasks can you easily access from the System utility? Choose all that apply.

   - Allow or deny remote access

   - Change the computer name

   - Create user accounts

   - Uninstall applications

   - View installed hardware

Module C: Command-line tools

All versions of Windows have a variety of command-line tools that you can use to perform all kinds of tasks, from copying files to troubleshooting a network connection.

In this module, you will learn:

- Learn about the purpose and function of Windows' most popular command-line tools.

- Understand the scenarios under which you'd use each tool.

Command-line tools

A command-line interface is a way of interacting with a computer. Instead of clicking around in windows and dialog boxes, you interact with a computer using lines of text called commands. The command-line interface could be called an old-fashioned way of executing commands on a computer, as this was the way computers were administered years ago. In many cases, these commands were replaced by the graphical user interface we've come to know in the Windows operating system, but they're still available to use at the command line in a Command Prompt window, part of which is shown in the following figure.

The command line in Windows 7

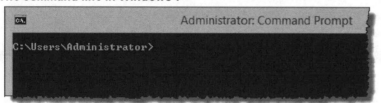

A more powerful command line is available using PowerShell. It accepts the same commands as Command Prompt, but adds additional features. PowerShell is available in Windows 7 and later; in Windows 10 it is the default command line, though Command Prompt is still supported.

PowerShell in Windows 8.1

Administrator: Windows PowerShell

```
Windows PowerShell
Copyright (C) 2013 Microsoft Corporation. All rights reserved.

PS C:\Users\Administrator> get-help

TOPIC
    Windows PowerShell Help System

SHORT DESCRIPTION
    Displays help about Windows PowerShell cmdlets and concepts.

LONG DESCRIPTION
    Windows PowerShell Help describes Windows PowerShell cmdlets,
    functions, scripts, and modules, and explains concepts, including
    the elements of the Windows PowerShell language.

    Windows PowerShell does not include help files, but you can read the
    help topics online, or use the Update-Help cmdlet to download help files
    to your computer and then use the Get-Help cmdlet to display the help
    topics at the command line.

    You can also use the Update-Help cmdlet to download updated help files
    as they are released so that your local help content is never obsolete.

    Without help files, Get-Help displays auto-generated help for cmdlets,
    functions, and scripts.
```

In Linux, you use the Terminal, shown in the figure below, to execute commands.

The Terminal in Linux Ubuntu

Many advanced computer professionals prefer to use the command line at least for some tasks, while most everyday users prefer graphical interfaces. Also, you can automate command-line tasks using scripts, making mundane administrative tasks easier and less time-consuming. One of the chief advantages of PowerShell over the Command Prompt is vastly improved scripting features.

Command line basics

In Windows, the following commands are some basics that will help you get around the command-prompt window and get the help you need.

Exam Objective(s): 220-1002 1.4.21, 1.4.22

Basic commands

Command	Use it when you want to...
`help`	Display a list of available commands and their descriptions.
`help commandname`	Display a description of a specific command.
command`/?`	Display a command's syntax and parameters/options.
`cls`	Clear the command-prompt window.
`exit`	Close the command-prompt window.

Most commands have parameters or options you can set. **/?** itself is one example.

- Parameters beginning with **/** or **-**, like **/F** or **-all**, change the options or functions of the command, sometimes drastically. In general, you can use multiple command options separated by spaces, but some combinations won't make sense.

- Parameters that don't begin with punctuation are frequently variables which represent input sources, output targets, or other named entities that the command should act on. For example, **nslookup www.google.com** will use the **nslookup** command to show you information about Google's web server.

- Some parameters might be mandatory for a given command, while others are optional. In help syntax, square brackets like **[option]** denotes an optional parameter.

When you use commands that perform administrative tasks, you'll need to run your command line interface with administrator-level credentials.

- In Windows, you can right-click Command Prompt or PowerShell in the Start menu and choose **Run as Administrator**. The entire session will then have administrative privileges.

- In Linux, there are two options for administrative commands:

  - Prefix the **sudo** command before any other command to perform it as an administrator.

  - Use the **su** command to change your current Terminal session to root or any other user you have credentials for.

File management tools

There are several command-line tools that you can use to manage files and folders on your computer. They're described in the following table.

Exam Objective(s): 220-1002 1.4.1, 1.4.16, 1.4.17, 1.4.18

File management commands

Command	Use it when you want to...
dir	View the contents of a directory (known as folder in the Windows interface).
md	Create a directory.
cd	Change from one directory to another.
rd	Delete (remove) a directory.
del	Delete files.
copy	Copy files from one location to another.
xcopy	Copy files, directories, and subdirectories.
robocopy	Copy files and directories. This command was introduced in Windows Vista and provides a more robust tool to replace **xcopy**.
extract	Extract files from a cabinet file, which have a .cab file extension.
expand	In Windows Vista, expands one or more compressed update files.

File management commands usually accept files or folders as arguments, such as a file you want to copy, or a folder you want to navigate to. There are a few guidelines to keep in mind when you write them out.

- If the location is in the current folder, you can usually simply type its name. Don't forget the file extension if it's a file.

- If the location is in another folder you can enter its position relative to the current folder, such as Sales\TargetFile.txt

  - You can use `..` to specify a parent folder. For example, **cd ..\Backups** would navigate one folder up, then to the Backups folder. If you just want to move up one folder you don't even need the space, so **cd..** would also work.

- Sometimes it's useful to use `.` to specify the current folder. `.\TargetFile.txt` would make it explicitly clear that you're referring to a file in the current folder.

- If you don't want to worry about the folder you're currently in, use an absolute file path beginning with the drive letter, or the computer name for a network share. For example, `C:\Backups\Old` or `\\FILESERVER\Marketing\Clients.xlsx`

- If any part of the location contains spaces, enclose the entire thing with quotes. For example, `"Eastern Locations.docx"` or `"C:\\Program Files\Microsoft"`

Disk management tools

There are several disk management tools that you can use to manage your hard disks from the command line. Most require administrative permissions for full functionality, and some may not run at all if you're not an administrator. They're described in the following table.

Exam Objective(s): 220-1002 1.4.8, 1.4.9 1.4.10, 1.4.11, 1.4.15

Disk management commands

Command	Use it when you want to...
diskpart	Create partitions on a hard disk.
sfc	Check your hard disk for corrupt files and repair them. The sfc command runs the System File Checker.
dism	Repair Windows images, Windows Setup, and Windows PE. You can use the dism command when **sfc** is unable to repair corrupted files.
chkdsk	Check a hard disk for file system errors and repair them. It also checks the disk surface for bad sectors. You can schedule chkdsk to run at regular intervals as part of a disk maintenance routine using tools such as Task Scheduler or third-party scheduling tools. In Windows 8 and Windows 8.1, **chkdsk** is scheduled to run at regular intervals in Task Scheduler.
format	Format partitions on a hard disk.

Miscellaneous tools

There are several other tools you should know about that don't necessarily fit into other categories, as described in the following table.

Exam Objective(s): 220-1002 1.4.7, 1.4.12, 1.4.13 1.4.14

Miscellaneous commands

Command	Use it when you want to...
gpupdate	Refresh Group Policy settings, both local settings and those applied at the domain level in Active Directory.
gpresult	Display the Resultant Set of Policy information for a specific computer or user account. You can use this command and **gpupdate** to troubleshoot the application of Group Policy settings for users and computers.
tasklist	Display a list of processes running on your computer to troubleshoot system issues.
taskkill	Stop a process on your computer if you think it is interfering with the system.
shutdown	Logoff the current user on the local or remote computer, or shut down the computer.
bootrec	Repair your Windows installation. The bootrec tool can troubleshoot and repair the master boot record (MBR), the boot sector, and boot configuration data. You'll need to boot the computer from the Windows installation disk to access this utility.

Working at the command line

To administer your computer from the command line, you enter commands in the Command Prompt window.

1. To open a Command Prompt window:

   - In Windows Vista and Windows 7, click **Start**, type cmd, and press **Enter**.

   - In Windows 8 and Windows 8.1, on the Start screen, type cmd, and press **Enter**.

2. At the command line, enter the command you want to execute and any options or parameters, using the command's syntax. You can see a command's syntax and available parameters by displaying its help information. An example of the md command is shown in the following figure.

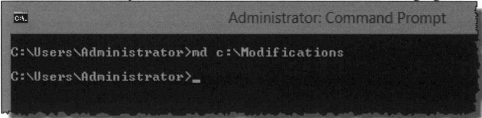

Exercise: Using command-line tools

Command-line tools allow you to interact with the computer outside of the GUI to complete administrative tasks. If you have a Windows computer available, have students complete the following steps

Do This	How & Why
1. Run **cmd**.	
2. Use the **dir** command to list the contents of the current directory.	
3. Use the **cd** command to move into the Documents folder for the current user account.	It's in C:\Users\<Username>\
4. List the contents of the Documents folder.	Make note of a file in this directory.
5. Use the **md** command to create a subdirectory called test.	
6. Use the **copy** command to copy the file you noted in the Documents folder to this test folder.	
7. Verify the file is in both locations.	If necessary, you can use cd.. to move to the parent directory, or ..\<path> to specify other directories in the parent directory.
8. Use the **del** command to delete the file from the test folder.	
9. Use the **rd** command to delete the test folder.	
10. Use the **chkdsk** command to check your hard disk for errors.	
11. Start Notepad from the command line.	
12. Use the **tasklist** command to view all running processes on your computer.	
13. Use the **taskkill** command to stop the notepad.exe process.	

Assessment: Command-line tools

1. If you want to copy a subfolder and its contents from one location to another, which file management command would you use? Choose the best response.

   - COPY
   - MD
   - MOVE
   - XCOPY

2. To get help with a particular command's syntax and parameters/options, simply type the command /?. True or false.

   - True
   - False

3. Which disk management command would you use to check your hard disk for corrupt files and repair them? Choose the best response.

   - bootrec
   - diskpart
   - chkdsk
   - sfc

4. Which command can you use to repair your Windows installation? Choose the best response.

   - bootrec
   - chkdsk
   - gpupdate
   - sfc

5. What command will change a Linux Terminal session to administrator privileges? Choose the best response.

   - admin
   - cls
   - su
   - sudo

Module D: Operating system troubleshooting

While most of the time you'll find your computer's operating system will present very few problems, there are times when you're going to encounter issues. To resolve those issues, you'll need to recognize some common symptoms, and you'll need to know which tools to use while you're troubleshooting problems.

In this module, you will learn:

- How to troubleshoot common symptoms of operating system issues.

- Which tools to use in your troubleshooting process.

Common symptoms

While you might encounter a unique problem that you need to troubleshoot, depending on your users and their functions in your organization, you'll find that you most often encounter some common problems that support technicians have encountered for years. In the following sections, you'll learn about some of those symptoms and how to use common tools to troubleshoot problems.

Windows startup

Beginning with Windows Vista, Microsoft changed the way a Windows computer boots, in part to add support for the Unified Extensible Firmware Interface (UEFI), a firmware interface that's designed to replace the traditional Basic Input Output System (BIOS) firmware interface that's been around for decades. So for Windows Vista, Windows 7, Windows 8/8.1, and Windows 10, the boot process is portrayed in the following figure.

Exam Objective(s): 220-1002 3.1.1.3, 3.1.1.4, 3.1.1.7, 3.1.1.10, 3.1.1.1.11

It's important to note that up until Windows Vista, NTLDR would read the boot.ini file to find the boot partition where the operating system files are stored. If either NTLDR or boot.ini is missing, Windows won't start. From Windows Vista on through Windows 10, the BOOTMGR file accesses the Boot Configuration Data file and starts up the files that load the operating system.

Windows boot process

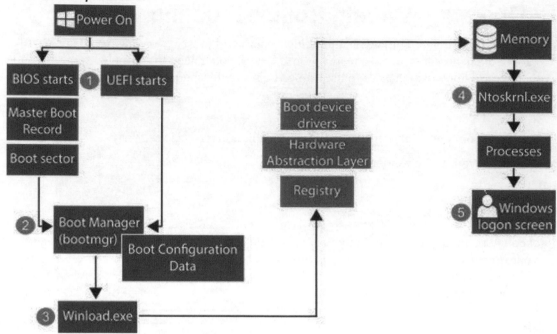

(1) After you press the power button on the computer, one of two things happens.

- If you have a BIOS-based system, the BIOS starts and searches the hard disk for the Master Boot Record (MBR). The MBR contains code that scans the partition table for the partition that holds the operating system and loads its boot sector. The boot sector then points to the Boot Manager file called bootmgr.

- If you have a UEFI-based system, it loads Boot Manager.

(2) Boot Manager reads the Boot Configuration Data file, and if there's more than one operating system that you can boot to, you're presented with a list of options to choose from. If there's only one operating system, or after you choose one from the list, Boot Manager loads Winload.exe.

(3) Winload.exe loads the hardware abstraction layer, the Registry, and boot device drivers into memory.

(4) Ntoskrnl.exe takes over and loads all the necessary operating system processes.

(5) After all the processes are loaded, you'll see the logon screen.

During the startup process, there are a few common errors that you might encounter. They're described in the following table.

Windows startup

Common symptom	Probable causes
<ul><li>Failure to boot</li><li>Missing operating system</li><li>Missing NTLDR (pre-Windows Vista)</li><li>Missing Boot.ini (pre-Windows Vista)</li></ul>	<ul><li>Missing or corrupt files that control the boot process and load the operating system.</li><li>Incorrect boot order in the BIOS (so the system boots to a non-system disk or device).</li></ul>

Common symptom	Probable causes
• Missing Graphical Interface (GUI) • Graphical interface fails to load	• Device drivers that prevent Windows from starting and loading the GUI. • Registry errors.
Very slow startup	• Errors with Fast Boot feature • Driver problems • Errors in startup applications, or too many startup applications.
Windows profile is slow to load after login	• Errors in a startup application. • Group policy misconfiguration • Corrupted user profile • For domain accounts, problem connecting with Active Directory server over the network, or profile errors caused by joining a new domain.

Troubleshooting Windows startup

You should take the following steps when troubleshooting problems with Windows startup. You don't have to follow the steps in order; take the actions that are most appropriate for your situation.

Exam Objective(s): 220-1002 3.1.2.6, 3.1.2.11, 3.1.2.14, 3.1.2.15

- To troubleshoot failure to boot and "missing operating system" error messages, follow these steps.
  - If Windows Recovery Environment (Windows RE), which is built on the Windows Pre-installation Environment, is installed, boot to Windows RE to diagnose and solve startup problems. Follow the prompts to repair the installation.
  - Use MSCONFIG to choose different types of startups to help isolate which files or services might be causing startup problems.
  - Boot to the system recovery image you created using the Windows Backup tool. Choose the option to repair the system.
  - Verify in the BIOS/UEFI that the computer is booting to hard disk or device with a system partition (a partition that holds the operating system files). Update the boot order if necessary.
  - Boot to a Windows Pre-installation Environment (WinPE). The WinPE will provide you with an interface that you can use to access the drive with the system files to correct any errors or to access the computer to remove data files.
    The NTLDR and Boot.ini files, Automated System Recovery, Recovery Console, and Emergency Repair Disks are associated with earlier versions of Windows that are not covered in the latest CompTIA A+ objectives.
- To troubleshoot a missing graphical interface:
  - Boot to safe mode, if possible. Use Event Viewer to attempt to isolate the problem. Use Device Manager to investigate and repair problems with devices and drivers.
  - Boot to the Windows Recovery Environment and use REGEDIT or REGEDT32 to restore the Registry from backup. If you can't use Win RE, use the command prompt.

- To correct problems with a slow Windows startup, examine the following options.
  - Use MSCONFIG to disable unnecessary startup applications and services.
  - Disable Fast Startup in your power profile.
  - Update drivers.
  - Perform a refresh or factory reset of your computer, after backing up data.
- When Windows user profiles prevent you from logging in, try one of the following options to rebuild the profile:
  - Use the `sfc` or `dism` utilities to search for and correct corruption problems.
  - Examine group policy settings.
  - Create a new account, and transfer files from the old account to the new one. Only copy folders with ordinary user data, such as Documents, Downloads, Pictures, and so on.
  - From another account, rename the user's folder, such as from `C:\Users\Student01\` to `C:\Users\Student01.OLD\`. When you reboot the computer, the profile will be recreated at login. Then you can transfer files from the old folder to the new one.
  - For domain accounts, check network settings, particularly DNS.

Entering safe mode

When Windows boots into safe mode, it loads a limited set of files and drivers, and applies highly compatible system settings so that configuration or driver problems won't get in the way of starting Windows and troubleshooting problems. There are a few points to keep in mind when using it.

- Safe mode itself loads a graphical interface but no networking support. Some safe mode boot methods include other options
  - Choose **Safe mode with networking** to load network drivers. This is useful if you want to access the internet for your troubleshooting process.
  - Choose **Safe mode with command prompt** to boot directly to the command prompt rather than the graphical interface. This is useful if you suspect graphics-related problems and think you can fix them from the command prompt.
- To enter advanced boot options, press **F8** or **Shift**+**F8** during the boot process, but before you see the Windows load screen.

  This takes careful timing, and on Windows 8 and 10 computers with the fast boot option enabled, it might not work at all. You'll need to use another option.
- If you can enter Windows and open **MSCONFIG**, check **Safe boot** on the boot tab.

  You can also set any other options you like.

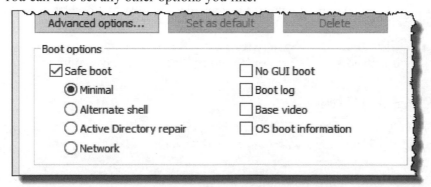

- From Windows or the sign-in screen, press **Shift**+**Restart** to enter the Troubleshoot screen.

a) Click **Troubleshoot** > **Advanced Options**.

b) Click either **Startup Settings**, or **See more recovery options** > **Startup Settings**.

c) Click **Restart**, then choose your preferred safe mode options.

- Windows 10 will automatically enter a repair mode after three failed startups. You can then perform the **Troubleshoot** > **Advanced Options** steps above.

  If all else fails, you can interrupt the startup process yourself using the reset or power buttons, forcing Windows to enter repair mode.

Windows operation

You'll encounter a wide variety of errors that occur during the day-to-day operation of a Windows computer. Of course, which types of problems you encounter depend on the type of population you're supporting, but the most common types of problems are described below.

Exam Objective(s): 220-1002 3.1.1.1,3.1.1.5, 3.1.1.6, 3.1.1.9, 3.1.18

Windows operation

Common symptom	Probable causes
Proprietary crash screen: Blue Screen of Death (BSOD)	- Device drivers. If you've just installed a new device or updated device drivers, this is the first thing you should check. - Memory. - A malware infection.
Improper shutdown	- Power failure. - Forced shutdown by user. - Application errors.
Spontaneous shutdown/restart	- Application errors. - Malware.
- Device fails to start - Device not detected	- Bad or incorrect drivers. - Disconnected devices. - Hardware errors.
Missing DLL	The necessary DLL has been deleted, overwritten, or corrupted.
Service fails to start	The service named in the error message, or one of its prerequisite services. Typically, you'll see error messages when a critical service fails to load and when you try to start a program that uses a particular service.

Common symptom	Probable causes
Application crashes	<ul><li>Application errors</li><li>Application configuration error</li><li>Conflicts with other applications</li><li>Driver or hardware error</li></ul>
Compatibility errors	The application was designed for Windows XP or an earlier Windows version.
Slow system performance	<ul><li>Application errors that are taking over system resources.</li><li>Heavily fragmented hard drive, or lack of free space on hard drive.</li><li>Malware.</li></ul>
System boots to safe mode	<ul><li>Bad driver.</li><li>Device error.</li></ul>
File fails to open	<ul><li>Incorrect file association in system settings.</li><li>Malware.</li></ul>
Multiple monitor misalignment or orientation	The settings in the Display properties are not configured properly.

Back up in the print queue

Causes and resolutions of items being backed up in the print queue

Cause	Resolution
Print job can't be interpreted by the printer or print server	Causes it to lock. Delete the print job from the print queue. If you can't delete the job from the queue, stop and restart the print spooler service.
Bi-directional printing is enabled but not supported by the printer	Turn off bi-directional printing.
Corrupt or incorrect print driver	Reinstall correct print driver.

Printer access denied

Causes and resolutions of accessed denied error

Cause	Resolution
Credentials were not saved properly when the printer was installed	Remove and then reinstall the printer, making sure to save credentials when prompted.
The user doesn't have access	Add the user to the printer's access list. Verify the user is not a member of a group that is denied access to the printer.

Cause	Resolution
Print server or host computer does not have correct print drivers for client	Using Printer Management, install the correct drivers.
Network and Sharing is not enabled	Enable the Network and Sharing feature.
Firewall is preventing access	Disable firewall software.
Anti-virus software is preventing access	Disable anti-virus software.

Printer won't print

Causes and resolutions of a printer not printing print jobs

Cause	Resolution
Out of paper	Add paper to the paper tray.
Out of ink/toner	Replace the empty cartridge.
The printer is not turned on	Power on the printer.
Loose or damaged data cable	Verify the data cable is securely connected. Try a different data cable. If the computer is connected via Wi-Fi, verify the Wi-Fi connection is working.
Incorrect or corrupt print driver	Download and reinstall the appropriate print driver for your specific print device and operating system.
Another printer is the default printer	Print job printed or entered the print queue for the default printer, not this one. Change the default printer or verify you have correctly selected this printer.
The printer is not an AirPrint printer	If you are attempting to print from a "i" branded device, they will only print to compatible AirPrinters.

Troubleshooting Windows operation errors

You should take the following steps when troubleshooting problems with Windows operation. You don't have to follow the steps in order; use the steps that are most appropriate for your situation.

 Exam Objective(s): 220-1002 3.1.2.1, 3.1.2.2, 3.1.2.3, 3.1.2.4, 3.1.2.7, 3.1.2.8, 3.1.2.9, 3.1.2.10, 3.1.2.12, 3.1.2.13

- To troubleshoot a BSOD, try the following approaches.
  - Reboot the computer to see if the problem is resolved.
  - Note the error on the blue screen and research in Microsoft's Knowledge Base. Apply the suggested solution.
- To troubleshoot improper shutdown:
  - Restart Windows normally, especially if the improper shutdown was due to a power failure or a forced shutdown by a user.

- Try booting into safe mode to see if the system will boot at all, and then restart Windows normally.
- Use System File Checker (SFC, or the `sfc` command in a command prompt window) to verify the integrity of system files.

- To troubleshoot spontaneous shutdown and restart:
  - Check Event Viewer to try to find the problem. Apply any appropriate fixes to solve the problem.
  - Scan the system for malware and apply the appropriate remedies.
- To troubleshoot device issues, use Device Manager.
  - Ensure that the device is enabled and its other properties are correctly configured.
  - Look for driver updates, or roll back a newly updated driver.
- To troubleshoot missing DLL files, first note the DLL's name and file location.
  - Copy and paste the same DLL from another computer into the correct location on the computer that displays the error message.
  - Look for associated services and runtimes which might supply the DLL. Many applications require some version of the Microsoft Visual C++ runtime, for example.
  - Use REGSRV32 to register the DLL, which is sometimes required before the file will run on the system.
- To troubleshoot services:
  - Scan for and remove malware.
  - Open Event Viewer to isolate the failed service.
  - If a service seems not to be responding, use `services.msc` to start it, or restart it if it's already running.
  - Examine the service's properties in the Services administrative tool, including dependencies. Reconfigure the service as necessary, or reconfigure a service upon which it depends.
- To troubleshoot application crashes or compatibility errors:
  - Apply application updates.
  - Perform a repair install of the application from Control Panel or Settings.
  - Change the operating mode of the application on the Compatibility tab of the application's Properties dialog box.
  - Open Troubleshooting in Control Panel. Select the option to run programs made for previous versions of Windows, and complete the wizard.
- To troubleshoot slow system performance:
  - Open Task Manager and look for applications that are consuming too much memory or processor resources. Resolve the issue by killing the offending application or process.
  - For a longer-term solution, uninstall applications you don't need, or update those which are causing problems.
  - Check how much free space is on the system drive, and free space if necessary.
  - Scan for and remove malware.
  - Update the operating system.
  - Check the level of fragmentation for magnetic hard drives, and defragment if necessary.
- To troubleshoot a system that boots into safe mode:
  - Check for and fix any errors in Device Manager by updating drivers or rolling back a recent driver installation.

- In MSCONFIG, on the Boot tab, verify Safe Boot isn't checked.
- Use System Restore to restore to a point in time when the system wasn't experiencing these problems.
- To troubleshoot problems right after a hardware or software change:
  - Uninstall and reinstall new hardware, drivers, or applications.
  - Roll back driver or operating system updates.
  - Use System Restore to restore to a point in time when the system wasn't experiencing these problems.
- To troubleshoot a file that fails to open:
  - Change the file association for the type of file that won't open, or if no association has been assigned, create one.
  - Troubleshoot the application you want to use to open the file, to make sure it isn't having other problems.
  - Scan for and remove any malware.
- To troubleshoot misaligned monitors or incorrect monitor orientation.
  - Open Display properties. Drag the monitors to align to them along the bottom or the top.
  - Change the orientation of one or more of the monitors to or from landscape or portrait.
- To resolve problems that are preventing Windows from starting or operating in any capacity, consider refreshing, re-imaging, or performing a clean reinstall of Windows. Make sure to retrieve important files from the computer or backup beforehand.

Mac OS and Linux

The following tables describe some common symptoms you might see when you encounter errors on Mac OS and Linux systems.

Mac OS

Common symptoms	Probable causes	Possible solutions
Proprietary crash screen: Pinwheel	<ul><li>Insufficient memory.</li><li>Slow processor.</li><li>Application error.</li></ul>	Test and upgrade memory or processor, if possible. Close any unused applications; keep open application to a minimum. Quit any frozen applications.
Kernel panic	Hardware or software failure.	Try rebooting. Update software and firmware. Test and replace RAM. Ensure the hard disk has plenty of free space.

Linux

Common symptom	Probable causes	Possible solutions
Missing GRUB/LILO	File has been corrupted or overwritten. GRUB is the boot loader in newer Linux systems, while LILO is the older.	Reinstall or recover GRUB or LILO.
Kernel panic	Hardware or software failure.	Try rebooting. Update software and firmware. Test and replace RAM. Ensure the hard disk has plenty of free space.

Mobile operating system and application issues

Mobile devices are small computers after all, and like desktop computers, they have their share of issues related to the operating system and installed applications. The table below lists some common symptoms and some probable causes. Just like with desktop PCs, mobile device problems sometimes can be fixed by simply restarting the computer.

Exam Objective(s): 220-1001 5.5.1 ; 220-1002 3.4.1

Many problems you might encounter are similar to those you'll find on desktop PCs and can be investigated the same way. Others are specific to, or just more likely on, mobile devices.

Mobile system and app issues

Common symptom	Probable cause
Application errors	Can have a variety of causes. The error message may give more details, but examining full application logs might require root access. Failure to launch at all can indicate a compatibility problem.
Slow performance	Device overheating, lack of sufficient storage, or too many apps running at one time.
No power, or battery not charging	Unplugged or defective A/C adapter, wet or damaged charging port. Battery damage or wear can impair charging as well.
Short battery life	Brightness settings set too high, or too many apps and services running at one time. Battery wear or defects can also degrade life over time, especially on an older device.
Swollen battery	Battery wear or defects causing gas buildup within the cell. **WARNING:** Using or especially charging a swollen battery can cause fire or explosion.
Overheating	Improper ventilation, excessive processor use, or too many apps and services running at one time.
Frozen system	Lack of sufficient storage, too many apps running at one time, or low battery.
System lockout	Security response to failed logon attempts.

Mobile I/O and connectivity issues

Common symptom	Probable cause
No display	Connection to external display, power failure, or display damage.
Dim display	Brightness settings or auto-brightness settings have been modified.
Flickering display	Improper display settings or driver, especially on a laptop. Flickering when the screen is moved usually indicates a hardware problem.
Cannot broadcast to external monitor	Broadcast settings have been misconfigured on the device or the external monitor, or there's a mismatch is screen resolution between the device and the monitor.
Stuck keys or buttons	Dirt or moisture in keyboard, or wear from rough/excessive use.
Touchscreen non-responsive or inaccurate response	Touchscreen is broken, dirty, wet, or miscalibrated in OS settings.
Drifting pointer or "ghost" clicks	Touchscreen driver interacting with mouse use, hand brushing laptop touchpad while typing.
No sound from speakers	Sound has been turned off or settings have been misconfigured, or the speaker hardware has failed.
Intermittent wireless	Items or structures blocking the signal between the device and the cell tower or a wireless access point.
No wireless connectivity	Wireless networking has been turned off, or a failure in the network card or antenna.
No Bluetooth connectivity	On the mobile device, Bluetooth may be disabled. Bluetooth devices themselves may be out of range, powered off, or no longer paired.
Unable to decrypt email	Incorrect email security configuration, mismatched encryption settings, or no S/MIME support.

Unable to decrypt email on mobile device

S/MIME enables users to send and receive S/MIME email messages from wireless email clients. S/MIME and digital signatures provide assurance the message is authentic. Without S/MIME, users are unable to read encrypted email and can't send encrypted email themselves. To fix this issue, you launch the mobile email client and verify S/MIME is installed. The exact steps depend on which mobile email client is installed. If your mobile email client doesn't support S/MIME and you want to use encryption, you'll want to install a client that does support it.

Troubleshooting a mobile device

If you are experiencing issues with your mobile device, follow these steps to see if you can resolve the issue:

1. When something isn't working right, it's possible a necessary feature has been disabled by mistake.

    • Features like Wi-Fi, Bluetooth, GPS, sound, and so on are often toggled by buttons on a touchscreen, or Fn key combinations on a laptop. Check onscreen icons.

- Num Lock and Cap Lock keys are easy to toggle on a compact laptop keyboard, and Num Lock in particular can change keyboard functions. Most keyboards have LEDs to show when these keys are activated.

- When you're sure the feature you need is enabled, you can look for other causes.

2. Many features and applications require network connectivity. Some require connection to specific networks such as cellular, Wi-Fi, Bluetooth, or GPS/Location services.

   - Ensure the service is enabled, and that you are receiving a strong signal.

   - For cellular networks, make sure that your device/SIM card is enrolled with your provider.

   - If a Wi-Fi network requires sign-in, make sure that your credentials are validated.

   - Wi-Fi hotspots, especially public ones, may still have low performance or block access to some network services.

   - Make sure that Bluetooth accessories are paired and turned on.

   - Many mobile devices use *Assisted GPS* (*AGPS*) to determine your location more quickly and precisely. AGPS uses GPS satellites, nearby cell towers, and Wi-Fi networks to lock onto your phone., so all three must be turned on for it to work.

3. Many issues such as slow performance, "stuck" applications, or non-functioning features can be solved by resetting the device.

   - Simply powering down and restarting the device can solve some problems without risk of data loss.

   - Look in the settings menu for a **Reset settings** option (or something similar) to return operating system settings to their defaults. This can solve more problems than a restart, but you'll lose settings you changed on purpose.

   - The **Reset network settings** option can fix network connectivity issues, but you will need to reconfigure your network settings just like when you connected for the first time.

4. When you suspect a problem with a specific application, repair or remove it.

   - A force stop can prevent an unruly app from causing system problems.

   - Ensure the app is up to date, but sometimes an app update may introduce new errors.

   - Clearing application cache or settings may correct lingering problems, but deleting app files may cause loss of application-specific data. Verify that important files are backed up.

   - Uninstalling and reinstalling problem apps can fix many problems. If you don't need the app in the first place, don't reinstall it.

5. Complete an Internet search for a resolution to your specific issue.
   Manufacturer sites, tech sites, and support forums have solutions to most all mobile device issues you will come across.

6. A hard reset of your device may solve problems if all else fails.

   - Hard resets are most useful for problems with touchscreens, navigation, and problems powering on, which don't point to specific apps.

   - Look up hard reset instructions for your specific device. Most require holding down multiple buttons during start, then navigating a recovery interface. There may also be a **Factory data reset** option in your Settings app.

   - Recovery environments can provide varying solutions including cache clearing and full factory resets. Be aware that some can delete all user data on the device, so backups are essential.

If a hard reset doesn't resolve the issue, there is most likely a hardware failure.

Exercise: Troubleshooting Windows

To resolve issues with the Windows operating system, you'll need to recognize some common symptoms and use the appropriate tools to troubleshoot the problem. If possible, have a Windows computer available with some solvable system problem to troubleshoot. If not, perform the following steps on a properly functioning Windows system:

Do This	How & Why
1. Boot to Windows RE and view how it can diagnose and solve startup problems.	
2. Run MSCONFIG to review startup settings and services.	
3. Verify in the BIOS/UEFI that the computer is booting to hard disk or device with a system partition.	
4. Boot into safe mode.	Try a variety of methods for doing so, if time allows.
5. Open Event Viewer and look for any entries that indicate a startup problem.	
6. Open Device Manger and verify there are no device issues reported.	
7. Run the System File Checker to verify the integrity of system files.	SFC, or the **sfc** command in a command prompt window.
8. Open Troubleshooting in Control Panel or Settings. Run the wizard to find compatibility problems with programs written for older Windows versions.	
9. Open Task Manager and look for applications that are consuming too much memory or processor resources.	
10. Run Windows Update to verify all system files are up-to-date.	

Assessment: Troubleshooting

1. When troubleshooting failure to boot and "missing operating system" error messages, which steps would you take? Choose all that apply.

   - Verify in the BIOS/UEFI that the computer is booting to hard disk or device with a system partition.

   - Boot to safe mode, if possible. Use Event Viewer to attempt to isolate the problem. Use Device Manager to investigate and repair problems with devices and drivers.

   - Boot to the Windows Recovery Environment and use REGEDIT or REGEDT32 to restore the Registry from backup. If you can't use Win RE, use the command prompt.

   - Use MSCONFIG to choose different types of startups to help isolate which files or services might be causing startup problems.

2. Which system utility would you use to repair the computer if it continues to improperly shutdown after a reboot? Choose the best response.

   - Device Manager
   - REGEDIT
   - REGSRV32
   - System File Checker

3. Which can cause a kernel panic error to occur on a Macintosh computer? Choose the best response.

   - Application error
   - Hardware or software failure
   - Insufficient memory
   - Slow processor

4. GRUB is the boot loader in newer Linux systems. True or false?

   - True
   - False

Summary: Windows management

You should now know how to:

- Use appropriate Windows features and tools to manage the operating system and the computer on which it is running.

- Use Control Panel utilities to modify Windows system settings or troubleshoot system behavior.

- Apply appropriate Microsoft command-line tools to perform a variety of Windows management tasks, from copying files to troubleshooting a network connection.

- Resolve PC operating system issues by recognizing common symptoms and using the appropriate troubleshooting tools.

Chapter 3: Windows networking

You will learn how to:

- Share and secure resources.
- Establish network connections.
- Troubleshoot network connection issues.

Module A: Network shares

Modern versions of Windows are designed to connect to many sorts of networks. While Internet connections are most popular for home users, they frequently coexist with connections to small LANs or centrally managed corporate networks. Each of these network types has different requirements for both connectivity and security, and sometimes one system will connect to or switch between multiple networks. Before you can effectively configure a Windows network, you need to know how different network and sharing types operate.

You will learn:

- About domains, workgroups, and homegroups
- About network locations
- How to share folders
- Hoe to share printers

Resource sharing

In modern versions of Windows, connecting a client workstation to an ISP is pretty simple and straightforward. Not that there aren't potential problems, but really most of the complexity and questions are about the nature of the LAN, and how to share resources with its other members.

Windows includes tools for a wide range of network services: while some of them are usable on the Internet, many others are intended for use within local networks. Some of them are widely used standards, and others use proprietary Microsoft protocols intended for Windows networks specifically. How they're used depends entirely on the size, security level, and organizational structure of your LAN.

Sharing models

Windows uses three different sharing models, depending on how computers are arranged within the network. Which you use can have a lot of impact on how you share resources and even how you use your computer.

Workgroup　　By default, every Windows workstation is configured for a peer-to-peer sharing method based on the *workgroup*.

- All systems in a workgroup must be on the same local network. Usually a workgroup has twenty or fewer machines.
- There's no password needed to join a workgroup, and no central administration.
- Each computer has its own list of user accounts, called local accounts. To log onto that computer, you need to have credentials for one of its accounts.
- Each computer is able to choose what it shares and with whom.

Domain   Domains are client/server networks centrally managed from one or more Windows servers.

- Domains can have thousands of computers spread across multiple local network segments, as long as all client systems can communicate with their servers.

- Domains are centrally administered from servers. Administrators create and manage accounts for the entire domain, including what resources each account is allowed to access.

- In general, only business editions of Windows can join domains, while home editions cannot. Business editions usually have "Business", "Professional", "Enterprise", or something similar in the name.

- With a domain-based account you can log onto any computer on the domain, whether or not you have a local account on the system. You can still log onto that computer's local accounts, but won't be able to access any domain resources.

- The resources shared by each computer on the domain, whether it's a client or a server, are centrally controlled by administrators.

- Domain users typically have limited permissions to change system settings.

Homegroup   Windows 7, 8, and 8.1 systems can join homegroups, intended to allow easier sharing of common resources like photos, videos, and printers on home networks. The feature was initially included in Windows 10, but was removed in 2018.

- Homegroups are created by one user, and can be joined by anyone with a shared password. The password is only needed once, when initially joining the homegroup.

- Computers already in workgroups can create or join homegroups. Computers in domains can join homegroups, but not create them.

- Home and business editions of Windows can join homegroups, but Windows Server editions might not be able to.

- Each user on the homegroup can choose whether to share any of a list of commonly shared items, such as photos, videos, music, or printers.

- Computers on a homegroup continue to use their local or domain accounts.

- Unlike workgroups and domains, homegroups don't have unique names.

Joining workgroups or domains

You can change your computer name, change your workgroup, or join a domain from the same window.

Note: Individual computers recognize each other by name on the workgroup or domain, so when configuring the network, it's important to make sure each system has a unique name. Otherwise, sharing might not work properly.

Exam Objective(s): 220-1002 1.8.2

1. Open the **System** Control Panel window.

Windows Vista or 7	Click **Start**, then right-click **Computer** and choose **Properties**
Windows 8 or 8.1	Type `System` at the Start screen, and click **System** when it appears.
Windows 10	Type `System` in the search box, and click **System** when it appears.

2. In the Computer name, domain, and workgroup settings, click **Change Settings**.
3. In the Computer name tab of the **System Properties** window, click **Change**.
4. Make the desired change.
   - Set the computer's name in the **Computer name** field.
   - Choose between domain or workgroup networks by clicking the appropriate radio button.

     Note: If you're in a home edition of Windows, Domain will be unavailable.
   - Enter the desired domain or workgroup name in the appropriate box.
5. Click **OK**.

If you're joining a domain, you'll be prompted for a user name and password. This isn't asking for the local user's credentials, but rather of a domain administrator with permission to join users to the domain.

6. Restart your computer for the changes to take effect.

The NETDOM command

It's usually easiest and most convenient to join a domain from the Windows GUI, especially for novice users. Advanced users, or those with more complex needs, can also use the command line utility, **netdom**. Netdom is included with Windows Server editions, and is activated on all systems installed as domain servers. For client versions of Windows, you'll need to install the *Remote Server Administration Tools* (*RSAT*) package, available from Microsoft. On any version of Windows, netdom requires administrative privileges, so needs to be run from an elevated command prompt.

The netdom command can be used for a variety of domain related tasks, but all follow the same basic syntax.

```
netdom command [computer] [{/d: | /domain:} domain ] [options]
```

netdom add	Adds a workstation or server account to the domain.
netdom computername	Manages both primary and alternate names for a domain computer.
netdom renamecomputer	Renames a domain computer (but not the domain controller) and its associated account.
netdom join	Joins a workstation or server to the domain, including making accounts if necessary.
netdom move	Moves a workstation or server from one domain to another, making accounts if necessary.
netdom remove	Removes a workstation or server from the domain.
netdom query	Queries the domain for membership and trust relationship settings.
netdom reset	Resets the secure relationship between a workstation and its domain controller.
netdom help <command>	Displays help information for a given command.

Network location

Every network you join has a *location type*, which is important in terms of network security. If you're connected to a domain, the location type will also be Domain, and its settings will be controlled by the network administrator. If you're not on a domain, you can choose which settings you want to use.

The Set Network Location window as seen in Windows 7.

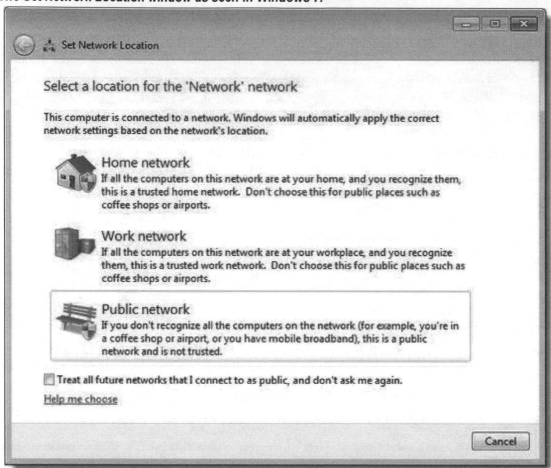

Exam Objective(s): 220-1002 1.8.9

In most Windows editions, networks can be either Public or Private. In Windows 7 Private networks are further subdivided into Home and Work networks. The difference between them is security vs. accessibility.

The Public location disables most workgroup and homegroup sharing features, and instructs Windows Firewall to use stricter rules. It's best when sharing on the local network isn't important and you're just using the LAN to reach the Internet, for example at a public Wi-Fi hotspot, or when directly connected to a broadband modem.

Private, Work, and Home locations all instruct Windows Firewall to use its generally less restrictive Private settings, designed for a network where you can control who else is connected. They also enable workgroup sharing features, including file and printer sharing as well as the *network discovery* service used to browse computers on the local network. The only difference between the three is that Home and Private networks allow homegroup membership if the operating system itself does, but Work networks do not. Domain networks are even less restrictive, enabling access to the network services that Active Directory domain controllers use to centrally manage the network.

When you first connect to a wired network, you'll be asked which location settings you want to use. Depending on your Windows edition and settings, you might be asked when joining a Wi-Fi network as well, or the location might automatically default to Public. You can change the location of a network whenever you like by clicking it

Public and private locations are each separately configurable in other network security settings. For example, Windows Firewall and folder sharing permissions both allow you to separately configure Public and Private networks.

Changing network locations

You might choose the wrong network location, or want to change it later. The steps to do so vary by Windows version.

- In Windows 7, click the network's location in the Network and Sharing Center to open the **Set Network Location** window.
- In Windows 8:

    a) Navigate to **PC Settings > Network > Connections**

    b) Click the network you're connected to.

    c) Turn the **Find Devices and Content** switch **On** for private networks and **Off** for public
- In Windows 10:

    a) Navigate to **Settings > Network & Internet > Status**

    b) Click **Change connection properties**.

    c) Choose **Public** or Private

Create or join homegroups

You can create or join homegroups from the Control Panel. If you're in a homegroup, you can easily share resources, or access shared resources, without sharing user credentials. All you need is to enter the homegroup's password when you first join it.

Note: Homegroups are available in Windows 7, Windows 8, and Windows 8.1. Homegroup support was removed from Windows 10 in the April 2018 update.

Exam Objective(s): 220-1002 1.6.11

Settings for an existing homegroup in Windows 7.

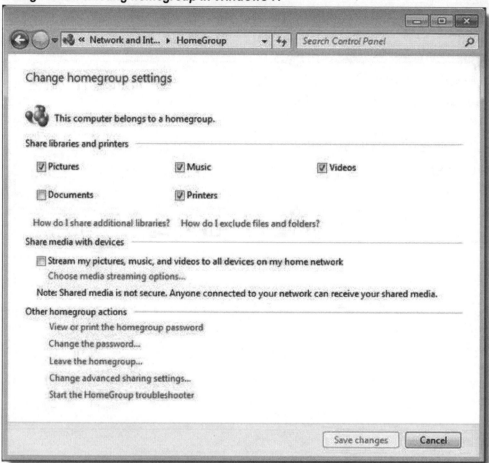

1. Make sure your network location is set to Home or Private.

2. In the Control panel, click **Network and Internet > HomeGroup**.

3. Create or join a homegroup.

   • To create a homegroup, click **Create a homegroup** and follow the onscreen instructions. You'll be given a password after setup.

   • To join a detected homegroup, click **Join homegroup** and follow the onscreen instructions. Enter the password when prompted.

   • If you're already joined to a homegroup, you can change what you're sharing, view the password, or leave the group.

   • If you created the homegroup, you can change its password.

4. Click **Save Changes**.

Exercise: Joining a workgroup

If your classroom has multiple networked computers, you can follow the steps below to set a unified workgroup for the entire class, with a unique name for each workstation.

Do This	How & Why
1. Check your network location.	
a) Right-click the network icon and click **Open Network & Internet Settings**.	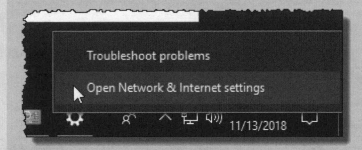
	The Network & Internet section opens in PC settings. The Status tab is selected.
	Note: If you were in Windows 7 or Windows 8, you would open the Network and Sharing Center this way instead.
b) In the View your active networks section, examine the network location.	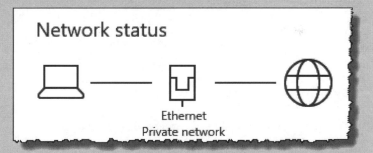
	If your network type is already Private, Work, or Home you don't really need to change anything, but you'll set your network location anyway.
2. Set your network location.	Changing network location is different for each Windows version.
a) Beneath Network status, click **Change Connection Properties**.	The **Network profile** window opens.
b) Click **Private**.	Windows 7 splits the Private profile into separate Home and Work profiles. Your computer is now discoverable and can be used for file and printer sharing.
3. Set your computer name and workgroup.	
a) In Control Panel, navigate to **System and Security > System**.	You can open Control Panel with **Start > Windows System > Control Panel**. Among other details, this window displays the computer name and workgroup.

Do This	How & Why
b) In the Computer name, domain, and workgroup settings, click **Change Settings**.	The **System Properties** window opens.
c) On the Computer Name tab, click **Change**.	The **Computer Name/Domain Changes** window opens. You can use it to name the computer, join a workgroup, or join a domain. To join a domain, you need an Active Directory controller.
d) Set your **Workgroup** as TUCANA, and choose something unique as your **Computer name**.	Or enter whatever your instructor supplies for you.
e) Click **OK**.	If you had joined a domain, you would have had to enter domain credentials. After a moment, you're welcomed to the TUCANA workgroup.
f) Click **OK** twice more.	You're also notified you need to restart your computer for changes to take effect.
g) Click **Close**, then **Restart Now**.	After restarting, your new name and workgroup membership is applied.
4. Close all open windows.	

The System window at the end of the exercise.

Computer name, domain, and workgroup settings

Computer name:	Mocha	🛡Change settings
Full computer name:	Mocha	
Computer description:		
Workgroup:	TUCANA	

Folder sharing

There are a number of ways you can share folders in a workgroup environment. Each has its own rules as to just what you can choose to share, and accessing each depends on different elements of network configuration.

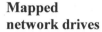 **Exam Objective(s):** 220-1002 1.8.1, 1.8.3

Shared folders   Ordinary shared folders take a little knowledge and configuration to use properly, but they give you the most control over just what you can share and who can access it. You can choose any folder on your computer and share it along with all of its subfolders. Depending on your exact sharing settings, you can control which users can access the folder, and whether they can modify the folder's contents or just read it.

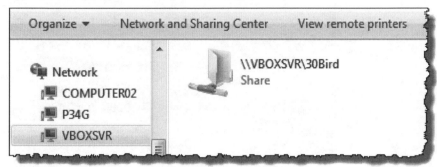

Mapped network drives   Navigating to network shares can be a little tedious, so when you access one frequently you can map it as a network drive. This doesn't change what it is or what you can do with it: it just assigns a drive letter to the folder so it appears like one of your local drives. Network drives appear in your drive listing in Windows Explorer.

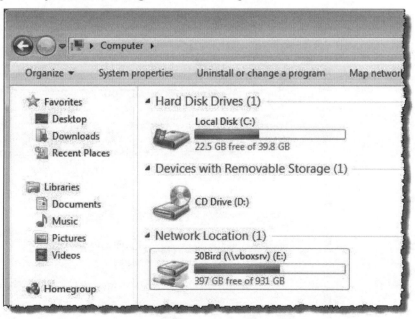

Public folders   Every version of Windows from Vista onward installs public folders, by default in `C:\Users\Public`. They're primarily designed for files shared between different local users, but you can also easily enable sharing of all public folders over the network. The Public folder can have subfolders, either installed by default or added by users, but that's not really important when it comes to sharing; either all public folders are shared to the network, or none are.

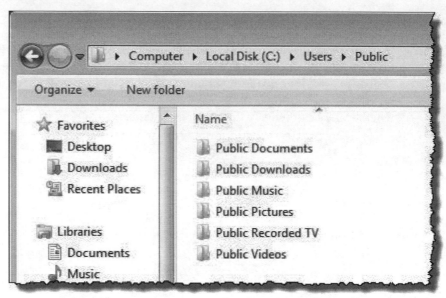

Homegroup folders   When you create or join a homegroup, you share your user folders and printers. By default, all your media folders are shared, but Documents is not, but you can customize the list as you like. Unlike workgroup sharing, anything you share with a homegroup can be accessed by any of its members with no additional credentials needed.

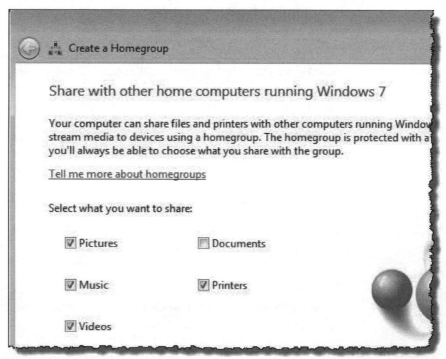

Administrative shares By default, all versions of Windows create *administrative shares* accessible only to users with administrative privileges. They're hidden, so they won't appear when you just browse available resources, and they're not accessible to ordinary network users, but they collectively provide total access to your computer. Administrative share names are easy to recognize because they end with $, for example C$ represents the C drive, and PRINT$ represents all installed printers.

> You can't permanently delete administrative shares: they'll just be recreated the next time you log on. You can disable them if you need the added security, but doing so can interfere with certain network functions.

Browsing networks

In general, you connect to shared resources on the LAN using Windows Explorer, just like resources on your own computer.

- In Windows Explorer, click **Network** in the navigation pane to view a list of all visible computers and network devices.

  - Double-clicking computers will navigate to their shared resources. Depending on permissions, you may need to enter user credentials.

  - Double-clicking other devices will depend on their nature. You might add a device to Windows Media Player, open a configuration window, or just view its IP address and other properties.

  - Shared folders and printers attached to a computer will appear inside that computer, while network printers or network-attached storage devices will appear as independent devices.

- You can type a network location into the Address bar using the format
  \\COMPUTERNAME\ResourcePath

- You can use the same process anywhere else that uses the Windows Explorer file browser, such as Open or Save As windows.

- Some applications integrate access to Windows shares in other ways. For example, Windows Media Player displays libraries in shared media devices.

- Just because a device appears on the network doesn't mean you can access it through Windows Explorer. To access web configuration for devices like routers and network printers, use your web browser instead.

Mapping network drives

When you use a shared folder often, you can map it as a network drive so it will appear in your normal list of drives.

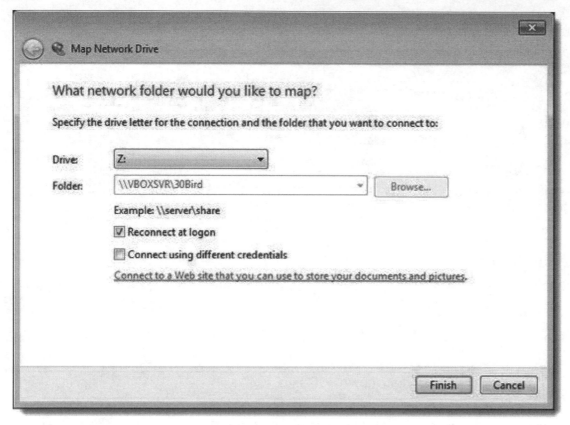

1. In Windows Explorer, right-click the shared folder and click **Map network drive**.

2. In the **Map Network Drive** window, set options.

   - From the Drive list, choose the drive letter you want to use.

   - Check **Reconnect at login** if you want the share to be permanent. Otherwise it will only last until you restart your computer.

   - Check **Connect using different credentials** if you want to connect to the share as a different user.

3. Click **Finish**.

Sharing folders

You can share individual folders to your workgroup or homegroup. Homegroup sharing only allows you to choose whether it is read-only or read-write access, while workgroup sharing allows you to set more detailed users and permissions.

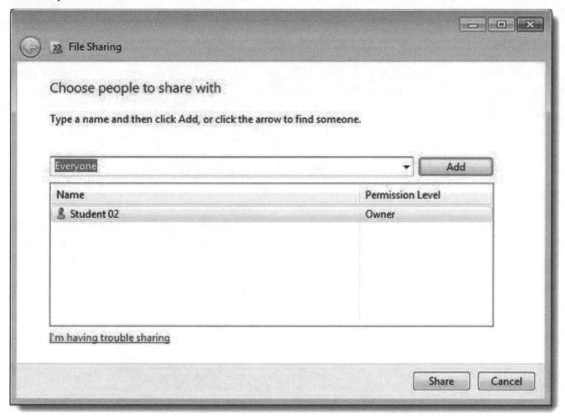

1. Select the file or folder you wish to share.

2. Open the **File Sharing** window.

   - In Windows 7, choose **Share With > Specific People**.

   - In Windows 8 and later, click **Specific People** on the Share tab.

   - In any version of Windows, right-click and choose **Share With > Specific People**.

   - If you're only sharing to your homegroup, choose **Homegroup (Read)** or **Homegroup (Read/Write)** in the Share with list, and you're finished.

3. Choose who you want to share with.

   - If you're on a workgroup, click the arrow, select a local user from the list, and click **Add**.

   - If you're on a domain, click the arrow, then select **Find People**. You can search for domain users in the **Select Users and Groups** window.

   - If you know the user you want to add, type the name into the box and click **Add**.

4. Choose permissions for each user by clicking in the permission level column.
   You can also remove users by clicking the permission level and choosing **Remove**.

5. Click **Share**.

Printer and multifunction print device sharing

There are several methods for sharing a printer or multifunction print device among multiple computers. When purchasing a printer, if you want to be able to print to it from multiple computer and other devices, you must identify the best method for sharing the printer to meet your specific needs.

Exam Objective(s): 220-1002 1.8.4

Network
Joins the printer to the LAN using an Ethernet cable or Wi-Fi connection. Users' network credentials determine whether they have been authorized to connect and print to a network printer. Depending on your network setup, the printer might be assigned an IP address automatically or you manually assign one in printer settings. When possible, you should assign a static IP address to the printer so that it always has the same IP address.

> **Note:** If you want to print via Wi-Fi to a network printer from an "i" branded device, such as an iPad, you must purchase an AirPrint-compatible printer.

Short-range wireless
Communicates with client computers via Bluetooth or IR. Once the printer is powered on and the device you want to print from is within range, you can create an ad hoc network connection between the devices and then print. Depending on the device, you might be prompted to accept the connection before your device will connect to the printer. Be aware that some printers labeled "Bluetooth printing capabilities" have the Bluetooth transceiver built-in, but others require you to purchase a separate adapter.

Shared printer
The printer is installed as a local printer on a client computer or a designated print server. The computer then shares the printer via its operating system software. When you share a printer, you can control which users can connect and print to it. A shared printer is only accessible when its host computer is powered on and connected to the network.

Bonjour is Apple's zero-configuration networking feature. On Apple computers, Bonjour is the service that assigns IP addresses, resolves host names, and discovers network services, such as network printers. Often, it gets installed on Windows computers as part of iTunes.

Sharing printers

You can share a printer from its **Properties** window.

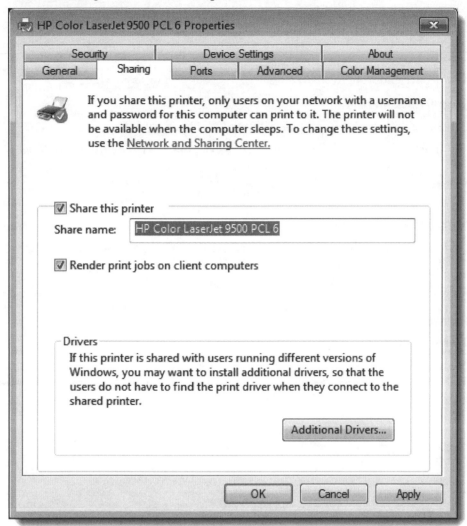

1. In the list of printers, right-click the printer you want to share and click **Printer properties**.

2. On the Sharing tab, check **Share this printer**.

3. Specify the share name if desired.

4. Click **Additional Drivers** to install drivers for other clients to automatically install on connect., for example to keep both x86 and x64 drivers.

5. Click **OK**.

Sharing a printer or multifunction print device in Mac OS X

This feature is used to share non-networked, non-wireless printers connected to a host computer with other network users and devices. To share a printer or multifunction print device in Mac OS X:

1. In the Dock, click **System Preferences > Sharing**.
2. Check **Printer Sharing**.
   If you have a multifunction printer and want to share the scanner, check **Scanner Sharing**.
3. In the Hardware section, select **Print and Scan**.
4. Select the printer you want to share and check **Share This Printer On The Network**.
5. If you have a multifunction printer and want to share the scanner, check **Share This Scanner On The Network** on the Scan tab.

Sharing a printer or multifunction print device in Linux

This feature is used to share non-networked, non-wireless printers connected to a host computer with other network users and devices. To share a printer or multifunction print device in Linux:

1. With the Dash open, type `printer`.
2. Click the printer tool to open system-config-printer.
3. Right-click the printer you want to share.
4. Check both **Enabled** and **Shared**.

Changing advanced sharing settings

Depending on your network you might need to fine-tune sharing settings more finely than choosing a public or private network. You can access advanced options from the Network and Sharing Center. In Windows Vista they'll be listed in the main window: in later versions you'll need to click **Advanced Sharing Settings**.

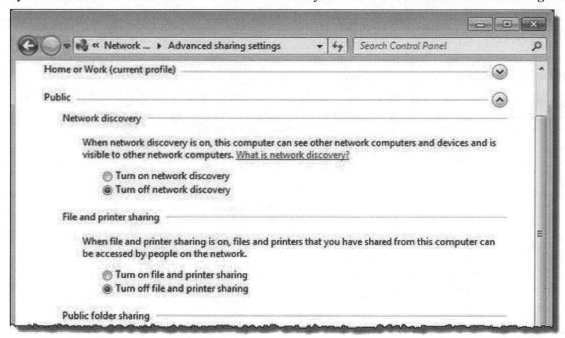

The advanced sharing options vary slightly between Windows editions: in particular, some editions let you change all settings separately for public and private networks, while in other editions some settings affect all networks. In Windows 7, you can change the following options.

- Configure **Network discovery** to change whether you can see or be seen by other computers on the network.

- Configure **File and printer sharing** to change whether your network shares can be accessed from other computers on the network. Remember that you still have to choose what folders to share.

- Configure **Public folder sharing** to choose whether network users can access the Public folders.

  Note: Local users can still access the Public folders regardless of the setting.

- Click **Choose media streaming options** to select how other network devices can play streaming media from your libraries.

- Configure **File sharing connections** to change encryption strength in network authentication. You should enable 128-bit encryption unless your network has very old devices that don't support it.

- Configure **Password protected sharing** to control whether network users must have local credentials on your computer.

  Turning password-protected sharing off is more convenient. Turning it on is more secure. You can create local users for network shares if you like.

- Configure **Homegroup connections** to decide whether homegroup connections are allowed, or whether all sharing is by workgroup methods.

Managing offline files

Network drives have some limitations. Namely, on slow networks response might not be very fast, and if your connection or the remote computer aren't constantly available you might lose access at any time. When you work with network files frequently you can designate them as *offline files* which will be stored as copies on your local computer even when you're not connected. When you are connected, Windows will synchronize your offline copies with those on the network. Offline files are especially useful for laptop users who may not always be connected to the work network, but frequently use network folders.

Exam Objective(s): 220-1002 1.6.18

Sync Center in Windows 7

You can control offline files from the *Sync Center* in Control Panel. It isn't listed in Category view, so either switch to icon view or use the Search box. In Windows 7 you can also navigate to **Start > All Programs > Accessories > Sync Center**

- Windows will automatically store offline copies of certain files, but most categories depend on network configuration. To make a network folder available offline from a client computer, navigate to it in Windows Explorer.

  Note: The files will need to download from the network before they are available offline.

  - In Windows 7, click **Sync > Always available offline**

  - In Windows 8, 8.1, or 10, click **Easy access > Always available offline** on the Home tab.

  - In any Windows version, right-click a folder or file and choose **Always Available offline**

  - If the option isn't available, you need to enable offline folders.

- Once you've made files available offline you can view their status in Sync Center.

  - Click **View sync results** to view any recent synchronizations or sync errors.

  - Click **View sync conflicts** to view file version conflicts. If any appear, click **Resolve** to view details and see resolution options.

- You can switch file access to offline mode at any time. You will then only be able to view files you've stored offline., and they will not synchronize with the server.

  - In Windows 7, click **Work offline**

  - In Windows 8, 8.1, or 10, click **Easy access > Always available offline** on the Home tab.

- Click **Manage offline files** to change how Windows handles offline folders.

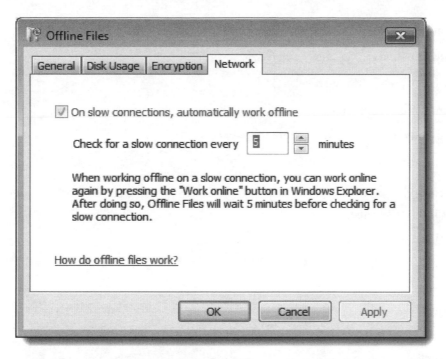

- Use the General tab to enable offline files, open the Sync Center, or view offline files.

- Use the Disk Usage tab to configure how much local space Windows will use for caching online files.

- Use the Encryption tab to encrypt offline files in case your computer is ever lost or stolen.

- Use the Network tab to configure how your computer manages file shares over slow network connections.

- You can also use Sync Center to synchronize files with compatible mobile devices. To do so, connect the device and click **Set up new sync partnerships**.

The NET command

You can manage network shares from within the Windows GUI, but you can also do so by using the command-line utility, **net**. Actually, net is a rather multifaceted tool. Not only can it manage your network shares and print jobs, it can control communication sessions, and even start or stop services on the local computer.

 Exam Objective(s): 220-1002 1.4.19, 1.4.20

You can use the command by typing net *command* . Typing net by itself will give a list of commands, while net help *command* will give detailed help for a specific command.

```
c:\Users\Public>net /?
The syntax of this command is:

NET
    [ ACCOUNTS | COMPUTER | CONFIG | CONTINUE | FILE | GROUP | HELP |
      HELPMSG | LOCALGROUP | PAUSE | SESSION | SHARE | START |
      STATISTICS | STOP | TIME | USE | USER | VIEW ]
```

Some common **net** commands include:

Net Share	Lists, creates, and removes network shares on the local computer.
Net Use	Displays or connects to shares on remote computers.
Net User	Adds, removes, and otherwise manages user accounts on the computer.

Net Share	Lists, creates, and removes network shares on the local computer.
Net View	Lists computers and devices on the network.
Net File	Shows or closes open files on a server.
Net Sessions	Lists or ends communication sessions with network computers.
Net Accounts	Sets logon and password requirements for users
Net Computer	Adds or removes a computer from a domain
Net Start	Starts a Windows service.
Net Stop	Stops a Windows service.
Net Pause	Pauses a Windows service.
Net Continue	Continues a Windows service.

Exercise: Sharing a folder

If students have network computers available, have them share a folder with another user.

To complete this exercise, you'll need to be connected to the same private network as a partner. For simplicity, you'll share a folder with very little security in place.

Do This	How & Why
1. Create a shared folder on your hard drive.	
a) Create a folder named C:\My shared folder	Navigate to C:\ in Windows Explorer and click **New Folder**. 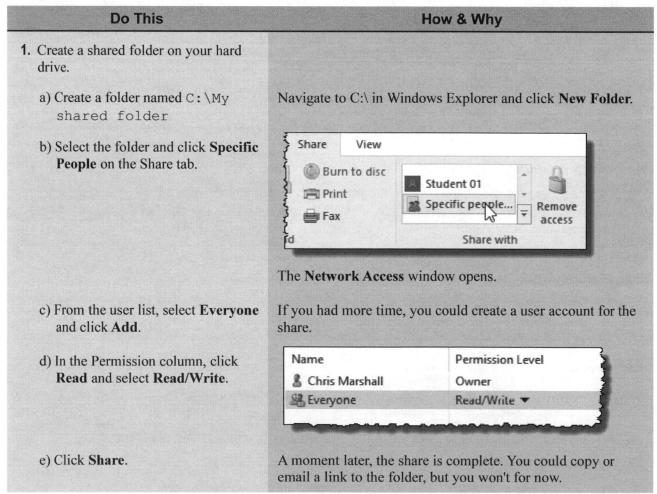 The **Network Access** window opens.
b) Select the folder and click **Specific People** on the Share tab.	
c) From the user list, select **Everyone** and click **Add**.	If you had more time, you could create a user account for the share.
d) In the Permission column, click **Read** and select **Read/Write**.	
e) Click **Share**.	A moment later, the share is complete. You could copy or email a link to the folder, but you won't for now.

Do This	How & Why
f) Click **Done**.	![0 items State: 👥 Shared]
	The folder is listed as shared in the Status bar.
2. Create a file named `C:\My shared folder\<Name's> file.txt`	Right-click in the folder and click **New > Text Document**. Use your name, but you don't need to edit the file.
3. Configure advanced sharing settings.	By default, password protected sharing means your partner will need local credentials on your computer, even to access a folder open to everyone. This is an important security feature, but you'll turn it off to make the sharing process easier to demonstrate.
a) Open the Network and Sharing Center.	In the Control Panel, navigate to **Network and Internet > Network and Sharing Center**.
b) On the left, click **Change advanced sharing settings**.	The **Advanced sharing settings** window includes separate configurations for public and private networks.
c) Under All networks, click **Turn off password protected sharing**.	In Windows 8 or later, it will be under All networks. Password protected sharing When password protected sharing is on, only peop computer can access shared files, printers attached other people access, you must turn off password p ○ Turn on password protected sharing ◉ Turn off password protected sharing
d) Click **Save settings**.	
4. Edit your partner's shared file.	
a) In Windows Explorer, click **Network**.	Your partner's computer, as well as any other systems on the local network, will appear. It may take a few moments.

Do This	How & Why

b) Double-click your partner's computer.

You can also navigate to \\Name using your partner's computer name, if it doesn't show up immediately.

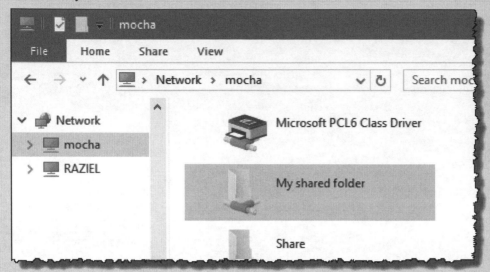

The shared folder appears.

c) Open the text file in My shared folder.

It should have your partner's name.

d) Change the file contents.

Type anything you like., save the file, and close Notepad.

5. On your own computer, edit your shared file.

It has your partner's message.

6. Close all open windows.

Assessment: Sharing and security

1. You're setting up a small office LAN, and you want individual users to independently share individual folders and printers. What kind of sharing model should you use? Choose the best reply.

   - Domain
   - Homegroup
   - Private
   - Workgroup

2. What network locations have network discovery enabled by default? Choose all that apply.

   - Domain
   - Home
   - Private
   - Public
   - Work

3. What can you manage with the net command? Choose all correct answers.

   - Network print jobs
   - Network security settings
   - Network shares
   - Windows services
   - Wireless network connections

4. Your office has enabled workgroup sharing of files and printers, and for security reasons password-protected file sharing will remain on. What rules will you need to keep in mind when supporting user problems? Choose all that apply.

   - Once a folder is shared, it's uploaded to a central file servers.
   - To access network resources, you must know a user name and password for the specific host computer.
   - To access network resources, you must know a shared password.
   - You can only access folders if the computer which originally shared them is powered on and connected to the network.
   - Your user name and password are good across the entire workgroup.

5. Your enterprise LAN uses a VPN so that users working from home can access shared Windows folders in the office, but it doesn't work as well for travelling employees in locations with unreliable or no internet access. What steps could remote users take to keep access to important folders on the road? Choose the best response.

   - Change the network location to Work
   - Configure a homegroup
   - Designate those folders as offline files
   - Map the shared folders as a network drive

Module B: Network connections

Windows today supports a wide variety of connection types, both in the physical and the logical sense. If you're on a typical Ethernet network, you might be able to just plug in and everything works, but for many others you'll need to configure NIC, IP, or other network settings.

You will learn:

- About the Network and Sharing Center
- How to create network connections
- How to manage network connections
- About Remote Desktop and Remote Assistance

The Network and Sharing Center

You can access most network tasks from the **Network and Sharing Center** window, whether you need to join a network or change settings for an existing one. The exact options vary depending on your version of Windows.

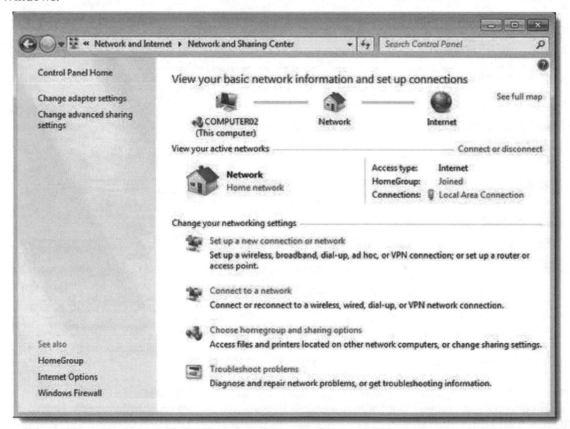

To open the Network and Sharing Center from Control Panel, click **Network > Network and Sharing Center**. You can also right-click the network icon in the system tray and click **Network and Sharing Center**.

Connecting to networks

When Windows automatically detects a network, or when it's been saved already, it's pretty simple to connect to it.

Available wireless connections in Windows 7 and Windows 10

 Exam Objective(s): 220-1001 2.3.5; CompTIA A+ 220-1002 1.8.5

- To join a wired Ethernet network, simply plug into it. Windows should detect the network and connect automatically.

- To join a Wi-Fi or WWAN network, click **Connect to a network** or click the wireless network icon in the system tray to view a list of available networks. Select the network you want and click **Connect**.

  Your first time connecting to a secured network, you'll be prompted to enter security credentials.

- To join other saved networks, click **Connect to a network**.

- If the network you want isn't visible, click **Set up a new connection or network** to view a list of available connection types.

Manually connecting to wireless networks

You might want to manually set up wireless networks if the network isn't currently available, if it is configured not to broadcast its SSID, or Windows fails to automatically detect its security settings.

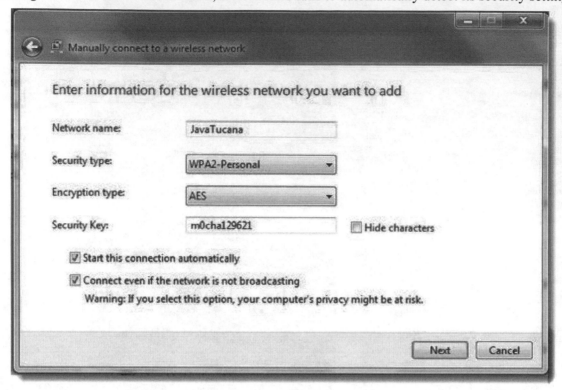

1. In the Network and Sharing Center, click **Set up a new connection or network**.

2. Click **Manually connect to a wireless network** and click **Next**.

3. Enter information for the wireless network.

   • Be sure to choose the right security type for the network.

   • Check **Start this connection automatically** if you want to connect to the network whenever it's in range.

   • Check **Connect even if the network is not broadcasting** if the network's SSID broadcast might be turned off.

4. Click **Next**. Windows will add the connection.

5. Click **Close**.

Setting up mobile hotspots

In Windows 10 you can set up a mobile hotspot in order to share your computer's network connection with other computers. You can use this for example to get Wi-Fi access from other computers when you're using a wired or 4G connection. Before setting up a mobile hotspot, remember that you can't share the same connection you're using to the internet. Mostly this is an issue if you're connected via Wi-Fi but also want to share to other computers via Wi-Fi. To do that, you'll need two Wi-Fi adapters. Alternatively, if your Wi-Fi adapter supports it, a dual-band adapter might be able to share 2.4 GHz internet over the 5GHz band, of vice-versa.

Creating a mobile hotspot

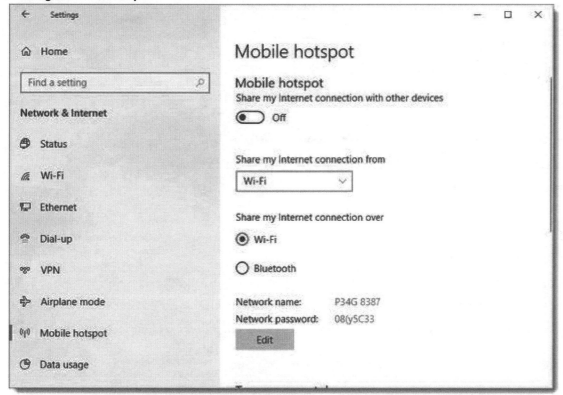

1. Navigate to **Settings > Network & Internet > Mobile Hotspot**.
   You can also click **Mobile Hotspot** in the Action Center.

2. Choose the network connection you want to share.
   This should be your existing internet connection.

3. Choose the connection you want to use for sharing.
   If you use Wi-Fi, Windows will generate a random network name and password. Click **Edit** if you want to change it.

4. Use the **Off/On** switch to toggle the hotspot.

To join a device to a Wi-Fi hotspot, use the network name and password you selected. To join a device to a Bluetooth hotspot you'll need to pair it with your computer.

Creating wired internet connections

If you need to connect to the internet using a dial-up connection, or if your broadband ISP requires a username and password, you can create the connection in the Network and Sharing Center.

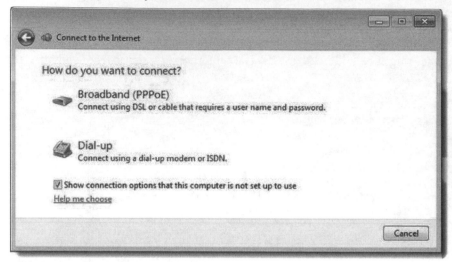

1. In the Network and Sharing Center, click **Set up a new connection or network**.

2. Click **Connect to the Internet**.

3. Click **Broadband** or **Dial-up**.

4. Enter your connection settings.

   • Name the connection if you like.

   • Dial-up connections will require a phone number, while broadband will not.

   • The first time you use a particular telephone line, click **Dialing Rules** to choose local dialing settings.

   • Click **Allow other people to use this connection** if you want other users on your computer to access this connection.

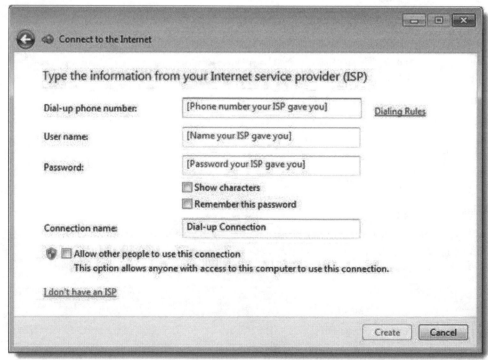

5. Click **Create**.

Creating VPN connections

Many workplaces use virtual private networks (VPNs) that allow you to join a LAN remotely via a secured internet connection. There are a variety of VPN technologies: some require third-party software, while others supported natively by Windows.

VPN setup in Windows 7 and Windows 10

You can use the same process for dial-up access into a corporate network by clicking **Dial Directly** instead of using your existing internet connection. In Windows 7, use the following process.

1. In the Network and Sharing Center, click **Set up a new connection or network**.

2. Click **Connect to a Workplace** then click **Next**.

3. Click **Use my Internet connection (VPN)**.

4. Enter your network properties and click **Next** or **Create**.

   - For a VPN, enter the network address; for a dial-up connection, enter a phone number.

   - Enter a network name if you want.

   - Check **Use a smart card** if the network uses one for authentication.

   - Check **Allow other people to use this connection** to make it available to all users on your computer.

   - Check **Don't connect now** to set the connection up without immediately connecting.

5. Enter your credentials, including destination domain if necessary.

6. Click **Connect**.

In Windows 10, you can still create VPN connection in the Network and Sharing Center, but you'll need to connect to it in **Settings > Network & Internet > VPN**. You can also use this screen to set up a VPN in the first place.

   - To connect to an existing VPN, click its name, then **Connect**

   - To create a new VPN connection, click **Add a VPN connection**. You'll need the same basic info to set up the connection.

Configuring proxy servers

If you're on a corporate network, whether you're connecting to the LAN or remotely, you might need to use a proxy server to browse the web. This is one setting you can't access from the Network and Sharing Center, since technically it's a web browser setting. Most browsers have their own proxy settings hidden in the options somewhere, but typically they'll default to using the system proxy settings used by Internet Explorer. You can find these in the **Internet Properties** window.

Exam Objective(s): 220-1002 1.8.6

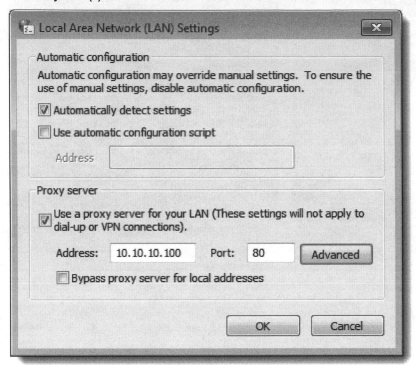

1. In Control Panel click **Network and Internet > Internet Options**.
2. View the Connections tab.
   - If you're on a VPN or dial-up connection, select the network and click **Settings**.
   - If you're on a direct LAN connection, click **LAN settings**.
3. Check **Use a proxy server**.
4. Enter the proxy server address and port provided by your network administrator.
5. Click **OK**.

Exercise: Creating a VPN connection

Using a VPN allows you to securely connect to a private network using a public network infrastructure. If students have Windows computers available, have them create a VPN connection using the following steps.

Do This	How & Why
1. Open the Network and Sharing Center	In the Control Panel, navigate to **Network and Internet > Network and Sharing Center**.
2. Create a new VPN connection.	It won't be a working connection, but you won't need to actually connect.
a) Click **Set up a new connection or network.**	The **Set up a connection or network** window opens.
b) Click **Connect to a workplace** and click **Next**.	

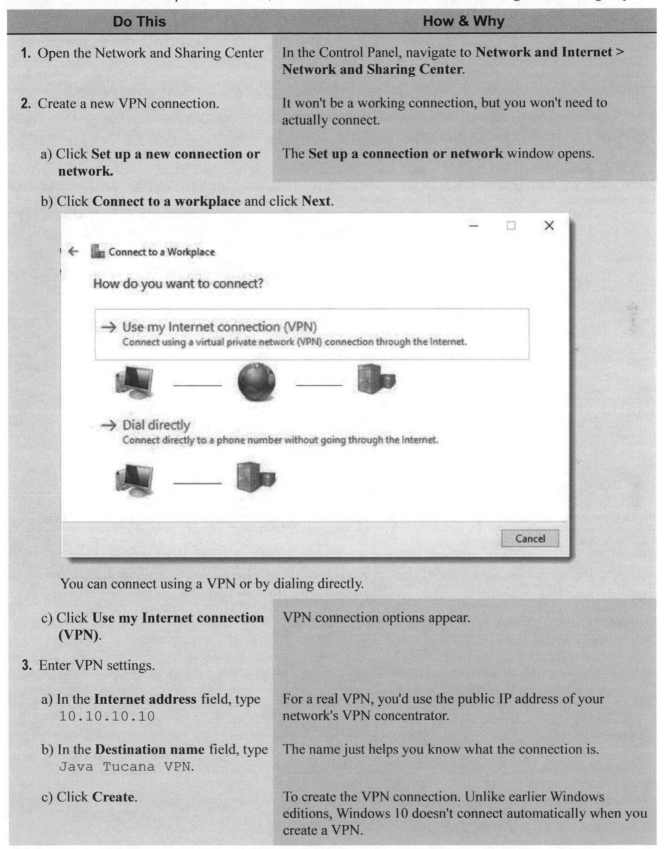

You can connect using a VPN or by dialing directly.

c) Click **Use my Internet connection (VPN)**.	VPN connection options appear.
3. Enter VPN settings.	
a) In the **Internet address** field, type `10.10.10.10`	For a real VPN, you'd use the public IP address of your network's VPN concentrator.
b) In the **Destination name** field, type `Java Tucana VPN`.	The name just helps you know what the connection is.
c) Click **Create**.	To create the VPN connection. Unlike earlier Windows editions, Windows 10 doesn't connect automatically when you create a VPN.

Do This	How & Why
4. Examine advanced VPN settings.	
a) In PC Settings, navigate to **Network & Internet > VPN**.	Press **Windows+I** to open Settings. The Java Tucana VPN is listed. You can also choose whether to allow the VPN over metered networks or while roaming.
b) Click **Java Tucana VPN**.	You can connect to it this way, but for now you'll check other options.
c) Click **Advanced Options**.	You can change settings or apply a proxy server to the VPN.
d) Click **Edit**.	To view the **Edit VPN Connection** window.
e) Click the **Type of Sign-in info** list	VPNs can use a variety of authentication methods.

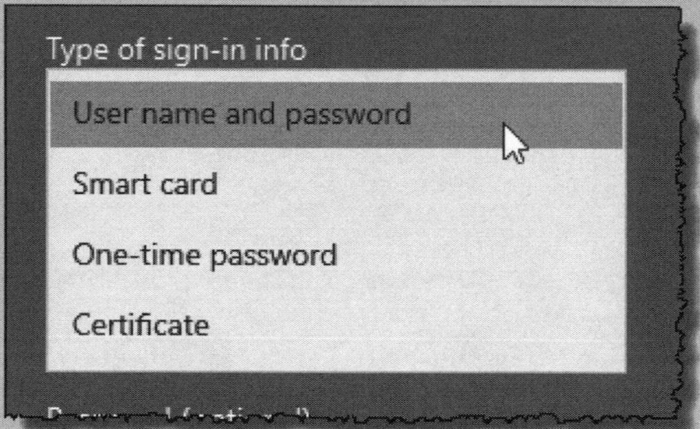

Type of sign-in info

User name and password

Smart card

One-time password

Certificate

f) Click the **VPN type** list.	VPNs can use a variety of different tunneling and encryption protocols.
g) Click **Cancel**.	To return to the VPN settings.
5. In the Network and Sharing Center, click **Connect to a network.**	Java Tucana VPN is now in the list of available networks.
6. Set up a proxy server for the VPN.	When you're connected to the VPN, you'll need to use Java Tucana's web proxy server.
a) From the VPN proxy settings list, select **Manual setup**.	Setting fields appear.
b) Set the Address to `10.10.10.20` and the Port to `80`.	
c) Check **Don't use the proxy server for local (intranet) addresses.**	Using the proxy server locally would interfere with LAN sharing.
d) Click **Apply**.	
7. Close all open windows.	

Proxy server settings for the VPN at the end of the exercise

VPN proxy settings

These settings will apply only to this VPN connection.

Manual setup ∨

Address
10.10.10.20

Port
80

Use the proxy server except for addresses that start with the following entries. Use semicolons (;) to separate entries.

☑ Don't use the proxy server for local (intranet) addresses

Optional Exercise: Connecting to a wireless network

For this exercise you will need to have a wireless adapter for each PC, as well as security settings for a WAP with SSID disabled. Since you don't need to actually connect to the network, you can complete the activity even without a real WAP, so long as the settings are valid. It can also be completed on a single PC as an instructor demonstration.

Do This	How & Why
1. If necessary, disconnect your wired network connection.	The wireless network icon only becomes visible when you're not connected to an Ethernet network, even though you can still connect to wireless networks
2. Connect to a wireless network.	
a) In the notification area, click 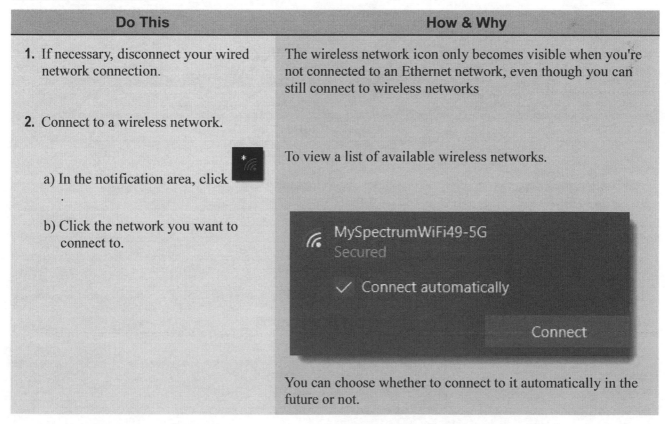.	To view a list of available wireless networks.
b) Click the network you want to connect to.	MySpectrumWiFi49-5G Secured ✓ Connect automatically Connect
	You can choose whether to connect to it automatically in the future or not.

Do This	How & Why
c) Click **Connect**.	Windows retrieves the network information, and asks you for the security key.
d) Click **Cancel**.	Instead, you'll manually create a connection.
3. Manually create a wireless connection.	You can manually create a wireless connection even if the WAP is currently out of range or if its SSID is hidden.
a) In the Network and Sharing Center, click **Set up a new connection or network**.	To view a selection of network types you can create.
b) Click **Manually connect to a wireless network**, then click **Next**.	When you manually connect to a Wi-Fi network, you can't retrieve security settings and other information from WAP itself. You're asked to fill in the network's information.
c) Enter the network's name, security type, encryption type, and security key.	Your instructor can supply the information.
d) Check both **Start this connection automatically** and **Connect even if this network is not broadcasting**.	This way you'll connect whenever you're in range of the WAP, even if its SSID is hidden.
e) Click **Next**.	
f) Click **Close**.	
4. If you've connected to a real wireless network, verify that you're connected.	
5. Close all open windows.	

Connection settings

The settings for configuring a given network connection are spread around a few interconnected windows, and they can have confusingly similar names if you think about them too casually. It doesn't get less confusing when you manage a computer with multiple network connections, or when they have similar names like "Local Area Connection" and "Local Area Connection 2".

You can reach all connection settings from the Network and Sharing Center, but some might take a few clicks or be reachable more than one way. In Windows 10 you can also access some of them by navigating to **Settings > Network & Internet > Status**.

Network connections	Clicking **Change adapter settings** will open the **Network Connections** window with a list of all your existing connections. From here you can enable or disable a connection, rename it, view its status, or change its properties.
<Connection name> Status	To view an enabled connection's status, click it in the Network and Sharing Center, or double-click it in the **Network Connections** window. Here you can view the connection's activity and details, or access its properties.
<Connection name> Properties	To view or change a connection's underlying properties, click **Properties** in either the connection's **Status** window, or in its context menu in the **Network Connections** window. Here you can access settings for the physical network adapter, as well as settings for network *protocol bindings*, such as TCP/IP.
Connection Properties (Windows 10)	In Windows 10 Settings you can click **Change connection properties** to view network properties or copy them for troubleshooting purposes. You can also change IP settings or network profile, and configure metered connections.

Connection properties in the Network and Sharing Center, and in Settings

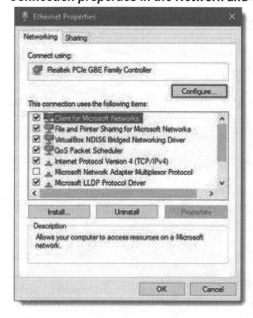 

 Note: Some settings might not be in the most intuitive place. If you can't find what you're looking for in one window, don't hesitate to check the others.

Managing network connections

The most central place for accessing connection settings is the **Network Connections** window. When you select a connection, a menu bar appears at the top of the window. You can also right-click a connection to view a context menu with similar commands.

- Double-click an enabled connection to open its **Status** window.
- Click **Enable** or **Disable** to toggle active connections.

    It's often a good idea to disable connections you're not using, and sometimes turning a connection off and on again can fix connection issues.

- Click **Rename this connection** to change a connection's displayed name.
- Click **Change settings of this connection** to open its Properties window.
- Click **Diagnose this connection** to run an automated troubleshooting tool.

Changing connection priority

Most of the time you'll only have one active network connection at a time, but when you have more than one, Windows needs to prioritize which connection to use for network traffic. For example, if your notebook uses the office Wi-Fi when you move around but you plug into the faster Ethernet connection at your desk, you could disable Wi-Fi whenever you're plugged in, or you could just configure the Ethernet connection to a higher priority so that whenever both connections are active, the wired connection takes priority.

In Windows 7, 8, and 8.1, you can also change the priority of network protocol bindings, for example IPv4 vs IPv6.

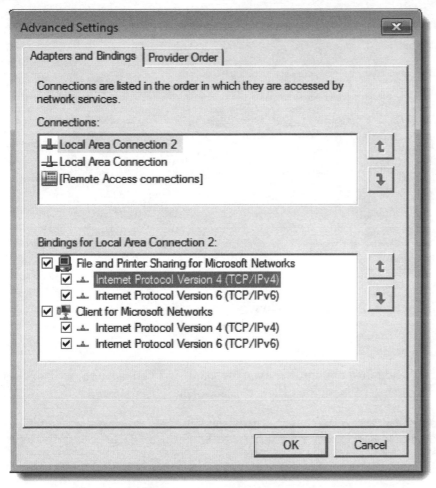

1. In the **Network Connections** window, click press **Alt** to activate the hidden menus.

2. Click **Advanced > Advanced Settings**.

3. In the **Advanced Settings** window, set priorities.

   • To change an adapter's priority, select it and click ⬆ or ⬇.

   • To change a binding's priority, select it and click ⬆ or ⬇.

4. Click **OK**.

Note: In Windows 10 you can't centrally change the priority of protocol bindings as you could in previous versions, and you're not likely to need to. If you must prioritize a particular protocol binding, open the **Properties** window for that protocol, then click **Advanced**.

Viewing connection status

The **Connection Status** window shows you the connectivity and activity of the selected connection. You can also view connection details and access properties.

The Connection Status and Connection Details windows

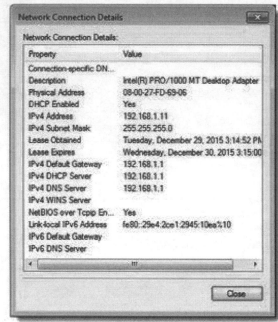

- Click **Details** to see addressing and other network details for the connection.

- Click **Properties** to open the **Connection Properties** window.

- Click **Disable** to disable the connection.

- Click **Diagnose** to launch an automated troubleshooting tool.

- Other connection types might have additional options. For example, on a Wi-Fi connection you can click **Wireless Properties** to view or change Wi-Fi specific connection and security settings.

Two tabs in a Wireless Network Properties window

Configuring NIC options

Both Ethernet and Wi-Fi connections on today's networks usually can take care of themselves at the network interface layer, but sometimes you might need to change NIC settings to ensure compatibility and performance with your network. The exact settings available, and the names they use, will depend on the network adapter. Not only will an Ethernet card have much different options than a Wi-Fi adapter, two different Ethernet adapters might have different options or the same options by different names.

Exam Objective(s): 220-1001 2.3.4; CompTIA A+ 220-1002 1.8.12

Note: Windows adapter settings only affect the NIC driver. An older Ethernet card might have some settings configurable through switches on the card itself, while a card integrated into a motherboard might be configurable in the system BIOS. At the least, the on-board NIC can be enabled or disabled in the BIOS.

Advanced settings for a typical Gigabit Ethernet adapter in Windows 7.

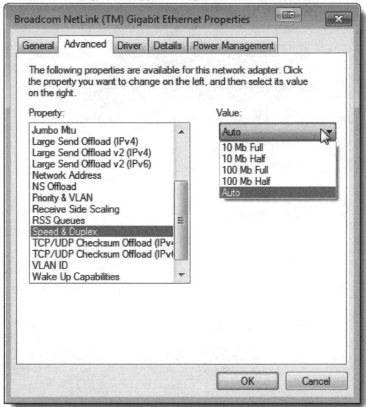

1. In the Network and Sharing Center, click **Change adapter settings**.
2. Right-click the adapter and click **Properties**.
3. Click **Configure**.
4. On the Advanced tab, select an option to access its settings.
   - To change speed and duplexing settings on an Ethernet adapter, click **Speed & Duplex Settings**.
   - To change speed settings on a Wi-Fi adapter, click **Wireless mode**,
   - To configure Ethernet QoS features, look for settings with **QoS** or **Priority** in their names.
   - To configure Wake-On LAN features, look for settings with WOL or Wake in their names.
5. When you're finished, click **OK** to save your changes.

Configuring IP addresses

By default, Windows configures connections to automatically obtain IPv6 and IPv4 addresses via DHCP. If a DHCP server isn't available, they'll choose a link-local or APIPA address which will allow only local connectivity. If you need to change settings, for example to set a static address assigned by your network administrator, you can do so from the **Connection Properties** window. In Windows 10 you can also do so from **Settings > Network & Internet > Status**.

Exam Objective(s): 220-1002 1.8.11

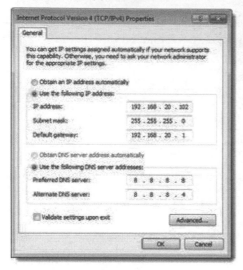 

1. Open the **Properties** window for the connection.

2. From the bindings list, choose the IP version you want to configure and click **Properties**.

3. Configure your addressing settings.

   - To use DHCP, click **Obtain an IP address automatically**.

   - 'To configure a static IPv4 address, click **Use the following IP address**. Then enter a valid IP address, subnet mask, and default gateway.

   - To configure a static IPv6 address, click **Use the following IP address**. Then enter a valid IP address, subnet prefix length, and default gateway.

   - To set a static IP address that takes effect when you can't locate a DHCP server, click the **Alternate Configuration** tab.

   - To add additional IP addresses, default gateways, or DNS servers, click **Advanced**.

   - To run an automatic check of your chosen settings, click **Validate settings upon exit**.

4. Configure your DNS settings.

   - To configure a DNS server via DHCP, click **Obtain DNS server address automatically**. This will only be available if your IP address is also supplied by DHCP.

   - To configure a static DNS server address, click **Use the following DNS server addresses** and enter at least one valid DNS server. You may use a static DNS server whether your IP address is static or dynamic.

Exercise: Configuring a static IP address

If your instructor has supplied you with valid static IP address settings, you can follow the steps below to configure a static IP address. If you don't have valid static IP address settings, enter whatever numbers you like, as long as click **Cancel** rather than **OK** at the end.

Do This	How & Why
1. On the left side of the **Network and Sharing Center** window, click **Change Adapter Settings**.	To open the **Network Connections** window.
2. Double-click the adapter you want to configure.	The Status window opens.
3. Click **Properties**.	
4. In the bindings list, select the IP version you want to configure, then click **Properties**.	Unless your instructor gave you an IPv6 address, click **Internet Protocol version 4**.
5. Set static IP information.	
a) Click **Use the following IP address**.	
b) Enter a valid IP address.	If you're not setting a real address, use 192.168.20.102 or another valid private address.
c) Enter the corresponding subnet mask.	If you don't have a real address, use 255.255.255.0.
d) Enter a default gateway.	If you don't have a real address, use 192.168.20.1.
6. Set static DNS information.	
a) click **Use the following DNS server addresses**.	
b) Enter a primary DNS server.	If your instructor doesn't provide one, enter 8.8.8.8.
c) Enter a secondary DNS server.	If your instructor doesn't provide one, enter 8.8.4.4.
	Note: 8.8.8.8 and 8.8.4.4 are public DNS servers administered by Google. You can use them if your normal DNS server isn't working right.
7. Click **OK**, then click **Close** twice.	**WARNING:** If you didn't enter a real, valid IP address, click **Cancel** instead of **OK**.

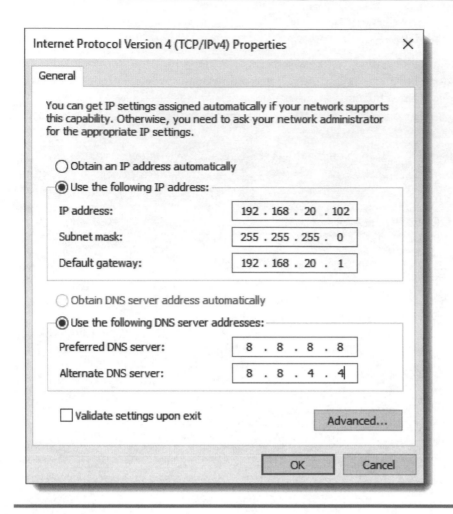

Remote Desktop Services

Remote desktop connections shouldn't be confused with ordinary network connections or even VPN connections. Instead, they're client applications that connect you to the desktop of a remote computer, controlling it as though you were physically there. They're generally not good for things like watching movies or playing games, but if your network connection is reasonably fast you can do almost anything else, and that includes accessing the resources and networks on the remote system.

There are a number of remote desktop solutions, but Windows natively includes support for Microsoft's Remote Desktop Services, using RDP. There are actually two primary applications that use Remote Desktop Services: each has its own purpose and limitations.

- *Remote Desktop Connection* is designed to log into unattended remote systems, for example to access your work computer from home. Any Windows edition can connect to a Remote Desktop Connection host system, but only business and professional editions can receive incoming connections.

- *Remote Assistance* is used for remote technical assistance connections, for example to let you access a friend or coworker's system and help directly. Any Windows edition can give or receive remote assistance, but the receiving system needs to actively request assistance.

Configuring remote settings

Settings for remote connections can be found on the Remote tab of the **System Properties** window. To reach it, click **Remote Settings** in the **System** window.

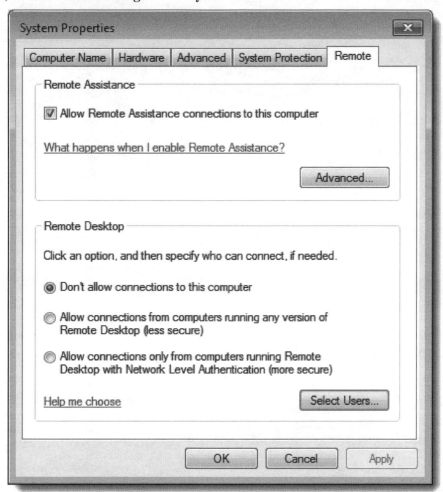

- By default, **Allow Remote Assistance** connections to this computer is checked.
- Click **Advanced** to configure rules about incoming Remote Assistance connections.
- If the Windows edition supports incoming Remote Desktop connections, they're still disabled by default.
  - Choose **Allow connections only from computers using Remote Desktop with Network Level Authentication (more secure)** if you only need to accept incoming connections from systems using Windows Vista or newer.

    Note: Windows 10 has a checkbox rather than radio buttons, but its function is the same.

  - Choose **Allow connections from computers running any version of Remote Desktop (less secure)** if you need to accept connections from obsolete Windows versions like XP.
  - Click **Select users** to restrict which users can log in remotely.

Requesting Remote Assistance

To establish a Remote Assistance connection, you first need to send the request from the receiving system. You'll need to share a file either by email or some other means, and a password. Alternatively, if you're both using Windows 7 or newer and if your network supports it, you can use the Easy Connect feature to send the file.

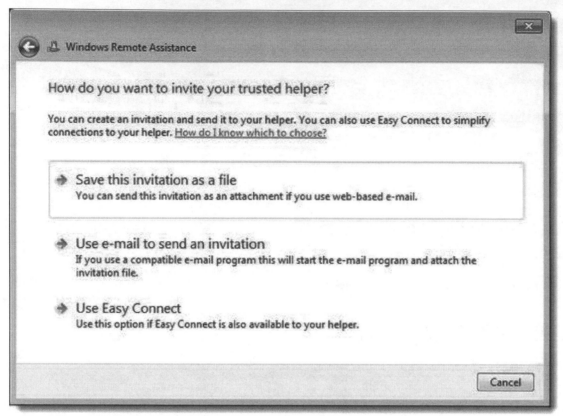

1. Open Remote Assistance.

   • In Windows Vista and Windows 7, click **Start > Help and Support**, then **More Support Options**, then **Windows Remote Assistance**.

   • In Windows 8 and later, click **System and Security** in Control Panel, then click **Launch remote assistance**.

   • For a quicker alternative, in any version of Windows type `msra` in the search bar or Start screen, then click it in the search results.

2. Click **Invite someone you trust to help you**.

3. Choose how you want to send the request information.

   • Click **Use Easy Connect** to check your network connection for Easy Connect compatibility.

- Click **Use e-mail to send an invitation** if you have a working network connection and a standalone email client such as Outlook or Windows Live Mail.

- Otherwise, click **Save this invitation as a file**. You can send the file by web-based email, another file sharing application, a shared network folder, or a removable drive.

4. Send the invitation file to the person helping you, according to your chosen method.

5. Separately communicate the displayed password to the person helping you.

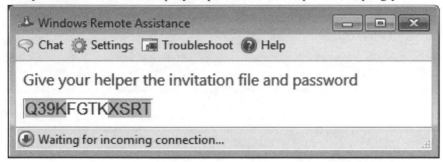

6. Leave the window open until the helper connects.

7. When asked if you'd like to give access or, click **Yes**.

At any point you can click **Pause** to stop the helper's view of your desktop or **Stop Sharing** to regain control.

Giving Remote Assistance

When you answer a Remote Assistance request, and the recipient gives you permission, you don't immediately have control of the remote computer. At first you just get to see the other computer's desktop. You can open a chat window, or request direct control, and the remote user can end the session at any time.

Exam Objective(s): 220-1002 1.8.8

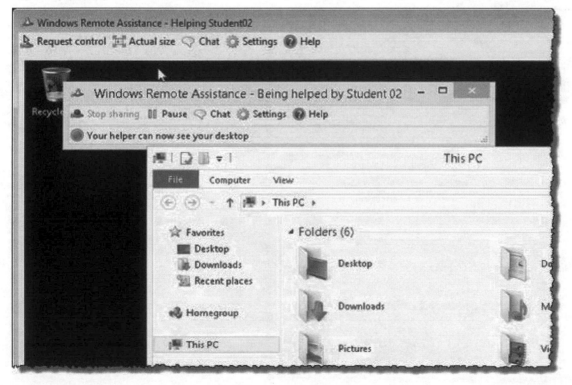

1. Double-click the invitation file you received from the recipient.

2. Enter the password and click **OK**.

3. Assist the recipient with their problems.

   - Click **Chat** to open a chat window.

   - Click **Request Control** to ask for control of the recipient's system.

   - Click **Settings** to configure connection settings, like performance options or session logging.

   - Even while you have control, the recipient can also still control the computer, so it's important not to both do things at once.

4. Close the window when you're finished.

Creating Remote Desktop Connections

Remote Desktop connections work much differently than Remote Assistance. The biggest difference is that while Remote Assistance requires someone actually at the remote system to allow you in, Remote Desktop Connection is just the opposite. Assuming the system is configured to accept incoming connections, all you need to get full control is valid credentials. Likewise, the control is full, just like if you had logged into the computer locally.

Exam Objective(s): 220-1002 1.8.7

In fact, if someone is logged on locally, they'll be returned to the login screen, just like if they'd chosen **Switch User** from the shutdown menu. This can actually be pretty valuable: For example, if you left yourself logged in at work, then logged in remotely from home, you can just take over your existing session from work.

Like Remote Assistance, Remote Desktop Connections can be opened by double-clicking a configuration file: the difference is that you're not prompted for a session password, just user credentials. If you don't have a file you can create a connection from any system: you just need to know the remote system's address and valid user credentials.

Note: You might have guessed this is why Remote Assistance is enabled by default and Remote Desktop is not: Remote Assistance can't be used to log into a remote system without the direct cooperation of its current user, while a computer open to Remote Desktop permissions is in danger of outside attack.

1. Type `remote desktop` in the search box or at the Start screen, and click **Remote Desktop Connection**.

2. Choose the type of connection you wish to make.

   - If you want to make a quick connection using default settings, enter the remote computer's address.

   - If you want to use custom settings or save a shortcut file for later use, click **Options**.

3. Configure options if necessary.

   - On the Display tab, configure resolution and color settings for the remote desktop.

   - On the Local Resources tab, configure use of your computer's resources over the connection, such as audio, keyboard/mouse, clipboard, printers, and shared drives.

   - On the Programs tab, choose any applications you want to automatically run on the remote system after you connect.

   - On the Experience tab, choose the Windows visual effects that you want to enable or disable, according to your network connection speed.

   - On the Advanced tab, configure additional security and network settings.

   - On the General tab, enter the address and user you want to connect as.

   - If you want to save the connection settings for later use, click **Save** or **Save As**.

4. Click **Connect**.

When you're logged into a remote desktop, you can close the connection by logging out, or choose Disconnect if you want to close an existing session without logging out the account.

Other remote access programs

Windows can act as a client or server for a variety of remote access applications, apart from Remote Assistance and RDP. Some common options include the following.

Exam Objective(s): 220-1002 4.9

Telnet	Provides command-line remote access using the Telnet protocol. Windows includes a command-line Telnet client; it includes a Telnet server which is not installed by default. Since Telnet provides no real security, you shouldn't enable the Telnet server, but you might use the client to connect to some remote systems such as certain network devices.
SSH	Provides command-line remote access using the SSH protocol; the related SCP and SFTP protocols can be used for file transfer if client and server support it. SSH includes strong security features, so should be used instead of Telnet wherever possible. As of 2018, Windows 10 includes the OpenSSH client. The OpenSSH server is included as an optional component but is not installed by default. You can use SSH to remotely issue commands to a computer, including Windows.
Third-party	In addition to third-party Telnet and SSH applications, there are a wide variety of applications which are designed to allow remote access, remote assistance, or just collaboration features such as screen sharing and file transfers. Some of these tools, like RealVNC or TeamViewer, are intended and marketed primarily as remote access and support tools. Others, such as Skype or Google Hangouts, are primarily collaboration tools and may not even allow remote control. Still others lie between the extremes. Any third-party applications can vary widely in underlying protocols and security features.

Security is a concern for any kind of remote access program. Any server program which allows remote access without the direct permission of a local user is especially at risk, but non-secure protocols like Telnet allow network attackers to spy on communications. Users can also be tricked into giving access or sending files to an untrustworthy party, such as one impersonating a technician. Even if you know exactly who you're dealing with, sharing your desktop isn't always safe if you're viewing sensitive materials - the other party may not be allowed to see them, or may be in a room with unauthorized viewers who can see the screen.

Exercise: Using Remote Assistance

Remote Assistance allows you as a repair technician to log into a user's computer remotely to diagnose and repair problems. If you and a partner both have a computer available, you can complete this hands-on exercise. You will also need a way to share files between those computers, like a shared folder or removable drive. If you performed the Sharing a folder exercise, use the same partner.

For this exercise, some steps will have to be performed on the recipient's computer (Computer A), and some on the helper's (Computer B).

Do This	How & Why
1. On Computer A, request a Remote Assistance session.	
a) In the search bar or Start menu, enter msra then click the result when it appears.	The **Windows Remote Assistance** window opens.
b) Click **Invite someone you trust to help you**.	You're asked how to invite your helper.
c) Click **Save this invitation as a file**.	
d) Save the file in a shared folder or removable drive.	Choose a unique name for the file. The **Windows Remote Assistance** window now displays a password.
e) Leave the window open.	Give your partner the password when asked.
2. On Computer B, open the Remote Assistance session.	
a) Double-click the shared file.	You're prompted for a password.
b) Enter the password from your partner and click **OK**.	The recipient will be asked whether to allow access.
c) On Computer A, click **Yes**. 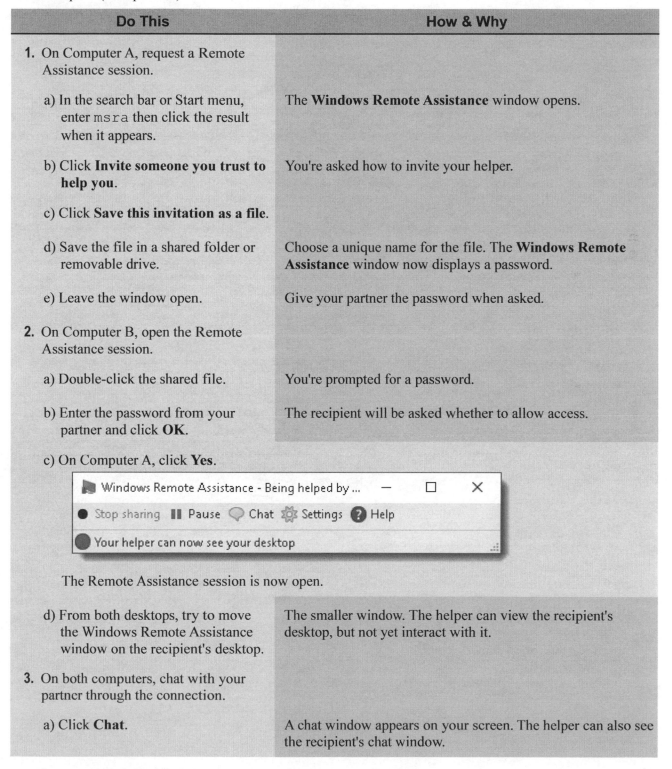 The Remote Assistance session is now open.	
d) From both desktops, try to move the Windows Remote Assistance window on the recipient's desktop.	The smaller window. The helper can view the recipient's desktop, but not yet interact with it.
3. On both computers, chat with your partner through the connection.	
a) Click **Chat**.	A chat window appears on your screen. The helper can also see the recipient's chat window.

Do This	How & Why
b) Type a message to your partner and click **Send**.	Windows Remote Assistance - Being helped by ▮ ● Stop sharing ▮▮ Pause ◯ Chat ⚙ Settings ❓ He **A Remote Assistance invitation has been opened. **A Remote Assistance connection has been established. ▮▮▮▮▮ : What are you having problems with? Chris Marshall: Inconsistent Wi-fi mostly
4. Give the helper direct control.	
a) On Computer B, click **Request Control**.	👤 Windows Remote ▶ Request control
	The recipient is asked whether to give permission.
b) On Computer A, click **Yes**.	◉ Your helper is sharing control of your computer
	The status bar now indicates that control is shared.
c) From Computer B, open an application on Computer A's desktop.	The controls might be a little slow, but the computer can be controlled remotely. If the recipient had a problem, you could fix it yourself.
5. From Computer A, explore other application options.	The helper can't use all of these, so it's easier this way.
a) In the Windows Remote Assistance window, click **Settings**.	You can change options for logging contact information sharing, and bandwidth usage.
b) Click **Cancel**.	To close the **Settings** window.
c) Click **Pause**.	The helper now can't see or control the recipient's desktop.
d) Click **Continue**.	The desktop is displayed again. Control is shared again as well.
e) Click **Stop sharing**.	Control is no longer shared, but the helper can still see the desktop.
6. From both computers, close the **Windows Remote Assistance** window.	The connection is closed.

Assessment: Network connections

1. Users from your office want to connect to the workplace LAN through their existing home internet connections. What kind of connection would allow them to do it? Choose the best response.

   - Dial-up
   - PPPoE
   - VLAN
   - VPN

2. Your company doesn't use Internet Explorer any more. Why should you still know how to configure its browser options? Choose the best response.

   - To configure dialup connections
   - To configure proxy settings
   - To manually connect to wireless networks
   - To use Remote Assistance

3. Which window would show you bindings for "Local Area Connection 2"?

   - Ethernet Properties
   - Local Area Connection 2 Properties
   - Local Area Connection 2 Status
   - Network Connections

4. You need to make sure an adapter is configured to use the network's QoS settings. Which advanced Ethernet property should you check? Choose the best response.

   - Duplexing
   - MTU
   - Priority
   - WoL

5. Which is true when configuring a static IPv4 address for a Windows workstation? Choose all that apply.

   - You can still use DHCP configuration for IPv6.
   - You can use DHCP to configure a DNS server automatically.
   - You must also configure a valid default gateway.
   - You must manually configure a DNS server.
   - Your IPv6 address must also be manually configured.

6. Which Windows editions can receive incoming Remote Desktop connections? Choose all that apply.

   - Windows 7 Home Premium
   - Windows 7 Professional
   - Windows 8.1
   - Windows 10 Pro

Module C: Connection troubleshooting

Network problems are common, and given how computers are used today, failure to connect often renders a system all but completely useless. Fortunately, most network problems aren't hard to solve, but you need to recognize common types of problems and the tools needed to correct them.

You will learn:

- How to use command line network tools
- How to troubleshoot network connections

TCP/IP tools

When you set up a network or troubleshoot problems, you'll need to verify settings and check connectivity. Even if it might seem old-fashioned at first, one of the best ways to do this is using the command-line utilities available in any Windows or Unix-like operating system with a TCP/IP stack. Their syntax is fairly simple, and they can often tell you more information more quickly than you can get by clicking around in graphical settings. The specific commands available, and exactly how they work, depends on your operating system and version.

 Exam Objective(s): 220-1002 1.4.2, 1.4.3, 1.4.4, 1.4.5, 1.4.6

ipconfig	In Windows operating systems, displays or refreshes IP settings for network interfaces.
ifconfig	In Unix-like operating systems, displays or configures IP settings for network interfaces.
nbtstat	In Windows, displays diagnostic information for NetBIOS over TCP/IP.
netstat	Displays a variety of network information including active connections, routing tables, and traffic statistics.
nslookup	Performs DNS lookups and displays the IP address of a given host name.
ping	Tests the reachability and latency of a given host.
traceroute/tracert	Displays the hop-by-hop path to a given host, along with the round-trip time to each hop.
pathping	In Windows, behaves similarly to tracert by pinging every hop along the route to determine relative latency.

Even where Windows and Unix-like operating systems use the same commands, the exact syntax often varies by exact version. If you're not used to using the command line, syntax diagrams either in books or in-line documentation can be intimidating, but there's generally a standard. The following descriptions will use syntax like in this sample command:

```
command -pip_address [interface_name] [/all]
```

- command is the command name.

- -p and /all are options or switches you can use to change the command's functions. You enter them exactly as they look.

- ip_address and interface_name are variables or arguments used with the command. In this case, you'd enter a remote IP address or a local network interface address, respectively.

- Brackets around any element indicate that it's optional.

ipconfig

In Windows, the **ipconfig** command is one of your prime tools for troubleshooting connectivity problems. It can be used to display network settings, as well as to fix some problems with DHCP and DNS settings. The command itself displays basic settings for all installed network interfaces, including IPv4 and IPv6 addresses, subnet mask, and default gateway. This means you can not only verify basic configuration, but also check whether the adapter is using a routable or self-assigned IP address.

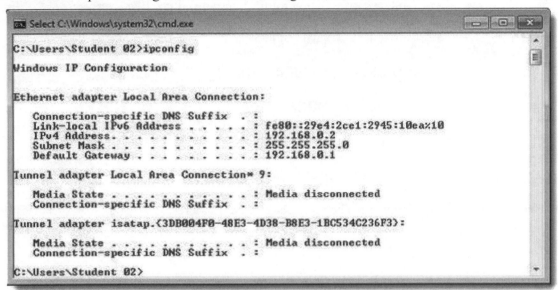

For more options, the syntax is simple. You can use any one of the following parameters.

Parameter	Description
/all	Displays additional information for each interface, including name, physical address, DNS, and DHCP settings.
/release [*interface*]	Releases the current IPv4 address for all interfaces, or for a single specified interface. Useful for removing bad DHCP settings.
/renew [*interface*]	Renews the current IPv4 or IPv6 address for all interfaces, or for a single specified interface. Useful for checking or repairing DHCP settings.
/release6 [*interface*]	Like /release , but for IPv6 address.
/renew6 [*interface*]	Like /renew , but for IPv6 address
/displaydns	Displays the current contents of the DNS cache.
/flushdns	Deletes the DNS cache. Useful when the current cache has incorrect entries.
/registerdns	Renews all DHCP leases and re-registers with DNS servers.

As you can see, **ipconfig** is most useful for computers with dynamic IP addresses. With static addresses you can still use it to view information and manage DNS settings, but it can't actually change IP settings.

ifconfig

Instead of **ipconfig**, Unix-like operating systems have the broader **ifconfig** command. It allows you to configure a wide variety of interface settings, even on static IP addresses. The command itself shows address and diagnostic information for all active interfaces. There are also a number of parameters you can use.

Parameter	Description
-a	Shows information for both active and inactive interfaces.
Interface up	Enables the specified interface.
Interface down	Disables the specified interface.
Interface dhcp release	Releases the DHCP lease.
Interface dhcp start	Leases a new DHCP address.
Interface ip_address	Assigns a static IP address.
Interface netmask *ip_address*	Assigns a netmask for a static IP address.
Interface mtu *value*	Sets Ethernet MTU.
Interface promisc	Enables *promiscuous mode*, allowing the interface to read all packets passing through the network segment regardless of where they're addressed. Important for running some diagnostic tools.
Interface -promisc	Disables promiscuous mode.
inet6	Inserted immediately after *interface* with any IPv4 related parameter, specifies the IPv6 equivalent.

Note: **ifconfig** has largely been superseded by the newer and more powerful **ip** command, but it's still installed and widely used on modern systems.

nbtstat

In Windows, **nbtstat** shows settings for NetBIOS over TCP/IP (*NBT*). NetBIOS was originally designed for early LANs: while NBT allows it to be used on modern networks, it's still increasingly seen as a legacy protocol, and you'll likely only encounter it working with older hosts and networks. The command-line utility is not generally found in Unix-like TCP/IP tools, but it's still a standard part of Windows. Without parameters the command only shows syntax information, but there are a wide number of optional parameters. You can use them alone or in combination, though the order can be important.

```
nbtstat [-a RemoteName] [-A IPAddress] [-c] [-n] [-r] [-R] [-RR] [-s] [-S]
[Interval]
```

Parameter	Description
[-a *RemoteName*]	Lists the NetBIOS table of a remote PC with the specified NetBIOS name.
[-A *IPAddress*]	Lists the NetBIOS table of a remote PC with the specified IP address.
[-c]	Lists the NetBIOS cache table, including both names and IP addresses.

Parameter	Description
[-n]	Displays names that have been registered locally.
[-r]	Lists names resolved by local broadcast or a *Windows Internet Name ServiceWINS* server.
[-R]	Purges and reloads remote cache name table.
[-RR]	Like -R , but first releases, then re-registers all NetBIOS names with the name server.
[-s]	Lists current NetBIOS sessions and statistics, using NetBIOS names.
[-S]	Lists current NetBIOS sessions and statistics, using IP addresses.
[*Interval*]	Repeats results at the specified interval (in seconds) until you press **Ctrl**+**C** to stop.

netstat

Never mind a busy server, even an ordinary user workstation today has a lot of network applications and services moving a lot of traffic over a large number of TCP/IP connections. The **netstat** command allows you to get statistics related to active connections and routing.

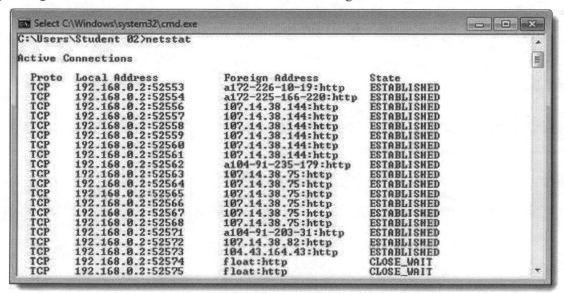

netstat itself displays a list of communication sessions along with source and destination hosts and ports. There are a wide variety of parameters available, depending heavily on your specific operating system.

Parameter	Description
-?	Displays system-specific help.
-a	Displays all connections and listening ports.
-b	In Windows, displays the executable which created each connection or listening port. In BSD-based operating systems, lists traffic quantity in bytes. (Linux uses -p for the Windows function.)

Parameter	Description
-e	Displays Ethernet statistics in bytes or frames sent/received.
-f	In modern Windows versions, displays FQDN for remote addresses.
-p *proto*	In Windows, shows connections for a particular Transport layer protocol. With -s , it can also include Network layer protocols.
-r	Displays the routing table.
-s	Displays statistics by protocol.
-t	In Linux, displays only TCP connections. **-at** for TCP and **-au** for UDP.

nslookup

If you want to perform DNS lookups on the command line, you can use the **nslookup** command. It can find the IP address of a given FQDN, so you can use it both to find addresses or use known names just to make sure your DNS settings are working properly. You can perform single lookups, or else you can enter an *interactive mode* that lets you just enter addresses until you press **Ctrl+C** to return to the command line.

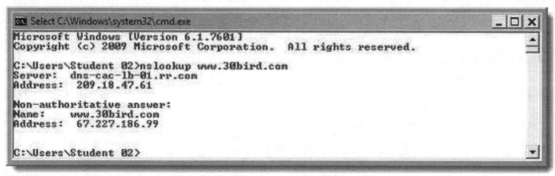

Command	Description
nslookup	Enters interactive mode using the default DNS server.
nslookup - *server*	Enters interactive mode using a specified server.
nslookup *host*	Performs a single lookup using the default DNS server.
nslookup *hostserver*	Performs a single lookup using a specified server.

ping

One of the most important command line tools is **ping**, which checks connectivity to a given host in terms of packet loss percentage, along with latency and number of hops traversed. Typically, one use of the command represents several individual echo request packets sent and measured individually. For basic functionality you only need an address to ping, but each operating system includes a number of optional parameters.

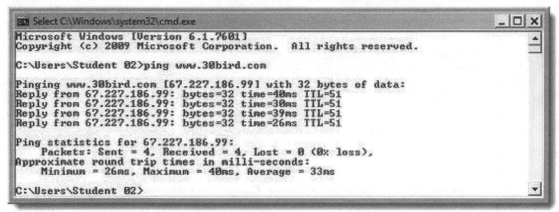

```
Select C:\Windows\system32\cmd.exe

Microsoft Windows [Version 6.1.7601]
Copyright (c) 2009 Microsoft Corporation.  All rights reserved.

C:\Users\Student 02>ping www.30bird.com

Pinging www.30bird.com [67.227.186.99] with 32 bytes of data:
Reply from 67.227.186.99: bytes=32 time=40ms TTL=51
Reply from 67.227.186.99: bytes=32 time=30ms TTL=51
Reply from 67.227.186.99: bytes=32 time=39ms TTL=51
Reply from 67.227.186.99: bytes=32 time=26ms TTL=51

Ping statistics for 67.227.186.99:
    Packets: Sent = 4, Received = 4, Lost = 0 (0% loss),
Approximate round trip times in milli-seconds:
    Minimum = 26ms, Maximum = 40ms, Average = 33ms

C:\Users\Student 02>
```

`ping [parameters] address`

Common parameter	Description
-n count	Sends a specified number of pings.
-t	Continues to ping until stopped
-a	Attempts to do a reverse DNS lookup of the IP address pinged.
-l size	Sets the size of the packet. (default 32 bytes.)
-f	Prevents packet fragmentation. With a large packet, you can use this to troubleshoot MTU problems.
-i TTL	Sets the TTL value of the packet. (max 255.)
-w time	Sets the timeout value for each packet in milliseconds (default 4000.)
-4 or -6	Forces use of IPv4 or IPv6. On some systems, the latter may just be called **ping6**.

For security reasons, the echo request packets used by ping are blocked by some hosts and firewalls. Inability to ping a particular target shouldn't be seen as proof that there's a more general network interruption.

traceroute

When ping isn't enough and you want to know the network path to a remote host, you can use the **traceroute** command, or **tracert** in Windows. It doesn't report only the round trip time and number of hops to the remote host, it also reports the name, address, and latency of each hop along the way. This lets you look for problems in the network along the path to your destination.

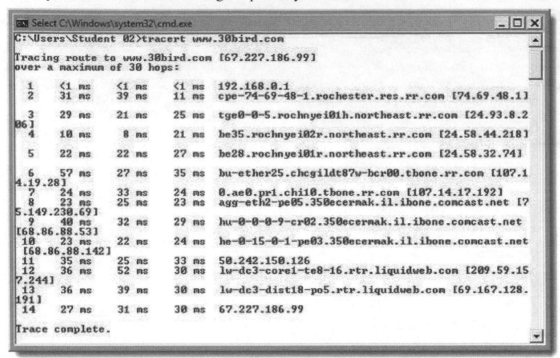

Like ping, the basic syntax of traceroute is `traceroute [options] address` Also like ping, different implementations use **tracert6**, **traceroute6**, or the `-6` parameter for IPv6 functionality.

Windows parameter	Linux parameter	Description
`-d`	`-n`	Doesn't perform reverse DNS lookups.
`-hmaximum_hops`	`-mmaximum_hops`	Specifies maximum TTL (default 30)
`-Wmilliseconds`	`-wseconds`	Specifies timeout (Windows default 4000ms, Linux default 5.0s)

Choosing command-line tools

Especially if you're using the divide-and-conquer approach to troubleshooting, you're often going to start by checking IP settings and connectivity. The answers you can get from a quick check at the command line can often tell you what's wrong, or where you need to look next. Don't hesitate to check settings in the Network and Sharing Center either.

- When you want to check end-to-end connectivity, **ping** is a great place to start.
  - Inability to reach only particular hosts or subnets suggests problems there, or at least somewhere on the way. Remember that ping is blocked by some firewalls.

- Inability to reach any hosts at all suggests a closer problem, possibly in the local host's IP settings or on the local subnet.

- If **ping** can't resolve host names but can reach known IP addresses, it suggests DNS server problems.

- High latency suggests network congestion, and especially when combined with high TTL it might mean routing issues.

- High packet loss can be network congestion, physical interference, or other reliability problems.

- If **ping** works normally, but applications are having connectivity problems, check at higher levels of the stack.

- Use **ipconfig** or **ifconfig** to check adapter settings.

  - Multiple active adapters can cause problems. Try disabling any that aren't in use.

  - An adapter with only link-local or self-assigned IP addresses won't be able to communicate outside its subnet.

  - An incorrect IP address, manual or dynamic, can cause various problems.

  - Remember to check subnet mask, default gateway, and DNS server addresses.

  - Try releasing and renewing DCHP leases if you suspect configuration problems. Inability to do so suggests server or physical connectivity issues.

  - Total lack of connectivity with valid settings suggests lower level problems.

- Use **nslookup** to test DNS server functions.

- If you suspect problems with address resolution, clear the DNS cache using the **ipconfig** or **ifconfig** command.

- Use **netstat** or GUI monitoring tools to examine existing network traffic. Performance problems can be caused by large amounts of unexpected traffic.

- To investigate potential route issues, use **traceroute**.

  - Assuming the route is good, traceroute can pinpoint just which link is failing.

  - Routing loops might render remote networks unreachable.

  - High latency hops suggest overloaded servers.

Exercise: Using TCP/IP tools

As an PC technician, you'll need to verify use TCP/IP tools to verify settings and check connectivity when troubleshooting network connection problems.

Do This	How & Why
1. In Windows 10, type cmd into the search box.	The command window opens.
2. Check your IP settings using **ipconfig**.	
a) Type ipconfig	The IP settings for all network adapters are displayed, including IPv4 and IPv6 addresses, subnet masks, and default gateways.
b) Type ipconfig /all	Scroll up in the command window if necessary. The /all parameter shows additional information, such as physical address, DNS servers, and DHCP settings.
c) Type **ipconfig /?**	The help option shows detailed command usage. You could also release or renew a DHCP lease, among other things.
d) How would your options differ if you were using **ifconfig** in Linux?	Apart from the syntax working a bit differently, you can also configure static IP address and a number of other interface settings.
3. Type ping www.weather.gov.	Your connectivity and latency to the National Weather Service website is displayed. Notice that the FQDN shown by ping isn't the same one you entered.
4. Type nslookup www.weather.gov.	Akamai Technologies is a content delivery service that among other clients hosts the NWS website. The DNS lookup data for the website is displayed. www.weather,gov is actually an alias for that particular akamaiedge.net FQDN.
5. Type tracert www.weather.gov.	**tracert** displays ping times to each router hop between you and the destination website, along with both the FQDN and IP address for each.
6. Type netstat.	**netstat** by itself displays your active network connections. You could explore other parameters for further network information.
7. Close the command line window.	

Network troubleshooting

Sometimes specific sites won't work, sometimes specific services, and sometimes just nothing seems to be responding. Any given symptom can have multiple possible causes, sometimes on different layers of the network. In Windows, it's often easiest to first look and see if the network icon in the system tray indicates a problem, before you go rooting around back for the network cable or restarting the computer.

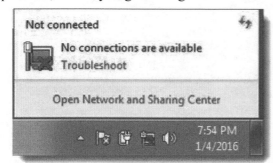
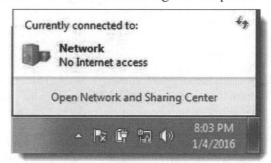

A red X indicates that Windows can't detect any connections. That could mean a physical problem, or just a disabled or misconfigured adapter, but it means you're probably entirely without network connectivity.

A yellow exclamation point indicates that Windows has limited or local connectivity, but can't reach the Internet or other larger network. This might be a problem with IP configuration or the local network, but it generally means the physical connection is working all right.

That isn't to say you can trust the connection icon entirely. Windows can make mistakes, and sometimes the connection will appear to be fine but something's still broken. An immediate glance also can't tell you where the problem is. If every computer in the office loses connection at once you can be pretty sure the problem is elsewhere in the network, but otherwise you should rule out local problems before looking further.

The simplest troubleshooting methods are the most obvious and least technical: make sure the network cable is plugged in, restart the computer, and so on. Windows can also perform automated troubleshooting: to do so, right-click the network icon and choose **Troubleshoot problems**. When those fail, or when you suspect a more specific problem, you can check network settings in Windows or at the command line.

A useful guideline for troubleshooting network problems is to follow the path of data to look for where the problem might be. There are multiple ways to do this:

- The *follow-the-path* approach tracks traffic through the network to look for what parts are working right and what don't. It's good for finding problems with faulty cables and misconfigured connections, but isn't very useful for a single network host that's having problems.

- The *top-down* approach moves down the network stack from network applications down through the operating system. It's best for solving problems that affect some network applications but not others, like if you can receive email but can't browse the web.

- The *bottom-up* approach moves up through the network stack from physical connection to NIC drivers and the operating system. It's best for solving problems that affect all network connectivity on a host, like if you can't connect to the network at all.

Troubleshooting connection status

When you can't achieve a network connection in the first place, or when you have intermittent connectivity or low performance, it might mean a problem with your physical connection, or at least with the adapter's configuration in Windows.

 Exam Objective(s): 220-1001 5.7.1.2, 5.7.1.4, 5.7.1.6; CompTIA A+ 220-1002 3.1.1.2

- Make sure the physical connection is secure. Check the cable and make sure the adapter's status lights show that it's plugged in.
- Verify that the adapter is enabled in Windows.
- If the adapter is enabled, try disabling it and re-enabling it in **Network Connections**. "Turn it off and on again" is only a tech support cliché because it works so often.
- Make sure that all correct drivers and device bindings are installed.
- Verify local network requirements. If the network uses custom Ethernet settings, MAC address filtering, or so on, you might need to reconfigure the adapter or the network.
- If your connection requires authentication, make certain you have the right credentials and security settings.
- If your computer has multiple network interfaces, make sure Windows is using the right one. Disable others if necessary.
- Intermittent drops and slow speeds can be caused by substandard wiring, improper duplexing settings, or LAN congestion or misconfiguration. Don't forget to look for other applications that might be consuming network bandwidth too.

Troubleshooting network settings

When you can achieve some sort of network connection, but can't reach the sites and services you want, there's probably a configuration issue somewhere. The best place to start looking is with TCP/IP settings, though it could be elsewhere in the network stack. If you find something out of place, update your network settings, and if necessary, restart the system.

 Exam Objective(s): 220-1001 5.7.1.1, 5.7.1.3, 5.7.1.5; CompTIA A+ 220-1002 3.1.2.5

- Improper IP address settings are the easiest way to foul up a physically functional connection.
  - IP addresses must be unique on the subnet.
  - APIPA or link-local addresses will allow communication on a local network, but not across routers.
  - If you're using DHCP, try releasing and renewing your lease.
  - If a DHCP server is not available, configure valid static settings.
  - IP address alone isn't enough: make sure the default gateway and subnet mask/network prefix are all correct as well.
- Ability to connect by IP address but not domain name suggests DNS problems.
  - Clear the DNS cache to remove potential bad entries.
  - If you're using DHCP, make sure automatic DNS servers are also configured.
  - Try an alternate DNS server. 8.8.8.8 and 8.8.4.4 are public DNS servers anyone can use.
- Remember that IPv4 and IPv6 must be configured separately, so know which one (or both) your network uses.
- A limited connection to local resources but not internet resources can have a variety of causes.

- Verify that IP address, gateway, and DNS settings are all correct.

- If your network uses a web proxy or requires other special client-side settings, verify they are correctly configured. This is especially likely when your web browser won't connect but other network services work.

- If multiple hosts on the same network are experiencing internet connectivity problems, check for router or WAN issues.

- If some applications connect to the network but others don't, verify your firewall and proxy settings.

- Inability to access resources on the local network even when you have network connectivity is likely due to network security settings. A common example is inability to connect to a shared printer or drive.

  - Make sure your network location is private and that network discovery is enabled.

  - Ensure that the target resource is powered on and connected to the same network.

  - On an Active Directory domain, verify domain membership.

  - On a Wi-Fi network, make sure you're not on a guest or isolated network.

  - Verify that you have the right credentials to access the resource.

- Inability to send or receive email may be due to firewall or spam filter settings, but the first place to check is in the email client itself.

  - Check the server name, port, encryption, and authentication settings for each server. POP3 and IMAP accounts both will have an SMTP server in addition to the POP or IMAP server.

  - The SMTP server will have a different port and possibly a different name. If necessary, enable SMTP authentication.

  - If the account has webmail access, check it to make sure the account itself is working.

- If nothing obviously seems wrong, try running the network troubleshooter in Settings or Control Panel. In Windows 10 you can also navigate to **Settings > Network & Internet > Status > Network Reset** to completely reset network settings to their defaults. You will need to re-apply any custom settings after.

- If you can't find anything wrong on the local system, escalate further into the network.

Troubleshooting wireless connections

Wireless network connections have unique properties both due to their physical nature and their commonly used connection protocols. This translates to different things which can go wrong, and different troubleshooting steps you'll need to take.

 Exam Objective(s): 220-1001 2.8.8, 5.7.1.6, 5.7.1.7

One of the most important is signal strength. While attenuation and interference are factors for any connection, they're a particular limitation in wireless networks. Windows gives a basic indication of the strength of a wireless signal, but it's not very detailed, or good at judging particular details of signal strength. This can be a problem, since a weak signal or interference can cause all kinds of problems even when everything is configured properly.

When you suspect signal problems, you might want to try a *wireless analyzer*. This might be a specialized hardware tool, but it can also be a software program running on a normal mobile device. Either way, it reads available wireless networks as well as their channels and signal strengths. More sophisticated analyzers can also tell you about network traffic: it's easy to read network performance when actually joined to a network, though some information can be gained even passively. Hardware-based analyzers often allow detailed RF spectrum analysis, giving detailed information on interference sources and other problems.

- Weak signals are often a case of attenuation or interference. Try moving the client or WAP if possible.

  - Thicker walls will attenuate signals more rapidly, as will brick, stone, or metal. Even glass has a surprising effect on Wi-Fi signals, especially when coated or tinted.

  - 5GHz signals attenuate more rapidly than 2.4GHz.

  - Interference sources can include other Wi-Fi networks, other wireless technologies, microwave ovens, and electrical motors or other devices.

  - Interference from other Wi-Fi networks can be minimized by making sure they're using different channels.

  - Antenna orientation for both the client and WAP can matter. If a device doesn't have an external antenna, try moving the device itself.

- Low performance can also be caused by network congestion or conflicting standards.

  - Wireless networks are particularly prone to congestion from too many clients.

  - Devices using older Wi-Fi standards can effectively slow the entire network by taking more time to transmit the same information.

  - Wireless repeaters or extenders half the bandwidth of the network.

- Network security settings can interfere with connection, especially if they're changed on the WAP.

  - When you can't find a network that should be reachable, it might not be broadcasting its SSID. Configure the network to connect even without SSID broadcast.

  - If an existing network stops connecting, verify that its settings haven't changed. Changes in password, or in encryption type, will require you to change settings or to remove and recreate the connection.

  - Public networks might require additional sign-in even when they're not encrypted.

  - Windows might automatically configure a wireless network as public even when it's private. If you need to use network discovery on a particular network, make sure it's set to a private location. If the network is public, keep it set so for additional security.

- Make sure you're connected to the right WAP, and not just one with a similar name. Some access points might not be connected to the right network, or even might be malicious impersonators.

- Ensure that the wireless connection itself is turned on.

  - Mobile devices can often be configured to turn off wireless adapters to save power, or as part of "airplane mode".

  - Sometimes wireless adapters are enabled or disabled by a button, switch, or keystroke combination so convenient that it's easy to toggle by accident.

  - Bluetooth and Wi-Fi might be controlled separately or together depending on the device.

  - Some wireless adapters have trouble reconnecting after sleep or hibernation: you may need to disable and enable them manually, or restart the device.

Discussion: Network troubleshooting

If possible, configure a computer with some sort of solvable network problem for students to fix. Otherwise, describe one or more sets of symptoms and ask students what they would check first.

1. What past network problems have you had that could have easily been solved by a top-down approach?

2. What past network problems have you had that could have easily been solved by a bottom-up approach?

3. What past network problems have you had that could have easily been solved by a follow-the-path approach?

4. Run the Network troubleshooter from PC Settings. What does it say?

Assessment: Connection troubleshooting

1. Which network tools are found in Windows but not typically in Unix-like operating systems? Choose all that apply,

    - ifconfig
    - ipconfig
    - nbtstat
    - ping
    - traceroute

2. You can't ping any other hosts, even on the local subnet. What should you check next? Choose the best response.

    - Application settings
    - DNS server
    - IP address settings
    - MTU settings

3. You can connect to the Internet, but not to local network shares. What should you check first?

    - DNS settings
    - IP address settings
    - Network location
    - Windows Firewall

4. On your laptop, you can see a couple of hotspots, but not the one you want to connect to. What can you try to fix it? Choose all that apply.

    - Double-check the encryption standard being used.
    - Make sure the adapter is turned on.
    - Move the laptop closer to the WAP.
    - Set the network to connect without SSID broadcast.

Summary: Windows networking

You should now know:

- About sharing and security on the network, including the different resource sharing models used by Windows, how to share folders and printers, and how to configure Windows Firewall.

- How to establish and maintain network connections in Windows, including LAN, Internet, dialup, wireless, and Remote Desktop Services.

- How to troubleshoot wired and wireless connections in Windows, using GUI and command-line tool.

Chapter 4: Security principles

You will learn:

- How to identify common security threats and vulnerabilities
- About common security control types

Module A: Threats and vulnerabilities

In this course so far, security's been mentioned but only as an aside. Partly that's because the details were being saved for this security chapter, but partly it's because for decades of computer and network design it was an afterthought. The engineers who designed the underlying standards of PCs and network technologies were focused on making things work in trusted environments, rather than on the many things which could go wrong. Today, complex and heavily networked computers holding valuable information mean that threats are everywhere, and everyone in the organization needs to know their part in securing IT resources.

You will learn:

- About the security goals of confidentiality, integrity, and availability
- How attackers threaten computers and data

About cybersecurity

Broadly speaking, security is the practice of protecting your assets from harm. Those assets can be almost anything, such as human health and safety, physical property, valuable information, and even stable business operations. *Cybersecurity*, often known as computer security or information security, is the practice of protecting information-related assets against whatever threatens them. Cybersecurity assets include computer hardware and software, data, network infrastructure, and the personnel who manage all of them. Cybersecurity threats include not just hackers and malware, but hardware and software malfunctions, physical attackers, natural disasters, and user errors.

Protecting physical equipment and human health is likely to be an important part of your job, but the asset that really sets cybersecurity apart is its focus on information; what computers store, what is transmitted over the network, and what users want to access. Think about it: even if your organization doesn't have information someone wants to steal, imagine the harm if an attacker broke into a server closet and stole the central network hardware, or if a virus on the sales manager's laptop wiped out all her presentations for the big conference. The overall damage for either could far exceed the cost of getting things up and running again.

The core of information security is commonly summed up into three components, known as the *CIA triad*. Designing networks with all three components in mind doesn't just protect them against known threats, it makes them less vulnerable to unknown dangers.

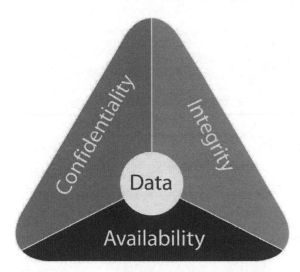

Confidentiality   Ensuring that information is viewable only by authorized users or systems, and is either inaccessible or unreadable to unauthorized users.

Integrity   Ensuring that information remains accurate and complete over its entire lifetime. In particular, this means making sure that data in storage or transit can't be modified in an undetected manner.

Availability   Ensuring that information is always easily accessible to authorized users. This means making sure that connectivity and performance is maintained at the highest possible level.

You might also hear about some other goals, and usually they'll fit into one of these. For example, *privacy* of personal information can easily be categorized as part of confidentiality. *Usability* is also important because security controls can get in the way of productivity, but that itself is related to availability. Regardless of how you define your goals, however, the important point is that you protect them throughout the entire information system.

Risk, threats, and vulnerabilities

Terms used to describe security challenges include risk, threats, and vulnerabilities. In casual use the three might be used imprecisely, or even interchangeably; however, while they're definitely related concepts, in security awareness they still mean very different things.

Risk   The chance of harm coming to an asset. Risk measurements can incorporate any combination of the likelihood of harm, the impact it will have on the organization, and the cost of repairing damage.

Threat   Anything that can cause harm to an asset. Threats can include *attacks* caused by malicious actors, but also human error, equipment malfunction, or natural disaster.

Vulnerability   Any weakness the asset has against potential threats. Vulnerabilities can be hardware, software, or human/organizational; likewise, they can represent errors or shortcomings in system design, or known tradeoffs for desired features.

The three factors are tightly intertwined. The end goal of cybersecurity is to minimize risk to critical assets, but to even calculate risk you need to know what threats you face, and where your organization is vulnerable.

Discussion: Security fundamentals

1. Consider a network service you use regularly, such as email.

a) How could its confidentiality be compromised?

b) Its integrity?

c) Its availability?

2. There's been a rash of burglaries in your area, and you notice that one door into part of the building with valuable equipment has a keypad lock set to '12345."

a) What is the vulnerability in this situation?

b) What is the threat?

c) What is the risk?

3. You've decided to correct the problem.

a) What changes should you make?

b) What kinds of controls are you changing or adding?

c) How will the change affect each of the three factors?

Common threats and vulnerabilities

Many users, home or business, might say "but my computer doesn't have valuable information, I don't care if the hackers get at it." It's a dangerous attitude: even such a computer likely has user credentials, saved passwords, and personal information that can be stolen and used elsewhere. Even if your computer doesn't, spyware can capture credentials when you log onto a company server or bank website. If nothing else, a virus or other attack can hurt your computer's performance or even render it inoperable, and cause you both immediate inconvenience plus the time and trouble needed to fix it, so you should always have security on your mind.

 Exam Objective(s): 220-1002 2.5.4, 2.5.10

Configuring computers properly will minimize the risk threats pose to them, and modern operating systems like include many security features by default, but they'll only be fully effective if their users also practice secure behaviors Some of the most common threats for user workstations include the following:

Malware	Malicious or unwanted software designed to steal data or impair your computer's performance. Malware is especially dangerous on Windows PCs and other computers that can run arbitrary software, but can be found on other systems as well.
Network attacks	Hackers, malicious software, and other automated attacks can try to access your computer over the network to steal data, or implant malware. When your data is passing over the network, attackers can also try to intercept it, modify it, or even impersonate someone else on the other end of a connection.
Unauthorized users	A malicious or even negligent user getting access to your account can do damage directly, or just weaken other security measures to make your data more vulnerable. Unauthorized users might physically log into your computer, or remotely gain access to either it or your online accounts. Intruders often rely on *social engineering*, con artist techniques used to trick legitimate users into trusting them and giving up access. Malicious employees within the organization are especially dangerous, since they already have some access.

Risk occurs when a threat intersects with a vulnerability. Some of the most common vulnerabilities in the enterprise include:

Insecure technologies	Older hardware, software, and network protocols commonly have outdated security features or known vulnerabilities that make them unsafe against modern threats. Even newer technologies may simply not be designed for the security standards you need. If you must use these technologies, you should use extra controls to reduce risk.
Weak configurations	Systems and software must be securely configured in order to minimize risk; many products with ample security features don't have them all enabled by default, and even secure settings might be changed during maintenance or user activity. Additionally, operating systems and other critical software must receive regular security updates to patch newly discovered vulnerabilities.
Non-compliant systems	Organizational security policies frequently define how systems are to be deployed. These policies can include supported operating systems, security features, updates, account management, and required or forbidden software. A system that isn't in compliance with these policies introduces risk, and not just because of insecure technologies or configurations in themselves. Administrators may not be aware of the risks it poses, or account for it in their overall security strategy.
Physical environment	Physical access to a computer, network, or storage device is a literal foot in the door to an intruder. Insecure physical environments let attackers bypass network-based access controls, implant malware directly, or simply make off with valuable equipment or data.
User behavior	Humans are one of the big weak links in any security system. Insufficient training can lead users to take actions that harm assets directly or just create security vulnerabilities; even experienced users can get sloppy or just make mistakes. Malicious insiders are a big risk, but so are social engineers who trick well-meaning users into risky behavior.
Weak documentation	Every aspect of cybersecurity relies on having security-related information at the ready, and without it you may never know you've got a security problem until it's too late. This includes training materials, configuration data, policies and procedures, and logs of user access and system activities. Security documentation must itself be secured, so it doesn't become a roadmap for an attacker.

For the most part, vulnerabilities are things which you can fix to minimize risk, but it's difficult unless you know the vulnerability is there in the first place. Cybersecurity is a constant arms race of attackers trying to find new vulnerabilities in common systems, while vendors and security professionals race to fix them. In particular, software updates and secure configuration guides alone won't protect you against *zero-day* attacks, which target vulnerabilities which have not yet been patched, and may not even be known to software vendors. Unknown risks like zero-day vulnerabilities are some of the most serious cybersecurity threats, and protecting against them requires securely designed informational systems managed by trained users who pay attention to detail.

Social engineering

Social engineering attacks take advantage of human behaviors to steal information directly, bypass security measures, or compromise systems against future threats. While hackers have been developing their techniques for years, conventional thieves and con artists have been honing their skills throughout human history. By tricking a technician or authorized end user into doing the damage, even an attacker with little technical knowledge can be a potent cybersecurity threat. Social engineering is one of the biggest sources of security threats, and one of the most consistently overlooked, so it's important to recognize attacks.

Exam Objective(s): 220-1002 2.5.1

The most common factor in social engineering attacks is impersonation. Whether in person, by phone, or by email, attackers pretend to be coworkers, technical support, bank workers, or other legitimate actors, just to get others to let their guard down. It's surprisingly effective to just ask someone for their password, if you have a good excuse about why you're not just a nosy stranger. Likewise, it's not hard to openly wander around many secure areas: most others will be too busy to notice unless you call attention to yourself. Another common factor is taking advantage of insecure behaviors in the real world: many users don't think of physical security and computer security as part of the same whole.

Shoulder surfing	Watching someone who is viewing or entering sensitive information, or eavesdropping on confidential conversations. It's easy to think of this as being literally over the shoulder, but people have been caught using binoculars or hidden cameras to steal password or ATM PINs. Shoulder surfing is especially a danger for employees doing work-related communications on mobile devices in public places.
Dumpster diving	Hunting for discarded documents and other media in a target's trash, looking for information. The most obvious target is confidential information that's valuable in itself, or security-related information that can be used to compromise the system, but it's not all that's valuable. Schedules, policy manuals, and personal information can also be used to launch further social engineering attacks.
Piggybacking / Tailgating	Getting into a secure area by tagging along right behind someone who has legitimate access, with or without their knowledge. A tailgater might join a crowd of authorized people that aren't individually checked, or even get a careless but polite person to hold a locked door open after entering.
Phone impersonation	Impersonating an authority figure or other relevant person over the phone and requesting sensitive information. This can be done in person, but the phone makes it harder to verify identity or spot suspicious elements. Help desk workers and other customer-facing employees are especially vulnerable to this, since they're trained to be friendly and helpful but might not be trained about what *not* to reveal.
Spam	Sending unsolicited emails or other electronic messages, with undesired or malicious content. Spam can be harmless noise, commercial advertisement, fraud attempts, or a way of delivering malware. Malicious spam uses social engineering to get users to read and act on it, and even the least harmful varieties generate network traffic and distract users.

Phishing

Using fake but official-looking messages to trick users into performing dangerous actions. Often phishing attacks are distributed via spam email: a common method is to claim to be a bank or legitimate online service, with a link to log into their website. The link actually leads to a fake page maintained by the attacker, even if it looks genuine at first glance. In truth, it either contains malware, or tricks users into entering their credentials or some other personal information.

Spear phishing

A variant of phishing that targets specific people, such as members of an organization or even individual users. Compared to a generic phishing message that could target almost anyone, a spear phishing attempt has personal or at least organizational information the attacker was able to gain beforehand and incorporate into the message. Spear phishing is an especially dangerous technique because those personal details can make even experienced users let their guard down and assume the attacker is a legitimate entity they should respond to.

Phishing emails often fool even experienced users

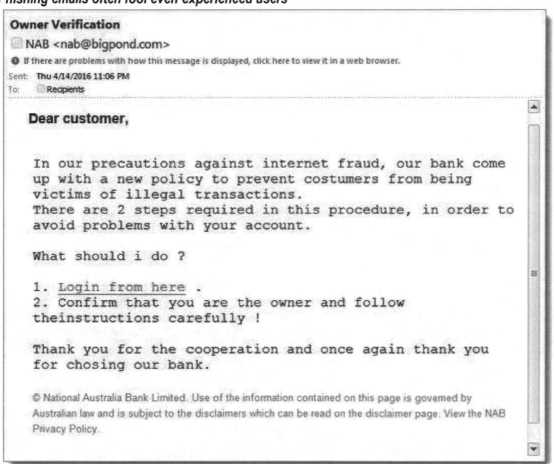

Malware

Malware is one of the biggest threats to endpoints like home computers and enterprise workstations, so as a PC technician you need to be ready to defend against infections and recognize them when they occur. There are many types, and they're constantly changing as their creators work around existing defenses. The first way to categorize malware is by how it spreads.

 Exam Objective(s): 220-1002 2.4.1, 2.5.11

Virus	Malware attached to an infected file, usually an executable program but possibly as a script inside a data file like an office document. The virus is harmless just sitting there on the drive, but when a user runs the program it becomes active. Then it can perform attacks, which very commonly include infecting other programs, corrupting data, or emailing itself to other users. Viruses were the first common malware, so sometimes "virus" gets used as a catch-all-term.
Worm	Malware that spreads without any human interaction. By using system vulnerabilities, it can replicate itself, spread to other systems, and run itself there. This makes worms capable of rapidly spreading through a network unassisted. Rapidly spreading worms can do damage just by the system resources they consume, but the most serious have malicious functions as well.
Trojan horse	Malware that appears to be a harmless or useful program, like a game or even an anti-virus application. It doesn't reproduce, outside of just tricking unwary users into installing it normally. Once it's running, its malicious functions take over. It might still be invisible to the end user, causing nothing more than system slowdowns or hidden vulnerabilities. Frequently a trojan will be attached to an email, masquerading as a useful file, funny video, or some other harmless program.

> **Note:** Closely related to traditional trojans are viruses installed on inexpensive USB flash drives, then left for someone to find. Unwary people who find a stray USB drive, especially one with an interesting label, will typically plug it in to see what's on it. If it's malicious, it will infect the computer.

You can also categorize malware by what it does once it's infected a computer. Some of it just impairs normal functions - invisibly consuming resources, causing more serious system slowdowns, corrupting critical data, or even deleting the entire hard drive. Some particularly nasty viruses can even take actions that physically damage hardware components. Other types are more specific.

Backdoor	In general, a backdoor is any hidden way into a system or application that bypasses normal authentication systems. Backdoors created by malware can be used to gather data, remotely control the computer, send spam email, or almost anything the computer itself can. They're frequently used with *rogue servers* that set up unauthorized network services on compromised systems.
Botnet	Many backdoors aren't intended primarily to let an attacker log into the computer. Instead, they turn the computer into a *zombie*: part of a large network of computers that performs distributed network attacks or other processing tasks on behalf of the botnet's controller. To the computer's user, the zombie might appear normal or just be unusually slow.
Rootkit	Malware that compromises boot systems and core operating system functions in order to hide from most detection methods. In extreme cases, rootkits can infect device firmware, requiring specialized equipment to remove. Rootkits and similar features have even been used in commercial software: even if there's no malicious intent from the vendor, they can compromise security other ways.

Ransomware	A particularly intrusive sort of malware that attempts to extort money from the victim in order to undo or prevent further damage. One common type of ransomware encrypts user files to make them unreadable, then demands payment to the malware's distributor in exchange for the decryption key. Another type is a bogus "free antivirus" program claiming it's detected an infection but that you need the paid version to actually remove it.
Spyware	Malware specifically designed to gather information about user and computer activities to send to other parties, often through a backdoor. Spyware can be used to track browser activity, redirect browser traffic, steal financial or user account information. *Keyloggers* which silently record all user input are a serious form of spyware. Sometimes tracking cookies used by web browsers are classified as spyware, though they tend to be more limited in capability.
Adware	Malware that delivers advertisements to the infected system, either as pop-ups or within browser or other application windows. Adware frequently has a spyware component, even if it's just to track user activities and choose targeted ads.

Forced access attacks

Just like many security threats in the real world involve someone trying to get past the lock of a door or safe, many digital threats involve someone trying to get into a secure system, encrypted file, or something else protected by some sort of access credentials.

Exam Objective(s): 220-1002 2.5.6, 2.5.7, 2.5.8

The easiest way for an attacker to bypass access controls is by choosing a target that doesn't have any. This is especially easy when a network has poor physical security, open Wi-Fi hotspots, or computers and network services without password-protected accounts. It's also a problem for unprotected data that can get in the hands of an attacker, like a database, USB drive, or the hard drive of a stolen computer.

If a system uses some sort of authentication system, or if data is protected by encryption, the attacker can try to use proper credentials such as a password. For this reason, stealing passwords and encryption keys is one of the most common goals of attackers: it literally unlocks the path to anything else they might want.

Attackers who can't steal passwords can just try to guess one, a process called *password cracking*. This can be surprisingly easy. Even outside of those who pick `12345` or `football`, many users will use the same password for every login they have - email, bank, credit cards, etc. - so an attacker who learns one password learns them all. Many network devices or services come installed with a default password, and administrators too often don't bother to change them. On many systems, there's nothing keeping an attacker from just trying one password after another until something works.

Automated tools are commonly used to speed the cracking process. Their methods aren't unlike manual ones, just faster and more tireless.

Brute force	The attacker tries every possible password or key in a methodical order, until finding the right one. Brute force can crack any password in theory, but it's a very slow method. Short passwords are very vulnerable to brute force cracking, but long passwords are much safer.
Dictionary attack	The attacker uses a word list, such as a literal dictionaries or list of common passwords. This approach won't easily guess random character strings, but are very effective against passwords comprised of words or names. More sophisticated dictionary attacks check for words with appended numbers, common letter substitutions, and so on. Even long passwords can be vulnerable to dictionary attacks if they use recognizable words or patterns.

Hash table   Many password-based authentication systems rely on *cryptographic hashes* generated from the password, rather than the password itself. Attackers can leverage this by pre-calculating hashes for all possible passwords, at least up to a certain length. While creating a hash table is slow, using a hash table to crack passwords is much faster. This makes them useful for attackers who want to crack a lot of passwords at once. Hash tables are very large; even for short passwords they can be many gigabytes in size.

Rainbow table   A more popular variety of hash table that's designed to use less disk space. It doesn't crack passwords as quickly as a full hash table, but it's still a lot faster than brute force attacks, so it's an appealing compromise for many attackers. Like brute force and hash tables, rainbow tables are most effective against short passwords. Some authentication systems are designed to protect against them.

Cracking isn't the only option. Attackers can also look for backdoors or use social engineering to get access to systems or passwords. Finally, just because you have access to a system doesn't mean you have authorization to do whatever you like. Many exploits rely on *privilege escalation*, or gaining additional permissions from an application or operating system. A privilege escalation exploit might allow a guest to have the privileges of a regular user, a regular user to have administrative privileges, or even just allow User A to access User B's private files.

Network attacks

Cybersecurity attacks like social engineering, password cracking, and malware can and often do take place over the network, but there are whole categories of attacks that rely on abuse of network protocols. Many of them target the core protocols that make TCP/IP work, or older application protocols designed before security was a major concern. Any protocol can have vulnerabilities, however.

Exam Objective(s): 220-1002 2.5.2, 2.5.3, 2.5.5, 2.5.9

Many network attacks are primarily the responsibility of network or server administrators to recognize and defend against, but others directly affect endpoints and users who access network services. Since malware-infected PCs are often used to launch network attacks, you might find an attack coming from your own system if you're not careful. End users and PC technicians should be aware of the following threats:

DoS   *Denial of service* attacks are designed to prevent legitimate users from accessing a network service or an entire network. The most common DoS technique attacks servers or routers with overwhelming or unusual traffic which consumes its resources and causes slowdowns or crashes. Other DoS methods include locking users out of accounts, or physically attacking hardware. Malware and forced access can also be used with DoS in mind.

DDoS   *Distributed denial of service* is a type of DoS where a single target is flooded by traffic from many individual computers, often spread across the internet. The number of attackers, and their distribution on the network, make the attack harder to defend against. DDoS attacks commonly use botnets directed by the actual attacker, and can overwhelm even powerful networks.

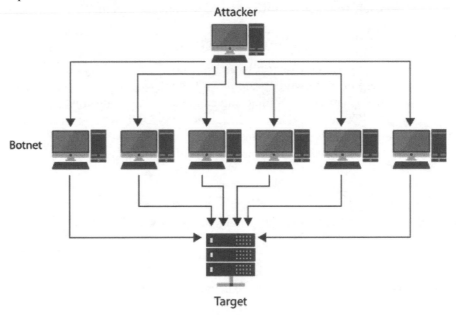

Eavesdropping   Any attack that intercepts or observes private communications. Eavesdropping is common for social engineering attacks like shoulder surfing, but on the network it's most common where an attacker can get access to unencrypted network traffic, such as from an unprotected switch or an open Wi-Fi network.

Man-in-the-middle   A form of eavesdropping where an attacker intercepts and relays communications between two points, often impersonating each party in the eyes of the other. This is much more potent than ordinary eavesdropping because the MITM can also insert or modify information in real time before it reaches its destination. Some MITM techniques are even designed specifically to attack protocols which are secure against ordinary eavesdropping. This type of attack is often directed at online banking and e-commerce sites, allowing the attacker to capture login credentials and other sensitive data. Sometimes the attack itself is a malicious script within the user's browser, rather than out somewhere on the network.

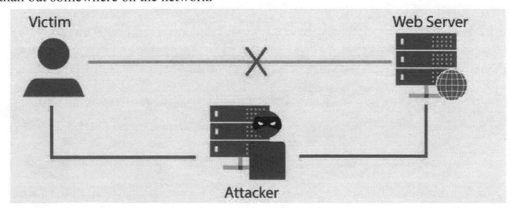

Spoofing	A technique that falsifies the origin of network communications, either to redirect responses or to trick users into thinking it comes from a trustworthy source. Spoofing attacks can apply to almost any protocol that specifies both a destination and an origin address: IP addresses on the internet, MAC addresses on the LAN, or specific applications such as email addresses or caller ID. Usually spoofing isn't an attack in itself so much as a way to enable other attacks like DoS or social engineering.
DNS hijacking	An attacker giving false replies to DNS requests sent by a host, in order to redirect traffic to a malicious or fraudulent site. Sometimes called *pharming*. When you or an application try to access a named host, you actually connect to the attacker's site which may host malware, perform MITM attacks, or just trick you into divulging sensitive information. DNS hijacking can occur via compromised DNS servers on the network, or DHCP servers that give hosts incorrect DNS settings., Hosts themselves can also be targeted by installing malware, changing network settings, or altering the `hosts` file the operating system uses to help resolve names.

Discussion: Threats and vulnerabilities

1. Would it be hard for an attacker to guess or bypass passwords on the hosts and devices you have access to?

2. What social engineering attacks have you encountered, in the workplace or your personal life?

3. Perform a web search for recent news stories about major cyber attacks. What techniques do they use?

4. Even assuming you don't have any malicious employees, how are inside attacks still a threat to the network?

Exercise: Identifying current virus threats

It's important to stay on top of known threats so that you can verify your systems are protected to the best of your ability. Many antivirus/anti-malware software companies help their customers do that by providing a comprehensive support area on their Website.

If you have Internet access, follow these steps to investigate current virus threats.

Do This	How & Why
1. Open an Internet browser and go to **www.symantec.com**. 2. Under Security Center, click **Threats**.	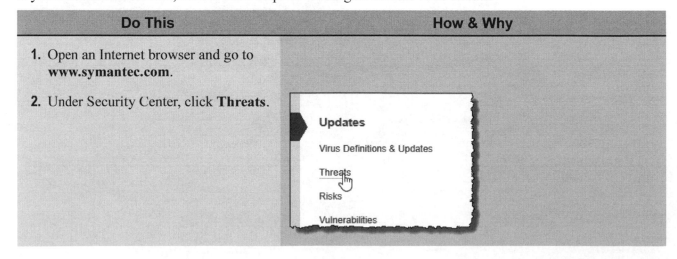

Do This	How & Why

3. Observe the list of current threats, threat type, and their severity.

4. Click any of the current threats to view the threat's details.

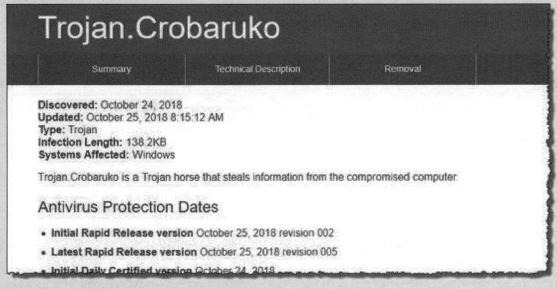

Trojan.Crobaruko

Summary   Technical Description   Removal

Discovered: October 24, 2018
Updated: October 25, 2018 8:15:12 AM
Type: Trojan
Infection Length: 138.2KB
Systems Affected: Windows

Trojan.Crobaruko is a Trojan horse that steals information from the compromised computer.

Antivirus Protection Dates

- **Initial Rapid Release version** October 25, 2018 revision 002
- **Latest Rapid Release version** October 25, 2018 revision 005
- **Initial Daily Certified version** October 24, 2018

You can view:

- A summary of the threat, including the systems it infects and when Symantec's antivirus solutions began protecting against it.

- Technical details, including what the threat does when it is executed and recommendations on what to do if your system has been infected.

- Removal details, along with how to reduce your risk of becoming infected by this threat.

5. Using the breadcrumbs, return to the Security Response page.

🏠 Security Center / Threats

6. Explore the **Risks** and **Vulnerability** tabs to observe the information they contain.

7. Click the **A-Z** tab.

All threats, risks, and vulnerabilities are listed here in alphabetical order. If you know the name of the malware you are looking for, you can search for it directly by name here.

Assessment: Security threats

1. What aspect of security does a keylogger primarily attack? Choose the best response.

   - Confidentiality

   - Integrity

   - Availability

2. Which types of attacks are thwarted by complex passwords that are combinations of upper and lower case letters, numbers, and special characters?

   - Brute force

   - Dictionary

   - Malware

   - Man-in-the-middle

   - Zero-day

3. As a user, what can you do to protect yourself from man-in-the-middle attacks?

   - Avoid connecting to open Wi-Fi routers.

   - Avoid following links in emails when possible.

   - Enable Firewall protection.

   - Install only the application software you need.

   - Use complex passwords that are combinations of upper and lower case letters, numbers, and special characters.

4. You receive an email about a new feature for an online service you use, and click the link for more information. Just before you sign into your account you notice the URL is wrong: it's actually a different site made to imitate the one you belong to. What attack were you targeted by? Choose the best response.

   - DoS

   - Evil twin

   - Phishing

   - Spoofing

5. What kind of attack is most likely when you're doing sensitive work on your laptop at a coffee shop? Choose the best response.

   - Piggybacking

   - Shoulder surfing

   - Smurfing

   - Wardriving

6. A user complains that every time they open their Internet browser, it no longer goes to their preferred home page and advertisements pop up in dialog boxes that they have to close. What is the likely cause?

- Spyware

- Trojan

- Virus

- Worm

7. A user logs into their computer and is presented with screen showing a Department of Justice logo indicating the computer has been locked due to the operating system being in violation of federal law. The screen gives several details of the violation and indicates that the user must pay a fine of $500 within 72 hours or a warrant will be issued for their arrest. The user cannot unlock their system. What type of malware is likely infecting the computer?

- Keylogger

- Ransomware

- Rootkit

- Trojan

- Worm

Module B: Security controls

The tools and measures used to achieve security goals are called *security controls*. A security control can be anything that protects your assets: the network firewall, the locks on the doors, even the company policy on data backups.

You will learn:

- About common security controls
- How to apply physical security
- About encryption
- About authentication systems

About security controls

The wide range of controls used by modern organizations means that a lot of effort has gone into categorizing controls by nature and function. One way is to categorize a control by the goal it furthers, such as confidentiality, integrity, or availability. Another is on the control's functional nature, such as physical, logical or procedural. Some important categories of security control you might encounter include:

- Physical security controls intended to protect against physical theft, intrusion, or vandalism. These might be used to protect facilities, secure areas, or portable hardware; they include locks, barriers, surveillance systems, and guards.

- Logical access control systems intended to prevent unauthorized access to computers and data in person or over the network. These controls include passwords, user accounts, operating system permissions, and a variety of other network and host-based functions.

- Data protection controls for both computers and networks. These controls include encryption to protect confidentiality, integrity monitoring to detect unauthorized changes, and data backups to provide recovery when important data is lost.

- Security hardware and software intended to protect against malware and network attacks, such as firewalls and antivirus software.

- Controls intended to prevent harm to equipment or associated business disruptions. These include environmental controls, backup power, and other redundant systems.

- Safety controls meant to protect against threats to human well-being.

- Policies and procedures used to reduce risks due to user error or insecure practices. These include system configuration guidelines, operational procedures, user training, auditing, and incident response.

A given control can fit into multiple categories, or work together with controls in other categories. For example, secure Wi-Fi networks have authorization to provide access control as well as encryption to protect transmitted data, and environmental control systems protect both sensitive equipment and human health.

Policies and best practices

Every organization with IT operations should have cybersecurity policies defining the organization's informational assets as well as the controls and procedures needed to secure them. If you're not in a position to be writing these policies from scratch, much of your work is going to be learning those policies, understanding what they mean, and putting them into action. A given organization might have a wide assortment of policy documents describing organizational goals, technological standards, operational procedures, and acceptable user behaviors. Failure to follow policies can compromise overall organizational security as well as have personal consequences for you, so it's your responsibility to know which ones are relevant to your duties.

Exam Objective(s): 220-1002 4.6.4

Policies themselves are often shaped by regulatory requirements defined by outside organizations, usually government agencies or regulatory groups. Regulatory compliance failures are threats in themselves, since even if no direct harm comes to your assets you and your organization can face civil or criminal liability. Regulatory compliance should be part of your organizational policies, but you should have some idea of the types of regulation your organization faces. Examples include:

SOX
The *Sarbanes-Oxley Act of 2002* is a US federal law designed to prevent fraudulent accounting practices. It applies primarily to financial records managed by companies that do business in the United States.

HIPAA
The *Health Insurance Portability and Accountability Act* is a US law governing health insurance coverage, but from an IT perspective it protects the privacy of patient records. It applies to any organization that stores or handles protected data.

GDPR
The *General Data Protection Regulation* is a newly enacted European Union regulation which protects the privacy of individual data related to EU residents. It applies not only to any organization in the EU which handles personal information, but specifically to foreign organizations that do business with or market to EU residents.

PCI DSS
The *Payment Card Industry Data Security Standard* isn't a law; instead, it's a set of shared rules developed by the world's major credit card companies and administered by the *PCI Council*. PCI DSS compliance is part of the contract an organization must sign before it is permitted to process payment cards.

When your actions aren't strictly defined by policies or regulations, you should follow *best practices* - methodologies which have been proven effective by other organizations and experts in similar situations to your own. One drawback is that best practices are often situational and have no central authority, so they often take a lot more research and judgement than following a formal procedure.

When policies, regulations, and best practices come in conflict, you need to determine a course of action. Where possible, you always must follow policies and regulations unless otherwise authorized. In some cases, you might be able to get a written *exception* from management when a formal requirement can't or shouldn't be met. Best practices that go "above and beyond" requirements are sometimes just fine, but in some cases might cause unforeseen problems or violations. When you have any questions about a security procedure, don't be afraid to escalate to an administrator, security officer, or compliance officer.

The principle of least privilege

Effective security policies and controls should be based on consistent risk management philosophies. One of the big dilemmas when designing secure systems is how best to restrict potentially unsafe behaviors without interrupting normal system functions. On a system without any security anyone is allowed to do anything and you trust them to avoid doing anything harmful, but that makes attacks and dangerous mistakes both easy. By contrast, secure systems define *privileges* or permissions which govern whether a specific action is allowed or not. Privileges determine whether a user can access a file or other system resource, run a program, or change an operating system setting. They also can govern what a program can do. While they're not usually called "privileges", network devices like firewalls apply similar rules to network traffic to decide what traffic is allowed through and what isn't.

 Exam Objective(s): 220-1002 2.2.18

The *principle of least privilege* is just what it sounds like - the idea that the privileges given to a user or other entity are restricted down to the minimum needed to perform necessary tasks. For a simple example, imagine a building where each room and storage cabinet has a different lock; least privilege is giving each employee only the keys needed for their typical workplace tasks. You'll find it employed in all sorts of secure systems including operating systems, applications, networks, data storage, and human organizations. The actual implementation varies with technical details.

Least privilege is a security goal rather than a strict checklist, and some systems enforce it more rigorously than others. In the example with the locks, a real building might use the same key for multiple rooms with similar security needs, and assign a standard set of keys for most users. While you definitely want to make sure the new interns don't have access to secret financial files, it's probably less of a problem if they work on the fourth floor but can still get into the second-floor breakroom.

Data classification

One of the big factors that drives cybersecurity practices is that not all data needs the same security. It doesn't even make sense just using the strictest possible security to protect your data, since high security systems are difficult to maintain and often inconvenient to use. Instead, organizations tend to use a classification policy which defines types of organization the data uses, and what kind of controls are needed to protect it.

Exam Objective(s): 220-1002 4.6.3

Governments have a long history of formally classifying information for military or other security purposes, so they're a good place to look for examples. For example, the US government classifies information according to what harm it could do to national security if revealed. Sensitive information is classified as Confidential, Secret, or Top Secret, and each category has stricter controls for who may access it and how it can be stored or transmitted. There are even guidelines for how classified documents can be destroyed. Beyond that, information at a given level might have restrictions on exactly who can access it based on need; military secrets aren't going to be stored in the same place or accessed by the same people as diplomatic communications.

To some extent, private organizations can define whatever classification schemes they want. For example, yours might use "High", "Medium", and "Low", or "Confidential", "Proprietary", and "Public." The same principles apply though: every piece of information must be assigned an appropriate sensitivity level, and everywhere that data is stored, transmitted, and used must have adequate protections. Similarly, private organizations often compartmentalize information based on its type or who needs it, even if the overall sensitivity is similar.

One exception to businesses setting their own classification schemes is where regulatory compliance is involved. Regulations frequently define types of data which must be protected, and a list of security standards or specific controls which must be applied to protect it. They often also require periodic evaluations or audits, along with associated documentation, to certify compliance. Important types of regulated information include:

PII   *Personally identifiable information* is information that can be used to uniquely identify an individual person, either on its own or in conjunction with other information. It can also mean information that specifically relates to an individual person. PII is a focus of many privacy regulations and the target of various attacks; since it is a legal term rather than a technical one, its definition varies by jurisdiction. PII examples include contact information like name and address, personal attributes such as age or gender, and other life details like grades or workplace.

PHI   *Protected health information* is PII which can be connected to an individual's health status, medical treatments, and health care payments. PHI is defined by HIPAA, and must be protected by any organization under the jurisdiction of that law. Similar laws apply to health care data in other countries, and there are corresponding laws for other industries like education.

GDPR   The GDPR itself is a broad set of privacy laws intended to make sure that businesses which make sure consumers are aware of what PII businesses collect about them, and to give them more control over what is collected and how long it is kept. It most visibly has come to apply to websites and online services which collect user data, but it affects other companies as well. Any collected PII related to EU consumers is covered by the GDPR.

PCI   PCI-DSS regulations apply to any information regarding payment cards issued by major credit card vendors, and the customers that pay using those cards. They are designed both to guarantee interoperability among various payment card systems, but also to make sure both payment card data and the systems which process them are safe against fraudulent purchases and identity theft. Any systems which store or handle such data must be PCI-DSS compliant.

As you can probably guess, some data and systems can fall under multiple regulations, which means you must comply with all of them. Less obviously but just as important, even "unclassified" data still needs to be protected. Product documentation hosted on a public website may not be confidential, but its integrity and availability are important to your business.

Discussion: Security controls

1.   Make a short list of security control categories. What controls in each category are in use at your organization?

2.   What formal policies and external regulations are important in your organization?

3.   How does your organization generally implement data classification?

Encryption

There are a lot of ways to maintain data confidentiality, but most rely on keeping an attacker from viewing the data in the first place. This isn't always practical, especially when data is on the internet or portable media. Solutions that protect data in plain sight usually use some sort of *encryption*. Typical encryption scrambles data with a mathematical formula called an *encryption algorithm*, and a unique *key* which serves the same purpose as a password. The intended viewer has the appropriate key to *decrypt* the message, but to an eavesdropper without the key, the message looks like random gibberish.

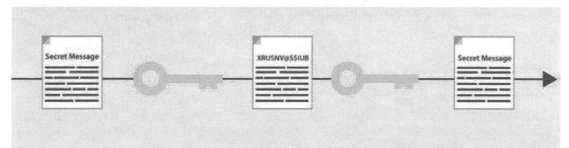

There are three basic cryptographic technologies that are used by computers and network protocols.

Symmetric   Uses the same key for both encryption and decryption. Also known as *private key cryptography* since the key must be kept secret for security to be affected. Symmetric algorithms are used primarily for encrypting bulk data, such as secure network communications and storage devices. They include AES, 3DES, RC4, Blowfish, and Twofish.

Asymmetric   Uses two mathematically related keys. Data encrypted with the first key can only be decrypted with the second, and vice-versa. Also known as *public key cryptography*, since typically only one key is kept private and the other is public knowledge. Asymmetric algorithms can be used to encrypt arbitrary data, but since that's more computationally expensive they're more often used to prove identity or securely exchange symmetric keys. They include RSA, DSA, ECC, and Diffie-Hellman.

Hashing   Converts data a unique signature called a hash. Hashes don't contain the original data and can't be reliably reversed. However, since any change to data changes its hash, data can be compared to a stored hash to verify its integrity. Hashes are important in data preservation, authentication, and system integrity checking. Common algorithms include MD5, SHA-1, and the SHA-2 family.

The strength of encryption depends on a few points. First, just like with passwords, longer keys (or hash sizes) provide stronger security, and since every extra bit in the key doubles the number of possible values, key strength is exponentially related to length. Second, the type and algorithm make a big difference. Not only does key strength have a much different meaning for symmetric and asymmetric algorithms, two symmetric algorithms can vary greatly in strength and performance.

Note: You might think it's best to just choose the strongest encryption possible. While that's often a good idea, very long keys and strong algorithms can run into performance and compatibility issues. Like every other part of security, you need to balance protection vs. usability.

Discussion: Encryption

1.   Why is it common for a communication session to use both symmetric and asymmetric encryption?

2.   Why wouldn't you just always use the most powerful encryption algorithm at the largest available key size?

3.   What is the difference between an asymmetric encryption algorithm and a hashing algorithm?

Access control

As great as encryption is for protecting data and communications, it alone can't solve all your problems, such as making sure the person you're talking with is who you think. Then if someone does slip past your guard, you need to minimize the potential damage. This is why secure communications setup requires a strict three-step access control process, which some protocols call *AAA*. AAA is used by network protocols, local logon systems, and often even human-focused physical security procedures. The process begins when a person, system, or any other entity wants to initiate communications or access resources. This entity is commonly called either a *security principal*, or simply a user.

Authentication	Positive identification of a person or system wishing to initiate communications, for example via a username/password or an ID card.
Authorization	Specifying the exact resources a given authorized user is allowed to access, such as file permissions on a hard drive.
Accounting	Auditing and logging the actions of an authenticated user for later review, such as operating system logs tracking logins and accessed files.

For a real world example of the AAA process, imagine you're guarding a security checkpoint to a restricted wing. Someone comes up and says "I'm Jim from sales" (identification), so you check his ID badge to make sure it's real (authentication), and now you know it's him. Then you look on the access list to make sure he's allowed in that wing (authorization), and finally have him sign the entry log (accounting.) In this case, you can also see his identification on the badge: that's why identification is sometimes folded into authentication.

Of the three, accounting is the least critical for security, but it's still very useful for security incidents or tracking resource use. Authentication and authorization are much more critical, and you'll find them used separately or together throughout PC and network technologies.

Authentication factors

Authentication requires at least one of three factors.

Knowledge	Something you know, like a password, PIN, or answer to a challenge question.
Possession	Something you possess, like a physical key, ID badge, or smart card. Traditionally, this includes any form of digital data a human can't be expected to memorize.
Inherence	Something you are; that is, a unique physical or behavioral characteristic, like a fingerprint, voice print, or signature. Inherence elements that are based on personal physical characteristics are called *biometrics*.

Some new authentication methods add others, such as behavioral recognition to recognize typing patterns, or location tracking features that let a system allow or deny access based on a user's physical location.

Authentication elements aren't always exactly the type of factor you'd think at first glance. Most obviously a slip of paper with a password written on it isn't a possession factor, since you're presumably expected to remember the password and dispose of the paper—the actual authentication system just wants you to type in the information. For another counter-intuitive example, a single-use PIN texted to your phone number when you try to log in isn't a knowledge element just because you type it in. It's a possession text proving that you're the person holding your phone.

Sometimes authentication factors are something you provide when you initially log in and then forget about as long as you remain at the system. With some new authentication systems, especially on the network, it becomes an ongoing process maintained throughout the session. Mostly it's handled out of the sight of users, but you might notice some exceptions. One example is an ATM requiring users to re-enter their PIN after each transaction; another is a computer that automatically locks itself after ten minutes of inactivity.

Multifactor authentication

Single-factor authentication is simple and easy, which is why it's so widely used. The problem is that authentication factors are imperfect. Knowledge factors like passwords are easily shared or even guessed. Possession factors can be stolen or duplicated. Even inherence factors can be falsified: a fingerprint scanner can potentially be fooled by using an existing fingerprint smudge and a little glue.

 Exam Objective(s): 220-1002 2.2.10, 2.3.2.1, 2.3.2.2

Research has shown that *multifactor authentication* with two or three factors is much stronger. For example, an ATM card and its PIN are much more secure than either would be apart. Two-factor authentication on a computer might require a smart card reader or fingerprint scanner in addition to a password. Other solutions don't require any special PC hardware, such as online services that require a password plus a one-use PIN sent to your telephone number or email address. Some systems might even require three-factor authentication.

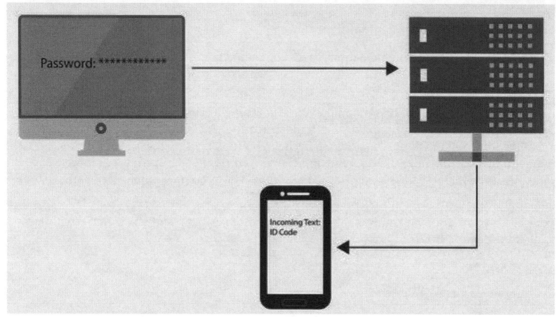

True multifactor authentication requires multiple elements of different factor types. For example, two passwords, or a password plus the answer to a security question, aren't multifactor since they're both knowledge factors.

Digital credentials

A lot of credential types are probably familiar to you, and don't need much explanation. Keys, ID cards, and passwords are doubtless part of your daily life. Even if you've never seen a fingerprint or retina scanner outside of a spy movie, the real-world devices follow the same principles. Some others need a little more explanation.

 Exam Objective(s): 220-1002 2.1.3, 2.1.6, 2.1.7, 2.1.12, 2.2.2, 2.2.6, 2.2.15

The first thing to keep in mind is that when you authenticate to a computer or other electronic device, any authentication factor needs to be digitized into data which can be stored on the computer and perhaps transmitted over the network. Even if it's reading biometric information like a fingerprint, your fingerprint pattern is going to be turned into a digital map that can be compared against the one stored on a device.

Especially when it comes to possession factors, there are several elements, or implementations, of digital authentication that you should be familiar with. You might find them used by computers, network services, electronic door locks, or anywhere authentication is needed.

Biometrics

Any physical property intrinsic to an individual human body, ranging from fingerprints to DNA to scent. Usually distinguished from behavioral characteristics like signatures and typing pattern. Contrary to some popular belief, biometric authentication isn't necessarily more reliable or harder to fool than any other type, but it's still useful. Common biometrics used on modern computers include:

- Fingerprint and palm scanners, which measure the unique patterns of ridges on a human hand.

- Retinal scanners, which shine infrared light into the eye to measure the blood vessel patterns on the retina.

- Iris scanners, which measure fine patterns of the iris of the eye. They often use infrared light as well, but are easier to implement than retinal scanners.

- Facial recognition systems which capture an image of the entire face to compare to a known photo. They have the advantage of working on any device with a digital camera and appropriate software.

- Voice recognition systems which measure unique voice patterns against a recorded sample. In theory, they work on any device with a microphone.

Digital certificate

A file created and signed using special cryptographic algorithms. The holder has both a public certificate which can be shared freely, and a secret encryption key which is never shared. Sample data encrypted with the secret key can be decrypted with the public certificate, proving the person or system presenting the certificate also holds the key. The authentication system can store certificates for allowed users, or submit a newly presented certificate to a trusted third party such as a certificate authority to verify its owner's identity. One common application of digital certificates is the one assigned to each secure website in order to prove its identity to visiting browsers.

OTP

A *one-time password* that is valid for a single session, so can't be stolen and reused. The OTP still has to be known to both the user and the authenticator somehow, so it's a challenge to accurately create one. An OTP can be generated independently on both ends by a sequential or time-based algorithm, or it can be generated by the authenticator and transmitted to the user out-of-band, such as to an email address or phone number.

Hardware token   Broadly speaking, any physical device used to aid authentication by containing secret information. A hardware token might have an LCD display to generate OTPs you can type in, or it might be a digital certificate securely stored on a USB key, RFID key fob, or scannable card.

Software token   A stored file that serves similar purposes to a hardware token. The term is a little flexible: usually it's applied to applications that allow a smartphone or other computer to serve as a hardware token, but it's sometimes used to describe temporary authentication and authorization data stored on and exchanged between computers in single sign-on environments.

Magnetic stripe card   A traditional machine-readable card, such as a bank or transit card, with a magnetic stripe to store user data. They've been around a very long time, and while they're useful they're not secure. They don't store very much data, and they're easy to clone. Magnetic stripe cards can still be used in multi-factor authentication, but they're not a very strong method on their own.

Smart card   An authentication card with an integrated circuit built in. At the least, a smart card's chip holds basic identifying information like a magnetic stripe would; it can also hold digital certificates, store temporary data, or even perform cryptographic processing functions to keep its data secure. Smart cards don't generally contain batteries, but instead receive power from the reader.

- *Contact smart cards* make physical contact with the card reader to receive power and transmit information.

- *Contactless smart cards* are powered by radio frequency induction from the reader, and communicate with it using NFC over a 1-3" (2-10cm) distance.

- *Proximity cards* work like contactless cards, but operate on different frequencies and hold less information. They operate at distances up to 15" (50cm) and are usually only used to unlock doors.

Smart cards are often built into human-readable ID cards or badges, such as the CAC and PIV cards used by US government organizations. Credit cards with chips are also smart cards. Another example of a smart card is the SIM card used to authenticate mobile devices on cellular networks.

Single sign-on

Traditionally, any network service requiring authentication would handle its own user authentication, but this has problems as networks become more interrelated, as users have more and more accounts to keep track of, and as security management becomes more complex and exacting. This has led to the popularity of *single sign-on (SSO)* systems, which allow one set of user credentials to give access to a large number of services. This can work two primary ways:

 Exam Objective(s): 220-1002 2.6.5

- In the strictest sense, SSO allows a user to sign in once to one of a group of mutually-trusting services, then seamlessly switch between services without being prompted for credentials again. For example, once you log into Gmail, you can freely switch to other Google services like YouTube or Google+, and you'll only be prompted for your password again if you try to access something like account or payment information. Behind the scenes, this all works by the servers communicating through tokens and certificates to make sure it's still you without interrupting you.

- SSO can also be used to describe systems where multiple independent services share authentication servers. For example, Facebook Connect allows third-party websites to offer a "Log In with Facebook" option. You still have to log into each site, but you can just use your Facebook credentials rather than creating a new account for each site.

Related to SSO is single sign-off. It's just what it sounds like: signing off one service also signs off of all related ones.

In Windows, one example of SSO is Active Directory domains. You need to log onto the domain by signing into Windows, but you won't be prompted for credentials when you access network shares, printers, or other resources, provided your account has access to them.

Implementing strong user authentication

Not all authentication schemes use user names and passwords, but it's normal for most computers and user-focused network services. When you manage a system or even just make your own account, you need to consider the best way to secure it.

Exam Objective(s): 220-1002 2.2.9

- Choosing a user name can itself affect security.

  - Attackers need to know a user name in order to attack it, so names transparently based on real name or role like john.smith, JSMITH, or DBAdmin can reduce security. At the same time, users need to remember their user names, especially for accounts they don't use daily. If you choose your own, pick something personal.

  - When centrally assigning user names, consider a pattern based on a consistent method which is not obvious to the casual outsider. For example, begin the user name with the month they started with the company, add first three characters of the last name and the first two characters of their first name, finish up with a building/floor/office number. You'll end up with something harder to guess such as 06SMIJI112, but users themselves can still easily remember their own.

  - If a computer or device comes with default accounts, change their names or disable them if possible.

- Passwords should be hard to guess or crack, but easy for users to remember.

  - Users often choose their own passwords based on something personal, such as their dog's name, daughter's birthday, or a maiden name. These passwords are very easy to guess if you know the user or use a dictionary attack, so users need to be discouraged from using them.

  - It's ideal not to assign passwords directly, both since administrators knowing passwords can compromise accountability and because administrator-assigned passwords are hard for users to remember. This leads to constant password resets or worse, users writing them down where they can be stolen.

  - You can implement password policies that require users to choose sufficiently long passwords that are a mix of upper and lower case letters, numbers, and special characters - referred to as a complex password. Complex passwords that might be easy to remember include: $peci@lK (Special K), Ih8pie$! (I hate pies!), or msJwbi97 (my son James was born in 97.)

- For extra security, consider multifactor authentication on systems which support it.

- User accounts should be used only by a single person whenever possible. If a user must temporarily share an account, the password should be changed afterward.

Discussion: Authentication

1. How are all three elements of the AAA process important to security?

2. Apart from passwords, what authentication factors are in use at your organization?

3. What network services have you used with single sign-on?

4. What multifactor authentication systems have you used in the past? Feel free to include those not related to networks.

5. What's the difference between a hardware token and a software token?

6. How could authentication systems in your organization be strengthened, or made easier to use?

Access control lists

Once you've authenticated your user, the next step, authentication, is all about determining what resources they're allowed to access. There are a number of ways to do this, but one of the most common is through *access control lists*. An *ACL* is a list attached to a resource, giving permissions, or rules about exactly who can access it. One of the most common uses of ACLs is in every modern computer's file system: each file and folder has an ACL specifying exactly which users can read it, modify it, and so on. Very often a file will be readable to anyone using the computer, but you could always configure a file to be readable only by its owner, or a program to be run only by someone with administrative privileges.

Exam Objective(s): 220-1002 2.2.14

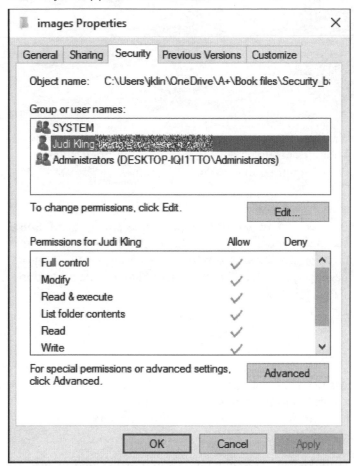

It's more than files though: ACLs are found everywhere in security. In networks especially, they're one of the main tools used to control traffic through routers and access points. This application is called packet filtering. ACLs can work for both inbound and outbound traffic: if you wanted to prevent network users from accessing a certain web site, you could block access to its IP address using an ACL. Routers and firewalls can commonly filter according to several criteria:

- IP address (source or destination)
- MAC address (source or destination)
- Port number (source or destination)
- Protocols used

A network ACL configured to filter traffic by protocol

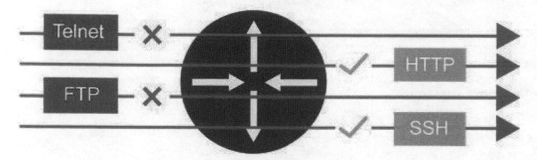

Both kinds of ACL are built on the same security principle of *implicit deny*, which is to say access is denied unless the ACL specifically allows it. Implicit deny policies provide better security than implicit allow policies, since it's harder to introduce a vulnerability by forgetting to configure the ACL.

User privileges

Every operating system and user-based application has its own model for how privileges are assigned. Some allow you to assign privileges to individual users piecemeal, and some simply have a divide between ordinary users and administrators. More complex schemes have *roles* or *security groups* representing a collection of related privileges. This makes administration easy because you can assign users to whatever roles or groups they need to perform their tasks. In most cases, you can assign new permissions or restrictions to a group in order to customize access controls for all users in it.

Exam Objective(s): 220-1002 2.6.1

For example, in local and domain accounts on modern Windows editions, you can assign permissions to an individual user, but apart from something like "access to a personal documents folder" that isn't recommended. Instead, each user belongs to one or more security groups that determine operating system privileges. If you belong to at least one group that has necessary privileges to perform the action, and you haven't been specifically prohibited from it, you can as well.

Administrators	Members of this group have full control of the computer, and they can assign user rights and access control permissions to users as necessary. The Administrator account is a default member of this group. Administrators can't actually do literally everything on the computer, since some privileges are reserved to specialized system accounts and should never be performed directly by users. However, they can perform administrative tasks such as installing applications and hardware drivers, creating and deleting user accounts, or changing sensitive operating system settings. Adding an account to this group makes it very powerful, and a potential security risk.
Domain Admins	Only found on Domain accounts. Members of this group have full control of computers throughout the domain. The Administrator account is joined to this group when a domain is formed. Privileges on an individual computer are similar to that of Administrators group members.
Users	Members of this group can perform common tasks and run most applications. However, they can't share folders, install printers, or generally change any system-wide settings that can affect other users or put system security at risk. Most newly created accounts are simply Users. In general, administrators as well as other privileged users also belong to the Users group, so a privilege added to this group applies to everyone.
Power Users	In older versions of Windows, members of this group had privileges beyond that of an ordinary user, but less than that of an administrator. In modern versions of Windows this group exists but has no special privileges. It can still be customized to make a general set of "privileged user" permissions.

Administrators   Members of this group have full control of the computer, and they can assign user rights and access control permissions to users as necessary. The Administrator account is a default member of this group. Administrators can't actually do literally everything on the computer, since some privileges are reserved to specialized system accounts and should never be performed directly by users. However, they can perform administrative tasks such as installing applications and hardware drivers, creating and deleting user accounts, or changing sensitive operating system settings. Adding an account to this group makes it very powerful, and a potential security risk.

Guests   Members of this group have much more limited permissions than Users. They can't customize settings, install software, or even change their own passwords. Guest accounts aren't protected by passwords and use a temporary profile that's deleted at logoff. Windows versions that include a Guest account generally disable it by default.

Backup Operators   Members of this group can back up and restore files from anywhere on the computer, regardless of individual file and folder permissions. While the Backup Operator privilege overrides any normal file system permissions, members of this group have no special power to change security settings.

Remote Desktop Users   Members of this group can log onto the computer remotely through Remote Desktop Services. This provides an easy way to control which accounts are allowed to use remote access, and which must be physically at the computer.

These are just the most common groups you're likely to encounter, but a variety of others are included with Windows. Most of them work a bit like Backup Operators, giving access to a limited subset of administrative tools. They're an example of least privilege - by adding users to one or more of these groups, you give them only the privileges they need without the risk of more administrators.

- Cryptographic Operators: Members of this group are authorized to perform cryptographic operations.

- Distributed COM Users: Members of this group are allowed to start, activate, and use DCOM objects on a computer.

- IIS_IUSRS: This is a built-in group that is used by Internet Information Services (IIS).

- Network Configuration Operators: Members of this group can make changes to TCP/IP settings, and they can renew and release TCP/IP addresses. This group has no default members.

- Performance Log Users: Members of this group can manage performance counters, logs, and alerts on a computer — both locally and from remote clients.

- Performance Monitor Users: Members of this group can monitor performance counters on a computer — locally and from remote clients.

- Replicator: This group supports replication functions. The only member of the Replicator group should be a domain user account that is used to log on the Replicator services of a domain controller.

- Offer Remote Assistance Helpers: Members of this group can offer Remote Assistance to the users of this computer.

Administrators can also create new groups and assign them whatever permissions they like. For example, on a shared computer you could create a Sales group which is allowed to access customer management software and a shared Sales folder, and add each salesperson's account to the group. This saves time over assigning permissions individually, and reduces the chance for error.

Responsible administrative account use

If you are an administrator, you should make a habit of logging on using a normal user account. If you are logged on as an administrator and are hit with malicious software, the software is running with your administrative access. If you are logged on as a normal user, the software won't have that higher-level access to the system. If while logged on as a normal user, you attempt to do something that requires administrative privileges, such as install software, Windows prompts you to enter the password for the Administrator account. Once you enter the password, it then lets you proceed. You can also use the **Run As** command to elevate your privileges to run that one program.

Exam Objective(s): 220-1002 2.6.7

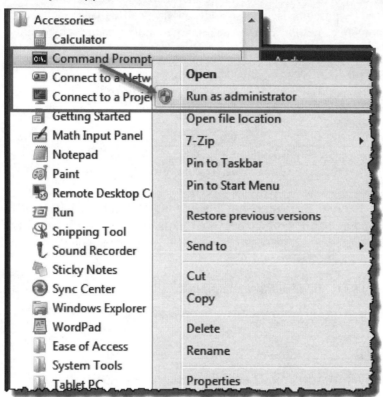

Even when you're logged in as an administrator, by default the User Account Control feature limits the permissions of programs you run. You'll still be prompted before making system changes, and you still need to launch most applications as an administrator if you want them to have administrative privileges. Since neither actually prompts you for a password, this is less secure than just logging in from a non-administrator account.

Trusted and untrusted software

Like users, software can be a security risk. Even if it's not malware or virus-infected, it can do unwanted things that compromise security, or allow users to bypass existing software limitations. Depending on the system, you can apply access control principles to software by limiting the privileges an application has, or by restricting the ability of users to install software. You can also use *application whitelisting* features to limit what programs an ordinary user can run in the first place.

Exam Objective(s): 220-1002 2.2.17

Even if you use all of the above, you still need to make sure the software you install can be trusted. Otherwise it might be compromised by malware, contain trojan horse features, or just not work as advertised. This is especially a problem for software you just download off a random internet site or get from some other untrusted source. Downloading from a trusted manufacturer website or installing from a commercially printed install disc is safer, but still not entirely foolproof. Stronger security measures use cryptography to authenticate that a software installer is genuine.

Many antivirus software providers incorporate a trusted software vendor list. This list helps the software decide if an executable file is safe to install or if it should be quarantined. Trusted software is identified as such using digital certificates. *Digital certificates* are widely used in various authentication processes.

- A *file hash* is provided with some software downloads so that you can manually make sure the file wasn't altered in transit. While this method is good for detecting corrupted downloads, it only proves the software is genuine if you can be sure the hash is from a trustworthy source.

- A *digital signature*, also referred to as a self-signed certificate, is a simply a statement of assurance. It allows a software, application, or plug-in publisher to identify themselves and verify the authenticity of their program. A digital signature doesn't authenticate an identity. The software publisher is basically saying "Trust me, I am who I say I am."

- A *digital certificate* is registered and signed by a central and respected *certificate authority (CA)* that can vouch for its authenticity. A number of third-party CAs offer certificate services to the public. Large organizations might set up and manage their own CA for internal communications. If a certificate is compromised, the CA can revoke it and issue a new one.

- A *code signing certificate*, also known as a software publisher's certificate, is a type of digital certificate. It contains information about the software publisher and the issuing certificate authority, and guarantees that an executable file or script hasn't been altered or corrupted since it was digitally signed.

One of the main benefits of app stores like the Microsoft Store, Google Play, and iOS App Store is that they are trusted sources with signed apps from verified customers. This doesn't make them 100% safe, but at least you know the vendor and that it hasn't been altered. If you're not using an app store, you can verify it other ways. When you install an application in Windows, the operating system will check its certificate to make sure that it was signed by a known software vendor and displays its information. If it isn't, you can still install it, but make sure you trust the software.

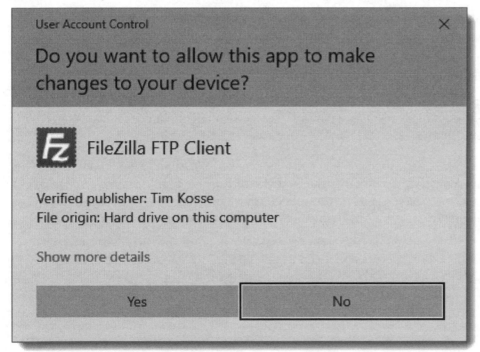

Signed software isn't limited to applications. On 64-bit Windows editions, you can't even install unsigned hardware drivers without changing your system settings, and UEFI firmware with secure boot features enabled checks the operating system for a valid signature before even loading it.

Discussion: Authorization

1. What's the difference between an ACL in a file system vs one on a network?

2. What's the difference between a power user and an administrator?

3. Why would backup operators need special privileges?

4. What methods do you use to make sure software is from a trustworthy source before you install and use it?

Physical security

One reason it's easy for people not to think of cybersecurity and physical security in the same terms is that they'll think of the former in terms of technical standards and network activities that aren't part of the "real world", and the second as a low-tech field that, important or not, is more about protecting people and physical valuables than data. In truth they're part of a unified whole, and in principle, they operate the same way. Physical controls extend beyond computers and policy statements and into the physical facilities of your organizations, and can be categorized in similar ways.

*   Access controls designed to keep people from going places or doing things they're not supposed to. They include walls and fences, secured doors, locked cabinets, and so on.

*   Surveillance systems designed to detect intruders whether or not they're successful in bypassing other security. Examples include cameras, motion alarms, and security guards.

*   Visible deterrents meant to discourage people from intrusion in the first place. Warning signs may deter accidental intruders, while visible cameras or guard dogs can discourage deliberate attackers in addition to their surveillance purposes.

Most other principles found in digital security have direct physical counterparts, but they rely on monitoring and restricting physical access. A physical facility is segmented into different security zones separated by secured entryways. You physically authenticate by having a door key or showing your ID badge to the guard. You're accounted for by signing an entry log or appearing on the surveillance camera.

For most PC technicians, the most important physical security tasks are making sure that doors are kept locked, unauthorized people aren't let into secure areas, and that equipment in non-secure areas isn't stolen or compromised.

Securing facilities and equipment

Physical access to network systems is a literal foot in the door for attackers. Given that and a little privacy, it's only a matter of time before even a strong system is compromised. It's important to restrict physical access to vulnerable network resources. Server rooms and network closets are the most vulnerable to attack, but anywhere that data is stored or can be accessed is a potential target. Even just access to a network drop or wireless broadcast is enough for a dedicated intruder. Depending on your organization's security requirements, the entire property might need strict physical access controls.

Exam Objective(s): 220-1002 2.1.1, 2.1.2, 2.1.4, 2.1.5, 2.1.8, 2.1.9, 2.1.10, 2.1.11, 2.1.13

- Where possible, move essential or at-risk systems into more secure areas.
- Control access into secure areas by using locked security doors.
  - Where possible, use electronic locks with entry codes, badge readers, keyfobs, or biometric scanners
  - *Mantraps*, or paired doors which allow only one person to pass at a time, are a way to prevent tailgating in high security environments.
  - Multifactor authentication is as valid an approach for physical locks as it is for system accounts.
- Use surveillance, security personnel, and employee awareness to keep track of who is in the facility.
  - Use CCTV or IP based security cameras to monitor critical areas.
  - Establish and enforce a visitor policy for any areas not open to the general public.
  - Keep an entry control roster to establish who is allowed into high security areas.
  - Hire security guards to authenticate users or monitor for intrusion
- Place network hardware into secure and locked network closets or cabinets.
  - Place Wi-Fi antennas so as to minimize broadcast into unsecured areas.
  - Physical access to WAPs should also be controlled, but note that WAP antennas often don't work well in a locked cabinet.
- Apply physical security to easily stolen equipment that must be kept in low-security areas.
  - Use cable locks or locked cabinets to protect workstations and lone servers
  - Issue cable locks to laptop users and require their use both in the office and on the road.
  - Use lockable or tamper-detecting cases to prevent unauthorized users from opening computers up to access internal components.
  - Block access to external ports, or use USB locks to keep users from adding or removing USB devices.
- Use *asset tracking tags* to keep tabs on mobile devices and portable equipment you can't lock down. Mobile computers may support tracking software.
- Use filters or *privacy screens* on displays used for sensitive tasks near unauthorized viewers.
- Put especially valuable items or data and documentation that doesn't need online accessibility in a locked safe or cabinet.
- Watch for signs of intrusion or social engineering attacks. Where security personnel are unaware, it's easy for someone pretending to be IT to just walk off with entire computers.

Discussion: Physical security

1. Does your workplace have clearly defined security zones?

2. What physical security controls are employed at your workplace?

3. Are computers and network equipment in your workplace physically secured?

User education

Human behavior is a frequent weak link of every security system, and social engineering attacks targeting the human element are constantly on the rise. Network security policies have to be implemented and enforced by technicians, overseen by managers, and followed by end users to be effective. All three categories of employee have blind spots, all three are subject to social engineering, and atop that they're busy people with other concerns: given a choice between doing their jobs efficiently and doing them securely they're all too likely to choose the former. It's vital to make sure that all users know their duties in maintaining organizational security, and that those duties not be too burdensome or confusing.

Exam Objective(s): 220-1002 2.4.2.5

- Educate all employees about security-related best practices and legal requirements for their job role, common social engineering attacks, and how to look for suspicious behavior.

- Alert users about newly discovered or trending attacks that might affect them, such as specific malware or phishing techniques.

- Tailor duties and education efforts to user roles and technical knowledge.

- Supply network security personnel with complete documentation about security policies.

- Provide technicians with detailed security requirements for systems they install and maintain.

- Advise management about overall goals and requirements for organizational security.

- Work with human resources staff to educate other employees and contractors, to respond to noncompliance issues, and to onboard and offboard new or departing users.

- Enforce separation of duties to prevent fraud or error by employees.

- Educate users about password policies and how to use other authentication systems securely.

- Establish clear policies for handling of organization equipment or data off premises, and of user devices or visitors on premises.

Assessment: Security controls

1. You require your users to log on using a username, password, and rolling 6-digit code sent to a keyfob device. They are then allowed computer, network, and email access. What type of authentication have you implemented?

   - Access control lists
   - Basic single-factor authentication
   - Principle of least privilege
   - Single sign-on
   - Multi-factor authentication

2. Which is a common method used to specify the resources a user is allowed to access?

   - Access control lists
   - Principle of least privilege
   - Share permissions
   - User groups

3. ACLs are based on which assumption? Choose the best response.

   - Explicit Allow
   - Explicit Deny
   - Implicit Allow
   - Implicit Deny

4. Right after you install an endpoint security suite it scans your computer and generates a database it can later use to detect any alterations to critical system files. What cryptographic method is it most likely using? Choose the best response.

   - Asymmetric encryption
   - Certificates
   - Hashing
   - Symmetric encryption

5. What AAA element specifies the exact resources a given principal is allowed to access? Choose the best response.

   - Accounting
   - Authentication
   - Authorization
   - Identification

6. Whenever you log into your account you need to press a button on your keychain, then type in the new set of numbers it displays. What kind of authentication factor are you using? Choose the best response.

    - Biometric

    - Digital certificate

    - OTP

    - Software token

7. Which user group has different default permissions depending on which Windows version you're using? Choose the best response.

    - Administrators

    - Guests

    - Power Users

    - Standard Users

8. The door to your floor's server room has an electronic lock; anyone on the approved list can swipe their ID badge to get in. After a temp worker got in with a "borrowed" badge, management wants to tighten security. What added feature would prevent that from happening again? Choose the best response.

    - Biometric lock

    - Entry control roster

    - Keyfob

    - Mantrap

Summary: Security principles

You should now know:

- How to distinguish between risk, threats, and vulnerabilities, and about common threats to cybersecurity,

- About security controls, including policies, data classification, authentication and access control, encryption, physical security, and user education.

Chapter 5: Security technologies

You will learn:

- How to enforce access control with core operating system features
- How to augment security with host software and network devices

Module A: Operating system security

Modern operating systems like Windows, Linux, or MacOS have a wide variety of logical security controls built into their core functions. The full list is beyond the scope of this course, but important elements for a PC support technician include file permissions, security policies, and account permissions. You can even manage operating system security across an entire network, such as with Active Directory domains.

You will learn:

- About file permissions
- How to manage file permissions in Windows
- About Windows security features
- About Active Directory and group policies.

Directory permissions

On some systems, such as Windows with NTFS and Linux, you can implement file and folder (also referred to as directory) permissions. With file and folder permissions, you either grant access permissions at various levels to individual users or groups of users, or you can explicitly deny access. If you explicitly apply the deny permission for a user or group, it overrides any other permissions they might have assigned. This adds a layer of security for access to your data.

Exam Objective(s): 220-1002 2.2.11, 2.6.2.1

NTFS permissions

Permission	Effect on folder	Effect on file
Read	User can view the contents of a folder and any subfolders.	User can view the contents of the file.
Write	Read permission, plus the user can add files and create new subfolders.	Read permission, plus the user can make changes (write) to the file.
Read & Execute	Read permission, plus the user can run executable files contained in the folder. This permission is inherited by any subfolders and files.	Read permission, plus the user can run a file if it is executable.
List Folder Contents	Read permission, plus the user can run executable files contained in the folder. This permission is inherited by subfolders only.	N/A
Modify	Read and Write permissions, plus the user can delete the folder.	Read and Write permissions, plus the user can delete the file.
Full Control	Read, Write, and Modify permissions and the user can delete all files and subfolders.	Read, write, modify, and delete the file.

Some caveats:

- If you don't assign a permission, no access is the default.

- A user's permissions are the sum of the permissions they have been assigned individually and obtained through any groups in which they are a member. This is called *effective permissions*. For example, if you assign Jake Read permissions to the Reports folder, plus Jake is a member of the Accounting group, to which you have assigned Modify permissions, then Jake effectively has Modify permissions on the Reports folder.

- The exception to the "permissions sum" rule is if individually or through a group, Jake was explicitly denied permissions to the folder. The Deny Access permission takes precedence over all other permissions a user might inherit.

File attributes

File attributes are settings associated with computer files that grant or deny certain rights to how a user or the operating system can access that file.

Exam Objective(s): 220-1002 2.6.2.3

File Attributes and Advanced Attributes

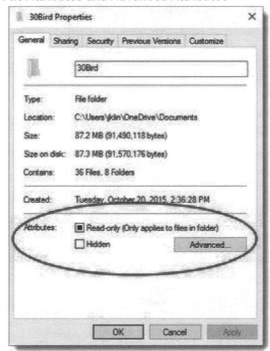

R   Read-Only - Allows a user or the operating system to read a file, but not write to it.

A   Archive - Specifies the file should be backed up.

S   System - Indicates the file is a system file and shouldn't be altered or deleted. By default, system files are hidden.

H   Hidden - Suppresses the display of the file in directory lists, unless you issue the command to list hidden files.

D   Directory - Indicates a folder or sub-folder, differentiating them from files.

I   Not content-indexed - Windows has a search function that indexes all files and directories on a drive to achieve faster search results.

Additional attributes are available on NTFS volumes:

C   Compressed - On an NTFS file system volume, each file and directory has a compression attribute. Other file systems may also implement a compression attribute for individual files and directories.

E   Encrypted - On an NTFS file system volume, each file and directory has an encryption attribute as part of the *Encrypting File System (EFS)* .

EFS Encryption has a few other rules you should keep in mind:

- When you encrypt a directory, all new files created in that directory are encrypted from that point forward.

- You can select to encrypt the directory's current contents when you perform the encryption.

- Encryption applies to the local system only.

- If you copy an encrypted file or directory to any other file system, the file or directory is no longer encrypted.

- A file can't be compressed and encrypted at the same time. The attributes are mutually exclusive.

In addition to using the Windows interface to modify file and folder attributes, you can also use the **attrib.exe** command. Its syntax is: **ATTRIB [+ attribute | - attribute] [pathname] [/S [/D]]**.

- + enables the attribute

- - clears the attribute

- pathname: drive and/or filename. For example: `C:\documents\*.doc`

- /S search the pathname including all subfolders

- /D includes directories in addition to files

Linux permissions

In Linux and other Unix-like systems, each file or directory (folder) has three basic permission types:

- Read (**r**): User can view the contents of a file.

- Write (**w**): User can write to (modify) the contents of a file or directory.

- Execute (**x**): User can run an executable file and view the contents of a directory.

Additionally, each and every file is owned by a single user and a single group, and has its own access permissions.

- *Owner* is the person who is responsible for the file.

- *Group* includes members of the file's group.

- *Others* includes all users who are not in the file or folder's group or the owner.

When you view folder contents in a Linux terminal, you'll see permissions written as a ten-digit string. The first is d for directories and blank for files, and the rest are blank (–). So a folder with all permissions set would read `drwxrwxrwx`.

Directory contents in Linux

```
total 16
drwxr-xr--. 6 waffle waffle   4096 Apr 21 16:18 proto
drwxr-xr--. 4 waffle archives 4096 Jul 31  2002 proto.old
-rw-r-----. 1 waffle sales      822 Apr 21 15:34 sales.txt
-rw-r-----. 1 waffle sales       10 Apr 21 15:33 sales.txt~
```

There is one qualifier. The *Security Enhanced Linux* (*SELinux*) component included with many Linux distributions allows more options for setting file and folder permissions. For example, you can allow or restrict a specific application's access to a folder. Rather than totally replacing traditional file system permissions, SELinux permissions work by adding additional security context labels to each file, folder, and other resource on the computer.

Share permissions

When a Windows computer is connected to a network, you can share its resources with other users on the network. This is referred to as a *local share* . A shared resource can be hardware (such as printer or disk drive), an application, or a file or folder. Similar to directory permissions, you assign or deny permissions for each shared resource.

Windows share permissions

Permission	Allows user to remotely
Read	• View file names and subfolder names • View data in files • Run program files Note: Read is the default Share permission assigned to the Everyone group.
Change	All Read share permissions, plus: • Add files and subfolders • Change data in files • Delete subfolders and files Note: The Change Share permission isn't assigned to any group by default.
Full Control	All Read and Change permissions, plus: • Change file and folder permissions (NTFS files and folders only) Note: Full Control is the default permission assigned to the Administrators group on the local computer.

Some things to know about share permissions:

- They apply only to users who gain access to the resource over the network. They do not apply to users who log on locally. NTFS permissions apply locally.

- They apply to all files and folders in the shared resource. If you need a more detailed level of security on subfolders and individual files, you will need to use NTFS permissions in addition to share permissions.

- It is the only method for securing shared resources on FAT and FAT32 volumes.

- You can specify how many users are allowed to access the resource at one time.

You can control access to shared resources using share permissions, NTFS permissions, or both. If you use both, be aware that the more restrictive permission always applies. For example, if the share permission is set at the default (Everyone has Read permissions) and the NTFS permission grant a user the Modify permission, the share permission applies. The user will not be able to make changes to the file.

Just like with NTFS file permissions, an explicit deny share permission overrides all other permissions to the shared resource. You'll specifically assign deny permission only when you want to override specific permissions that are already assigned.

Administrative shares

Windows automatically creates hidden network shares that allow users with administrative privileges to access the system remotely. These special shares are called *Administrative shares*. Common administrative shares include:

- Disk volume administrative share: *volume_letter*$, for example C$ or D$.

- Windows OS administrative share: admin$

- Printers folder administrative share: print$

The $ at the end of the share name indicates that is a hidden share.

Disabling the administrative shares

While the shares are hidden, they are well known and could present a small security risk. You can't delete these shares, but you can disable them if they aren't needed in your environment. This requires a change in the Registry.

1. Open the Registry Editor.
    regedit.exe

2. Navigate to **HKEY_LOCAL_MACHINE | SOFTWARE | Microsoft | Windows | CurrentVersion | Policies**

3. Select **System**.

4. Double-click **LocalAccountTokenFilterPolicy**

5. In the Value Data field, enter **0**.

6. Click **OK**.

7. Restart the computer.

Note: Some programs use the administrative shares, so disabling them can cause these programs to fail or generate error messages.

Discussion: File permissions

1. On an NTFS volume, all users on your team have full access permission to the project folder. The one problem is that it's really easy to delete important files and you'd rather make sure the new guy can read and edit but not delete anything. How can you do this?

2. On a Linux volume, what do r, w, and x stand for?

3. How can you secure access to files on a FAT32 volume?

Inherited permissions

Inherited permissions are permissions assigned to a parent object that flow down and apply to a child object. The exact rules depend on operating system, file system, and sometimes system settings. In Windows, there are a few basic rules.

Exam Objective(s): 220-1002 2.6.2.2, 2.6.3.3

- An object inherits NTFS and share permissions from its parent object when you create it.

- When you copy or move an object, the resulting NTFS and share permissions depend both on whether you're moving or copying it, but also what kind of volume the destination folder is in.

The effect of copying or moving files on their resulting permissions

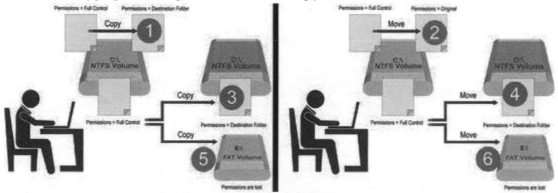

For this example, imagine that your computer has two NTFS volumes named C:\ and D:\, and one FAT32 volume named E:\ You have a folder named C:\Source\Docs which you'd like to move or copy. The action you take, and the destination, determine its resulting permission.

- If the destination folder is on the *same* NTFS volume as the source location, the result depends on whether you move or copy. So, if you put the folder in C:\Destination...

  - A copied object inherits the permissions of its new parent object. In example ①, C:\Destination\Docs will inherit the permissions of C:\Destination.

  - A moved object keeps its original permissions. In example ②, C:\Destination\Docs will have the same permissions C:\Source\Docs did.

- If the destination folder is on a *different* NTFS volume, the object always inherits the permissions of its new parent object.

  - Since it doesn't matter if you're moving or copying, in both ③ and ④, D:\Destination\Docs will inherit the same permissions as D:\Destination.

- If the destination is on a FAT volume, all permissions are stripped away. This is simply because FAT doesn't support file permissions.

  - In both ⑤ and ⑥, E:\Destination\Docs will have no file permissions. This means any user has full access to it.

- Some utilities allow you finer control of permissions when you copy or move files. For example, the **xcopy** command allows you to copy objects while preserving their existing permissions.

Stopping permissions inheritance

In Windows, if you want to assign different permissions to child objects, you must stop permissions inheritance. In most Windows versions, you break this link by clearing the **Include inheritable permissions from this object's parent** check box in Advanced Security Settings. If you attempt to make a change to a child object's permissions and the boxes are grayed out as shown in the following figures, this is your clue to stop permission inheritance.

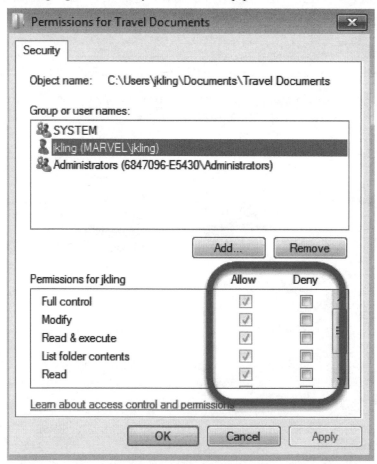

1. Right-click the parent folder and choose **Properties**.

2. On the Permissions tab, click **Change Permissions**.

3. In the Advanced Security Settings dialog box, clear the **Include inheritable permissions from this object's parent** check box.

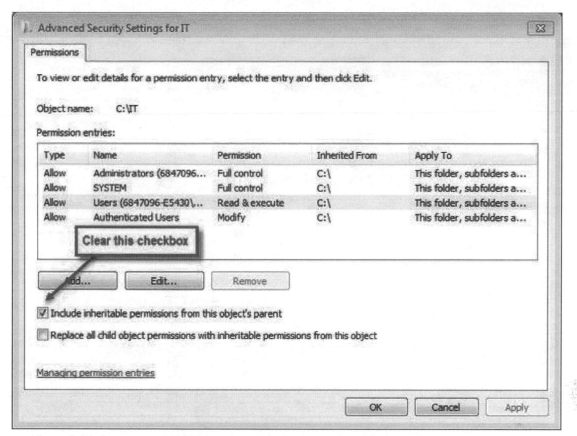

Once you've cleared this box, any child objects' permissions are cleared.

4. If you want to copy the parent permissions as a starting point to customize the child objects' permissions, check **Replace all child object permissions with inheritable permissions from this object**.

   This gives you an editable set of the parent permissions on child objects.

5. Click **OK**.

6. Click **OK** again.

Be aware that once you break the link, the child object won't inherit any permission settings from the parent object unless you specifically force inheritance again by rechecking the **Include inheritable permissions from this object's parent checkbox** or propagating permissions.

Propagating permissions

When you change the permissions of a parent folder, you have the option of applying that change to all subfolders. This is referred to as *permission propagation.* To propagate folder permissions down a structure where permissions inheritance has been broken, you use Advanced Security Settings.

Exam Objective(s): 220-1002 2.6.3.2

1. Right-click the parent folder and choose **Properties**.

2. On the Permissions tab, click **Change Permissions**.

3. Select the desired Access Control Entry, and click **Edit**.

4. Set the desired permissions and check `Apply these permissions to objects and/or containers within this container only`.

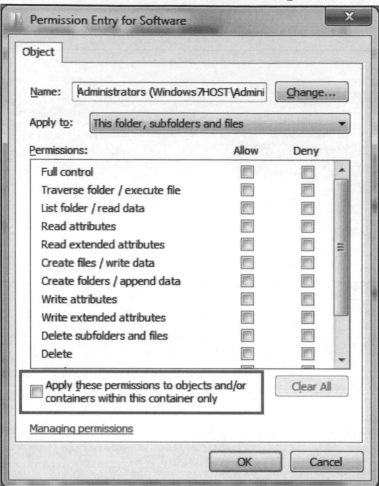

5. Click **OK**.

6. Click **OK** again.

Never assume a permissions change will be inherited or propagated, always check the child's permissions to verify.

Exercise: Examining NTFS permissions

In this exercise, you'll explore how to view and assign permissions for an NTFS folder.

Do This	How & Why
1. In File Explorer, create a file named `C:\NTFS lab\Sales data\Customer list.txt`	You'll have to create the NTFS lab and Sales data folders.
2. Change group permissions for the `Sales data` folder.	You want to make sure all users on this computer can create and edit files in the folder.
a) From the NTFS lab folder, right-click **Sales data** and click **Properties**.	The **Properties** window opens. It displays a list of group and user names on top, and a list of permissions below.
b) In the **Group or users names** list, click each entry in turn.	The list of permissions below changes. For example, the Users group is allowed to read from the folder but not write or modify.

c) Click **Edit**.	The **Permissions** window looks almost exactly the same, except that you can change Allow and Deny permissions.
d) Select the **Users** group.	Notice that there are Allow permissions with gray checkmarks. These permissions are inherited from parent folders, so you can't remove them. You can only add new ones.

Do This	How & Why
e) Next to the Modify permission, check **Allow**.	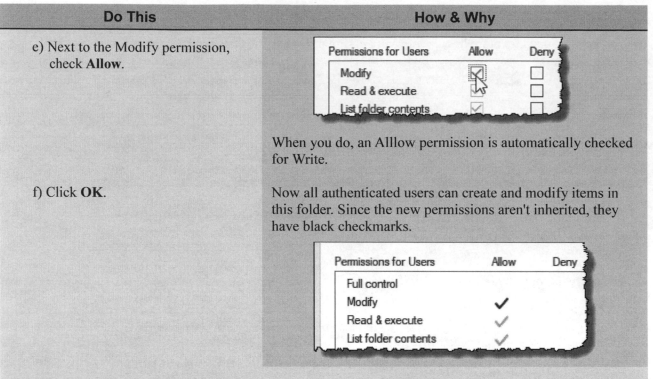
	When you do, an Alllow permission is automatically checked for Write.
f) Click **OK**.	Now all authenticated users can create and modify items in this folder. Since the new permissions aren't inherited, they have black checkmarks.

3. On the Security tab, click **Advanced**.

The Advanced Security Settings window gives you more detailed control of permissions. It shows which folder each permission is inherited from. You can also disable inheritance entirely for the folder.

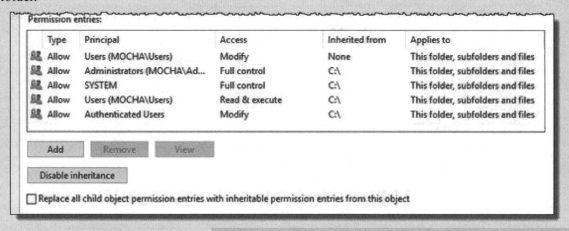

4. Click **OK** twice.			To close the Properties windows.	
5. Check permissions for `C:\NTFS lab\Sales data\Customer list.txt`			The Users group can read, write, and modify this file. If you check the Advanced permissions, you'll see that the Modify permission is inherited from the `C:\NTFS lab\Sales data\` folder.	
6. Close all open windows.				

Windows security features

In addition to ACLs placed on files, Windows itself has a number of important tools and settings throughout the operating system. You'll encounter some in using the Control Panel or System Settings, like Windows Firewall, Windows Defender, and tools to create and remove user accounts. Behind those are a variety of other background features and administrative tools that can configure and maintain system security.

Windows registry A database containing low level settings for all aspects of the Windows operating system as well as for some installed applications. Individual entries or *keys* in the database can be restricted by ACLs, just like Windows services and NTFS files.

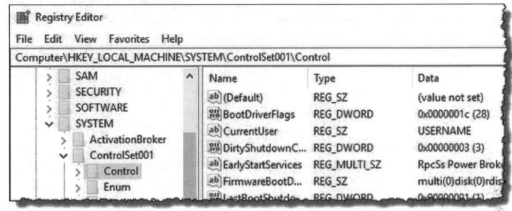

 Note: You can edit registry settings with **REGEDIT**, but it's usually a means of last resort if you can't change a given setting from some other utility.

Local Users and Groups An MMC snap-in (also available in Computer Management) which allows you to centrally manage users and groups on the computer. You can use it to create, rename, or delete users and groups; add users to groups; and set other user settings such as password policies, logon scripts, and folder locations.

Local Security Policy A utility which allows you to configure a wide range of security settings for the local computer, including those related to account management, default user rights, network functions, and so on. It works primarily by changing registry settings, but provides a much safer and more focused interface than **REGEDIT**.

Local Group Policy Editor A utility which allows you to edit *group policies* for the entire computer. Local group policies include the same settings as the local security policy, but also many other Windows settings. Critically, they can apply to specific users or groups, rather than all users on the computer. Group policies don't actually edit the registry directly. Instead, when a group policy is loaded its settings override the corresponding registry keys.

Security Account Manager A database which stores user passwords and performs authentication of local users. Users don't directly interact with the SAM. It just stores passwords in a hashed format that can't easily be extracted.

Credential Manager A Control Panel utility which allows individual users to access their stored user names, passwords, and certificates. These may be from websites, or from other network services. Unlike SAM, you can view your passwords and other credentials in Credential Manager, but Windows still protects them from view by any other user.

User Account Control Notifies you when an action will change Windows settings and gives you an option to stop. This applies even when you are logged on as an administrator. By default, UAC only notifies you when an application wants to change Windows settings on your behalf, but you can configure it to also notify you when your actions will change system settings.

Windows Resource Protection	A feature that runs in the background to protect critical system files, folders, and registry keys from unplanned alterations. WRP uses a combination of ACLs for each resource, and backed up copies of files and settings to restore from in case one is altered. Even the Administrator can't directly alter resources protected by WRP; instead, changes must go through the Windows Module Installer service.

Active Directory

When you configure independent Windows computers to behave as part of the same workgroup, each computer can share folders and printers, but there's no central management. If you want to have the same account on two separate computers, you have to configure it separately on both. The same is true for Windows settings. You can't even find out what shared resources are available without finding and querying each computer on the network. As networks grow, central control is required to maintain usability and security. A popular way to do this is with a *directory service* that maps out what resources are available, where they can be found, and any other information that's associated with each resource.

Windows domain networks use *Active Directory* as their directory service. It doesn't just map out network resources, but allows a central server called a *domain controller* to centrally control accounts, user authentication, and Windows settings for the entire domain. Active Directory is based primarily around three network protocols: LDAP for resource directory services, Kerberos for SSO authentication through the domain, and DNS for mapping the server namespace.

A domain controller stores the Active Directory Domain Services database that stores information about all computers, users, and other resources that are available on the domain. When you join a computer to a domain, the domain controller takes over account management and user authentication from the local machine. Likewise, the domain's security policies and group policies supersede that of the local computer. In fact, there are features to allow the domain controller to perform almost every aspect of Windows management on each PC joined to the domain.

A domain can contain many computers spread across multiple physical sites, provided that they all share a common directory database and set of security policies. For larger or more complex networks, you can create a hierarchical *tree* by joining domains themselves in parent-child relationships. The full extent of an Active Directory network with multiple domains or trees is called a *forest*.

Active Directory accounts

In Active Directory domains, account management is centralized. Local accounts created in Control Panel or System Settings can still exist on the computer, but they have no meaning on the domain and can't be used to access its resources. Instead, you can create or manage user accounts in the *Active Directory Users and Computers* window on the domain server. It works much like Local Users and Groups, but with more functions relevant to the domain.

 Exam Objective(s): 220-1002 2.2.1.2, 2.2.1.5, 2.2.1.6

Active Directory Users and Computers in Windows Server 2012

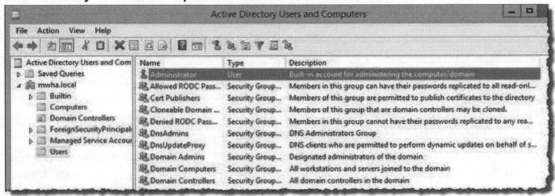

Active Directory defines multiple types of *objects* relevant to users and security, all managed centrally from the domain controller. In addition to users themselves, important object types include computers, printers, network share locations, and *security groups* which can contain other objects.

One thing to remember about domain accounts is that the account details, password, and permissions are stored in the Active Directory database, but files and folders are not. This has three consequences that are important to remember.

- You can log onto a domain account from multiple computers, but the first time you log on from a given computer you must have network access.

- Account details are cached locally at logon. This means you can log onto the computer without access to the domain controller, but you won't be able to access domain resources, and account changes made since you last logged in will not apply.

- By default, all personal folders, like Documents, are stored on the local computer and will not be accessible from other computers. Alternatively, administrators can configure domain accounts to store data on file share on a central server where it can easily be backed up and accessed throughout the network. There are multiple methods to do this. Each impacts user functionality.

  - An account can be set with a *roaming profile* which uses the remote share to store all personal folders, desktop contents and appearance, Windows personalization, and application settings. When a user logs from a client on the network, profile data is copied to the local machine. When the user logs off, changes are merged back to the central server. This allows a consistent user experience on any computer, but copying a large profile can take a lot of time and network bandwidth.

  - An account can be also configured with a *home folder* which maps the remote share as a network drive and sets it as the user's Documents folder. This approach only stores the Documents folder itself on the network so the user can access it from any computer. Other profile data is stored locally and not shared between computers. A drawback is that it requires constant access to the network share.

  - *Folder redirection* is a more flexible approach which allows an administrator to decide which folders are stored only on the network and which are copied locally. Typically, small and frequently accessed folders can be stored on the local computer, while large ones are kept on the network. Unlike roaming profiles, it can synchronize data in the background during the user session.

Active Directory security features

The core functions of Active Directory allow an enterprise to extend Windows security functions out to the domain by centralizing account management, group policies, and management of shared resources like folders and printers. In addition to those, AD provides some features that aren't really analogous to anything on standalone copies of Windows.

- *Active Directory Lightweight Directory Services (AD LDS)* provides directory services independent of the Windows domain model. You might find it used it networks which need authentication for distributed applications, or when it's useful to install a directory on a computer that isn't a domain controller.

- *Active Directory Federation Services (ADFS)* is a single sign-on system that uses the common internet standard *SAML* instead of LDAP. Unlike LDAP it is intended for use over the internet, and for integrating services with other organizations. You're likely to find it used to integrate web applications with Active Directory, especially those which aren't directly compatible with Windows authentication systems.

- *Active Directory Certificate Services (AD CS)* allows the Active Directory network to maintain a public key infrastructure. It creates, validates, and revokes digital certificates wherever they might be needed on the network - to identify users or computers, encrypt files or email, or establish secure VPN connections.

- *Active Directory Rights Management Services (AD RMS)* is an information rights management service that can encrypt and limit access to specific types of information on the domain, such as emails, Word documents, web pages, and so on. It can be used to centrally secure access to sensitive information wherever it is stored on the domain.

Group policies

One of the most valuable tools for establishing security baselines and enforcing user permissions in Windows is the Group Policy feature. Group policies let you centrally control how users can access Windows features and resources. For example, you can use Group Policies to enforce password policies, set firewall rules, block access to folders or network shares, or restrict use of particular desktop features like Task Manager. Even on an isolated Windows system the Local Group Policy Editor is a valuable security tool, but the *Group Policy Management Editor* available in Active Directory gives much more flexibility for controlling settings, including security, across the entire network.

The Group Policy Management Editor in Windows Server 2012

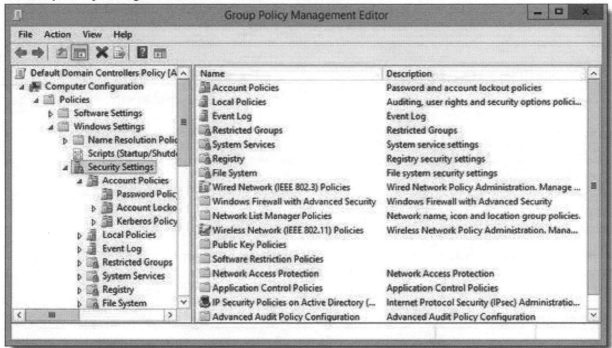

In Active Directory, you can set separate *group policy objects* (*GPOs*) for sites, domains, or *Organizational Units* using the Group Policy Management Editor. Without Active Directory you can only configure local GPOs for one computer at a time, but you can manually export settings from one computer and import them on another. This can save a lot of time when you want to configure the same security settings on every computer.

GPOs allow you to change thousands of settings affecting all sorts of Windows functions. The settings in a GPO are divided into two categories.

- *Computer Configuration* settings apply to all computers affected by the GPO, regardless of who are logged in. Commonly configured categories include startup and shutdown scripts for the computer, automatic deployment and configuration of software, account security policies, Windows Firewall rules, and restrictions on what software can run on the computer.

- *User Configuration* settings apply to all users affected by the GPO, regardless of the computer they use. Common categories include logon and logoff scripts for users, folder redirection, user-specific software deployment and settings, and settings that control what features the user can access from the Start menu, taskbar, desktop, and Control Panel.

Group policy management

One of the benefits of GPOs is that you can configure them at multiple levels: Domains, local computers, or physical sites. You can also create *Organizational Units*. An *OU* is a little like a security group in that it's a container which can hold users, computers, groups, or child OUs. Unlike a group it can't be directly assigned permissions via an ACL - instead, OUs can be assigned GPOs. For example, if you wanted to make a group policy for all computers used for software development, you could create a "Development" OU and add all relevant computers to it. You can even create new GPOs on an existing level to apply together.

Exam Objective(s): 220-1002 2.2.1.3, 2.2.1.4

This can make security challenging, since multiple GPOs means a chance for one with weak security settings to override one with strong settings, or for one with strong security settings to cause usability issues on a computer that doesn't really need them. When multiple GPOs apply, Windows processes them in the following order, meaning that each subsequent GPO overrides the one before.

1. Local GPO (set on the current computer)
2. Site GPO
3. Domain GPO
4. Organizational unit GPO
5. Child OU GPO

If multiple GPOs apply on the same level, each has a different *link order*. Higher link orders process first, and lower last.

If you're not a domain administrator you probably won't be designing GPOs, but when you troubleshoot computer problems on a domain, or set up user accounts, you need to be aware of which GPOs apply to a specific case. If some setting "isn't taking" it's entirely possible it's being overridden by a GPO higher up the priority list.

Updating group policies

Group policies can be changed at any time by a domain administrator, but they're not instantly propagated through the network. By default, Windows checks for GPO changes on login and then refreshes policy settings every 90 minutes in the background. If a troubleshooting process leads to GPO changes, or if you think there's some problem with group policy settings, you can also manually force an update using the **gpupdate** tool from any Windows edition that supports domain membership.

You can type **gpupdate** from any Command Prompt or PowerShell window. By itself, the command will simply check for all applicable User and Computer policies, and apply only those which have changed since the last refresh. Policies that apply only during logon or computer startup, like logon scripts and software installation, won't be applied until the next time a user logs on or the computer reboots. You can also use the following options:

- `/Target: Computer` or **`/Target: User`** will load only Computer or User policies, as applicable.
- **`/force`** will reapply all policies, even those which haven't been changed. After completing, it asks if you want to restart the computer.
- `/logoff` will automatically log the current user off if any changes apply only at user logon, such as a new logon script or folder redirection. If there are no such changes, the option won't do anything.
- `/boot` will automatically restart the computer if any changes apply at boot, such as startup scripts, or software updates. If there are no such changes, the computer won't reboot.

Logon scripts

Logon scripts are a useful addition to group policies, since they allow Windows to automatically take a defined set of actions when a user logs in. Popular uses for logon scripts include mapping network drives and printers, gathering information about the computer, or logging access for security reasons, but really you can perform almost any task that's available from a command line.

Exam Objective(s): 220-1002 2.2.1.1

You can configure a logon script in either Group Policy Management Editor or Local Group Policy editor by navigating to **User Configuration > Policies > Windows Settings > Scripts**, then double-clicking **Logon**.

Note: You can also set them on an individual user's Profile tab in Users and Computers, but in general it's better to use group policies.

Logon Script settings in a Group Policy and in account properties

A group policy allows multiple scripts to run, and scripts can be in .bat, .vbs, or .ps1 format. You can choose the order in which to run scripts. If your list includes both PowerShell and non-PowerShell scripts, use the PowerShell tab to choose whether PowerShell scripts should run first or last.

Logoff scripts work the same way as Logon scripts. So do Startup and Shutdown scripts - the only difference is that they're in **Computer Configuration > Policies > Windows Settings > Scripts**

Configuring account security policies

If you're managing a Windows Active Directory domain, you can configure user security policies such as password strength from the Group Policy Management Console. If you're managing local user accounts on a workgroup you're not entirely out of luck: Some versions of Windows include much of the same functionality in the Local Security Policy Console. There are some limitations: Local Security Policy only applies to a single computer, and the console is only available in business-oriented Windows versions: basically, any with "Business", "Professional", "Enterprise", or "Ultimate" in the name.

To open the console, type `secpol.msc` in the Search box or Start screen.

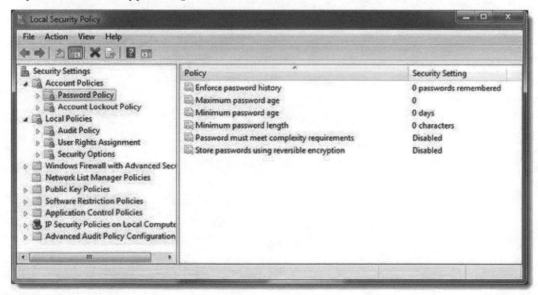

To use the console, navigate to folders in the left pane, then double-click items in the right pane to configure them. Some options can only be disabled or enabled, while others have numerical or other values.

- Navigate to **Account Policies > Password Policy** to change password requirements.

  - Set **Minimum password length** to set the smallest number of characters a password can have. For strong security, choose a value between 8 and 12.

  - Enable **Password must meet complexity requirements** to enforce complexity requirements. If it is enabled, all passwords must be at least six characters, not contain the user's user name, and contain any three of uppercase letters, lowercase letters, numbers, and special characters.

  - Set **Maximum password age** to set a maximum length of time users can use a password without changing it. Lower values are more secure, but can be irritating to users.

  - Set **Enforce password history** to specify a number of previous passwords Windows remembers for the user, in order to prevent users from reusing the same passwords. Higher numbers are more secure since users can't just cycle through the same couple of passwords.

  - Click **Minimum password age** to set a period that users must wait between password changes. This prevents users from changing passwords several times to cycle through the password history.

  - Enable **Store passwords using reversible encryption** to change how Windows stores passwords. This method is less secure, so you should only do it if a program requires it.

- Navigate to **Account Policies > Account Lockout Policy** to lock accounts after repeated failed logon attempts.

  - Set **Account lockout threshold** to set how many failed attempts are needed to lock the account. The default of 0 disables lockout. Lower values are more secure, but also make it easier for user error to cause lockouts.

  - If a lockout threshold is set, click **Account lockout duration** to specify a time in minutes the account will be locked out. If the value is 0, only an administrator can unlock the account.

  - If a lockout threshold is set, click **Reset account lockout counter after** to specify a time in minutes for the failed attempts counter to reset. If the lockout duration is non-zero, this value must be less than or equal to the lockout duration.

- Navigate to **Local Policies > User Rights Assignment** or **Local Policies > Security Options** to configure more advanced security options. For example, you can restrict what users can log on remotely, or specify advanced User Account Control settings. You can also rename the Administrator and Guest accounts here.

     Note: In general, you shouldn't touch these unless you have specific security needs and know what you're doing.

The same basic functions, plus more, can be found in Local Group Policy Editor, and on a domain controller in Group Policy Management Editor. The overall interface is similar.

Exercise: Using Windows security features

Do This	How & Why
1. Use the Registry Editor.	**REGEDIT** allows you to access almost all Windows settings, but there are reasons it should seldom be your first choice.
a) Click **Start > Windows Administrative Tools > Registry editor**.	You could also search for **regedit**.
b) Navigate through the tree in the navigation pane.	The folders, or *keys*, on the left form a large hierarchical database containing settings, or *values* on the right. You can create or edit keys and values, but there's not much indication of what each means.
c) Close the Registry Editor.	You might need this tool some time, but if you don't know what you're looking for it's hard to find important values and easy to cause system problems by making the wrong change.
2. Examine the local security policy.	The Local Security Policy utility allows you to change security-related registry settings in a more user-friendly interface.
a) Click **Start > Windows Administrative Tools > Local Security Policy**	Or search for **SECPOL**.
b) In the navigation pane, select **Local Policies > Security Options**.	Unlike the Registry Editor, this utility arranges security settings in a user-friendly name and arrangement.
c) Navigate to **Account Policies > Password Policy**.	This folder contains policies for password creation, such as length, complexity, and when they must be changed.
d) Double-click **Password must meet complexity requirements**.	To open a **Properties** window. You can change the settings, or click the **Explain** tab for details and advice on what each setting means.
e) Click **Cancel**.	
f) Close Local Security Policy.	Since you're using Windows 10 Pro, you'll use the Group Policy Editor instead of making changes here.
3. Edit the local group policy.	The Local Group Policy Editor allows you to change more settings than the Local Security Policy, and it's a better introduction to the Group Policies used on Active Directory
a) Search for **gpedit** and click **Edit group policy**.	It's the same console interface as Local Security Policy, but has different contents.
b) Expand **Computer Configuration > Windows Settings > Security Settings**.	The Security Settings folder has the same contents as Local Security Policy. Anything you could change there, you can also change here.

Do This	How & Why
c) Navigate further to **Account Policies** > **Password Policy**.	According to the present configuration, there aren't any rules for minimum password length, complexity requirements, or enforcement history, but passwords must be changed every 42 days

Policy	Security Setting
Enforce password history	0 passwords remembered
Maximum password age	42 days
Minimum password age	0 days
Minimum password length	0 characters
Password must meet complexity	Disabled
Store passwords using reversible	Disabled

Do This	How & Why
d) Edit the Enforce password history setting to **10** passwords remembered.	Double-click it and edit the field.

Local Security Setting | Explain

Enforce password history

Keep password history for:

10 passwords remembered

Do This	How & Why
e) Click **OK**.	To close the Properties window. Now it will be harder for users to reuse the same password.
f) Set Minimum password age to **1** day.	To keep users from just changing passwords repeatedly until they cycle back to the original.
g) Set Minimum password length to **8** characters.	You could set it higher for even more security.
h) Enable password complexity.	

Policy	Security Setting
Enforce password history	10 passwords remembered
Maximum password age	42 days
Minimum password age	1 days
Minimum password length	8 characters
Password must meet complex...	Enabled
Store passwords using reversi...	Disabled

Do This	How & Why
4. Examine other group policy settings.	Group policies include many settings which aren't found in the Local Security Policy. If you were on a domain controller you could layer multiple policies for sites, domains, and OUs.
a) Expand **Computer Configuration** > **Administrative Templates**.	You can use Group Policies to configure many other Windows settings.

Do This	How & Why
b) Inside Administrative Templates, navigate to **Windows Components > Windows Update**.	Notice that the default state for most is "Not configured". That way if you don't actually change a setting it can't override other group policies or user settings.
c) Navigate to **User Configuration > Windows Settings > Scripts (Logon/Logoff)**.	You could configure scripts to run whenever a user logs on or off.
d) Navigate to **Computer Configuration > Windows Settings > Scripts (Startup/Shutdown)**.	You can also configure scripts that run when the computer starts up or shuts down.

5. Close all open windows.

Assessment: Operating system security

1. You share a folder on your computer and assign the following permissions: 1. Share permission "Change" to the Everyone group. 2. NTFS permission "Read" to the Accounting user group. 3. NTFS permission "Full Control" to Tamara, who is a member of the Accounting group. When Tamara connects to the shared folder, what are her effective permissions? Choose the best response.

   - Read
   - Read & Execute
   - Change
   - Full Control

2. You should always disable the administrative shares on your computer to improve security. True or false?

   - True
   - False

3. You have a folder called Accounting with a dozen subfolders, each of which will have its own custom access restrictions. To start, you broke permissions inheritance so you can configure them individually, but you want to give the Accounting user group Modify access to both the Accounting folder and all of its subfolders. What is the quickest way to make that change? Choose the best answer.

   - It is not possible to make the change at the parent Accounting folder and have it automatically apply the change down to the subfolders. You must make the change at each folder individually.
   - Make the change to the Accounting folder, re-enable inheritance on the Accounting folder, and then apply the settings from the parent folder to the child folders.
   - Make the change to the Accounting folder, then propagate that change from the parent folder to the child folders.
   - Select all folders in File Explorer, open the Properties window, and apply the permissions you want.

4. What password policies can you enforce from the Local Security Policy Console? Choose all that apply.

- Account lockout settings
- BIOS/UEFI password
- Minimum password length
- Password complexity
- Screen saver password protection

5. In an Active Directory environment, what order does Windows process GPOs in?

1. Child OU GPO
2. Domain GPO
3. Local GPO
4. Organizational Unit GPO
5. Site GPO

6. Why would you set a minimum password age in the GPO? Choose the best response.

- To keep users from choosing simple passwords
- To keep users from bypassing history requirements
- To prevent attackers from easily cracking passwords
- To make sure users change their passwords regularly

Module B: Security hardware and software

Some security tools are built into core operating system or software functions, but others are built into network devices like routers, or are run as host applications which monitor system activities to look for threats. Even on host PCs, many security tools are focused on securing against network-based attacks.

You will learn:

- How antivirus software and email filtering block malware
- How firewalls, IDS, and IPS protect against network attacks
- How DLP technologies prevent sharing of sensitive data
- About VPN connections
- About other network security appliances

Antivirus/Anti-malware

An antivirus/anti-malware program scans your computer system for viruses/malware and removes them if they are found. As part of your digital security protection program, you'll want to install a good *antivirus/anti-malware program* on all systems. Look for the following characteristics when selecting an antivirus/anti-malware program:

Exam Objective(s): 220-1002 2.2.7, 2.4.2.7

- Desirable basic features include:

    - Performs scheduled and on-demand scans, including options for file types to scan or exclude.
    - Scans compressed files, downloads, emails, and removable media
    - Performs boot sector and startup scans, and create emergency repair disks
    - Defends against specialized attacks such as rootkits and ransomware
    - Generates scan logs and reports.

- For more comprehensive *endpoint security suites* look for additional features:

    - Integrated firewall to protect against network attacks
    - Email filtering
    - Browser exploit protection
    - *Secure DNS* features to protect against DNS hijacking

- A high detection rate, but a low rate of false positives.

    - Products from major vendors will receive frequent virus definition updates. You'll need network access to receive them.
    - Advanced products will have sophisticated *heuristic analysis* to identify unknown threats and new variations of existing threats.

- A limited impact on system performance. Antivirus resource use can be a burden on older computers, or even newer ones that don't have a lot of processing power or memory available.

- Easy to use and administer.

  - For standalone products, make sure that it's easy to configure settings, that updates and scans are automated, and that it's easy to safely access or recover a file that's been quarantined by mistake or still has valuable data.

  - For enterprise products, look for products suited to centralized deployment and administration.

Email filtering

In addition to antivirus/anti-malware software, a companion method of keeping viruses or malware from entering your network through your email system is to use email filtering. *Email filtering* is a software-based tool that can sort or block email from being delivered to a user's inbox based on configured criteria. It can be a separate program or a feature of your email program. Mail filters can scan both inbound and outbound email, preventing a virus or malware from entering your network and from spreading from your network. You can set filters based on IP address, sender email address, or any other identifiable characteristic of the email. Typically email filters are managed by individual users, but you can also implement them at the server level and apply them at a company level.

Setting an email filter in Outlook

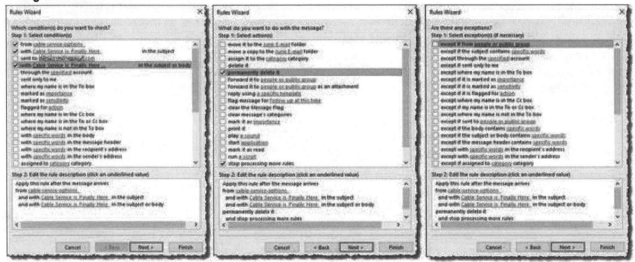

For example, while the Microsoft Outlook email client doesn't have the same email filtering features as an antivirus program with email protection, it still allows you to create email rules that fulfill as similar rule. In Outlook, a rule consists of three parts: A condition that triggers the rule, an action the rule takes, and exceptions which can override the rule.

Firewalls

A firewall controls incoming and outgoing traffic, preventing unauthorized access to or from your network. You establish certain rules, often referred to as a policy, which categorizes various types of network traffic as good (and thus allowed through to your network) or bad (and thus blocked from passing through to your network.) As part of your digital security protection program, you'll want to install a *firewall* .

Exam Objective(s): 220-1002 2.2.8, 2.4.2.6

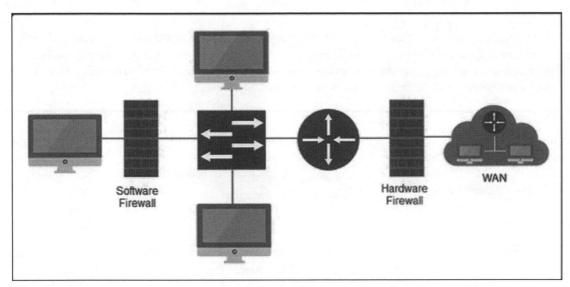

There are two types:

- A *hardware firewall* is a specialized network device that sits between your internal computer network and the Internet. It's much like a router with security features, and in fact firewalls are commonly built into routers. Hardware firewalls are a great solution for organizations need a single firewall system that protects multiple computers. The downside to them is that they can be expensive, complicated, and difficult to upgrade. They also can't protect against some attacks, like malicious traffic within the LAN.

- A *software firewall* is traffic control software that you install on an individual device. The benefit of a software firewall is that it is portable and local - it will protect the host on any network, whether attacks come from the internet or the same LAN. Software firewalls are built into most operating systems and available from third parties. Both are easy to update and configure from within the host.

Hardware and software firewalls are not mutually exclusive. A typical SOHO network has a software firewall on each host, and a hardware firewall built into the router.

Disabling ports

Your firewall has a variety of ports that are each used by a particular type of traffic. In total, a computer has 65,536 TCP ports and 65,536 UDP ports. The port numbers in the range from 0 to 1023 are the *well-known ports* or *system ports*. They are used by system processes that provide widely used types of network services. The five most common Internet traffic types, along with their default port number include:

- World Wide Web (using the Hyper-Text Transfer Protocol, or HTTP): port 80

- E-mail (using the Simple Mail Transfer Protocol, or SMTP): port 25

- File transfer (using the File Transfer Protocol, or FTP): port 20 for data transfer, port 21 for control

- Hostname/IP address translation (using the Domain Name Service, or DNS): port 53

- Remote terminal access (such as Telnet and Secure Shell): port 23 for Telnet, port 22 for Secure Shell

Ports are either in allow (open) mode or deny (closed or blocked) mode. If your mail server set up to receive SMTP traffic, it is what is referred to as *listening on port 25*. This means port 25 is open.

Applications such as peer-to-peer file sharing or video conferencing software often open ports without your knowledge or permission, as does outright malware. Each of those open ports becomes a security gap, unless you take proactive steps to close them. Several Internet sites list port numbers that hackers commonly exploit. You want to close any ports you aren't using on firewall or gateway computers. The best way to do this is to close all ports, then specifically open those you know you need.

Firewalls can block both incoming and outgoing ports. Usually, outgoing ports are less restricted since being very strict can impair local client applications from working properly, but it's a good idea to block outgoing traffic if you have reason to believe it's undesirable. One common application is to block outgoing ports commonly used by malware, such as *beaconing* messages sent by botnet malware to its controller. For this reason, software firewalls often work in conjunction with antivirus software.

Switch security features

Network ACLs are most commonly associated with routers and other more "intelligent" network devices. Despite this, switches and non-routing access points have traffic direction functions which lend themselves to security features similar to ACLs. Most of them are only important to network administrators, but a couple can have a major impact on endpoint systems and other hosts.

Exam Objective(s): 220-1002 2.2.4, 2.2.5

Port security   A switch feature that tracks device MAC addresses connected to each port on a switch, and allows or blocks traffic based on source MAC addresses. This can be used to restrict devices which connect to the network, or to detect and block some attacks using spoofed MAC addresses. It can also prevent multiple MAC addresses from connecting to a single physical port, such as if a user attached an unauthorized hub or switch to a network drop.

MAC filtering   On Ethernet networks this is another term for port security, but it's more commonly used for a similar feature on WAPs. It's still useful, but much easier to circumvent because a WAP transceiver only has one "port" and it's easier for an attacker to watch for legitimate MAC addresses to imitate.

Both port security and MAC addresses can use two approaches.

- Allow traffic unless it comes from a MAC address that's been *blacklisted*, or forbidden. This is less secure, but it's easier to maintain, especially if devices frequently join or leave the network.

- Block traffic unless it comes from a MAC address on a *whitelist* of approved devices. This gives more security, but it means new devices can't join the network without an administrator adding them to the list.

Even if you use whitelisting, it's not hard for an unauthorized address to spoof the MAC address of a legitimate one. This means neither port security nor MAC filtering are strong security measures on their own. However, both are still a useful extra layer to add to overall network security.

Intrusion detection and prevention

Intrusion detection systems (*IDS*) and *intrusion prevention systems* (*IPS*) are closely related to both firewalls and antivirus, but perform a different role than either. Like firewalls, they are designed to monitor network traffic to look for signs of intrusion or other unwanted activities. The actual evaluation is more like antivirus software; instead of network traffic being evaluated by a set of rules based on addresses and ports, it's evaluated by rules based on the signatures of known attacks, or by heuristic analysis which can recognize unusual or suspicious activities. While antivirus is focused specifically on recognizing suspect files and programs, IDS and IPS focus on network communications, system changes, or user actions.

Exam Objective(s): 220-1001 2.5.2.2, 2.5.2.3

IDS and IPS differ primarily in what they do on detecting a potential threat.

- IDS are passive monitoring systems designed to alert administrators when something suspicious happens, but take no action on their own. This has some advantages both in performance, and in the fact that an IDS can't disrupt normal activities by mistaking them for a threat.

- IPS are active protection systems which can block traffic, disconnect users, or take other corrective actions against an attack. While this has obvious security advantages, it can cause performance slowdowns due to processing time or even disrupt normal services due to false alarms.

Much like firewalls, IDS and IPS can also be placed on the network or on a specific host.

- Network-based NIDS and NIPS are placed on the network like routers or network firewalls, and protect entire subnets against outside attack.

- Host-based HIDS and HIPS are installed applications which protect individual hosts, like software firewalls. They can detect attacks from the local network, or even by users logged into the computer. They're also a good way to provide custom protection to specific high-value servers.

Data loss prevention (DLP)

Data loss prevention (DLP) software is used to classify and protect your organization's confidential and critical data. Within the software, you create rules that prevent users from accidentally or maliciously sharing particular types of data outside your organization. For example, a DLP rule might prevent users from forwarding any business emails outside of the corporate mail domain. Another DLP rule might prevent users from uploading files to a consumer cloud service, like OneDrive or Dropbox. Yet another type of rule would prevent users from copying files to removable media.

Exam Objective(s): 220-1002 2.2.13

An example of DLP being used for email

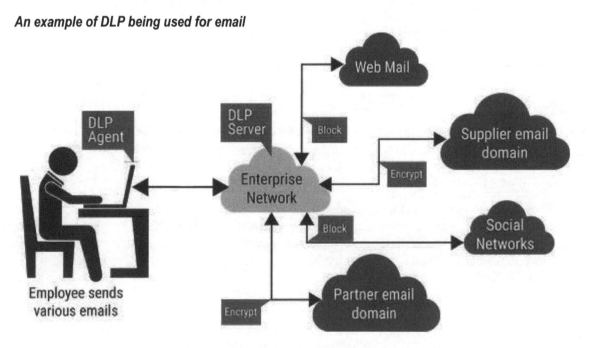

Windows Firewall

All modern versions of Windows include Windows Firewall, a host-based firewall application which protects all network connections by default. In general, Windows Firewall blocks all incoming connections not needed for important network functions, while allowing outgoing connections used by installed client applications. Like most firewalls, Windows Firewall allows you to configure rules, or *exceptions*, that apply to specific types of traffic.

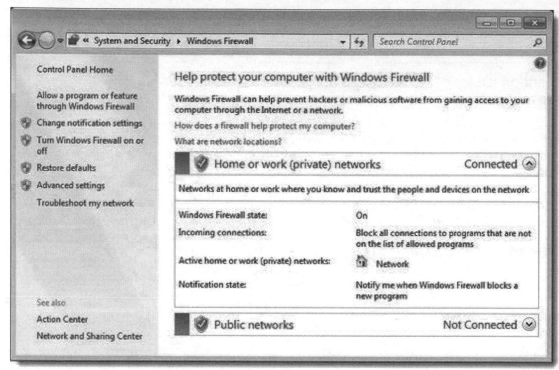

Windows Firewall maintains separate sets of rules for Public and Private network locations. By default, they're pretty similar, but Private networks are a little less strict: the ports used for network discovery and file sharing on LANs are blocked on Public networks.

Like most firewalls, Windows Firewall isn't just intended to protect against outside attacks, but also to prevent malicious programs like malware from communicating over the network. When Windows Firewall detects an unfamiliar program attempting to communicate through the network, inbound or outbound, it will ask whether you want to allow it. When a certain application can't connect to the network, it's usually worth making sure the firewall isn't blocking it.

Configuring Windows Firewall

You can access Windows Firewall through the Control Panel. In Windows Vista, click **Security**, then **Windows Firewall**. In other Windows editions, click **System and Security**, then **Windows Firewall**.

 Exam Objective(s): 220-1002 1.8.10

- Click the arrows next to Public and Private networks to hide or view current settings for each location.
- To change firewall status and notification settings, click **Change notification settings** or **Turn Windows Firewall on or off**.

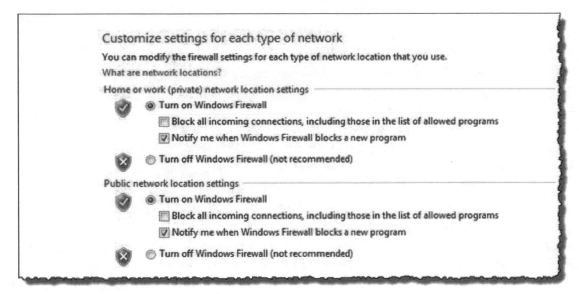

- To allow a specific application through the firewall, click **Allow a program or feature through Windows Firewall.**

- To access more detailed security rules, click **Advanced Settings**.

- To undo all firewall changes you've made, click **Restore defaults**.

Allowing programs through Windows Firewall

You can set Windows Firewall to allow or block network access to a given program. Each program can be allowed or blocked for public networks, private networks, or both.

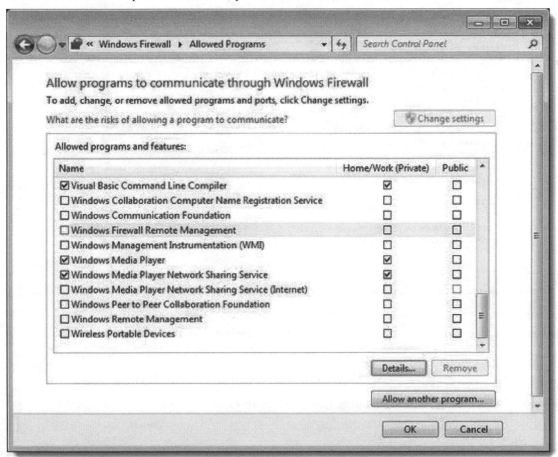

1. In Windows Firewall, click **Allow a program or feature through Windows Firewall.**

2. Configure each application you want to allow or block.

   - Check the Public or Private column for each program you want to allow.

   - If you're not sure what a program is, select it and click **Details**.

   - If the list isn't available, click **Change Settings**.

   - If the program you want isn't in the list, click **Allow another program** to search for it.

3. Click **OK**.

Using Windows Firewall with Advanced Security

Windows Firewall's normal configuration settings are designed to be easy for novice users, but under the hood the application supports pretty sophisticated features. Not only can you create rules based on location and application, but also on ports, protocols, IP addresses, and all sorts of other features supported by other enterprise firewall software. To access them, you need to open **Windows Firewall with Advanced Security**. To do that, simply click **Advanced settings** in Windows Firewall.

Windows Firewall with Advanced Security isn't actually a separate application from Windows Firewall, nor does it use a different set of rules. It's just a different interface that gives you more detailed access to the program's underlying features and the types of rules you can create.

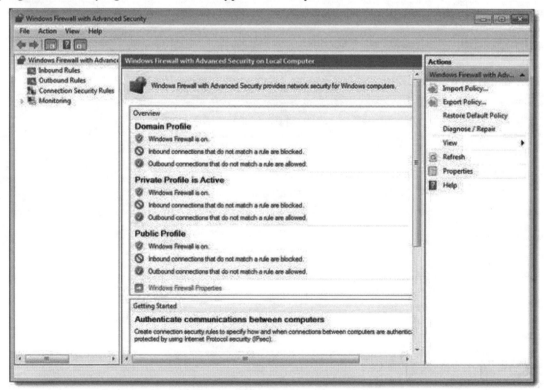

1. Use the navigation pane to select the kind of rules you want to view or change.
   Available rule types include inbound, outbound, connection security, and monitoring.

2. View or select existing rules in the center pane.

3. Click commands in the Action pane. The available commands will vary depending on context.

   - Click **New Rule** to open a wizard for creating new firewall rules.

   - Use the **Filter** commands to help filter long lists.

   - Click **Properties** to open or edit an existing rule.

Exercise: Configuring Windows Firewall

Typically, you manually add an exception to Windows Firewall to allow incoming connections to a given program or port.

In this exercise you'll configure Windows Firewall to make sure you can connect remotely to your computer using Remote Desktop Protocol, as well as the WebSocket protocol, but only if you're on a private network.

Do This	How & Why
1. In Control Panel, click **System and Security** > **Windows Defender Firewall**.	Windows Firewall opens, showing its current status. By default, it blocks all incoming connections that aren't explicitly allowed, and all rules can be separately configured for public and private networks. If you were signed into an Active Directory domain, there would be a third set of rules.
2. Add an exception to Windows Firewall.	By default, Windows Firewall uses a simple interface designed for end users not very experienced with networking.
a) In the left pane, click **Allow an app or feature through Windows Firewall**.	A list of installed programs is displayed. Those allowed to communicate through the firewall are checked.

b) Check **Private** next to both Remote Desktop and Remote Desktop (Websocket)

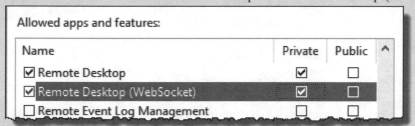

You may need to click **Change settings** first.

c) Click **OK**.	To save your changes and return to the status screen.
3. View Windows Firewall's underlying rules.	
a) On the left, click **Advanced settings**.	**Windows Firewall with Advanced Security** opens. This mode allows you to view and specify rules specific to ports and protocols, and not just associated programs.
b) On the left, click **Inbound Rules**.	Outbound traffic has its own list of rules, but the format is the same. To view a list of rules for inbound traffic.
c) Scroll through the list.	Rules can be used to allow or deny traffic, and can be for private, public, or Windows Domain networks. Enabled rules are checked in green; the others are configured but disabled.

Do This	How & Why

d) View the Remote Desktop rules.

They're about 2/3 of the way down the list.

Inbound Rules

Name	Group	Profile	Enabled	Acti
✅ Remote Desktop - Shadow (TCP-In)	Remote Desktop	Private	Yes	Allo
Remote Desktop - Shadow (TCP-In)	Remote Desktop	Domai...	No	Allo
Remote Desktop - User Mode (TCP-...	Remote Desktop	Domai...	No	Allo
✅ Remote Desktop - User Mode (TCP-...	Remote Desktop	Private	Yes	Allov
✅ Remote Desktop - User Mode (UDP...	Remote Desktop	Private	Yes	Allov
Remote Desktop - User Mode (UDP...	Remote Desktop	Domai...	No	Allo
Remote Desktop - (TCP-WS-In)	Remote Desktop (We...	Domai...	No	Allov
✅ Remote Desktop - (TCP-WS-In)	Remote Desktop (We...	Private	Yes	Allo
✅ Remote Desktop - (TCP-WSS-In)	Remote Desktop (We...	Private	Yes	Allov
Remote Desktop - (TCP-WSS-In)	Remote Desktop (We...	Domai...	No	Allo

Remote Desktop is allowed for private networks, and disabled for public and domain networks. Any changes in Windows Firewall, even the basic interface, are reflected in the underlying rules.

Do This	How & Why
e) Scroll horizontally to view all columns.	Each rule can include a wide variety of criteria, such as local and remote port, local and remote address, program, protocol, and user. Remote Desktop uses TCP port 3389, so these rules specify that for the protocol and local port.
f) In the right pane, click **Filter by State > Filter by Enabled**.	Only enabled rules are displayed. By default, most of them are in the Core Networking and Network Discovery groups that you need for normal network functions.
g) Click **Clear all filters**.	To show all rules again.
4. Close all windows.	Remember that to accept incoming connections from the Internet, any network firewalls will also need to be configured to allow them.

VPNs

A *Virtual Private Network (VPN)* describes a network scenario where a secure connection is created between multiple computers or LANs across an insecure external network. This is different from just connecting using a secure application protocol like HTTPS: Instead, it can protect all network communications between VLAN members, just like if they were connected on the same physical LAN. For example, this allows remote users to connect to resources on the enterprise LAN from home or on the road without compromising security. A VLAN doesn't even have to be across the internet. You can also use it to join two high security networks across a larger and less secure enterprise network.

 Exam Objective(s): 220-1001 2.6.7; CompTIA 220-1002 2.2.12

Multiple remote users connecting to a VPN server

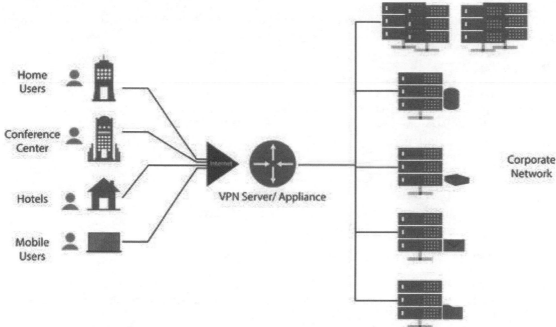

VPNs generally use secure transport protocols that provide secure data transmission over a non-secure network. Data is commonly secured using an encryption protocol such as IPsec or SSL/TLS, along with a *tunneling* protocol that allows other protocols to be carried through the connection even when they're insecure, non-routable, or non-TCP/IP.

The VPN itself generates a point-to-point connection across the larger network. Each end of the tunnel can be either a single host, or a *VPN gateway* that connects to an entire network. The VPN protocols are managed either by software running on a host or router, or on a specialized hardware appliance called a *VPN concentrator*.

There are typically two components to a VPN:

- A VPN Gateway: A networking device, such as a router, server, firewall, or similar device with internetworking and data transmission capabilities that sits at the external edge of a secure internal network and requires an external device to identify and authenticate itself before the gateway creates a connection allowing access to internal network resources.

- Secure transport protocols: Communications protocols that provide secure data transmission over an unsecure network. Data is commonly secured using an encryption protocol such as IPsec or a tunneling protocol such as SSL/TLS.

VPNs are pretty simple from the user perspective. In fact, site-to-site VPNs are totally transparent to end users and host computers. If you're connecting an individual host to a remote VPN, it's just a matter of running a VPN client and entering your authentication credentials. The client might even be included with your operating system. Once you connect, the remote VPN gateway will validate your identity and exchange encryption keys with your computer. As long as you remain connected to the VPN, any information you send to or receive from the remote network will be protected from external eavesdropping. VPN tunneling also means that you can use protocols which are normally only used on the LAN, such as SMB file sharing.

RADIUS

Authentication can be a challenge over the network, since credentials have to be presented remotely, and you might have a network that supports a wide variety of clients.

Exam Objective(s): 220-1002 2.3.2.3, 2.3.2.4

Remote Authentication Dial-In User Service (*RADIUS*) was initially designed to provide full AAA support for users joining the network over dialup connections. Since then it's been expanded to use for other point-to-point connections, such authenticating remote users in a VPN, or by ISPs to authenticate customer connections. One of the most common uses of RADIUS is as the authentication back end for Wi-Fi networks using WPA Enterprise security.

A RADIUS system consists of three basic parts:

Users   Endpoints that connect to the system. For a remote access VPN or WAP, users are individual workstations and mobile devices.

RADIUS Server A server on the internal LAN which provides AAA functions.

NAS   The *network access server* relays all communication between users and the RADIUS server. It's the device users directly connect to, like a dial-in server, VPN endpoint, or WAP.

RADIUS can use a wide variety of network protocols for authentication, such as PAP, CHAP, and EAP. Users might only need to know passwords to connect, or might have to have certificates or other credentials ready to use.

While it's a common standard, RADIUS has some limitations when it comes to scalability, flexibility, and usability. Some enterprises use other protocols with similar functions:

TACACS+   *Terminal Access Controller Access Control System* is a proprietary Cisco protocol with some performance and security benefits over RADIUS. Drawbacks include more complex configuration, and incompatibility with some network configurations.

Diameter   An open standard with similar improvements to TACACS+, named for being supposedly twice as good as RADIUS. While it has a broad feature set, it's also harder to configure and maintain. This means it's more often used on large carrier networks than in typical enterprise situations.

Security appliances

Network security functions can be built into a server that relays and evaluates network traffic, just like a router can. They can also be placed into a specialized hardware appliance, or in some cases placed in a VM that's run on the network. For the most part, they're managed by network administrators, but as a PC technician you should still know the roles they play and how they can affect network functions and security from the endpoint perspective.

The most familiar network security appliances are firewalls, IDS, and IPS. Others include:

WAF
Web application firewalls are specialized firewalls that can evaluate rules based on higher level protocols used by web servers. They have some overlap with IDS in that they are designed to recognize web attacks. A WAF can be placed protecting a single web server or a subnet with multiple web servers.

Network antimalware
Describes a variety of roles ranging from appliances that monitor network traffic for virus-related activity, to appliances that centrally monitor and update antivirus suites on all network hosts. If your organization uses network antimalware, make sure that hosts are configured to take advantage of it.

Spam filter
Performs ingoing and outgoing email filtering for an entire organization, usually by connection to a specific email server. Misconfigured spam filters can block important email or allow excessive spam through.

Content filter
Filters designed to prevent access to certain types of content. Spam filters are one kind of content filter; others block user access to content judged inappropriate for workplace use - adult websites, digital piracy tools, or social media. Poorly configured content filters can block access to legitimate sites.

Proxy server
Intercepts and mediates communications between internal and external hosts on the network. Often a proxy server also performs network address translation.

- *Forward proxies* mediate communications between internal clients and external servers, especially web servers. They're often used in conjunction with DLP and content filters. If your network uses a forward proxy, you may need to configure host browsers to be aware of it.

- *Reverse proxies* mediate communications between external (internet) clients and servers on the LAN. They're often used in conjunction with load balancers, IDS, or WAFs. You probably only need to worry about reverse proxies if you're supporting servers protected by one.

Unified security solutions

Security is no exception to the general IT trend of combining multiple related functions into a single product, whether to save costs or reduce administrative overhead. A well-designed integrated solution also allows multiple separate functions to complement and communicate with each other, providing more unified security.

Exam Objective(s): 220-1001 2.5.2.1

On individual hosts, the trend has been toward *endpoint security suites* that combine virus detection and removal with a host-based firewall, anti-spam, browser protection, DLP, and *file integrity monitors* that detect alterations to critical system files. In the enterprise, they may be placed under central control and monitoring, allowing administrators to easily get the big picture of threats to hosts throughout the network.

On the network, all-in one solutions are often called *next-gen firewalls* or *unified threat management* (*UTM*) firewalls. A UTM solution might incorporate any combination of advanced firewall, IDS/IPS, content filtering, NAT or proxy server, DLP, VPN endpoint, or other components.

Discussion: Researching security tools

1. What kinds of security hardware are in use in your organization's network?

2. Why is RADIUS still so popular when alternatives like TACACS+ and Diameter have more robust features?

3. Does your workplace use VPN connections for remote access? If so, what clients and technologies do they use?

4. In a browser, look for a comparison of endpoint security suites. Evaluate products based both on antivirus performance' and other capabilities.

Assessment: Security hardware and software

1. You want to prevent unauthorized traffic from entering your network by disabling unused ports on your firewall. The best way to accomplish this is to go down the port list and close each one you aren't using. True or false?

   - True
   - False

2. Which set of Windows Firewall rules is generally least permissive?

   - Incoming connections on private networks
   - Incoming connections on public networks
   - Outgoing connections on private networks
   - Outgoing connections on public networks

3. Windows Firewall with Advanced Security can be seen as a more powerful interface to the same Windows Firewall application. True or false?

   - True
   - False

4. Which of the following describes a network scenario where a secure connection to your internal network is made over an insecure external network?

   - Data loss prevention (DLP)
   - Digital security
   - Hardware firewall
   - Virtual private network (VPN)

5. Your wireless network is configured in 802.1X mode. What kind of server does it most likely use as a backend? Choose the best response.

   - KERBEROS
   - RADIUS
   - TACACS+
   - TKIP

6. You want to replace the network firewall, IDS, and content filter with a single device which will provide comprehensive network security protection. What sort of product should you look for? Choose the best response.

   - DLP
   - Endpoint security suite
   - TACACS+
   - UTM

Summary: Security technologies

You should now know

- About core operating system features to enforce access control, such as file permissions, account security policies, group policies, and protection of critical resources.

- How to augment security with host software and network devices, such as antivirus, firewalls, VPNs, and network security appliances.

Chapter 6: Securing devices and data

You will learn:

- How to secure workstations and data
- How to secure mobile devices
- How to secure network devices
- How to troubleshoot security issues

Module A: Workstation security

Workstation security is essential for the sake of the individual users and the overall organization. Workstations are the systems most often exposed to malware infestations, and most easily compromised by user error. Many users, home or business, might say "but my computer doesn't have valuable information, I don't care if the hackers get at it." It's a dangerous attitude: even such a computer likely has user credentials, saved passwords, and personal information that can be stolen and used elsewhere. Even if it doesn't, spyware can capture credentials when the user logs onto a company server or bank website. If nothing else, compromised workstations are difficult and time-consuming to fix, so preventative measures and secure practices are cost-effective.

You will learn:

- How to prevent malware infection
- How to prevent unauthorized access
- How to protect data

Threats to workstations

Securing anything, whether it's a computer, network, building, or organization, begins the same way. Look at what could go wrong. On a workstation, there are several obvious avenues you should watch out for: how likely each is depends on your organization and what the computer is being used for.

- Physical attacks to steal or damage hardware
- Network attacks to gain remote access or install malware
- Local logon by an unauthorized or malicious user
- Legitimate user error leading to compromised security settings or malware installation
- Theft of unsecured data

The next step is to identify and configure security controls which can minimize the risk of each threat.

- Physical security can prevent theft or damage: secure location might do for desktop systems, while laptops might need measures like locks, tracking software, and an alert user.
- Firewalls, anti-malware applications, and security updates can protect against network attacks.
- Strong passwords and access control can limit the risk of unauthorized logon.
- Restrictive permissions can reduce the impact of user errors.
- Encryption and secure disposal of data minimizes its risk of exposure.
- User and other organizational policies can enforce good security practices that reduce risk.

Securing the software environment

Malware and other network attacks work by exploiting software vulnerabilities on the system. If you harden a workstation against those threats, you can then focus the rest of your efforts on more unpredictable human threats to security. That isn't to say you can just install security software and walk away: maintaining a hardened system requires regular monitoring and updates.

 Exam Objective(s): 220-1002 2.7.5

- Make sure that firewall software is installed and enabled.

- All modern versions of Windows include Windows Firewall, but some security software includes a third-party firewall which replaces it.

- Both malicious and legitimate software can configure or request firewall exceptions. Periodically examine the firewall's configuration to make sure there aren't any undesired openings.

- Install and configure anti-malware software including real-time anti-virus monitoring.

  - The version of Windows Defender included with Windows 8 and later has anti-virus scanning. The version included with Windows 7 and Windows Vista is a more limited anti-spyware application, so you'll need to install separate anti-virus software such as Microsoft Security Essentials or a third-party application.

  - If your organization requires or licenses a particular anti-virus product, use it. Otherwise, a large variety of commercial or free products are available. Many secure other applications as well, such as browsers and email clients, or perform additional security functions.

  - Configure the software to regularly download updates and run system scans. Modern anti-virus software vendors commonly release daily definitions updates to keep up with constantly changing threats.

  - Review scanning logs and quarantine notifications regularly to review detected threats.

  - While you should only run one real-time monitoring program, you can enhance security by installing a second anti-malware program for manual or scheduled scans.

- Regularly download and install operating system updates. By far, most updates are security patches designed to prevent known exploits.

  - To prevent falling behind, configure updates to install frequently and automatically. Be sure to restart the system to apply them.

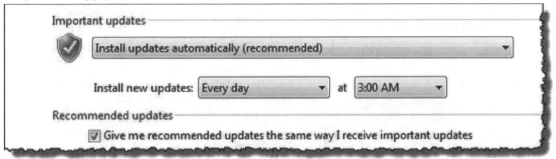

- If automatic updates aren't feasible, for example because some updates interfere with legacy software, review and perform manual updates on a frequent schedule.

- If the operating system is old enough to no longer receive security updates, consider an upgrade.

- Legacy and embedded systems that cannot be upgraded or replaced must be secured other ways, such as by increased monitoring, network isolation, or heightened physical security.

- Ensure that other applications are kept secure and up to date.

  - Web browsers and other software that access the network are especially at risk. This includes browser plugins and add-ons.

  - Enable automatic updates where possible.

  - For larger networks, use patch management software to centrally manage both application and operating system updates.

  - Configure application security settings to be as restrictive as possible without interfering with normal tasks.

- Control use of network servers and remote access programs.

  - On many workstations you can safely disable network servers and remote desktop connections, though you may want remote assistance features for technical support.

  - Restrict installation of third-party applications offering remote access.

  - Securely configure tools which are allowed. Ensure they have strong authentication, use encrypted protocol, and log access. You may also be able to limit screen sharing and file transfers.

- Ensure that only authorized applications are installed on the computer.

  - Your organization's policies might require or forbid certain applications on company workstations, or even personal computers connected to the enterprise network.

  - Even on home computers, make sure that applications come from trustworthy sources and have been scanned for malware.

  - Before installing an application, consider how it will affect overall system security, both on the host itself and the wider network,

  - Only run an application as an administrator if it's strictly necessary for compatibility reasons.

- Disable AutoRun or AutoPlay for removable media. In particular, executable files from removable media should never run automatically.

Disabling AutoPlay

When Windows detects a new drive or other removable storage device, the AutoPlay feature (called AutoRun in older Windows editions) automatically scans its content and takes or suggests actions based on the drive's content. For example, AutoRun might suggest running an installer on a CD, transferring photos from a camera, or watching video on a DVD.

Exam Objective(s): 220-1002 2.7.3

AutoPlay in Windows 7

This is all very convenient, but removable media can contain viruses or trojans that will infect your computer if you automatically run them. This was especially a problem in Windows XP and earlier when the feature was called AutoRun, and it was easy for an attacker to burn a disc that would automatically run malicious executable programs. AutoPlay, included with newer versions of Windows, prevents the worst problems, but it's still a potential vulnerability. Malware scanners might prevent this, but you can maximize security by disabling AutoRun or at least restricting it. You can disable AutoRun on the computer or domain level by using the Group Policy Editor or Regedit, but the simplest way to configure it for a given user is the AutoPlay Control Panel applet.

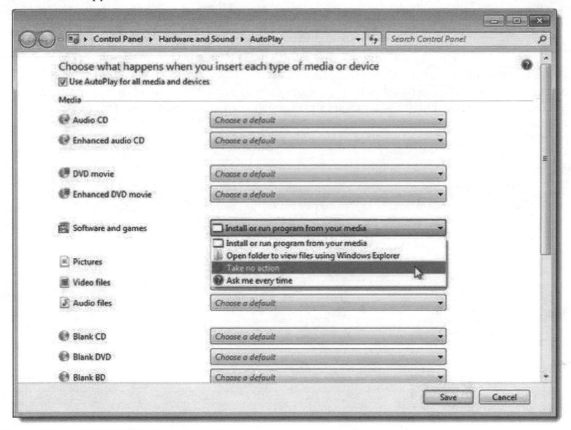

To configure AutoPlay in Windows 7:

1. In Control Panel, Click **Hardware and Sound > AutoPlay**.
2. Choose AutoPlay options.
   - Click the list next to a media type or device to select an AutoPlay default.
   - To disable AutoPlay entirely, clear **Use AutoPlay for all media and devices**.
   - Scroll to the bottom of the list to view installed devices such as cameras and smartphones.
3. When you're finished, click **Save**.

 Note: Even if you have malware scanners and have disabled AutoPlay or AutoRun, it's a bad idea to insert removable media you don't trust. Since burned discs or even flash drives are so cheap, it's not uncommon for attackers to just "lose" infected media somewhere a likely and curious target will pick it up.

Using account-based security

Hardening your workstation against outside attack is great, but if that's all you do it's easy for anyone else to walk up when you're away and access or change anything they like. It's even easy for you to accidentally install a program or change settings that compromise security without thinking about it. In the past, client operating systems such as older Windows versions had very little internal security: there might be only one user account without password protection, or all accounts would have full access to the system. Modern operating systems give you the tools to fix all of these, but only if you actually use them. In modern versions of Windows, you can follow these guidelines, but other operating systems have analogous features.

Exam Objective(s): 220-1002 2.7.1, 2.7.2.1, 2.7.2.4, 2.7.2.6

Account management in Windows 7

- Each user on a workstation should have a separate account.
    - If the workstation is a member of a domain, all domain users can log on using their own credentials.
    - If the workstation is not a member of a domain, each user will need a local account.
    - Windows 8 and newer allow you to add online Microsoft accounts that can be accessed from multiple devices.
- Each account should have appropriate user permissions.
    - Only administrative accounts should have administrative privileges. Even if a workstation has only one user, it's most secure to normally use a standard account, and only enter the credentials of the Administrator account when necessary.

- User Account Control settings can be adjusted to change when users have to manually confirm permission to change Windows settings.

- The optional Guest account has more limited access than a standard account, though it's not without security risks and should be disabled when not needed.

- Additional restrictions on accounts can be applied using domain or local security policies, or parental controls. One example is restricting valid logon times to work hours.

- Accounts should be protected by strong passwords or other authentication methods.

  - Default user names and passwords included with newly installed workstations or other devices should be changed to something unique. You can even rename the Administrator and Guest accounts built into each Windows computer.

  - Password-protected screensavers should be used to automatically lock the workstation whenever the user is away.

  - For extra security, workstations can be configured to lock accounts after a sufficient number of failed login attempts.

  - High security systems should use two-factor authentication requiring smart cards, one-time passwords, biometrics, or other factors as well as a conventional password.

  - BIOS or UEFI passwords can be set to restrict access to computer setup.

- Passwords should be easy for the user to remember, but hard for anyone else to guess or learn.

  - In general, longer passwords are stronger. So are passwords with multiple character types, such as lowercase, uppercase, numbers, and special characters.

  - Passwords consisting of dictionary words, names, or things people familiar with the user would guess are weaker than those with more random strings of characters.

  - Using the same password for multiple different accounts or systems means that someone who learns one can access them all.

  - A password should always be changed if there's reason to believe someone else has learned it.

  - Windows policies can be set either on the domain or local level to enforce minimum password requirements and require users to change them regularly.

Managing account settings in Control Panel

You can manage local account settings from the Control Panel. In Windows 7 and Windows 8, click **User Accounts and Family Safety > User Accounts**. From here, you can add and remove accounts, add or change passwords, configure User Access Control, and change account types.

In Windows 10, click **User Accounts > User Accounts**, for many of the same features, but other elements are found in Windows Settings, under **Accounts**.

Exam Objective(s): 220-1002 1.5.1.16, 1.6.3, 2.7.2.2, 2.7.2.3

User Accounts in Windows 7

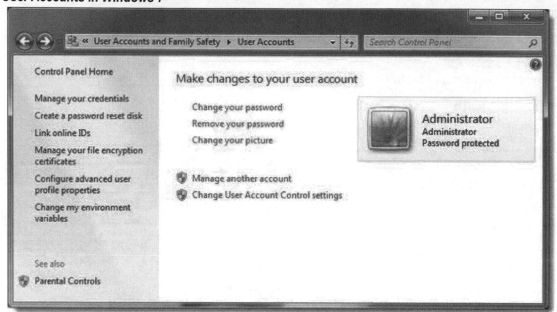

- By default, your own account will be displayed. To add or change your password, click **Add a password** or **Change your password**.

  - You must enter your old password before you can change it.

  - In Windows 7 and newer, you must enter a password hint.

  - Choose strong account passwords:

    - At least eight characters long

    - Does not contain any complete words

    - Does not resemble the user's real name, user name, or company name

    - Contains a mix of uppercase and lowercase letters along with numbers and special characters

    - Is easy enough to remember that the user won't try writing it down.

- Click **Change User Account Control settings** in order to adjust when Windows notifies you of changes.

User Account Control settings in Windows 7

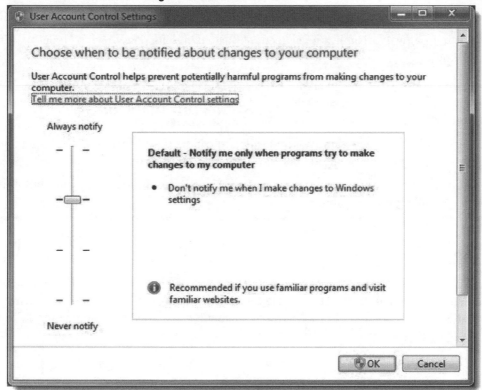

- The precise settings available depend on your Windows edition and whether you are logged in as a standard user or administrator.

- You should only reduce security from the default if it's necessary for compatibility with legacy applications.

- To add a new account, click **Manage another account > Create a new account**.

- To change settings for another account, click **Manage another account**, then click the account you want to manage.

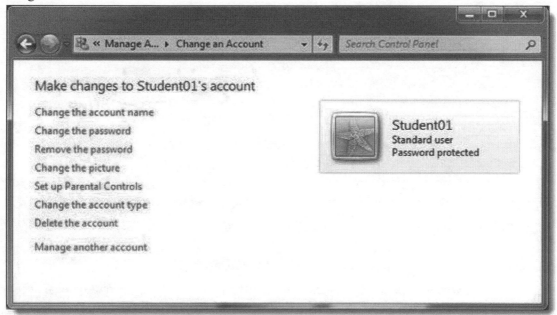

- You can change account names, passwords, and pictures just like your own.

- Click **Change the account type** to switch between standard and administrator accounts.

- Click **Delete the account** to remove it permanently.

   Note: To temporarily disable a local account, just change its password to something its owner doesn't know.

- Click **Set up Parental Controls** to add additional restrictions on an account. While this feature is intended primarily to restrict child accounts on family computers, in the workplace you can use it to restrict access after work hours or to block access to certain applications.

- The Guest account is disabled by default. While limited, it can be used by an attacker to gain additional access, so either leave it disabled or strictly configure its security options.

- The built-in Administrator account cannot be deleted or changed to a standard account, but it can be disabled if there's another administrator.

Managing accounts in Windows Settings

In the most recent feature updates for Windows 10, more account settings have been moved or added to Windows Settings rather than Control Panel. The precise options will be different depending on whether you have a local, domain, or Microsoft account. For a Microsoft account, some specifics include the following:

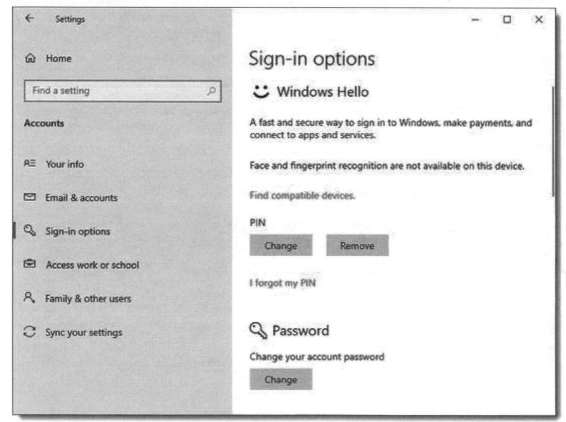

- Click **Family & other users** to add users on the computer.

  - Click **Add a family member** to add a Microsoft account for a family member. Family members can set parental controls and use shared calendar and Skype functions.

  - Click **Add someone else to this PC** to add non-family Microsoft accounts, or any local account.

  - Click **Assigned Access** to configure the computer as an interactive or non-interactive public kiosk.

- Click **Sign-in options** to set your sign-in options.

    - By default you will have an account password and a device-specific PIN.

    - Depending on your available hardware you might be able to use a photo, fingerprint scanner, or face recognition to log in.

    - The Dynamic lock feature will automatically lock the computer when your linked Bluetooth device, such as a phone, goes out of range of the PC.

- Click **Email & accounts** to manage accounts linked to the user, such as email, calendar, and Microsoft accounts.

- Click **Access work or school** to join a domain or connect to another enterprise network.

- Click **Sync your settings** to change how Windows settings are synchronized with other devices.

Managing stored credentials

Windows uses Credential Manager to store credentials you use to access other Windows computers and their shared resources, as well as certificates and passwords used by other network services. In Windows 8 and later, Credential Manager can also store website passwords.

 Exam Objective(s): 220-1002 1.6.9

Credential Manager in Windows 10

To access Credential Manager, either click **Manage your credentials** from your user account screen in Control Panel, or navigate directly to **User Accounts > Credential Manager**. You can only access credentials for your own account, even when you're an administrator.

- In Windows 8 and 10, click **Web Credentials** or **Windows Credentials** to switch between credential types.

- Click **Add** next to any credential category to input new credentials.
  - For most credentials you'll need an address, user name, and password.
  - To add a certificate-based credential, the certificate must already be saved in your personal store in Certificate Manager.
- To view details about a specific credential, expand it.
  - Click **Edit** to change its settings.
  - Click **Delete to remove it.**
- Click **Back up Credentials** to save stored credentials to a file.
  In Windows 7, click **Back up vault**.
- Click **Restore Credentials** or **Restore vault** to load saved credentials from a file.

Password-protecting screensavers

Unlike older CRT monitors, today's LCDs aren't harmed by showing the same image all the time. While the transition turned screensavers from valuable preventive maintenance to basically ornamentation, by configuring a workstation to lock itself whenever the screensaver becomes active you don't have to worry about someone walking away while still logged in. If you don't want the visual distraction, you can just set a blank screensaver, or configure power settings to turn off the screen quickly too.

Exam Objective(s): 220-1002 2.7.2.5

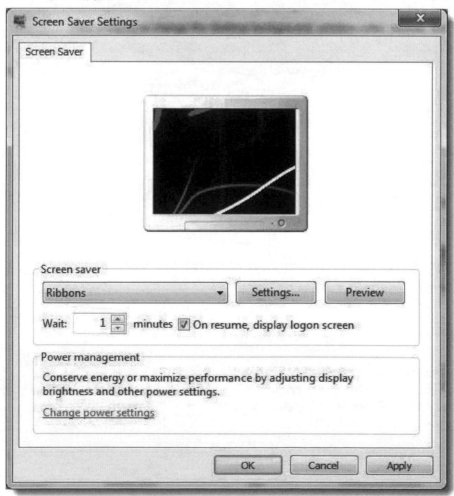

1. Open the Screen Saver Settings window.

   - In Windows 7, open Control Panel and click **Appearance and Personalization > Change screen saver**.

   - In Windows 10, open PC Settings and click **Personalization > Lock screen > Screen saver settings**.

   - In any Windows version, search for **Screen Saver** in Control Panel.

2. Choose a screensaver.

3. Select a time value in the Wait field.
   Shorter times are more secure, but can be annoying for users.

4. Check **On resume, display logon screen**.

5. Click **OK**.

Managing Users and Groups

You can create and manage local users and their group memberships from the in the **Local Users and Groups** snap-in in the **Computer Management** window. While this isn't intended for managing your own accounts like Control Panel or Windows Settings, when you're managing multiple users on the computer it gives you some options those do not.

 Exam Objective(s): 220-1002 1.5.1.3

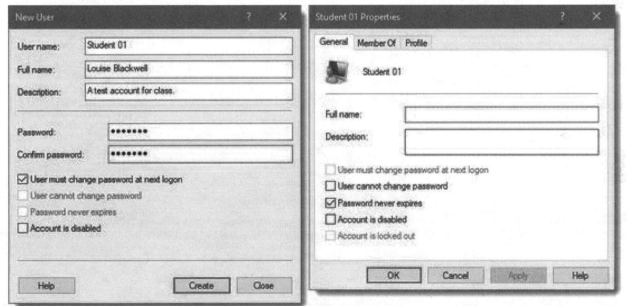

In Windows 10 Pro or Enterprise, open Computer Management and navigate to **System Tools > Local Users and Groups**.

- To create a new user, click the Users folder, then click **Action > New User**.

  - Check **User must change password at next logon** when you want users to have passwords which are private even from administrators. You must still assign a starter password they use for their first logon.

  - Check **Account is disabled** when you want to create an account but keep anyone from logging into it just yet.

- You can perform basic management of an account by right-clicking it to view a context menu.
  You can rename the account, delete it, or set a new password.

- To perform more detailed management of a user, double-click it to view the **Properties** window.

  - On the General tab you can set name and description, change password policies, and disable the account.

  - Click the Member Of tab to add or remove the user from groups.

  - Click the Profile tab to change the profile path or set a home folder.

- You can't create a Microsoft account from Local Users and Groups, but if it already exists you can still perform management tasks relevant to the local computer.

- To create and manage groups, click the **Groups** folder.

  - Create a group by clicking **Action > New Group**.

  - To change group membership, open it then click **Add** or **Remove**,

Managing Active Directory accounts

You can create and manage Active Directory objects in the **Active Directory Users and Computers** window. In Windows Server 2012, open Server Manager and click **Tools > Active Directory Users and Computers**. It's very similar to managing local users, but with additional options and commands.

Exam Objective(s): 220-1002 2.7.2.7

Creating new users or groups

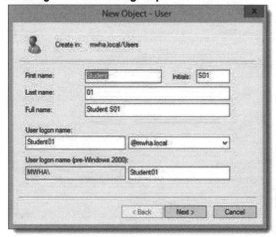
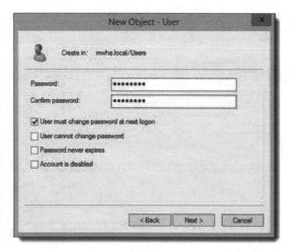

- To create a new user, click a container in a domain, then click **Action > New > User**.

  - The **New Object - User** has two screens. The first lets you set user name information, and the second lets you set a password and password-related options.

  - Check **User must change password at next logon** when you want users to have passwords which are private even from administrators. You must still assign a starter password they use for their first logon.

  - Check **Account is disabled** when you want to create an account but keep anyone from logging into it just yet.

- You can perform basic management of an account by right-clicking it to view a context menu.

  - Click **Disable Account** or **Enable account** to disable or enable user logon.

  - Click **Reset Password** to change a password that's been forgotten or compromised. You can also unlock the account if the user was locked out by too many failed logons. Just like when creating an account, you can require the user to change their password at their next logon.

- Click **Add to a group** if you want to add the account to a group and gain that group's permissions. This will not remove it from existing groups. For example, adding an account to the Domain Admins group will make it a domain administrator.

- Click **Delete** to permanently delete the account. If you're not certain you want to delete an account, it's safer to disable it.

- To perform more detailed management of a user, double-click it to view the **Properties** window.

  - You can set account details, user and contact information, remote access settings, and profile location.

  - On the Account tab, click **Logon Hours** to restrict when the user can log onto the network. You can use this to restrict users from logging in unobserved after business hours.

  - Click **Log On to** to restrict which computers the user is allowed to log onto.

  - Click the Profile tab to set a home folder on a network share.

Exercise: Securing the Windows environment

In this exercise you'll make some system configuration changes that reduce system vulnerability to malware and social engineering attacks.

Do This	How & Why
1. Disable AutoPlay.	While AutoPlay in Windows 10 is less of a vulnerability than in older versions, you'll still turn it off.
a) In Control Panel, click **Hardware and Sound > AutoPlay**.	To view AutoPlay options. You can set Autoplay defaults separately for multiple media types.
b) Next to any media type, click **Choose a default**.	Each media has its own options, but they might include opening File Explorer, importing photos, or doing nothing.
c) Next to Software and games, choose **Take no action** from the list.	The "Install or run program" option could lead to a malware infection.
d) At the top of the list, clear **Use AutoPlay for all media and devices**.	On second thought, you'll turn off AutoPlay entirely. Users who want to access external devices can navigate to them manually.

Choose what happens when you inse

☐ Use AutoPlay for all media and devices

e) Click **Save**.	
2. Enable a password-protected screen saver.	Locking the computer when you're away keeps someone from sneaking in and accessing it.
a) In Control Panel, search for Screen saver.	

Do This	How & Why
b) Click **Turn screen saver on or off** under Power Options.	The **Screen Saver Settings** window opens.
c) Choose any screen saver and wait time you like.	Choose 1 minute if you want to test the screensaver. Otherwise choose 5 or 10 minutes so it won't lock whenever you pause from work.
d) Check **On resume, display logon screen**.	Now whenever the screensaver activates, you'll need to enter your password,
e) Click **OK**.	
3. Examine account settings.	
a) In Control Panel, navigate to **User Accounts > User Accounts**.	To view settings related to your account. It should be a password-protected Administrator account.
	Chris Marshall chris.m███████████@gmail.com Administrator Password protected
b) Click **Manage your credentials > Windows Credentials**.	To view your saved credentials. You probably don't have any stored web credentials, but your stored Windows credentials include your Microsoft account. You can add new credentials, back your credentials up, or restore them from a backup.
c) Click **Back**.	
d) Click **Change your account type**.	You could make this account a standard account to enhance security. However, that would be a bad idea now since there aren't any other accounts on the computer.
4. Create a new local account.	
a) From the User Accounts screen, click **Manage another account**.	You'll have to click **Back** first. You can manage existing accounts in Control Panel, but starting in Windows 10 you can't create them here.
b) Click **Add a new user in PC settings**.	Settings opens, to the **Family & other users** section.
c) Click **Add someone else to this PC**.	By default, Windows prompts you to create a Microsoft account. You want to make a local one instead.
d) Click **I don't have this person's sign-in information > Add a user without a Microsoft account**,	You're prompted to enter a name and password.

Do This	How & Why

e) Enter a name and password.

Windows 10 requires you to set security questions for local accounts.

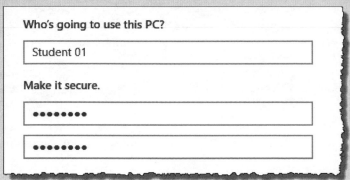

f) Choose three security questions and their appropriate answers.

These prevent you from being locked out of the account, since local passwords can't be reset from the network.

g) Click **Next**.

To create the account. It's not an administrator, so it only appears as "Local Account" in the list.

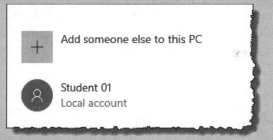

5. Examine Local Users and Groups.

Local Users and Groups gives a more streamlined interface for managing accounts, and is similar to the tools used to manage domain accounts in Active Directory.

a) Open Computer Management.

Click **Start > Windows Administrative Tools > Computer Management**.

b) Navigate to **Local Users and Groups > Users**.

In addition to your account and the one you just created, there are the default Administrator and Guest accounts, and a couple of system-managed accounts.

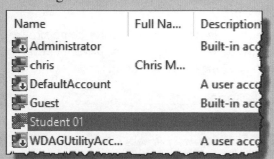

c) Double-click the **Guest** account.

You can view its general properties, group memberships, and profile settings. The Profile tab is another place you can add a logon script.

Do This	How & Why
d) Check **Account is disabled**.	The Guest account has limited permissions, but it's still a security risk.
e) Check **OK**.	
f) In the navigation pane, click **Groups**.	To view groups defined on your computer. You can open a group and add users or groups as members.
6. Close all open windows.	

If time allows, log in from your new local account. Try changing Windows settings, or using online features like the Microsoft Store and OneDrive.

Data security

System hardening and account protection are necessary to protect any workstation, but if systems are used to store sensitive data, it also needs to be protected. If the system contains certain types of data, like medical files or payment information, you might even be required by law or industry agreements to ensure that it's stored securely. Data stored on removable media is most at risk since it can be stolen by anyone with physical access, but even what's stored on the workstation itself needs to be kept safe both from intruders and legitimate users that don't have reason to access it.

The simplest way to protect data is by use of access permissions. Sensitive data shouldn't be stored on shared network folders unless it must be accessible over the network; if it must, the folder should be secured so that only intended users can access it. Locally used data should likewise be stored in folders only readable by users who need it. If data only needs to be accessed by its owner, that's simple: By default, each user's personal folders are readable only by that user, so private documents can be stored there.

Access permissions aren't very strong protection: anyone with administrative credentials can override them, as can anyone who physically steals the drive and installs it in a different computer. A safer solution is encrypting the data so that it's unreadable without the correct decryption key, such as a password or certificate. While no security method is perfect, data protected by strong encryption can be kept safe from all but the most determined attackers.

Note: Remember that losing data can be as bad as having it stolen. Part of secure data storage is keeping regular backups of important data, and keeping the backups themselves secure from threats.

Encryption tools

In the past, encryption had a reputation for being slow and cumbersome to use, and strong methods faced strict legal restrictions. These problems haven't entirely gone away, but there are many options for strong encryption today, some of which might already be installed on your workstation.

Exam Objective(s): 220-1002 2.6.8, 2.6.9, 2.6.10, 2.7.4

Since removable storage is at the greatest risk, some USB flash drives have built-in encryption. When you insert the drive, you can only access a read-only partition holding the encryption software: you need to supply the key in order to access the rest of the drive. Some include encryption hardware that improves performance and security.

When you're transporting files or storing them long-term, you might already compress them into archive formats like .zip or .rar. Most archive applications allow you to encrypt archive files with a password, but you need to be careful if you rely on them for security. Traditional .zip archives don't hide the names of files in the archive, and the content encryption is extremely weak by modern standards. Newer compression programs can create .zip files with AES encryption that's almost impossible to break with a strong password; alternate formats like .rar or .7z use AES and even allow you to hide file names.

For more flexible protection of data, especially if you also want to access it normally on your own computer, there are software applications that will seamlessly encrypt files and folders on your hard drive, or even encrypt entire drives and systems. Some even make use of hardware acceleration or key generation systems built into many computers, making it fast and more convenient. There are a variety of commercial solutions available, such as Sophos SafeGuard and Symantec Endpoint Protection; while the popular freeware TrueCrypt has been discontinued, other non-commercial options are available.

If you're lucky, your operating system might already include encryption support. There are two encryption systems included with some Windows editions.

EFS *Encrypting File System* allows encryption of individual drives and folders on any NTFS volume. It is included with Business/Professional/Enterprise/Ultimate editions of Windows, as well as all editions of Windows Server.

BitLocker Encrypts entire NTFS volumes, including the system drive. It is available on Enterprise and Ultimate Editions of Windows Vista and 7, Pro and Enterprise versions of Windows 8 and later, and all editions of Windows Server 2008 and later.

BitLocker-To-Go A BitLocker component used to protect removable drives, such as USB flash drives. It can encrypt drives formatted as FAT16, FAT32, and ExFAT as well as NTFS. It is included in Windows 7 and later systems which include BitLocker.

It's not a matter of which is better, and even if both are available, you'll find that they have different requirements and serve different purposes. Depending on your needs, you might prefer one or even use both together.

- EFS is intended for personal files and folders, while BitLocker protects entire drives with personal and system files alike.

- EFS-encrypted files are unreadable to other users on the same computer. All users on a BitLocker-encrypted system can access the full system, subject to normal user permissions. Bitlocker-To-Go drives can be accessed by whoever has the drive's password or smart card.

- Any user can independently encrypt files using EFS or encrypt a removable drive with Bitlocker-to-Go, while BitLocker must be enabled for the entire computer by an administrator.

- Each user account has a separate EFS key stored in its settings, and decryption operates transparently from that user's perspective. BitLocker uses a key for the entire system, which is stored either on a *Trusted Platform Module* (*TPM*) chip in the computer, or on a USB flash drive. For additional security, BitLocker can be configured to require a PIN, password, or smart card on system startup. BitLocker-To-Go uses a key for the individual drive, which may be password protected or stored on a smart card.

In modern versions of windows, both EFS and BitLocker use strong encryption, so if you lose the key your files might be gone forever. You can export both EFS and BitLocker keys for backup purposes, or assign them to data recovery agent accounts on a domain. In Windows 8 and later, BitLocker keys can also be stored on a Microsoft account for recovery.

Encrypting files and folders

You can encrypt personal files or folders from the **Advanced Attributes** window.

1. In Windows Explorer, right-click the file or folder and choose **Properties**.
2. Click **Advanced**.
3. In the **Advanced Attributes** window, check **Encrypt contents to secure data**.
4. Click **OK** twice.

    • If you encrypted a file, you'll be asked whether you want to encrypt the file alone, or its entire parent folder.

    • If you encrypted a folder, you'll be asked whether you want to encrypt the folder alone, or all of its subfolders and files.

5. Choose the option you want and click **OK**.

Encrypted file and folder names are green in Windows Explorer.

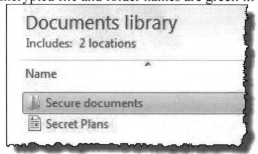

The first time you use EFS, you'll be prompted to back your key up. You can also back it up at any time by entering the **User Accounts** window and clicking **Manage your file encryption certificates**.

BitLocker

BitLocker is an entire volume encryption feature included with Windows Vista and Windows 7 Ultimate and Enterprise editions, and Windows 8 and higher Professional and Enterprise editions. Encrypting the entire volume protects all of the volume's data, including operating system files, the Windows registry, all temporary files, and the hibernation file, ensuring the integrity of the trusted boot path (BIOS, boot sector, etc.) and protecting against boot sector malware.

Exam Objective(s): 220-1002 1.6.17

To enable or configure BitLocker, navigate to **System and Security > BitLocker Drive Encryption** in the Control Panel.

By default, BitLocker uses a *Trusted Platform Module (TPM)*. TPM is a microchip installed on the motherboard of desktop and portable computers, which stores critical encryption keys in hardware inaccessible to the operating system or most attackers. If you don't have a TPM or don't want to use it, you can store the encryption keys on a USB flash drive. To do so, you must first configure BitLocker to work without a TPM using a group policy or script, and then you must insert that flash drive into the computer whenever you want to access the encrypted volume.

BitLocker can encrypt whatever NTFS volumes you like, including the system volume. However, it requires a smaller boot volume with at least 100MB of free space in order to perform the decryption routines which allow you to access the system drive.

There are three ways BitLocker can authenticate:

- *Transparent operation mode* allows the user to start up the computer and log into Windows as normal. BitLocker operates behind the scenes to verify that boot files have not been tampered with before releasing the encryption key and loading the operating system.

- *User authentication mode* prompts the user for a PIN or password on startup. When the password is entered, BitLocker releases the key and loads the operating system.

- *USB key mode* stores a startup key on a USB device. In order to boot, the key must be inserted, and the BIOS must be set to boot from USB.

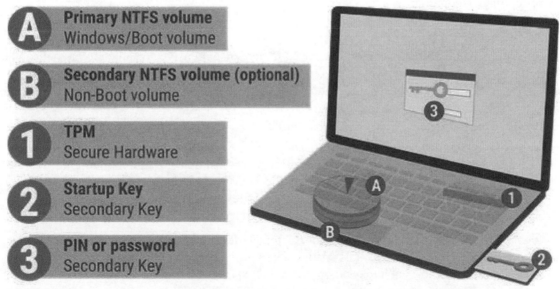

BitLocker can be configured to use a combination of the above modes. While you can store a single key in either TPM, USB, or password, you can also combine the TPM with a PIN, USB key, or both for extra security.

Note: BitLocker Drive Encryption is compatible with EFS. You can use BitLocker and EFS together to get the protection offered by both features

Secure media destruction

Data, and its storage media, can be most vulnerable when you throw it away. If data is worth securing in the first place, it has to be disposed of in a secure fashion as well. For the simplest example, imagine paper documents holding company secrets. If you just throw them away when you're done someone might literally dig them out of the trash and make off with them. Instead, you should make sure they're safely shredded. Thanks to modern scanning and image recognition technology, a conventional ribbon shredder isn't enough for highly sensitive documents. More secure solutions shred paper into confetti before either feeding it into an incinerator or a wet pulping process to leave nothing readable behind.

 Exam Objective(s): 220-1002 2.9.1

The same thing is true of digital media. Not only can valuable files remain on a discarded CD, flash drive, or hard drive, but the firmware on a computer, router, or other device might have system configuration or other data useful to an attacker. The surest way to ensure the data is destroyed is to destroy the media or device itself, and the best way to accomplish this depends on the media and your resources.

- Optical discs are rather fragile: not only can some consumer shredders destroy them, you can also cut them up with scissors, use something rough or sharp to scratch the upper metallic layer that stores data, or even put them in the microwave for a flashy, if potentially unsafe, show.

- Backup tapes can be thoroughly destroyed by tape shredders or incineration, though since some media releases toxic chemicals when burned the latter may be forbidden by local regulation.

- *Degaussers* use powerful electromagnets to destroy all data on magnetic media like tapes and hard drives, but not optical or flash storage. Some media can be easily reused after degaussing, but others, like most hard drives, require specialized tools to reformat

- Industrial shredders can destroy flash drives, hard drives, or even entire computers.

- Simple hammers and drills can easily destroy flash chips or hard drive platters. With hard drives, it's usually easier if you first open the drive cover with a Torx driver.

If you have a lot of media to destroy, it might require a lot of work or specialized equipment. An alternative is to hire a data destruction service: many offer on-site services and provide *certificate of destruction* documents for legal liability or regulatory compliance.

Securely erasing data

If your security needs aren't that extreme, you might not want to destroy expensive erasable media that can be repurposed, resold, donated, or otherwise recycled. In general, you can do this safely, but you need to use secure procedures to make sure the original data is genuinely inaccessible.

 Exam Objective(s): 220-1002 2.9.2

This isn't as easy as it sounds. Imagine you want to delete some private files from your hard drive before selling your computer to somewhat untrustworthy acquaintance. If you just delete them, they might go to the Recycle Bin where they're easily restored. Even if you empty the Recycle Bin, that only removes the file system's pointer to the data location: if it's not written over by new files, data recovery software could find and restore it. Even a quick drive reformat only replaces the file system, not the underlying data.

In the end, the only way to be really sure data is gone from a storage device is to make sure that every single bit of it is overwritten with new data, even if it's just writing a string of zeros. For additional security you can overwrite the same data multiple times, but it takes more time and experts are divided on how much benefit it gives.

- To securely delete files on an active computer, install a secure deletion program. Popular options include SDlelete, CCleaner, Eraser, and File Shredder. Some will also overwrite all free space on your hard drive, allowing you to ensure that previously deleted files are gone forever.

- To securely erase an entire hard drive, you'll need a formatting tool that overwrites the entire drive. For large drives, this can be a time-consuming process.

  - Most operating systems default to "quick formats" that don't actually delete existing data on the drive. If you use standard formatting tools make sure to perform a "full format" that rewrites the entire drive.

  - Some drive utilities from manufacturers or third-party vendors can perform a *low-level format* which writes zeroes to the entire drive and restores it to its newly installed configuration. Historically, a true low-level format also defined the tracks and blocks drives use to store data. On today's drives this isn't generally possible outside the factory, but the term is commonly used for anything that operates "below" the high-level format of the operating system.

  - Data destruction utilities can achieve the same result, and usually have other features oriented toward data disposal rather than drive diagnostics. Examples include DBAN, HDShredder, and KillDisk.

- In order to maximize the limited lifespan of flash memory, SSDs move data around as it's written and deleted. The details aren't important for most users, but an unfortunate side effect is that it makes it difficult to be sure any particular data is really gone. Some SSD manufacturers offer utilities for secure drive wiping.

- One benefit of using full disk encryption is that securely erasing just the drive's decryption key will quickly and effectively perform a secure wipe. The challenge is being certain that the key is not recoverable.

- Wiping or overwriting data can be a very lengthy process on large volumes, especially when policies or regulatory requirements specify multiple passes. It may be cheaper to destroy and replace a hard drive than it is to securely wipe and re-purpose it, once you account for time and labor.

Exercise: Enabling BitLocker

On a computer with a TPM it's easy to enable BitLocker from the Control Panel. If you don't have one, you'll need to configure it in Local Group Policy Editor, and store the key on a removable drive.

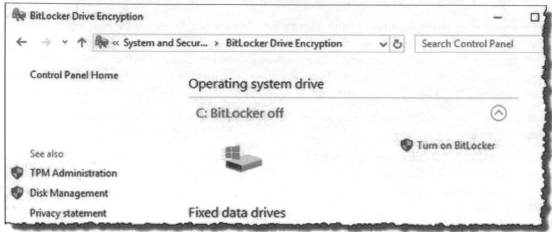

Do This	How & Why
1. Search for `gpedit` and click **Edit group policy**.	The Local Group Policy Editor window opens.
2. Configure BitLocker to operate without a TPM.	You'll enable boot using a password.

a) In the Navigation Pane, navigate to **Computer Configuration > Administrative Templates > Windows Components > BitLocker Drive Encryption > Operating System Drives**.

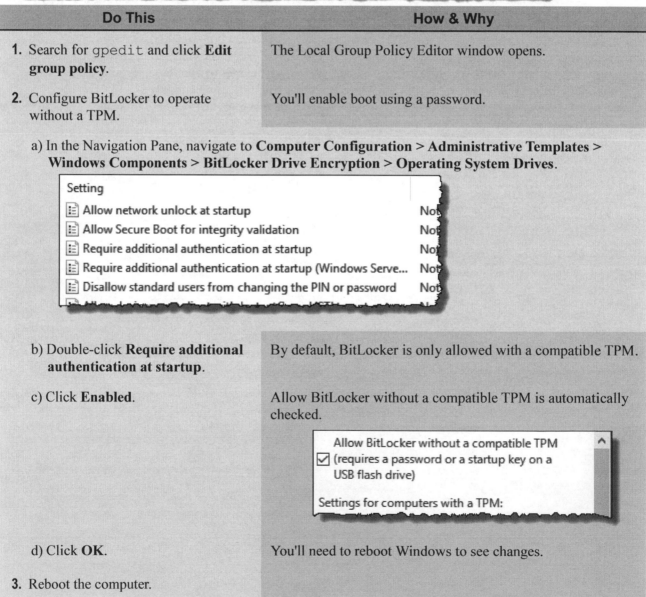

b) Double-click **Require additional authentication at startup**.	By default, BitLocker is only allowed with a compatible TPM.
c) Click **Enabled**.	Allow BitLocker without a compatible TPM is automatically checked.
d) Click **OK**.	You'll need to reboot Windows to see changes.

3. Reboot the computer.

Do This	How & Why
4. Configure BitLocker. a) In Control Panel, navigate to **System and Security > BitLocker Drive Encryption**.	
b) Click **Turn On BitLocker**.	Windows tests to see if your system is compatible with BitLocker. After a little while, the **BitLocker Drive Encryption** window appears.
c) Click **Enter a password**, then type a password in both fields.	It doesn't need to be that strong since you aren't securing your real system.
d) Click **Next**.	The next screen asks you how you would like to store your recovery key.
e) If you have an external drive or network share available, save the file there.	You can't save it on an internal disk.
f) Continue through the wizard by clicking **Next** three times and reading each screen.	You can choose what data to encrypt and what encryption modes to use.
g) When asked if you're ready to encrypt this drive, click **Cancel**, then **Yes**.	You won't really take the time to encrypt your system drive.
5. Open the recovery file you created earlier.	It contains an identifier and recovery key. You can use it to unlock the drive if you lose your password or encryption key.
6. Close all open windows.	

Assessment: Workstation security

1. By default, AutoPlay and AutoRun only run media files, not executables, and so aren't a real security risk. True or false?

   • True

   • False

2. In general, you should leave the Guest account in Windows disabled. True or false?

   • True

   • False

3. Which are characteristics of EFS? Choose all that apply.

- Encrypts entire drives, including removable drives.

- Encrypts files based on user account, which provides security for an individual's files on a multiuser computer.

- Requires administrative-level privileges to turn encryption on and off.

- Doesn't require any special hardware.

4. Which Windows encryption feature can you use to encrypt files on your USB drive? Choose the best response.

- BitLocker

- BitLocker-To-Go

- EFS

5. When you enforce password complexity in Windows, you can't edit the precise complexity requirements True or false?

- True

- False

6. Low account lockout thresholds are _____. Choose the best response.

- Less secure, and less trouble for users

- Less secure, but more trouble for users

- More secure, but less trouble for users

- More secure and more trouble for users

7. Your organization has a degausser in the basement. What media can you use it to securely destroy? Choose all that apply.

- Backup tapes

- CDs and DVDs

- Hard drives

- Paper documents

- SSDs

8. A full Windows format of a hard drive will securely remove sensitive files. True or false?

- True

- False

Module B: Mobile device security

Even if modern mobile devices are full-featured computers in their own right and face the same kinds of threats as workstations, the actual risk posed by a given threat might be very different. Mobile operating systems are pretty hardened out of the box, so the risk of malware and network attacks is greatly reduced if not quite eliminated. On the other hand, compared to a desktop a smartphone or tablet is incredibly likely to be lost or stolen. This is one reason it's even more important to use backup functions or cloud storage on a device storing important data. It's also why mobile devices have many operating system functions, hardware features, and software applications designed to make devices and their contents useless to a thief or nosy discoverer.

You will learn:

Mobile authentication

There are a lot of dilemmas involved when designing a mobile operating system, even once you're used to a workstation OS, and a number of them are related to security. One of the big ones is that it's far easier to set a phone or tablet where strangers can try to get access, or just walk off with it to guess passwords at their leisure. At the same time, while you might log on to your workstation for hours at a time, you probably often use your phone for just a moment while hurrying through your day, so making it difficult to access undermines a lot of its advantages. On top of that, while most mobile devices are only regularly used by a single person so aren't configured with multiple user accounts, now and then you might want to let someone borrow yours for a bit even if you don't trust them to go sifting through everything you have on it.

Exam Objective(s): 220-1002 2.8.11

Mobile operating systems, and to some extent laptops running workstation operating systems, use a combination of operating system features and third-party apps to address these problems. First, mobile operating systems by default quickly activate a *screen lock* on idle devices. In principle it's just like a password-protected screensaver, but in addition to passwords lock screen can also be secured by PINs or patterns easier to enter without a keyboard. Alternatively, the device can have a biometric scanner allowing a fingerprint or even the user's face to unlock it. To allow temporary access for users, you could lock the device while allowing access to a single app, or mark specific apps as requiring special authentication.

The challenges of mobile authentication shouldn't be confused with the separate and opposite trend of mobile devices themselves being used as authentication factors, typically as part of a multi-factor authentication system. Effectively, a particular device becomes a possession factor, proving identity by something you own. An example is an *authenticator application* which securely generates one-time passcodes, such as Google Authenticator or Microsoft Authenticator. Mobile payment apps such as Apple Pay or Google Pay are also authenticator apps, but instead of generating passcodes they allow the device to function like a contactless payment card Mobile authentication might not even need an app: some web authentication systems ask for a password, and additionally send a numeric passcode to the user's phone via SMS or internet.

Screen lock options

Every mobile operating system includes screen lock features. Windows tablets simply use the same lock screens workstations do. With iOS the exact options available will depend on your OS version and the model of your device. With Android, you also can download third party apps, and your device manufacturer might have installed custom software already. On a modern device, several options might be available. Multiple methods might even be used as part of a multifactor authentication system.

Exam Objective(s): 220-1002 2.8.1, 2.8.5, 2.8.8, 2.8.10

Swipe screen	Swipe a finger across the screen, or a certain part of the screen, to unlock. This doesn't offer any security against intrusion at all: at best, it prevents accidental input.
Password	A strong password provides very strong authentication, but it's more trouble to enter on a touchscreen keyboard than a physical one, especially if it includes mixed cases and special characters.
Passcode/PIN	Unlock the device with a numeric passcode. Not as strong as a password, but easier to enter, and even a four-digit PIN allows for 10,000 combinations.
Pattern	Unlock the device by drawing a predefined pattern over points on the screen. This can be easier than a passcode, but choosing a pattern that's both easy to enter and hard to guess might be challenging.
Fingerprint	A biometric device with a fingerprint scanner isn't entirely foolproof—it's not just spy movie stuff for a clever hacker make a "fake finger" from some glue and an existing fingerprint smudge on the screen. That said, it's strong protection against most intruders.
Face	Uses the device camera and face recognition software. Can potentially be fooled by using a photo, but newer versions add additional measures like requiring the user to blink. Cameras with infrared (IR) sensitivity are especially effective for facial recognition under varying light conditions.

Some screen locks have additional security features. Commonly, too many failed attempts will temporarily lock the phone entirely in order to prevent brute force hacking—you'll have to wait anywhere from thirty seconds to an hour to try again. In iOS, and some Android apps, you can even configure the device to permanently erase all data after sufficient (usually ten) failed attempts. This can be very potent protection for important data, but it makes it easy for a child or mischievous adult to wipe the whole device. Another feature is a little more subtle: By configuring the camera on the front of the device to take a photo of anyone entering a wrong code, you can see who it was later.

Many people don't use strong, or often any, security on mobile devices because it's a pain to unlock. As one way around this, some devices let you add widgets to the lock screen that show commonly accessed data. For example, you could check the time and weather on your phone without unlocking it. Others allow shortcuts to functions that can be used without unlocking, like taking photos or making phone calls. Some of these options can compromise security so should be used with care.

Configuring screen locks in iOS

In iOS 9, you can change passcode and screen lock settings by navigating to **Settings > Passcode**. If your device has a fingerprint sensor, it will appear as **Settings > Touch ID & Passcode**

- To add a passcode, tap **Turn Passcode On**.
  - By default, passcodes are six digits.
  - Tap **Passcode Options** to select a longer, shorter, or alphanumeric passcode.
- To change a passcode, click **Change Passcode**. You'll have to enter the old one.
- By default, you need to enter a passcode to unlock the screen even if you've just locked it. If you want to set a delay before the code is required, tap **Require Passcode**.
- Use sliders to enable certain functions when the phone is locked, such as voice dialing, Today, Notifications View, and Siri.
- Activate **Erase Data** to erase the device automatically after ten failed attempts.

Configuring screen locks in Android

Since Android devices are less unified and more customizable than iOS, screen lock procedures and options vary. While the feature comes with the operating system, it can be changed or replaced by device manufacturers or third-party apps. Additionally, it varies by OS version.

For example, in Android 5.1, you can access screen lock options from **Settings > Lock Screen**.

- To choose a screen lock, click **Screen Lock** and choose a lock type.

- To change a screen lock, click **Screen Lock** and choose a lock type. You'll need to enter your existing credentials.

- Biometric locks might require additional setup. For example, before using fingerprint verification, click **Settings > Fingerprint.** to register your fingerprint and set a backup password.

- Enable **Phone shortcut** or **Camera shortcut** to make those features available without unlocking.

- Tap **Additional information** for widgets you can display on the lock screen.

Mobile data protection

On its own, even a strong lock screen shouldn't be seen as real protection for a device or its data: any system is much easier to break into when the thief can take it home and work on it at leisure. Simple passcodes can be eventually broken, and thieves are always compiling or researching security vulnerabilities. SD cards can be removed and accessed in other devices; while accessing internal memory on a mobile device is harder than taking the hard drive out of a workstation, it's not impossible either. If you really want your device and its data to remain secure, you'll want to do more than set a passcode.

Exam Objective(s): 220-1002 2.8.2, 2.8.3, 2.8.4, 2.8.9

The best option is to recover the device itself, especially if it's just lost rather than stolen. As long as the software's set up ahead of time, Apple's Find my iPhone and Google's Android Device Manager both allow you to use networking and location features to find where a device was last located from any web browser. If it's on and connected to the network, you can also remotely lock it, wipe its data, or, if you might have just left it in your other coat, make it ring remotely.

Even if you can't recover the device, you can recover data using remote backup applications. On an iOS device, you can configure a daily backup of data to via the iCloud service. Android includes automatic cloud backup of contacts, calendars, and mail, but more complete solutions are available as apps. Some of these features can even be used to track a phone too, for example if a thief turned the device on long enough that it backed itself up.

To make sure the data is safe from attackers, most modern devices allow full device encryption to protect all stored data and even that on SD cards. By using a key which is built into the device and cannot be extracted, full device encryption can protect all data on the device with strong encryption. All iOS devices running version 8 or newer have encryption enabled by default, so as long as you use a strong passcode the data is protected. By contrast, almost all Android devices support encryption, but few have it enabled by default so you'll need to set it up in **Settings > Security**.

Remember, all of these methods need to be configured before the device is lost: if you wait, there's not much you can do.

Hardening mobile operating systems

Compared to their desktop counterparts, especially in the past, mobile operating systems are fairly well hardened. By default, user accounts don't have root access, and apps run in *sandboxes* fairly separated from each other, each with its own well-defined permissions. On top of that, most people get apps from trusted sources like the Apple, Google, or Amazon app stores, all of which carefully monitor products for any sign of malware. Finally, on the network mobile devices are less likely to run network server applications or old insecure protocols than even desktop workstations: this means they're not subject to network attacks exploiting server processes.

Exam Objective(s): 220-1002 2.8.6, 2.8.7, 2.8.12, 2.8.13

None of this is to say that you shouldn't actively secure a mobile operating system, especially in a high security environment. It's just that the newest smartphone is going to be a lot safer to just put on the network than an old Windows XP desktop.

- Apply security patches and updates as soon as they're available.
  - Android manufacturers commonly push updates to owners when they're released, but you can manually check by tapping **Settings > System Updates**.
  - To manually update an iOS device, tap **Settings > General > Software Update**.
  - OS updates can be large, so perform them over Wi-Fi to avoid data charges.
  - Mobile updates are usually quick and painless, but it's safest to back up data beforehand in case something goes wrong.
- Apps typically update automatically whenever a new version comes out. Updates might include boosted security features.
  - By default, apps only update on Wi-Fi to save data charges.
  - When a new app version requires additional permissions, you'll need to approve the update. Review changes to make sure they're permissions you really want the app to have.
- Consider the need for antivirus software.
  - Despite some malware being discovered in the past, Apple considers iOS secure enough that vulnerabilities can be fixed through OS updates alone. Consequently, they don't allow antivirus software on their app store.
  - Some Android vendors pre-install antivirus software, and others are available on Android app stores. Note that the sandboxed nature of apps makes Android antivirus apps less able to actually remove potential malware than desktop antivirus.

- Be careful not to install apps from untrusted sources, like poorly verified third-party app stores or private developers.
  - iOS by default only allows installation from Apple's App store. Getting around that usually requires jailbreaking the phone, specifically permitting an app, or running an "app" that's really just a website.
  - Android allows apps from third-party stores without much trouble, which is convenient but a potential security risk. To ensure that only apps from trusted sources can run, tap **Settings > Security**, and clear **Unknown Sources**.
- Firewalls beyond built-in OS features are not generally necessary on mobile devices, but third-party apps are available for Android. Some require rooting the phone, but others do not.
- Be careful when joining unfamiliar or unsecured Wi-Fi networks: they could allow others to spy on your communications. For regular communications over unsecured Wi-Fi, consider configuring a VPN.

Mobile device policies

To maintain a secure IT organization, it's important to apply a consistent security policy to all devices on the premises, on the network, or otherwise coming into contact with sensitive information. In the old days this was easy: employee workstations and the occasional laptop were all owned by the company and could be controlled as strictly as desired. The popularity of mobile devices doesn't make this strictly impossible— secure facilities might ban private devices from the premises or at least from accessing company resources— but it's no longer the normal assumption.

Exam Objective(s): 220-1002 2.8.14

Some organizations today actively encourage *bring your own device* (*BYOD*) policies, in the idea that letting employees use their personal devices freely for work both saves money and increases morale. Others fall in between: they might have a mixed environment of personal and corporate mobile devices, or they might subsidize employee-owned devices that are used for work. Even when devices are strictly corporate owned, it may or may not be permitted for employees to use the same device for personal purposes. Allowing devices which are used both for work and personal tasks poses several challenges both for keeping the organization secure and to avoid conflict between employees and management. Mobile device policies might include the following:

Permitted devices	Required features, operating systems, or models for a device to be allowed under the policy.
Support	Who supports which aspects of device functions. IT may not have the time or training to support everything that can go wrong on a wide range of user devices.
App and data ownership	Policies should clearly specify what apps and data are company property, for example work email messages and corporate documents. Mobile *containerization* technologies can even allow part of an employee-owned device's memory and storage to be securely set aside for corporate purposes, or vice-versa.
Privacy	Employees should expect some privacy with personal activities and data on their own devices, but at the same time it might be limited during work hours or on company networks. The policy should spell out employee privacy expectations.
Network access	Some workplaces may choose to limit personal devices to limited access or guest networks. This can limit their usefulness, but makes it easier to secure them.
Onboarding and offboarding	There should be a set process for how an employee needs to prepare a device to join the program, and another for what happens when an employee leaves or just stops using a particular device for work. Offboarding should also address what happens with devices subsidized by the company.

Profile security requirements

Regardless of who owns the mobile devices employees are using, you need to ensure that they all are consistently secured. Useful policies to standardize include:

- Passcode requirements
- Device encryption and other security settings
- Certificate distribution
- Backup policies
- Update policies
- Required or forbidden apps
- Physical security procedures
- Acceptable use

Exam Objective(s): 220-1002 2.2.3

Especially in a large organization, it's easiest if you can centrally administer devices in order to assign device permissions, verify security compliance, apply updates, or even monitor activity. Software designed for these tasks is called *Mobile Device Management* (*MDM*) and encompasses a wide variety of features. Some MDM solutions are primarily designed to configure multiple devices remotely, while others primarily manage permissions granted to different devices on the corporate network.

Enterprise MDM software typically operates using security profiles, typically text-based files encoded in XML format. A given profile might apply to a specific category of user, or role of device; it can include security settings, apps, network access permissions, and anything else needed to configure the device to the profile's needs. A given device might have multiple profiles applied—sometimes this means having to resolve conflicts between them. As you might imagine, BYOD devices are likely to have different profiles assigned than corporate-owned ones.

Discussion: Securing mobile devices

1. What locking method do you use on your mobile device?

2. How is your mobile data backed up?

3. What anti-theft measures do you have installed, such as tracking or encryption?

4. What policies does your organization have regarding use of mobile devices?

Exercise: Securing a mobile device

Mobile devices are small and easily stolen or left behind. It's critical that the data these devices contain do not fall into the wrong hands. If you have a mobile device such as a smartphone or tablet, view its security features.

Do This	How & Why
1. Configure one or more screen lock options. If you try more than one, compare their security and ease of use.	
2. Verify that the system is up to date.	
3. Log into your associated online account to make sure you can find your device's physical location.	
4. Examine data protection settings such as device encryption, remote wipe, and advanced locking features.	

Assessment: Mobile device security

1. What mobile operating system includes pattern lock in a default installation? Choose the best answer.

    *   Android
    *   iOS
    *   Windows Phone
    *   All three

2. Both iOS and Android include a built-in feature to find and secure a lost device. True or false?

    *   True
    *   False

3. Both iOS and Android enable data encryption on most devices by default. True or false?

    *   True
    *   False

4. What are important security steps on all mobile devices? Choose all that apply.

    *   Configuring antivirus software
    *   Configuring remote backup features
    *   Installing a firewall app
    *   Regularly applying operating system updates
    *   Using biometric authentication

5. What kind of policy governs a user-owned device on the corporate network? Choose the best response.

    *   Acceptable Use
    *   BYOD
    *   MDM
    *   Offboarding

6. What kind of policy governs removal of sensitive data and credentials when a user device is no longer used for company business?

    *   Asset tracking
    *   Offboarding
    *   Onboarding
    *   Storage segmentation

Module C: Network security

All security is protecting against attacks and misuse. On an isolated system that's complicated enough, between threats like physical threats, unauthorized users, and damaging malware. The network doesn't just add a powerful new vector for attacks, but it means there are more devices that need protecting. Securing a SOHO network usually isn't as daunting as a larger one, but you still have to use tools, and modes of thinking, that aren't necessary for securing an individual host.

You will learn:

- About defense in depth
- How to secure network hosts
- How to secure network infrastructure
- How to secure wireless networks

Defense in depth

Some early network experts saw security as a "hard shell" to put around the network, defending it from outside attacks without disrupting normal internal operations. It didn't work very well: not only are many threats on the inside, but any crack in that outer shell makes it easy for an external threat to become an internal one. Today, network experts recommend a defense in depth strategy, where security is applied throughout the network and the entire organization. That way, an attacker who breaches one layer of defense still has to overcome the rest.

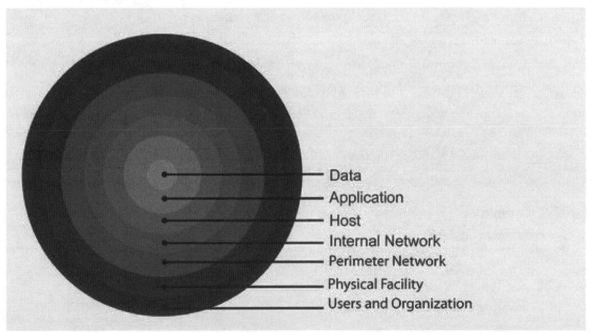

- Data
- Application
- Host
- Internal Network
- Perimeter Network
- Physical Facility
- Users and Organization

Don't take the diagram too literally when you think about security plans: it's not a video game where an attacker has to fight through each room in sequence to get the treasure, it's just an effort to make sure that no one flaw will compromise everything. That's not easy. The data attackers are ultimately after may "live" on servers but it's also flowing through wires, carried on users' personal devices, and literally flying through the air. Likewise, an attacker who gains too much physical access or employee trust can use them to bypass many other security methods.

Also remember that security risks aren't just about theft of data, but about attacks or other incidents that will disrupt network functions. On every level, you need to identify *critical assets*: the ones that can't be easily replaced, or which will immediately disrupt organizational functions if they're compromised. For the network especially, this often means the *critical nodes* the network needs to function, like essential servers or backbone routers. When possible, you should consider redundant systems for any critical assets, so that an accidental or deliberate outage won't disrupt business functions for long.

Exactly how far you need to take security precautions on any of these levels depends on the precise needs of your network. A lot of security measures are meant for highly secure networks facing extreme risks, or for large and complex networks. Others are good practice even if you just need to secure a few workstations and the router that connects them to the internet.

Securing network hosts

Even with computers not attached to the network you should secure data, applications, and the operating system itself against attackers or malware. If you're doing that, you're on a good start to securing network hosts as well, though on the network the risk of attack is higher and more varied.

Exam Objective(s): 220-1002 2.10.5, 2.10.7, 2.10.8

- Make sure the system has a firewall installed and configured.
- Close unnecessary network services and ports.
- Configure network applications to be as secure as possible without interfering with normal functions.
  - When possible, choose applications and protocols with strong authentication and encryption features.
  - Use high browser security settings.
  - When appropriate, install content filtering or parental control software on the host or network which will restrict access to malware sites and vectors.
  - Don't enable remote desktop connections unless you frequently need to use them.
- Don't install software from the Internet unless it's known and verified to be safe.
  - Restrict user permissions to prevent unauthorized software installation.
  - Ensure that downloaded software comes from a trusted source.
  - Scan installer files with antivirus software before running them.
  - Use similar caution with email attachments, even those which at first appear to be document rather than executable files.
- Make sure that network shares are properly secured, especially those holding sensitive data.

Securing network devices

On a SOHO network you're not likely to have a number of security zones and subnets, but you still need to secure network devices, and to understand how secure and trusted a given part of the network is.

Exam Objective(s): 220-1002 2.10.2, 2.10.3, 2.10.4, 2.10.6, 2.10.9, 2.10.10

- Harden network devices like switches, routers and firewalls in much the same way as hosts, by keeping them up to date and disabling unnecessary services.
- Change default user names and passwords for device administration.
- Disable remote management of routers and other network devices from the internet if possible. If you must, make sure you're using strong passwords and secure protocols.
- Install network-based security systems. At the minimum, configure network firewall settings on your router; you might also consider content filtering, network-based antimalware or IDS/IPS, or even a UTM solution.

- Configure port forwarding and triggering rules only where needed for necessary services. Disable UPnP if you don't use it.
- Consider restricting client connections to the network by enabling MAC filtering or configuring static IP addresses.
- If certain hosts or servers require less restrictive internet access permissions, consider putting them on a perimeter network outside the trusted part of the LAN rather than loosening security to the rest of the network.
- Secure physical access to network devices and ports: it's much easier to compromise any system with direct access to the hardware.
- Watch for unauthorized network devices or services on the network.

Securing wireless networks

Wireless networks have additional security measurements. While enabling strong Wi-Fi encryption is a good start, there's a number of other steps you can take. Note that most of these won't greatly enhance security on their own, especially against determined attackers: they're more designed to add more discouragements from casual intrusion into your network.

Exam Objective(s): 220-1002 2.10.1

- Change the default SSID, but avoid names that hint at your network's nature or contents.
- On private networks, disable SSID broadcast.
- Disable WPS if possible.
- Enable MAC filtering for client authentication.
- Consider using WPA Enterprise authentication for more flexible security settings.
- If the router supports a separate guest network, make sure it's isolated from the private network and uses a different password.
- Place the access point not only to maximize coverage in the desired area, but to minimize coverage in undesired or insecure areas. If your Wi-Fi isn't available on the street, people on the street can't try to hack into it.
  - Use a Wi-Fi analyzer to check coverage areas.
  - Reduce radio broadcast power if your coverage area is much larger than it needs to be.
  - Place access points in physically secure locations, but be mindful of their effects on coverage. A metal cabinet or locked electrical closet might hurt signal strength.
- Scan periodically for rogue access points connected to your wired network. Even if they're not malicious in nature, they can introduce security vulnerabilities.

Discussion: Network security

1. Why is it so important to specifically restrict software that's run from the internet?

2. Describe the steps you'd take to make sure a computer on your home network was properly secure.

3. How would you tighten security on your work network?

4. Why won't measures like MAC filtering and disabling SSID significantly increase network security?

5. What examples have you seen of serious security incidents that resulted in part from not using defense in depth policies?

Assessment: Network security

1. Defense in depth is a good idea for any network, but not all layers are equally important on every network. True or false?

   - True

   - False

2. You've set a Wi-Fi password, but you'd like some extra protection against unauthorized clients connecting to the network. What feature should you enable? Choose the best response.

   - Content filtering

   - DHCP server

   - MAC filtering

   - Port forwarding

3. You've just installed a router fresh out of the box. Which configuration changes should you make to improve its default security? Choose all that apply.

   - Change the default user name and password

   - Close unnecessary ports and services

   - Configure QoS

   - Disable remote administration

   - Enable UPnP

4. Your WAP uses WPA2-AES and WPS. SSID is disabled. Which change should you make to increase security? Choose the best answer.

   - Disable WPA

   - Disable WPS

   - Enable SSID

   - Enable TKIP

Module D: Security troubleshooting

The first sign of a security failure can be anything from a missing computer to a nearly invisible sign of intrusion tucked away in a system log. While you and network administrators should be on the lookout for all of them, as a network technician the most common security problem you'll have to troubleshoot is malware on user workstations. Malware itself can be painfully obvious, but it even more often can be easily mistaken for general performance and reliability problems. What this means is that you need to be ready to expect malware whenever you troubleshoot a system.

You will learn:

- How to recognize malware infections

- About malware detection and removal tools

- How to safely remove malware

Common malware symptoms

When you're troubleshooting a system, either because of a user complaint or because you notice something odd yourself, there are a variety of issues that should make you immediately think of malware. For other symptoms, malware is one of multiple possible causes, but you still need to keep it in mind. Sometimes even if a symptom isn't caused malware it still might reflect a security related issue such as unauthorized access, inappropriate user activity, or configuration errors.

Exam Objective(s): 220-1002 3.2.1

File alteration	Any unexpected alteration to files can be indicative of malware. They might be renamed or deleted suddenly, or vanish gradually over time. Changes in file permissions, either removing restrictions or sudden access denied errors, are also potential signs of infection. Deleted or renamed system files in particular can cause the system to become unstable or even unusable.
Unfamiliar programs	Programs that shouldn't be installed can indicate malware, either because they were installed by existing malware or because a user carelessly installed a compromised application. Especially dangerous are unfamiliar antivirus or other security applications: these are commonly *rogue antivirus* malware that fakes system problems or virus detection in order to make you buy paid security scanners or further compromise the system.
Security alerts	If your antivirus scanner occasionally detects and quarantines threats you should review the log to see what they were. Frequent alerts could represent network vulnerabilities, or some other, undetected malware that's opened a backdoor into the system. Security alerts are also another sign of a rogue antivirus program, since some of them very closely resemble legitimate software or even Windows functions. Make sure it's the right security application before taking action.
Log errors	You should review system and application logs periodically or whenever things seem to be behaving strangely, using Event Viewer or other tools. Frequent errors or unusual events might be a symptom of malware, but could also be caused by corrupted files, improperly configured applications, or other system problems.

Browser oddities Malware frequently attacks or affects web browsers. This might manifest as something as simple as excessive or unusual pop-up ads, or new toolbars and add-ons in the browser. Your default search engine might be changed, or worse, search requests redirected to new and unfamiliar websites. Familiar-seeming websites showing certificate errors are another possible sign of browser or network tampering—at the least, they mean you shouldn't hang around the site. Certificate errors in any application are a potential sign of security problems, in fact, though they can be caused by innocent mistakes like an improper system clock or misconfigured server.

A certificate error in Internet Explorer

Email issues Receiving excessive spam isn't necessarily a sign of malware, but it can increase the risk of contracting it: consider client protection and spam filtering if it's a problem. On the other hand, malware can hijack an infected system's email and use it to *send* spam. Stolen email account credentials can also be used by malicious users to spy on activities, commit fraud, or make other attacks. Signs of hijacked email include unfamiliar messages in sent mail folders, reports from email contacts of unusual messages such as spam or malware, or automated responses to messages the user never sent.

Stability and performance Malware can cause all sorts of problems with overall system performance: application crashes, operating system lockups or reboots, network connectivity problems, or just performance slowdown. When a computer "just isn't working right" but there's no clear cause, be sure to look for malware.

Failed updates To prevent detection or removal, malware will frequently disable tools that can fight it. Operating system updates can fail, or refuse to launch. Antivirus or other security applications might be disabled or stop updating. Browsers can block access to security-related websites.

Malware removal tools

Removing malware safely and completely can be challenging, enough that some organizations don't even take the risk—if a computer is infected it's wiped and restored from a clean image. You still can use that approach even if policy doesn't demand it, but if restoring would be a lot of work or if the computer has files and settings you don't want to destroy, cleaning might be your best option.

 Exam Objective(s): 220-1002 2.4.2.1, 2.4.2.2.2.4.2.3, 2.4.2.4

You'll need antimalware software to detect and remove the threat, of course, but you might need other operating system tools or even third-party utilities in order to guarantee the process and restore the system to normal working order. General purpose scanners and utilities can be part of your regular software toolkit, while you might need to research and download specific removal tools as you need them.

Antivirus scanner Real-time, scheduled, and manual anti-virus scans are the first line of defense against malware. If one product can't find the infection you can always try another. For some rootkits or other disguised malware, you might need to run a scanner from bootable media you're sure is clean.

Antimalware software Apart from traditional antivirus scanners, some products specialize in detecting a broader range of threats, such as changes made by spyware, adware, or rootkits. Other tools are designed to remove specific threats.

Event Viewer Used to detect and diagnose unusual system behavior. System logging software won't remove malware, but it might show you how it was contracted or what changes were made.

System Restore Saves and restores system files and settings, allowing you to recover from some harmful changes—even those you might accidentally cause in the cleanup process.

System backups Restoring from data backups can recover data lost to malware, and restoring from a complete system image is even a valid form of malware removal. One problem is that if you don't notice malware immediately, recent backups may themselves be infected.

Terminal As useful as GUI tools, some troubleshooting is easier when you're familiar with command-line tools. Sometimes you might even have to boot to a command prompt to salvage a damaged system.

MSCONFIG Allows you to change boot options. Malware frequently changes boot settings, or adds malicious programs or services to the startup process. MSCONFIG also is one way to enter safe mode or other controlled startup environments.

Installation media If system files are missing or damaged, you might be able to restore them from an operating system installation disc or flash drive.

Recovery environment If the computer won't boot or if malware has compromised the operating system enough to prevent repair, you'll need an alternate boot environment. Windows XP included the Recovery Console environment for repairing boot options or corrupted system files. Newer versions of Windows include the more comprehensive Windows Recovery Environment or System Recovery Options: these include automated diagnostic and recovery options as well as full command line access.

Rescue disk A combination of antimalware and system repair tools on a bootable disc or flash drive. There are many free preconfigured products, some from antivirus vendors: they include PC Tools' Alternate Operating System Scanner, Kaspersky Rescue Disk, and Microsoft's Windows Defender Offline. If you have the technical expertise you can even create your own, for example using the *Windows Preinstallation Environment* (*WinPE*) used by both Windows setup and Windows Recovery Environment. Either way, since you need updated antivirus definitions and can't rely on contacting the network, you'll probably have to download or create a new rescue disk whenever you need one.

Mobile security symptoms

When it comes to mobile devices like smartphones and tablets, malware isn't the top security threat most people's minds. Partly this is because theft or unauthorized access are such big risks, but also because mobile operating systems were designed from the start with modern security threats in mind. Most software is downloaded directly from well-monitored app stores, and system permissions are more tightly controlled: even a device's owner might not have the ability to download an app from a random website or give a trojan horse the keys to the boot sector.

 Exam Objective(s): 220-1002 3.5.1

That isn't to say mobile devices are safe: malware aimed at mobile operating systems is rapidly growing and evolving, and attackers are constantly finding new exploits to install adware and spyware or even gain root access to take control of devices. Trojan horses are common too, either compromised legitimate apps on third-party app stores, or seemingly legitimate applications that ask for permissions they don't really need to gain more information or compromise performance. It doesn't even take malice for mobile apps to become a problem: if an app keeps secretly turning on your phone's location tracking in a misguided attempt to be helpful rather than to nefariously report on your activity, it's still running down your battery.

The symptoms of mobile malware are similar or analogous to that on the desktop. Performance problems, altered operation, ads, or other unexpected behaviors can all be warning signs. A lot of specific details are related to features common on mobile devices or operating systems.

Device and network performance	Heavy resource utilization, slow network speeds, and rapid battery drain can suggest either malware or just a misbehaving application. At the same time, it could also be a weak signal or radio interference: mobile devices can consume a lot of power just trying to maintain connectivity far from a WAP or cellular tower. Then again, dropped signals can themselves be related to malware.
Exceeded data limits	Most mobile plans have monthly limits for data use. Even when they don't, providers and devices can monitor data usage. Unexpectedly high network use can be a sign of an application transmitting or receiving large amounts of data.
Unexpected feature activation	Some mobile features, while very useful, can consume battery life and compromise security or privacy. It's easy and good practice to turn some of these off when you don't need them, such as Wi-Fi, Bluetooth, or location tracking. If they turn on without you noticing, it suggests either malware, or legitimate software that's inadvertently been given system permissions to do so. Likewise, cameras or microphones activating when you're not deliberately using them is a sign of spyware.
Surveillance risks	Mobile devices make perfect surveillance devices in the hands of malicious or unwary users. Even if features like cameras, microphones, and location tracking aren't turned on by malware, it's easy to leak sensitive data using these features in normal applications. If your organization uses mobile devices in any sort of sensitive environment or occupation, review organizational policies for data leaks.
Changed app permissions	For security reasons mobile apps should only be given permissions they need to function. For example, you shouldn't give an app access to the camera or ability to place calls unless you trust it and it actually needs that capability. If apps have changed or excessive permissions, look to see if anything else is out of order.
Unintended Wi-Fi access	Joining an untrusted Wi-Fi network is a security risk. Unencrypted Wi-Fi networks can leave your network communications open to eavesdropping, and even a "secure" hotspot run by a malicious party might be used to steal data or perform network attacks. Some malicious hotspots are even "evil twins" imitating a specific valid network. When troubleshooting a device, you can review its saved networks and Wi-Fi control history.
Unintended Bluetooth pairings	Whether caused by malware or not, pairing with an unfamiliar or unintended Bluetooth device can endanger security. Review paired Bluetooth devices and investigate any unexpected entries.
Unauthorized root access	Not only can malware force root access, but a device jailbroken or rooted by a legitimate user can be more vulnerable to malware. While the device owner can know this and take the risk anyway, this might be prohibited under a BYOD policy, never mind on a company-owned device. When troubleshooting, watch for apps that require root access.
Suspicious apps	Apps the user doesn't know about, or that come from third-party app stores or websites, might be a security risk. With so many available apps it can be hard to tell what's unusual, but investigate anything that sticks out.
Unauthorized account access	On network-centric mobile devices, there can be many signs of unauthorized access from outside sources. Unexpected activity on online accounts, unauthorized mobile payments, or personal data turning up where it shouldn't all point to a compromised device even if it seems just fine to its user.

Leaked data

Mobile devices are easy ways to leak personal or business data. Not only can it be stolen from the device itself or a cloud backup, the device can be used to smuggle data from inside a secure enterprise network. Data loss prevention software can help notice when a leak has happened, but it's more important to make sure security settings like device encryption and multi-factor authentication are in order beforehand.

The tools and operating system functions you need to troubleshoot and repair mobile devices are also similar in purpose to those on the desktop, just designed for different operating system and hardware features.

Antimalware

Just like on the desktop, you can use anti-malware software to monitor the system or actively scan for signs of malware. Apple claims that iOS devices are not vulnerable to malware and does not allow malware scanners in its App Store, but a variety are available for Android and Windows Phone.

App scanner

Other scanners don't look specifically for malware such as for app problems or changes. They can help notice unusual activities even if they're not strictly malware.

Wireless analyzer

To verify signal problems, you can just try moving the device. You can also use a Wi-Fi analyzer or cell tower analyzer, either as a specialized appliance or an app on another mobile device. If the problem device shows signal strength or connection speed problems even where you know there's a good signal, you know there's a hardware or software issue.

App control features

If you think an app is having problems, you can force stop it from within the operating system, or uninstall and reinstall it. You can even uninstall apps remotely from iTunes or the Google Play Store. Mobile device management apps, like Apple Configurator, let you centrally manage multiple mobile devices owned by your organization.

Backup and restore

You backup and restore mobile data and settings to and from your desktop, and you can also store it using cloud services like Google Sync, iCloud, or OneDrive. This reduces danger of data loss on the device, but be careful you haven't backed up anything that's compromised.

Factory resets

Mobile devices are easy to reset to a freshly installed state, deleting user data, installed apps, and, hopefully, any installed malware. If you have recent and trustworthy backups, this can be the simplest way to fix a compromised device.

Removing malware

The process for repairing an infected system is pretty straightforward, but even if you follow it precisely that doesn't make it easy. Wiping away some malware is a simple process, but others can dig very deeply into the operating system and take elaborate or creative methods to remove.

Exam Objective(s): 220-1002 3.3

1. Identify symptoms that suggest the presence and nature of installed malware.
2. Quarantine the infected system.
3. In Windows, disable System Restore.
4. Repair the infected system.

   a) Update anti-malware software.

   b) Use scanning and removal tools.
5. Update the system and schedule future scans.
6. Enable System Restore and create a new restore point.
7. Educate the end user and document findings.

Quarantining systems

Once you've determined that a system likely has malware, you need to immediately quarantine it until the situation is resolved. If you don't, the malware could easily spread through the network or storage devices.

- Isolate any removable storage devices that have been recently connected to the computer, or backups that might have been made since infection. They'll need to be scanned, and shouldn't come into contact with other systems.
- Disable all network shares, file sharing applications, or other ongoing connections to other computers.
- Identify and isolate other computers that might be infected. Any systems that regularly share files or synchronize data with the infected system are at risk. Contact other technicians or network administrators to see if similar symptoms have appeared elsewhere.
- Limit network connectivity. Disconnecting from the network entirely is the surest way, but if you need to download tools or definition updates from the infected computer, just do your best to isolate it from other computers on the local network.

Disabling System Restore

System Restore, or any other application that backs up files and settings, is a powerful tool for recovering from system damage whether it's caused by malware or not. The problem is that if you back up infected files, then restore them later, you'll just re-infect the whole system. For this reason, you need to disable System Restore or similar applications while the system is infected. With System Restore in particular, disabling the feature also deletes existing restore points: a potential risk since it removes a safety net, but at least it makes sure you won't restore malware by mistake.

System Restore settings in Windows 7

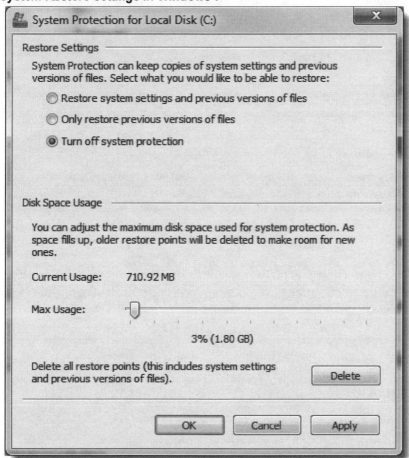

While System Restore has been around since before Windows XP, the precise steps needed to disable it vary by operating system. In Windows Vista, 7, and 8 the steps are very similar.

1. In the **System** window, click **System Protection**.

   - In Windows 7 and 8, open Control Panel and click **System and Security** > **System**.

   - In Windows Vista, open Control Panel and click **System and Maintenance** > **System**.

2. In the **System Properties** window, select your system drive.

3. Disable System Restore for the drive.

   - In Windows 8, click **Configure**. Select **Disable System Protection**, and click **OK**.

   - In Windows 7, click **Configure**. Select **Turn off System Protection**, and click **OK**.

   - In Windows Vista, uncheck the drive, then click **Turn System Restore Off**.

4. Repeat the process for all other drives that have System Restore enabled.

Remediating infected systems

Actually removing malware is its own troubleshooting process. You'll have to choose tools, verify findings, and apply creative solutions as necessary. there are some general steps and techniques you'll have to keep in mind.

- Always use updated tools. Effective security software is updated frequently, even with daily definitions. Outdated software can be useless against a new threat.

- Combine multiple tools, especially when the system might have multiple separate infections. Specialized antispyware scanners can find what common antivirus monitors do not, and even two different brands of the same type of scanner might find very different results. Run one tool, then the other: trying to scan the system with two at once can hurt the performance of both.

- Run multiple scans to verify malware removal. In particular, if you think the system is clean, reboot and then scan it again.

- If the system won't boot normally, or if particularly well-protected malware can't be completely removed, try safe mode, restore environments, bootable rescue discs, or removal tools targeted to the specific infection.

- Don't forget to scan removable media that may have been infected.

- After the malware is removed, you may need to reconfigure or reinstall services and applications affected by it, or restore data from a clean backup.

Securing repaired systems

Odds are that a newly repaired system is going to encounter malware again, and if it got infected last time it's likely it's still vulnerable. Immediately after the repair process, you need to harden the system again and make sure it's more secure than it was when it was infected.

- Update all potentially vulnerable software: not only the operating system and antimalware applications, but network applications such as browsers along with their add-ons and plugins.

- Schedule regular security scans and definition/OS updates. Even if a program doesn't include scheduled scans, you can run it through Task Scheduler.

- Prevent worms by disabling unnecessary services and tightening firewall protections.

- Examine system and application settings to look for other security problems.

- If you can find out how the system was infected, take more specific measures to prevent recurrence. For example, if users are installing trojan horse programs, you might consider restricting user permissions or revising user policies to prohibit unauthorized software.

Following up on repairs

Your work isn't done once the system is working. Especially if user error led to the infection or delayed its discovery, you need to notify the user. You also need to document your findings, and present them to system administrators or management.

- Discuss your findings with any users that might be involved with the infection.

  - Try to learn more about when and how the problem began, and what actions the user took.

  - Instruct the user about your organization's security policies, as well as best practices to avoid future infection from the same or similar threats.

  - Describe what signs there might be if the threat wasn't completely removed, and ask the user to contact you if there's any recurrence.

- Document your findings and the steps you took to resolve any problems.
- Report your findings to network administrators and other appropriate management.
  - Include any potential risks elsewhere on the network.
  - Notify them of any provable or suspected human attacks or policy violations.
  - Point out specific policy changes or technical controls which could reduce chances of the event recurring.

Exercise: Using Windows Security

In different versions of Windows, the central location for security tasks might be called the Action Center, Windows Defender Security Center, or just Windows Security. In all versions it allows you to recognize security problems, check for malware, and access security settings.

Windows Security in Windows 10

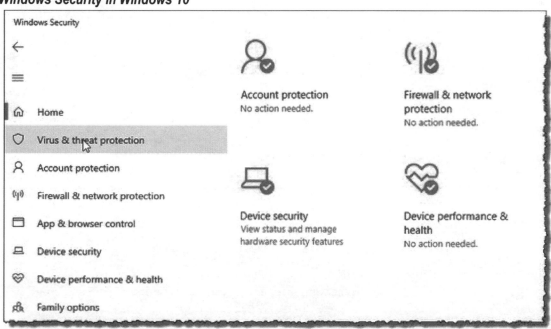

Do This	How & Why
1. Open Windows Security.	
a) Click **Start > Windows Security**.	You can also open the app from **Settings > Update & Security > Windows Security**. It shows various security categories and any known problems in each. If you're lucky, all will have green check marks.
b) Maximize the window.	If necessary, to see the Navigation pane labels.
c) Click each category in the Navigation pane.	You can access virus protection, account protection, firewall, app & browser control, device security, device performance & health, and family options.
2. Perform a manual virus scan.	In Windows 7, Windows Defender was very limited. In Windows 8 and later it's a fully-featured antivirus scanner with real-time protection. You can still scan manually.

Do This	How & Why
a) Click **Virus & threat protection**.	To View Windows Defender Antivirus settings.
b) Click **Check for Updates > Check for Updates**.	Windows Defender regularly updates itself, but you can manually check before a scan if you think there's a reason it might be out of date.
c) Click **Back**.	
d) Click **Scan options**.	In addition to the default quick scan, you can perform a deeper full scan, a custom scan, or an offline scan that can remove some malware ordinary scans will not.
e) Perform a quick scan.	Select it and click **Scan now.** A progress bar appears, but you can still use your computer for other tasks while the scan continues.

Quick scan running...
Estimated time remaining: 00:00:26
635 files scanned

Cancel

f) Wait for the scan to complete.	The scan shouldn't find any threats, but if it did you would be asked how to respond to them.
g) Click **Back > Manage settings**.	You can change advanced settings here, such as real-time protection, exclusions, controlled folder access, and cloud functions. You shouldn't need to change these.
3. Close all open windows.	

Assessment: Security troubleshooting

1. What was the first version of Windows to include real-time antivirus scanning? Choose the best response.

   - Windows XP Service Pack 2
   - Windows Vista
   - Windows 7
   - Windows 8
   - Windows 8.1

2. Order the steps of the malware removal process in Windows.

   1. Disable System Restore
   2. Educate the end user
   3. Enable System Restore
   4. Identify symptoms
   5. Quarantine the system
   6. Repair the system
   7. Update the system

3. When quarantining a system, you should consider disconnecting from the network entirely. True or false?

   - True
   - False

4. Disabling System Restore also deletes existing restore points. True or false?

   - True
   - False

5. On scanning a system, you've recognized a spyware program that inserted a malicious service into Windows startup. Apart from a malware scanner, what tool could disable the program? Choose the best reply.

   - Event Viewer
   - MSCONFIG
   - Recovery Console
   - WinPE

6. It's generally a good idea to run scans using multiple separate antimalware applications, even if you only need one real-time scanner. True or false?

   - True
   - False

Summary: Securing devices and data

You should now know:

- How to minimize security risks to workstations and data by hardening the operating system, restricting account permissions, applying strong password policies, encrypting stored data, and securely disposing of media holding sensitive data.

- How to secure mobile devices by using strong authentication, enabling device encryption, configuring anti-theft applications, and implementing organization-wide mobile device policies.

- How to apply a defense in depth strategy to a SOHO network in order to secure hosts, network connections, physical hardware, and wireless communications.

- How to troubleshoot security issues such as malware infections

Chapter 7: Operational procedures

As you work as an A+ support technician, you'll experience a wide variety of situations beyond just working with hardware and operating systems. You'll also need to obtain and perfect the skills necessary to work with people and the procedures to deal with safety and professionalism.

You'll learn how to:

- Interpret and create policies and other documentation.
- Respond to incidents involving prohibited content and activities.
- Perform backups and recover lost data.

Module A: IT operations

No organization of any size has employees so skilled that they don't need some formal policies to keep them on the same page. To achieve a smoothly functioning IT infrastructure you need to have documented guidelines for user behavior, technical procedures, and regulatory compliance. Just as importantly, IT operations will frequently change as technologies, threats, and organizational goals evolve. When they do, you need a change management process that makes sure operational, policies, and documentation remain aligned.

You will learn:

- About policies and procedures
- How to manage system and network documentation
- How to apply a formal change management process.

About policies

When you approach a complex organizational goal like maintaining secure and consistent IT operations, you need to have a documented plan for every important step of design, standard operations, and even response to unexpected events. These documents should cover systems and data, the security controls protecting them, and how both inside and outside users should interact with them. They should also include a description of the organization's overall business goals, to give context that ties all of those details together.

In other words, these documents are the components that turn computers and technicians into a functioning IT department. You might hear them called frameworks, policies, controls, procedures, guidelines, standards, and so on. Each of these has a specific meaning, even if there's a lot of overlap between them.

Policy
A statement describing how management intends the organization is to be run. Compliance with a policy is mandatory for all employees or users falling under its scope. "User accounts must be protected by strong passwords" might be found in a policy.

Standard
A technical definition of specific methodologies or requirements which are needed to satisfy policies. Standards are also mandatory. A standard might be something like, "Passwords must be at least eight characters long and contain letters, numbers, and special characters." Many standards are defined by outside standards bodies.

Guideline
A description of *best practices* or recommendations for achieving a certain policy goal. In theory, guidelines unlike standards are optional and leave room for interpretation. Advice on how to avoid an easily guessed password might be found in a guideline.

Procedures
Specific and ordered instructions for complying with a particular element of a policy or standard. Procedures are mandatory, and written for whoever will actually perform them. In general, a procedure represents a short-duration task, while long tasks are called *processes* and contain multiple procedures. The steps needed to change or reset a password would be written as a procedure.

Policy documentation needs to be taught to all personnel and users who fall under its scope, and should be readily available to anyone that has a compliance question. At the same time, some documents are sensitive information. As important as it is for a system administrator to have procedures for hardening a web server, the same document might give an attacker clues on how to compromise it.

Typical policies

Ideally, an organization's policies should form an integrated consistent whole governing business operations, networks and computers, operational procedures, security, user behaviors, and interactions with clients and customers. For a policy like that to be effective it needs input from administrators, human resources, senior management, and legal staff, and it has to address both organizational goals and technological details. Even a component of overall policies, like "network policy", exists on multiple levels; it affects a lot of different people and assets with different roles and knowledge levels. It also needs to cover both broad guidelines and goals as well as specific details and procedures. This means that the policy isn't likely to be a single document, but rather a set of interrelated and evolving documents. Every part needs to be written in language that will be clear to those it affects. You might find the following components in a complete set of network security policies:

- For managerial staff, the policy needs to include a high-level outline of the organization's goals, and the steps that will be taken to achieve them. This outline will be used as the guiding principle for the others. Important components include the issues which the policy is meant to address, legal or regulatory requirements relevant to it, what actions will be necessary to enact the policy, how employees are expected to comply, and the consequences for non-compliance.

- For IT administrators and technicians, the policy itself needs to include technical documentation about how the network will be secured. Important components include general guidelines about security goals and best practices, technological standards used on the network, guidelines for the maintenance of network diagrams and, procedure documents for specific operational tasks. It also needs to include policies for managing user permissions and securely disposing of data.

- *Acceptable use policies* (*AUPs*) target end users, who may be employees or customers using hosted services. Each of the two will likely have a different AUP. An AUP includes procedures and guidelines for use of network resources written in terms appropriate to the user's access level and technological knowledge, such as password creation and responsible network use. It also includes consequences for noncompliance.

- *Privacy policies* govern codified expectations of user privacy and consent to security-based monitoring of user activity. They target both inside employees and outside customers or other individuals, and must be in compliance with any applicable privacy laws. Privacy policies targeting users might be included in the AUP. Privacy policies for customer data include both internal policies for securing such data, and external statements to customers explaining their privacy rights and expectations.

- *Incident response policies* specify exactly what steps will be taken in response to a security incident, in order to minimize and repair damage without exposing the network to further risk. They include elements such as incident documentation, regulatory reporting requirements, and securing forensic data that may be needed for legal proceedings

- *Disaster planning* and *business continuity* policies specify the steps that will be taken to secure assets, protect staff, and maintain business operations in terms of natural or artificial disasters and disruptions.

- *Change management* policies provide guidelines for updating policies and procedures to suit changing needs, without introducing new vulnerabilities.

- *Standard operating procedures* (*standing operating procedures* in military organizations) are lists of step by step instructions to perform routine tasks. Procedures aren't traditionally considered policies themselves, but policies should specify how procedures are developed, stored, and taught to employees.

Depending on your role and organization you may or may not be in a position to help design policies, but you it's your responsibility to know what policies apply to you and to users you support. You should also know where to take policy questions, or feedback when a policy seems inappropriate or out of date.

Acceptable use policies

Every organization needs a formal *acceptable use policy* (*AUP*) specifying how employees are allowed to use company resources, such as hardware, software, and network services. If your organization provides user services to outside customers, they'll need their own, separate AUP.

Exam Objective(s): 220-1002 4.1.5

The goal of any AUP is to prevent user behavior that compromises security, hurts performance, or damages your corporate reputation. For instance, even in the most permissive workplace it's still unacceptable if users install questionable software on company workstations, spend all day on social networking sites instead of working, or use a work account to send harassing email to people. One user might find that to be common sense, but to another it might need to be spelled out.

For an AUP to be enforceable rather than a list of friendly suggestions, it must specify what consequences management will take in case of violation. Additionally, users must be required to sign or otherwise provably affirm that they have read it before they access any company resources. Otherwise, you might not be able to do much about abuses: firing an employee for "policy violations" without being able to show just what terms the employee agreed to then violated can be grounds for an unlawful termination suit. For internet or remote access services, you'll also need to specify the legal jurisdiction, generally your central location, which governs any legal action resulting from policy violations.

Acceptable use policies vary widely between organizations, depending on their security needs and management philosophies, but they typically include use of the following:

Internet	A restrictive internet policy could prohibit any personal internet use on company systems. More often, personal use is allowed with restrictions on inappropriate or offensive content, resource-intensive or legally questionable P2P file sharing, and excessive time spent on social networks or personal email during business hours. Network policies might also define the remote access or VPN solutions used by employees who are traveling or working from home.
Company accounts	Use of company email accounts, website or social media accounts, or any other resources that associate the user with the organization itself need special scrutiny. Misuse of these resources can cost money, damage business relationships and public reputation, or even open the organization itself to legal consequences—users given access to them must agree to use them appropriately.
Hardware and software	Policies should define both what hardware and software users have access to and what changes they can make. A restrictive workplace might prevent any changes to workstation configurations and strictly define what software can be used for what tasks. Even a permissive company should regulate employee software installation or configuration changes that might hurt performance or compromise security.
Privileged users	Administrators and other privileged users can easily do damage to network function or security than ordinary users, so they should face additional impressibilities and obligations. Privileged user agreements should cover when privileged accounts should and shouldn't be users, what actions require special authorizations, and ways privileged users are subject to additional monitoring and review.

Hand-in-hand with an AUP you need to establish a *privacy policy* defining just what user information and activities will be recorded and monitored, and how it will be used by the company. Users naturally assume that their behavior and information will be private and untraced, even when they're using secure corporate systems that must carefully log user activity, and they might unreasonably resent even mild monitoring when it comes to light. Laws and industry regulations might restrict how user data, especially of outside customers, can be collected or shared without explicit consent. To avoid misunderstanding, policies should not only be made clear to all users, but any changes in them should also be communicated.

IT personnel must be familiar with the AUPs and privacy policies applying to the users of any systems they maintain and support, both in order to abide by them and to help enforce them. In particular, if your duties involve interaction with users you need to know how to advise them on how to comply with policies, and how you should respond upon encountering policy violations.

Password policies

Passwords are widely used throughout information security, by administrators and end users alike. They're the easiest kind of credentials to implement, and when used properly provide strong security. Unfortunately, when misused passwords are very easy to compromise.

Exam Objective(s): 220-1002 4.1.6

One half of the problem is administrative. Passwords are prime targets for data theft, and a number of high-profile data breaches in recent years have resulted in the theft of unsecured or poorly secured user data. Even on interior servers, passwords need to be stored securely, typically in hashed and salted form. They should never be transmitted in clear text over the network.

The other half is user policies. Users today might have to manage a lot of passwords in their daily lives. If left to themselves, they'll use very simple passwords, reuse them for account after account, and share them with others. It's not hard to tell that that's a security nightmare. The traditional solution is to require or assign complex passwords, change them frequently, and require different passwords for each service. That just adds another problem: users can't keep up and just write their passwords down somewhere or otherwise undermine the policy.

There isn't an easy solution, and there's a lot of debate among security professionals how to use passwords in the workplace. Whatever approach your organization uses, you must comply with its password policies and, if necessary, follow additional best practices which don't violate the formal policy. As strong password policy addresses the following needs:

- Passwords should be easy for the user to remember, but difficult for an attacker to guess.

  - Short or commonly used passwords are easy to crack. So are passwords related to the name, family, or other real-world facts about the user.

  - Using the same password across multiple accounts or services means an attacker who accesses one account can easily gain access to the others.

- Passwords should never be shared between users or given to unauthorized people.

- If passwords must be stored anywhere but in the owner's memory, they should be kept under appropriate security.

- A password should be changed if there's any reason to believe it should be compromised.

- Passwords alone are a single factor which can be easily compromised, so secure accounts should augment them with multi-factor authentication or other security measures.

- Single sign-on is an effective solution to users struggling with multiple separate passwords, but it also increases the impact of a single compromised password.

Regulatory compliance policies

Policies designed by the organization must also be in compliance with applicable government and industry regulations, as well as agreements with business partners. Regulatory compliance is particularly important for organizations that handle a lot of data owned by other people, do work in specific sensitive fields, or need to integrate their operations with common industry standards.

Exam Objective(s): 220-1002 4.1.4

Regulations depend both on your organization and the legal jurisdiction it's in, but in the US some examples include *FISMA* for all federal government agencies, *HIPAA* for patient data in health care systems, *Sarbanes-Oxley* (*SOX*) for corporate financial data, and *PCI-DSS* standards for systems handling payment card data. You'll also have to deal with international export controls if you deal in materials and information importance to national security, or trade with specific foreign countries.

Any of the above regulations can have broad or highly-specific requirements on security controls, data retention requirements, vulnerability management programs, and just about anything else you can imagine. Failure to comply with those requirements can lead to stiff fines and other legal penalties, even if you never actually suffer an attack that compromises the protected data. Policy design and enforcement must take applicable regulations into account, and all personnel must know their responsibilities regarding regulatory compliance. Heavily regulated industries may also have specific compliance policies and training managed by the chief compliance officer.

Discussion: Policies

1. What's the difference between a policy and a procedure?

2. Why would a CEO, a network technician, and a sales representative each need to refer to a very different security policy document?

3. What insecure password behaviors have you seen in the past, and what sort of policies would correct them?

4. What acceptable use policies are in place at your organization?

5. What asset management and data disposal policies docs your organization have?

Network and system documentation

To effectively enforce policies or perform procedures, you need to make decisions based on exactly how the existing network is put together. It's not just security: you'll face the same questions when making changes, replacing components, just trying to join a new system to the network. This means you need to keep thorough documentation about the network, starting when you begin the planning process. It should include, but not necessarily be limited to:

- Physical and logical diagrams of the network

- A list of IT assets including hardware and software

- Vendor documentation and configuration baselines for listed assets

- Vendor documentation for deployed assets

- Assigned MAC and IP addresses, and available IP addresses

Importantly, the documentation itself needs to be considered secure data. Even basic network configuration data can be useful to an attacker, so the more that is kept on a need-to-know basis the more secure the network will be.

Network diagrams

It can be hard enough to come back to a home entertainment center and remember exactly how everything is connected together, let alone an office network of any real size. When you need to clearly understand network layouts or share them with other people, you should use network diagrams that visually represent important components and connections.

 Exam Objective(s): 220-1002 4.1.1

Like a policy, the detail level of a network diagram depends on its intended audience and purpose. An initial plan or basic overview might just show the general structure, but maintenance documentation for technicians could include every last component and connection, along with complete labeling for each. Network diagrams also can focus either on the network's physical or logical topology. Each type needs to convey different types of information.

- Physical diagrams focus on the physical arrangement of network components such as hosts, network hardware devices, ports, and cables. Details might include cable lengths, port locations, and specific hardware standards in use. Physical diagrams are important for technicians who need to connect or troubleshoot physical components of the network.

- Logical diagrams focus on the flow of data through the network. As well as devices such as routers and firewalls, they include elements such as subnets, VLANs, IP addresses, and protocols used for transport and routing. Logical diagrams are important for planning and troubleshooting issues related to data flow.

Either type of network diagram should be created with consistent tools, using consistent symbols and labeling styles in order to reduce risk of confusion. Technicians should learn the style in place both to read it accurately and in case they need to make updates.

Safety plans

A comprehensive safety plan protects your employees and your equipment. It is important that you document the safety procedures you want your employees to follow, and then make sure they are trained appropriately. Refresher training should be conducted at regular intervals. Some components that you'll want to consider including in your safety program include:

- Personal safety. This includes using the appropriate personal safety equipment and personal safety guidelines when working with equipment.

- Equipment grounding. All equipment should be properly grounded to reduce the risk of electrocution or component damage.

- Safe component handling and storage.

- An injury incident reporting system.

- Toxic waste handling and disposal.

- Compliance with all government regulations - federal, state, and local.

Knowledge bases

By contrast to internal documentations, your organization might use a public facing *knowledge base* to communicate system and product information to users or customers. The knowledge base is a collection of articles that serves as a first line of customer support, helping them to educate themselves about your products and services, and ideally solve their own problems before calling the help desk. If the knowledge base isn't informative, accurate, and easy to use, customers won't use it, or might follow its guidance into further mistakes you'll need to spend extra time correcting.

Exam Objective(s): 220-1002 4.1.2

When you develop or contribute to knowledge base articles, keep the following ideals in mind:

- Articles should be written with the target audience in mind. Highly technical articles might suit a highly technical user base, but will confuse many end users. Very simple articles may not answer the questions an advanced user is asking.

- When your goal is to reduce technical support workload, it's a good idea to make articles to address common questions and problems. Even if simple questions are just listed in a FAQ, answering them once in the knowledge base can save a lot of calls later.

- Articles need to be easy to read and extract useful information from, even when they address complex topics.

  - Keep writing concise and well-organized.

  - Instead of explaining every detail, consider links to other articles or external sources for relevant information

  - Use diagrams, screenshots, or other graphics for concepts that are hard to convey in text.

- The knowledge base as a whole should be easy to navigate, with a clear organizational hierarchy and search functions.

- The knowledge base should be kept up to date. When an article is rendered obsolete by system changes it should be updated or deleted. If an article is still valid for old products or legacy systems it should be marked as such.

Inventory management

Another area of IT where documentation is essential is in inventory management. Managing sale inventory is essential for any business that sells goods, but the same principles apply to *IT asset management* (*ITAM*) for any organization with IT assets it needs to keep track of. ITAM is more work than you might think, especially for an organization with many similar devices which might be moved or borrowed throughout the organization. Even worse, you also need to track non-physical assets such as software licenses.

Exam Objective(s): 220-1002 4.1.7

Some approaches that will help you manage IT inventory include:

- Track each asset through its life cycle, from acquisition until disposal.

- An IT asset list can be very large, so don't be afraid to place higher scrutiny on expensive or critical assets than on less important ones.

- Use a *configuration management database* (*CMDB*) to track all assets in an automated fashion.

- Keep regular inventory of physical assets.

  - Barcode tags and scanners can both automate the process and help differentiate multiple copies of the same hardware model.

  - RFID tags and scanners are even more powerful approaches which allow you to locate devices at a distance.

- For software licenses, tracking what you own is often more critical than tracking what you have deployed, and more likely to cause legal problems.

Discussion: Documentation

1. Does your organization have a consistent standard for network diagrams?

2. How different would a physical diagram of your LAN be from a logical diagram?

3. How would you improve your organization's knowledge base? If it doesn't have one, what knowledge bases have you used that you would like it to emulate?

4. What IT inventory management practices does your organization use?

The change management process

Hardware, software, and business practices are always temporary. When problems crop up, or your organization's needs evolve, you need to be ready to make changes. Regardless of the reason for any particular change, you should perform it with a consistent process in order to achieve your goals while reducing the risk of unforeseen consequences. The general steps are the same for any type of change and any organizational scope, but the formality and time needed for each depend entirely on the size of the network, the scope of the change, and the policies and needs of your organization.

Exam Objective(s): 220-1002 4.2.1

1. Identification	Identifying and documenting the reason why a change is necessary.
2. Change request	Researching and documenting the steps needed for the change, its potential impact, and who will be affected.
3. Approval	Going through your organization's approval process for the specific change.
4. Preparation	Gathering necessary resources, scheduling the change, and notifying users.
5. Implementation	Making and testing the change.
6. Followup	Monitoring for negative impacts and changing network documentation.

You could say the process begins before you recognize the need for a change. Change management is easiest when systems are designed with future changes in mind. You also need a strong understanding of its existing state - not only the elements you're considering changing, but any related elements that might be affected. Without that knowledge you'll be working in the dark from the moment when you start guessing what the problem is, right until the end when you're not sure how much good the change did. Preparing for change is one more reason you need to have complete and accurate documentation of your existing business processes and the IT infrastructure that supports them.

Identifying changes

For small changes where you have the authority, the process from noticing something that needs to be changed to starting the actual preparations might be more of a thought experiment than a formal process, but that doesn't mean it's not important. Considering any change to network configuration carefully is key to avoiding unintended side effects and needless service disruption, and that starts with knowing just what you want to fix.

1. Verify that there is a present or future problem which needs to be addressed.

2. Identify the options for correcting the problem.

3. When an option seems promising, examine it more closely by asking questions in an informal process.

   • Will it fix the problem?

   • Will it introduce compatibility issues or other new problems?

   • How many users and systems will be affected?

   • How much time and resources will it take?

   • Can it be reversed if something goes wrong?

4. As necessary, seek opinions or advice from colleagues or technical support resources to verify your decision.

Requesting changes

Before you officially request a change, much less implement it, you want to know the full details of what it entails. Many organizations use a formal document structure for network changes, called a *Request for Change* (*RFC*) or something similar. Even if yours doesn't, a structured and detailed document serves as much to help you in the rest of the process as it does to convince your superiors to approve the plan.

Exam Objective(s): 220-1002 4.2.2, 4.2.3, 4.2.4, 4.2.7

Which leads to the next part - the decision for a serious change generally shouldn't be up to one person. The accepted practice is to designate a *change advisory board* (*CAB*) which has both the skill and authority to determine whether the request is reasonable and necessary, and to identify any oversights or errors the original proposal might have. The CAB should represent a variety of viewpoints. In addition to a designated change manager and technical personnel it should include experts on accounting, customer management, regulatory compliance, or whatever else might be relevant to the specific change. For some changes, outside expertise is valuable. Once a CAB is convened its members should continue to meet and communicate not only throughout the approval process, but also to oversee the change as it is implemented and tested.

Whether you're preparing a change request or serving as a member of a CAB, you need to consider the following questions and concerns:

- Clarify the purpose of the change.
  - What is the problem being addressed?
  - What will happen if no change is made?
- Examine the necessary scope of the change.
  - Exactly what needs to be changed?
  - What users or systems will be affected?
  - How expensive, in money and other resources, will the change be?
  - Is it possible the scope of the change will increase on further examination?
- Examine the potential impact of the change through a *risk analysis* process that evaluates possible outcomes.
  - What are the short- and long-term benefits of the proposal?
  - What immediate disruptions might the change cause?
  - What long-term consequences or side effects might result?
  - How reliably predictable are both the benefits and costs of the change?
  - Is there a *backout plan* to reverse the change if something goes wrong?
  - If the change is successful in the short term, how will it affect the system's ability to deal with future changes?
- Develop a timetable and operational plan for the change.
  - What resources are needed?
  - What personnel will participate in the process?
  - Who needs advance notification of potential disruptions?
  - When can the change be implemented?

Preparing for changes

Once you've received approval for a change, you need to prepare for it before you touch any active systems. As with every other step, the more critical the system and the more expansive the change, the more rigorous your preparation has to be. Some large-scale changes may need to be broken up into multiple phases, each with its own preparation and implementation cycle.

Exam Objective(s): 220-1002 4.2.5

- Purchase or prepare any resources you need for the change.

- Make sure all IT staff and relevant users are trained to perform their roles during and after the change.

- Choose a time for implementing the change.

  - When possible, choose a period of low maintenance and without critical operations occurring.

  - Schedule a *maintenance window* allowing time to implement changes as well as some leeway for delays or minor problems.

  - Authorize downtime in coordination with appropriate system administrators.

- If possible, test changes in an isolated test environment. Unfortunately, this is often more difficult for network-wide changes than those on individual hosts.

- Make sure that all affected users receive advance notification of the upcoming changes and of any possible service disruptions.

- Immediately before the change, make backups of any systems or configuration settings that will be changed.

Finalizing changes

With a large change, just the testing and adjustment after the fact can be a project in itself.

Exam Objective(s): 220-1002 4.2.6, 4.2.8, 4.2.9

1. Test the results of the change, enabling systems and services as necessary.
   - Verify that the changes operate as planned.
   - Check for anticipated side effects.
   - Verify overall system functionality.
   - If problems are detected, either make corrections or in the worst case proceed with your backout plan to roll back changes.
2. When services are restored, notify users and administrators. Include relevant results of the change.
3. Continue a review process for as long as required.
   - Observe system functions, making adjustments or fine-tuning as necessary.
   - Pay close attention to user reports regarding the change and its results. No change is really successful unless it has passed *user acceptance testing* by the end of implementation.
   - Review the change process with other staff and/or the CAB to identify lessons learned.
4. Update any relevant documentation to reflect the new state of the overall system. Be sure to change them based on your final results, not your initial plan.
   - Physical location changes
   - Added systems or services
   - Changed configurations

- New user or maintenance procedures
- Performance baselines

Discussion: Planning changes

(Question/answer exercise.)

1. Consider a past business change you've implemented or participated in.

    a) Identify each step of the change process as it happened.

    b) Did the change go as planned?

    c) What could have been done differently?

2. In a web browser, look up change request document templates, and consider what would fit your organization.

Assessment: IT operations

1. Which of the following items should be considered as part of a comprehensive safety plan?

   - Injury incident reporting system.
   - Personal safety
   - Regulation compliance
   - Safe component handling and storage
   - Toxic waste disposal

2. What is most likely to be part of an AUP? Choose the best response.

   - How often employee evaluations should be conducted
   - What to do when a workstation shows signs of malware infection
   - Whether you can access streaming music services from your workstation
   - Who is in charge of a critical database

3. Experts agree that very demanding password policies are the best way to maintain security. True or false?

   - True
   - False

4. Order the steps of the change management process.

   1. Approval
   2. Change request
   3. Followup
   4. Identification
   5. Implementation
   6. Preparation

5. Your company's network topology diagrams aren't very detailed so you're helping to improve them. The new set will have separate physical and logical diagrams. Which of the following should you make sure to put in the logical diagrams? Choose all that apply.

   - Ethernet cable standards
   - IP subnets
   - Patch panel port mappings
   - VLAN trunk links
   - WAP serial numbers

Module B: Incident response

During your career, you're likely to encounter situations where users possess prohibited content, from that prohibited by the company, to content prohibited by law. You must follow corporate end-user policies and security best practices when responding to security incidents and when dealing with licensed content and personal information of customers, clients, or patients.

You will learn how to:

- Respond to incidents involving prohibited content.
- Explain the concepts of licensing and privacy.

Incident response

In IT terms *incident* is an event or series of events that is unexpected, unusual, and that poses some meaningful threat to the organization's functions, performance, or security. Incidents can be almost anything, but categories you're likely to run into include:

- Hardware and software malfunction, on individual PCs or the network
- Viruses or indication of network attack
- Human error or operator negligence
- Health and safety violations of any origin
- Violation of company policies, such as inappropriate use of internet or other resources
- Criminal behavior such as illegal financial dealings, child pornography, or terror threats

IT personnel are likely to encounter these incidents first, so need to be ready to act as *first responders* who can identify when something is wrong and either take action or escalate it to someone who can.

The goal of incident response isn't just to correct the problem, especially when it's something like a policy violation rather than software troubleshooting. You also want to understand what led to the problem, notify management of what happened, and gather any necessary evidence needed for policy changes, disciplinary actions, or even legal proceedings.

Responding to an incident

The exact procedure you need to follow in order to respond to an incident depend on exactly what it is, but for something involving policy violations or prohibited content you might follow the following procedure.

 Exam Objective(s): 220-1002 4.6.1

1. Identify the problem.
   - Identify the type of violation which has happened
   - Once you recognize that an incident may have taken place, begin to document each step you take, regardless of the incident type.
2. Report the incident through the proper channels. You'll need to review your company policies to determine what channels those are.
   - Escalate to superiors
   - Report to human resources personnel or law enforcement
   - Be ready to hand the investigation over to more qualified responders.

3. Preserve the data and devices involved in the incident. Criminal investigations and other formal procedures rely on preserving a *chain of custody* that verifies evidence was collected properly, then stored unaltered from its discovery to its use in court.

- Don't collect relevant data or tamper with devices holding it unless you're trained in applicable forensic procedures.

- Physically secure workstations, mobile devices, or removable media which may contain relevant material or evidence.

- If appropriate, isolate affected systems from the network or other sources of outside interference.

- Keep all evidence in a safe location.

- For each piece of evidence, document where it was found, what you did with it, and to whom you gave it.

Documenting incidents

The incident response process relies on documentation. Documentation should begin when the incident is discovered, whether or not it's something you immediately need to report to your superiors or legal authorities. You should continue documenting new discoveries and your actions throughout the incident response process, culminating in an *incident report* which can be used to prevent similar incidents in the future. The incident report isn't just a summary of the incident itself, but is used to document and evaluate the response process itself.

Exam Objective(s): 220-1002 4.1.3

Your incident documentation should comply with any organizational policies or regulatory requirements, but in general you should include the following information, and be ready to answer related questions.

- A general description of the incident
  - Timeline of events
  - Involved parties, internal and external
- The total impact of the incident, including its scope, cost, and duration
- Policies which may have been violated
  - For security incidents, specify data types or classifications at risk.
  - For legal or regulatory violations, specify laws or regulations involved.
- Problems with the response process
  - Insufficient preparation
  - Slow detection
  - Communication difficulties among the response team
- Recommendations for preventing recurrence
  - User education or revised procedures
  - New policies or security controls

Discussion: Incident response

1. What is the difference between a chain of custody and just keeping evidence safe?

2. Identify the response steps you've taken, or seen taken, for a past security incident. Consider both what happened, and how the process could have been improved.

3. If you discovered a serious incident at your workplace, what reporting procedures would you need to follow?

Assessment: Incident response

1. A few years ago, a disgruntled employee at your organization caused a major data breach by sabotaging network security systems. Even worse, there were several errors in the incident response process. One of the most serious meant that the activity logs proving the employee's involvement were ruled inadmissible in court. Which of the following errors was the biggest contributor to that ruling? Choose the best response.

    -   Confusion in the reporting process meant the incident was escalated to the wrong department and law enforcement was not quickly informed.

    -   First responders initially identified the sabotage as a software bug.

    -   The activity logs were stored unattended, in an easily editable format.

    -   The incident report didn't clearly state the policies which were being violated.

2. Which of the following is not true about writing an incident summary report?

    -   It isn't the appropriate place to point out shortcomings the response process.

    -   It should contain a detailed list of actions taken during the response process.

    -   It should list any remaining vulnerabilities or steps that could be taken to prevent recurrence.

    -   It should list exactly which policies were violated by involved parties.

3. In which stage of the incident response process should you begin documenting your actions? Choose the best response.

    -   Identifying the incident

    -   Preserving systems and data

    -   Reporting the incident

    -   Writing an incident report

Module C: Backup and recovery

Systems will inevitably fail. Computers will break, power outages will disrupt operations, and data will be lost when a hard drive fails or a virus corrupts it. You might also be unable to retrieve valuable data simply because no one knows a valid password for it. Planning in advance will minimize both the risk of lost data, and any related downtimes.

You will learn:

- About fault tolerance and recovery
- How to back up data
- How to plan for account recovery

Recovery concepts

In security terms, disaster prevention and recovery is all about maintaining the availability and integrity of your organization's assets, especially critical services and irreplaceable data assets. Generally, this is best achieved by two strategies. First, you can maximize availability by choosing systems that are less likely to fail and ensuring that they can be quickly restored when they do. A high availability system can be achieved through a combination of more robust components, redundant components that compensate for individual failures, and development of quick and effective repair procedures. Second, you can maximize the integrity of valuable data by choosing backup procedures that minimize the data loss from any particular disaster.

When you deal with disaster planning and recovery procedures, you're likely to see a number of terms used to describe hardware and services, and it's useful to know what they mean.

RTO *Recovery time objective* is the maximum expected amount of time needed to fully restore service after a disaster. RTO is determined by your disaster recovery procedures, and lower is better.

RPO *Recovery point objective* is the maximum period of data which will be lost in the case of a disaster. RPO depends on your backup frequency, but lower is better.

MTTF *Mean time to failure* is the average amount of time between when you install a device and when it will fail. MTTF is usually used to describe non-repairable components like light bulbs and hard drives, and higher is better.

MTBF *Mean time between failures* is the average amount of time a component or system can remain online before it needs to be taken down for repair. Higher is better.

MTTR *Mean time to repair* is the average amount of time a component or system will remain offline for repair in the event of a disaster. Lower is better.

Fault tolerance The ability of a system to continue operating in at least partial capacity despite the failure of one or more components. It can be achieved through redundant components or the system's ability to cope with errors. For example, a CPU might detect overheating from a failed fan and slow itself down to avoid hardware damage without stopping, and RAID allows a storage system to keep working without data loss when an individual drive fails.

Maximizing availability while minimizing recovery time is always ideal, but doing so requires prior planning and ongoing preparation. The higher the standards you want to maintain for a given system, the more expensive and labor-intensive it becomes.

Redundancy

Redundant components or even entire systems are a good way to achieve fault tolerance. If the component is hot-swappable, you can repair or replace it with no service interruption. If it isn't, you can at least get by until it's a better time to do maintenance. Redundancy can be applied to physical components, entire systems, or support services. A wide variety of redundancy solutions are popular in modern IT operations. Some you might encounter include the following:

- Backup power systems such as UPS or generators

- RAID storage systems that can compensate for the failure of a single drive

- Multiple NICs or network connections that can function when specific links or nodes fail

- Multiple redundant servers that use *load balancing* technologies to boost performance and compensate for individual failures

- Virtual or cloud-based systems which can be activated quickly when primary systems fail

- Backup sites or distributed facilities which can compensate for a sitewide disaster

Some redundant solutions take over automatically when the primary component fails, while others require human response. Both kinds need to be tested, updated, and otherwise maintained much like primary systems are. You should learn what redundant systems are in use in your workplace, and understand your responsibilities in maintaining and using them.

Data backups

Redundant systems can reduce the chance of service interruptions or data loss, but won't eliminate them entirely. It's especially important with valuable data, since a failed RAID controller, malware infection, or natural disaster can overcome a single redundancy solution. You should always perform periodic backups to external media so that if won't be lost if something happens to the system. How often you should back up important data depends on how often it changes, and how critical it is to minimize the chance of any particular changes being lost. For example, while you might back a transaction database up nightly, or even constantly to the cloud, a user workstation that doesn't host irreplaceable local data might just need a system backup immediately after its configuration is changed.

There are many ways to perform backups, so there's really no excuse not to perform them regularly. Most operating systems come with some sort of backup software built in. While it's usually pretty basic, you can find third party solutions meant for home users or enterprises of any size. With most solutions you don't need to actually interrupt service to perform backups, so you can choose to perform backups at otherwise slow times or even continuously in the background.

Backup types

Backup strategies can be categorized according to what kind of data is preserved, how multiple backup copies are managed, and where backup data is stored. The first of the three is rather straightforward:

Exam Objective(s): 220-1002 4.3.1

- *File level* backups preserve important files or folders so that they can be restored to the same or a different system when needed.

- *Image level* backups copy entire hard drives or other storage volumes. In addition to backing up important files, a *system image* allows you to quickly restore a fully configured computer to an operative state.

- *Application-aware* backups are designed to back up application servers running database software or other critical, constantly running applications. These backups can preserve even application state information and other data held in RAM, which would be lost by a file or image level backup.

Unless you're just taking an image of a newly configured system, backups aren't a one-time event. If you're performing backups frequently you should keep multiple copies, just in case the latest backup doesn't work or if the data you want was already gone or changed when it was taken. Since full backups consume a lot of space and time, backup software tends to allow options to track and back up data only when it changes.

In Windows file systems, for example, each file has an *archive bit* in its file properties. Windows sets the archive bit whenever a file is created or modified so that backup utilities know it's changed, and the utilities can then clear the bit again. Typical Windows backup software might include the following options for a file level backup:

Full   Backs up all files that are included in the backup policy regardless of their archive bits, then clears the bit for all files. It's typical practice to perform a full backup first and at periodic intervals thereafter.

Incremental Backs up only files with a set archive bit, then clears the bit. Incremental backups save all changes since the last full or incremental backup. They're quick to create, but a long series of incremental backups makes recovery more time-consuming.

Differential Backs up files with a set archive bit, but does not clear the bit after. Differential backups save all changes since the last full backup. Each differential backup will be larger than the one before, but it's quicker to recover from a differential backup than an incremental one.

Other backup technologies might use their own options and terminology, but behind the scenes the functions will usually be similar. *Continuous backup* software that never runs a discrete backup process may not rely on the archive bit, but it still watches for files that have changed, and backs up a fresh copy to the archive.

For any of the above methods, backup software will eventually run out of space. Depending on your methods, deleting old backups might be a manual process, or it might automatically happen on a set schedule or just when space starts to run out.

Backup destinations

You can store backups almost anywhere you can store data in general, but the method you choose can greatly affect the logistics of the process, and what kind of protection it gives your data. The simplest way for most users is to back up data to an external hard drive, or even a flash drive. If the backup volume isn't too large, it's an affordable solution that doesn't require any special hardware, and you can just leave the drive in place for scheduled automatic backups. The main disadvantage is that it's not the safest backup strategy. If the backup drive is stored in your office, a fire that destroys your computer could easily destroy all your backups. If the backup drive is left plugged in full time, ransomware or some other attack could corrupt the backups too. For that matter, backup hard drives can fail just like main drives, and anything that happens to the drive will affect all backups on the same disk.

Exam Objective(s): 220-1002 4.3.5

For larger enterprise backups the traditional solution is to use magnetic backup tapes. While less convenient, tapes are less expensive per gigabyte than hard drives, and no moving parts means less to fail. Since they're intended to be removed from the drive and can be write protected, they're also less subject to corruption via malware or localized physical damage. For small backups, optical discs have similar advantages.

You can also perform backups over the network, whether to a network file share or to a network-based tape drive. This approach has some important advantages; the backups are physically separated from the original computer, and you can configure regularly scheduled backups for a whole network full of individual systems to the same backup volumes. One drawback is that network backup can impact network performance, especially where bandwidth is limited. Another is that the central backup location itself is a high value data repository that you need to protect.

For particularly high value data you should keep at least one set of *offsite backups* that will be safe even some sort of disaster strikes your entire facility. You can perform offsite backups by simply sending copies of tapes to a secure storage facility, or by choosing a backup location in a remote rather than local network. The cost for either can be higher than local networks, but it reduces risk further.

Cloud backups are an increasingly popular offsite backup solution that can work for enterprises and individual users. To some extent, any cloud file storage service such as Dropbox, Google Drive, or OneDrive is a cloud backup service which continuously protects any data you choose to sync to the cloud. With compatible software you can also use cloud storage to store actual backup archives just like an ordinary network share. Some cloud backups are even more focused, preserving account and application settings for a cloud-enabled account regardless of whether user data is backed up as well. Best of all, as long as you have a stable internet connection, it's easy to set up cloud backups that happen automatically with no real work on your part.

Cloud backups still aren't a perfect solution. They consume internet bandwidth, and cloud storage can be more costly than local storage. Regulatory requirements might limit cloud storage of some data. Finally, when you back your data up to the cloud it's only as safe as the cloud provider makes it. A system failure or cyberattack could compromise it. You should only choose a provider you trust to keep your data available to you and safe from attackers, and who will assume reasonable liability if it is lost.

Managing backups

The process for making backups and restoring from them depends entirely on the software you use. However, there is some advice that applies to any solution.

Exam Objective(s): 220-1002 4.3.2

- Before performing any workplace backups, check your organization's policies and procedures, and if necessary applicable laws and regulations.

- Data backups should be determined by a written policy. The policy should identify the following points:

  - What data should be backed up
  - What methods should be used
  - How long backups should be retained
  - How backup data should be secured.

- Backups are as sensitive as the original data and should be protected in the same way. For network backups, this includes secure protocols for the backup process itself.

- Backups are useless if you can't restore data from them. Worse in fact, since you'll have a false sense of security.

  - Regularly verify the integrity of backup media
  - Securely discard old and worn out media
  - Regularly practice restoration procedures, both to make sure the data is secure and that personnel are accustomed to doing it.

- Before performing cloud backups, choose a provider you trust, and verify that your business agreement and any relevant laws and regulations clearly specify the responsibilities and liabilities for both parties.

Windows backup features

Windows includes backup software that's sufficient for many users, but the available options depend on which version of Windows you're using. By default, the backup tools in all versions of Windows back up the common Windows folders, including Desktop, Documents, Music, Videos, and Pictures. You can choose other files and folders, but for ease of use, you can just store files and folders in the common Windows folders for automatic backup. In Windows 8 and later, File History will also backup OneDrive files that are available offline on your computer. Windows system settings are not backed up when you back up files and folders, but some user settings are preserved on the network if you use a Microsoft or domain account.

In addition to backing up files and folders, you can create a backup image that contains system settings and applications that you can use to restore a Windows installation if it ever fails to run.

When you need to restore files and folders, you can use the same tools to access the file backups and restore them to their original locations or alternate locations, depending on your situation. You might need to restore the files to a different computer if you lost your original computer to a system malfunction, physical loss, or theft.

Backing up files and folders

The exact backup procedure will depend on your version of Windows, but the procedure generally includes the following steps.

1. Open your backup tool.

   - In Windows 7, the default backup tool is Backup and Restore, which can be used for file or image level backups.

   - Windows 8, 8.1, and 10 still include Backup and Restore, but the new *File History* feature is a more streamlined option for many users.

2. Choose a location to store the backed up files.

   - Choose a local removable device if you want to have the backups close at hand and easily portable.

   - Choose a local network share if you want easily accessible files under your organization's complete control.

   - Choose an internet location if you want off-site backups available from anywhere with an internet connection. Make sure you have adequate bandwidth and trust the remote hosting site.

3. Choose the files you want to back up, if you want to back up files that aren't in the common Windows folders.

4. Set a schedule for the backups. You can typically choose anywhere from hourly to daily.

5. Start the backup, if it doesn't start automatically.

Creating a system recovery image

Creating a system recovery image can vary between Windows versions, but it follows these general steps

1. Open Backup and Restore.
   In Windows 10 it is called Backup and Restore (Windows 7)

2. Click **Create a system image**.

3. Select a location to store the image.

   - An NTFS-formatted hard disk.

   - One or more DVDs. (You'll need a DVD burner and sufficient blank discs)

- A network location. (You'll need to provide an appropriate username and password for the network location.)

4. Complete the wizard and start the backup.

Restoring files and folders

While the exact steps to restore your files will depend on your operating system and your backup settings, you will generally follow these high-level steps.

1. In the same utility which created the backup, start the wizard to restore files.
    File History, Backup and Restore, or a third-party tool.

2. Select the option to restore files.

3. Select the files you want to restore.

4. Complete the wizard to restore the files.

Recovering accounts

Losing access to a user account can have a similar impact to a failed hard drive or system. Inability to log in causes a service disruption, and if you can't recover access to the account you might permanently lose some associated data such as other stored credentials or encrypted files. Account recovery is easiest when you're in a centrally managed environment, but even there prior planning is essential.

Exam Objective(s): 220-1002 4.3.6

Account recovery options vary depending on the operating systems, applications, and services they apply to, but in a typical Windows environment you can apply the following guidelines:

- For domain accounts, an administrator or anyone else with appropriate privileges can reset accounts or unlock passwords from Active Directory.

- Microsoft account passwords can be reset from any device with internet access, including the device you're trying to log into. You'll need to prove your identity to Microsoft using your associated email address or phone number, so make sure you have access to those.

- Local accounts cannot be remotely unlocked or reset, so it's especially important to maintain access to the computer.

  - A local administrator can reset other user passwords.

  - You can create a *password reset disk* on a removable drive, then use it to regain access to your computer if you forget the password. To do so, navigate to User Accounts in Control Panel. You must create the password reset disk before forgetting your password.

  - Restoring from a system image backup with a known password can restore access, but be careful not to lose data changed since the backup.

  - Some recovery CD tools allow you to reset user passwords. One example is Microsoft Diagnostics and Recovery Toolset (*DaRT*) but there are third party tools. Some can even decrypt existing passwords.

    Note: These tools are part of why physically securing a system is essential to real account security.

- Certificates and other stored credentials are encrypted with the Windows password, so an external password reset (as opposed to a user-initiated password change) will cause them to be lost. Most visibly, this means the password reset will render all EFS-encrypted files inaccessible. The only way to prevent this is advanced preparation.

- You can back up locally stored credentials to a removable drive or network location. From the User Accounts screen in Control Panel, click **Manage your credentials** or **Manage your file encryption certificates**

- You can retrieve stored credentials from a system image, provided you have valid credentials from when the backup was made.

- On a domain, centralized certificate services allow the certification authority to invalidate and reissue certificates. This can be used to reset certificate-based logon credentials.

- Even on a domain, EFS-encrypted data can't be accessed simply by issuing a new certificate. Instead, the domain administrator must designate a *data recovery agent* before the EFS certificate is created. The DRA has special permissions to decrypt EFS files. Some Windows editions designate a DRA by default, while others require administrator access.

- Don't reset an account for someone else unless you're certain of their identity and follow all required organizational procedures.

- Store backup credentials with the same security you would store all the data they can be used to access. While the above advice applies to Windows accounts, similar rules apply to almost any identity system. Administrators and automated systems might be able to reset accounts after proof of identity, but losing local passwords can lead to an unusable device. Even if you can reset the account, there may be consequences such as lost data if you don't prepare in advance.

Exercise: Configuring backups

For this exercise you will need a storage device other than your system drive. The exercise is written assuming a USB flash drive, but you can use any internal, external, or even network drive you can access.

Do This	How & Why
1. Create a file on your desktop.	You need a file to test your backup with, so you'll create one.
a) On your desktop, create a text file named Backup.	Type anything you want in Notepad.
b) Save the file and close Notepad.	
2. If necessary, insert your USB drive.	You can also use a second internal drive, network partition, or blank optical disc.
3. Configure a backup location.	
a) In Control Panel, navigate to **System and Security > Backup and Restore (Windows 7)**.	The content pane shows that Windows Backup has not been set up.
b) In the content pane, click **Set up backup**.	To view available drives. You can also add a network location.

Do This	How & Why

c) Click your chosen backup drive in the list. then click **Next**.

You might see a warning that the drive doesn't have enough space to store a system image. That's okay for now.

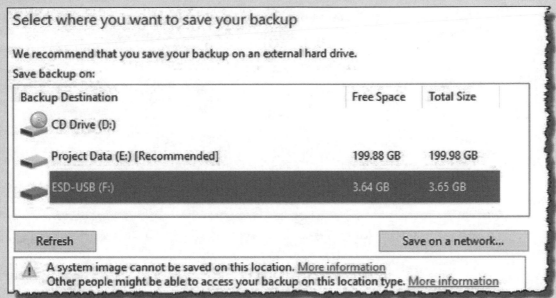

By default, Windows backs up the contents of your desktop, libraries, and personal folders. It also creates a system image, if there's enough space.

d) Click **Let me choose**, then click **Next**.	You'll customize exactly what you back up instead. 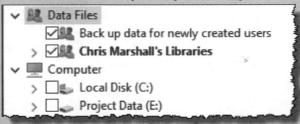 By default, user data files are backed up, but you can add or remove any folder on your computer.
e) Below the list, clear **Include a system image of drives: System Reserved, C:**.	While you'd include these in a real backup of your computer, for now you'll save the space and time.
f) Click **Next**.	To review your backup settings. By default, your backup will run once a week, but you can change the time and frequency if you like.
g) Click **Save settings and run backup**.	After a short time, the backup completes. The **Backup and Restore** window now shows statistics about your backup schedule, location, and status. **Note:** If you receive a write protection error, open OneDrive settings and disable files-on-demand.

Do This	How & Why
4. On your desktop, delete `Backup.txt`.	Imagine you deleted this by accident, or overwrote it with the wrong file. Now you can look in the backup.
5. Restore Backup.txt.	
a) In Backup and Restore, click **Restore my files**.	The **Restore Files** window appears.
b) Click **Browse for Files**.	The **Browse the backup for files** window opens. It's like an Open or Save window, but you can only navigate through your backup files.
c) In the Navigation pane, click **<Username's> backup**.	To view your personal folders. They all contain the contents of those folders at the time the backup was made.
d) Navigate to your Desktop folder.	It's probably in **OneDrive > Desktop**
e) Select **Backup.txt**. and click **Add files**.	The file now appears in the **Restore Files** window.
f) Click **Next**, then **Restore**.	You could also restore it to a new location if you wanted. Backup.txt reappears on your desktop.
6. On your desktop, double-click **Backup**.	If necessary, move or close windows to see it. It's just like it was when you saved it.
7. Close all open windows.	

Assessment: Backup and recovery

1. In terms of time, how does a differential backup plan generally differ from an incremental backup plan?

   - It's quicker both to create backups and to restore data

   - It's quicker to create backups, but slower to restore data

   - It's slower to create backups, but quicker to restore data

   - It's slower both to create backups and to restore data

2. While most of the Windows 10 computers at your workplace use Pro or Enterprise editions, some use Windows 10 Home. You want to use a standard backup method for all of them. What built-in utilities can you use? Choose the best response.

   - Backup and Restore

   - File History

   - Either, depending on your specific needs

   - Neither; you will need a third-party utility

3. For years, the network administrator at your company performed off-site backups by putting a set of tapes in his home safe every weekend. Now that he's retired, his replacement is evaluating cloud backups instead. What drawbacks is this likely this have? Choose all that apply.

   - Incompatibility with conventional archival formats and software

   - Increased network bandwidth

   - More labor intensive

   - More vulnerability to natural disaster

   - Potential regulatory violations

4. Your personal workstation has a variety of applications with additional plugins and custom configuration options. Even if you only use those applications occasionally, it would take a long time to configure them on a new computer. What kind of backup would save you that time on restoring from a hard drive failure? Choose the best response.

   - Application-aware

   - Continuous

   - File

   - Image

Summary: Operational procedures

A+ technicians experience a wide variety of situations beyond working with inanimate objects such as hardware and operating systems. An A+ technician's world includes interacting with people, and following procedures and guidelines outlined by their company to keep employees and equipment safe.

You learned how to:

- Interpret and create policies and other documentation.
- Respond to incidents involving prohibited content and activities.
- Perform backups and recover lost data.

Chapter 8: Safety and professionalism

When troubleshooting an issue with a computer or peripheral device, you need to work methodically and safely to identify the cause of the problem and then make repairs.

You will learn how to:

- Follow appropriate safety procedures when working on computers and peripheral devices.

- Protect personnel and equipment from hazardous environmental conditions.

- Demonstrate proper communication techniques and professionalism.

Module A: Safety

Computers and other peripheral devices are powered by electrical current. Some devices, such as printers, have moving parts that can catch foreign objects. When working on computers and other peripheral devices, you must be careful to protect yourself from injury, as well as protect the computer and device components from becoming damaged.

You will learn how to:

- Protect computer components from damage during troubleshooting.
- Protect yourself from injury during troubleshooting.
- Safely dispose of components containing hazardous materials.

Safety procedures

Even if it's not on anyone's list of most dangerous jobs, IT technicians commonly find themselves in unsafe conditions. Important hazards include electrical shock, dust and debris, heavy objects and equipment, and materials that can be hazardous either during careless exposure or when improperly disposed of.

 Exam Objective(s): 220-1002 4.4.5

For all sorts of safety-related procedures, it's important that you know the best practices to protect yourself, others, and valuable equipment from harm. Beyond that you need to know organizational policies and government regulations relevant to any equipment, materials, and procedures in your workplace. Even if your actions are safe in themselves, failure to comply with policies and regulations can still get you in trouble. Depending on the workplace you might be able to check formal policies or ask a safety officer, or you might have to perform research on your own.

Component safety

The most common cause of damage to computer components during installation or repair is electrostatic electricity. Damage occurs when one object builds up more electrons on its surface than another object. When the two objects meet, the objects attempt to balance the difference in electrical charge by transferring electrons from the object with more to the object with less. When you are one of the objects, you'll sometimes feel a "static shock." Be aware that you don't need to feel or see the static shock for the transfer of electrons to cause damage to sensitive computer components. There are several tools that you can use to keep yourself and your equipment properly grounded.

Exam Objective(s): 220-1002 4.4.1, 4.4.2

- *Antistatic bags*: A bag typically made from plastic polyethylene terephthalate (PET) used to store components that are sensitive to electrostatic discharge. The bags are slightly conductive, forming what is known as a *Faraday Cage* around the component, protecting it from any electrostatic discharges occurring on the outside of the bag.

- *ESD straps*: Devices worn by the user on their wrist, ankle, or heel and then attached to a ground source away from sensitive internal components. The most common ESD strap used in PC repair is the wrist strap. Any buildup of electrical charges on the user's body is channeled through the strap on the user's wrist to the computer's metal chassis, protecting any internal components the user touches from static discharge. You wear an ESD wrist strap on the wrist of your non-dominant hand. For example, if you are right-handed, wear the strap on your left wrist.

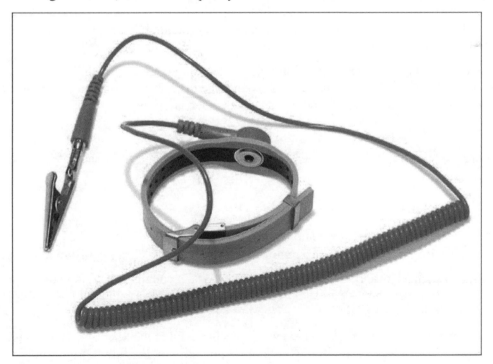

- *ESD mats*: A special electrically grounded mat designed to place computer equipment on while you are working.

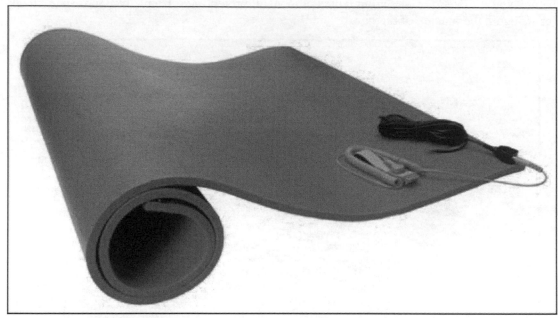

If you don't have an ESD device, you can protect your equipment by "self-grounding." Self-grounding is where you touch a grounded metal object, such as the computer's chassis, prior to working on sensitive components. The grounded metal object must be unpainted with a clear ground path. This is a quick and easy option, and many people build computers without taking any other precautions. However, there's a risk that self-grounding will not be enough to protect sensitive components.

Finally, don't forget that grounding is important for operating equipment as well, in order to prevent electrical shock during operation. Some specialized equipment may have grounding requirements in its setup instructions, but more commonly it is provided through the ground wire of a three-prong electrical outlet. So-called "ground plug" adapters can allow you to physically connect a grounded device into a non-grounded (two-prong) outlet, but they are not safe and generally provide no actual grounding.

When buildings are constructed or modified without attention to building codes, even an outlet that looks grounded might not be. If you have reason to suspect the ground line of an outlet might not be connected, an inexpensive *receptacle tester* will check for grounding as well as other safety issues.

Personal safety

When working on computer equipment and peripheral devices, you need to keep yourself safe. Follow these guidelines to prevent injury:

 Exam Objective(s): 220-1002 4.4.4

- Disconnect the power before repairing a computer or other device. Electricity can be provided by a wall outlet or battery. It's just as important to remove the battery as it is to unplug from a wall outlet.

- Remove loose items such as jewelry, scarves, or ties that could get caught or bang on components. Remember to secure loose clothing - for example, placing rubber bands around your wrists if you are wearing a shirt with loose sleeves.

- Use proper lifting techniques when moving heavy equipment. Bend at the knee and squat to pick up the item. Lift using your legs, not your back. Don't turn or rotate until you are fully upright. For large or bulky items, team lift.

- Be aware of weight limitations. Your company might have policies about the maximum weight employees are allowed to lift unassisted. Use the proper tools such as a hand truck or mechanical lift to move heavier equipment.

- Be prepared for electrical fires. Have a Class C (in the US) fire extinguisher handy. They are made for fires involving electrical devices and their contents have passed required electrical conductivity measurements. Look for one of these symbols on your extinguisher:

- Secure loose cables out of the way. You need to make sure they are not causing a tripping hazard. Also make sure you can't get a hand caught in the cables, which could cause you to pull the device, knocking it over or into other components.

- Wear safety goggles. Workplace eye injuries are common. If you are using chemicals or heat to clean or repair a component or device, you should wear safety goggles to protect your eyes from cuts, scrapes, and burns.

- Wear an air filter mask. If you are using chemicals or heat to clean or repair a component or device, you should wear an air filter mask to protect your lungs from any harmful fumes.

Toxic waste handling

Computers and peripheral devices are full of materials that are hazardous to humans and our environment. Before you dispose of a computer, device, or individual component, check your local government regulations for disposal requirements. Many municipalities no longer allow you to throw these items in the trash. They must be taken to the appropriate recycling facility. Three items that shouldn't be placed in the trash, regardless of local regulations include:

Exam Objective(s): 220-1002 4.4.3

- Batteries. Batteries include heavy metals such as lead, cadmium, zinc, lithium and mercury. If batteries are sent to the landfill, the battery casing corrodes and the metals can leak causing soil and ground water pollution. The same heavy metals cause air quality issues if the batteries are incinerated.

- Toner cartridgcs. Printer cartridges are made up of a complex combination of plastics, metals, foam, ink and toner, and are not biodegradable. If sent to a landfill with other trash, they take up land fill space for practically forever. When you recycle an ink toner cartridge, manufacturers can reuse it up to ten times without product degradation. Many ink toner dealers will pay for used ink toner cartridges.

- CRT displays. CRT displays contain leaded glass, which if broken can cause soil and water contamination. Many states and local municipalities have banned CRTs from being collected with trash, and require that you dispose of them through an authorized recycling facility.

- Cell phones and tablets often contain toxic materials including non-removable batteries. Since they're small and easy to throw away, it's important not to put them in the trash.

  - Some electronics stores and mobile device vendors will accept them for recycling, even if they don't accept larger electronics.

  - Relatively modern devices in good condition can be donated to charity.

  - If a device has any valuable data on it, perform a factory reset or physically destroy it before disposing of it. Be careful not to smash or puncture a device while a battery is still inside.

Discussion: Safety procedures

For this discussion, have some safety procedures and equipment available for review and demonstration, if possible.

1. What safety hazards are there in your workplace?

2. What safety equipment have you used to protect yourself or valuable equipment?

3. What disposal or recycling guidelines are there for hazardous materials in your workplace?

4. What safety regulations apply to your workplace?

Assessment: Safety

1. Which safety device is used to protect sensitive components from electrostatic discharge during transport and storage?

   • Antistatic bags

   • ESD straps

   • ESD mats

   • Self-grounding

2. Which class of fire extinguishers is used on electrical fires?

   • Class A

   • Class B

   • Class C

   • Class D

3. Which items can cause soil and water contamination if they are sent to a landfill?

   • Batteries

   • CRTs

   • Magnetic tapes

   • Toner cartridges

Module B: Environmental factors

It's sometimes easy to overlook how the environment and computer systems are linked together. It's important to understand the impacts of environment on computer and electronics, and how both can impact the environment around them. Take care that any actions you take that may impact the environment comply with all local and federal government regulations. If there's any doubt, be sure to consult local authorities.

You will learn about:

- Temperature and humidity controls.
- Power protection.
- Impacts from particles in the air.

About environmental factors

When it comes to computers and other electronics, "environmental impact" can mean a lot of things. When you're using or disposing of electronics it can mean health or ecological damage caused by toxic materials. In the operational environment, it's usually more the opposite, referring to how computer operations are affected by their surroundings. Important environmental factors include:

 Exam Objective(s): 220-1002 4.5.6

- Temperature and humidity
- Airborne contaminants and air quality
- Dust and debris
- Electrical power
- Hazardous chemicals in or around electronics

All of these environmental effects can affect equipment function and human health, so you should keep best practices and company policies in mind in your workplace. It's also essential that your operational environment, and your maintenance and disposal procedures, comply with all local and federal government regulations. If there's any doubt, be sure to consult appropriate authorities for guidance.

Temperature and humidity

The right environment is important for the health of the electronic equipment at a given location. Three aspects of the environment that are important are temperature, humidity, and proper ventilation.

 Exam Objective(s): 220-1002 4.5.2

Environmental variable	It's important because...
Temperature	Electronic equipment, especially older computers and high-volume servers, generate a lot of heat, and they don't do well in high-temperature environments. Electronic equipment must be kept in typical office environment, where temperatures don't fluctuate much between 65 to 85 degrees. But dedicated server rooms can generate plenty of heat that needs to be dissipated through a well-ventilated HVAC system.
Humidity	Humidity above 50% to 60% can cause condensation, which can destroy electronic equipment. On the other hand, low humidity breeds static electricity, which can fry delicate computer components.

Environmental variable	It's important because...
Ventilation	A good air flow not just in an office but around specific components can prevent overheating of both the components and the surrounding environment. Good ventilation can also reduce humidity to proper levels.

Power surges, brownouts, and blackouts

Delicate electronic components prefer a steady supply of electricity, and when the electric supply exceeds or falls out of normal ranges, you can experience not just data loss when equipment fails, but permanent equipment damage. Look out for these three power supply problems:

Exam Objective(s): 220-1002 4.3.3, 4.3.4, 4.5.3

Power surge — An increase in voltage that can last several seconds and damage equipment. Short intense power surges may also be called *power spikes*.

Brownout — A drop in voltage, which may cause electronic devices to fail or behave unpredictably. Typically, "brownout" means a voltage drop lasting minutes or hours, while a short-term voltage drop is called a "sag" or "dip." Power companies sometimes use intentional brownouts during emergencies to reduce load on the electrical grid.

Blackout — A complete interruption of the power supply, lasting any duration. Electrical devices without alternate power will fail.

To protect against problems with the power supply, consider these tools:

- A surge suppressor, or surge protector, prevents power surges or spikes from reaching sensitive equipment. A surge suppressor can be a single strip designed to protect a few devices, but you can also purchase whole house or building suppressors which an electrician installs on the main power supply lines for the building.

  Note: Not every power strip is a surge protector, and surge protection degrades over time. Make sure to purchase a surge protection with a guaranteed rating, and if you can't test it regularly replace it according to industry recommendations.

- An uninterruptible power supply (UPS) is a battery backup which instantly takes over during blackouts or brownouts. Depending on its battery capacity, a UPS might just give you time to save your data and shut down gracefully, or it might allow you to work through a moderately short blackout. A UPS can protect a single computer or a whole facility, and most include surge protection.

- Electrical generators can provide protection against longer term power outages. Since generators take time to turn on, they're often used along with short-term battery backups.

A UPS is bulkier than a simple surge protector

Installing a UPS

Universal Power Supply devices provide temporary battery power to your computer and other devices. They provide enough power to allow you time to save any work and then complete a graceful shutdown of your operating system during a power outage. Often, they come with monitoring software that reports when power has been lost or a surge has occurred.

They also protect your equipment from power surges. to install a UPS:

1. Plug the power cords for the computer, display, and any externally powered devices into the UPS.
   There are usually two sides. One side continues to provide power temporarily so that you can complete a graceful system shutdown. The other side provides basic surge protection.

2. Plug your network cable into the UPS, then run another network cable from the UPS to your computer's network port.

3. If you have a POTS phone, you can plug the phone line into the UPS, then run another phone cable to your phone.
   If your phone requires power, you can protect it by plugging it into the UPS as well.

4. Run the USB cable from the UPS to a USB port in your computer.

5. Plug the UPS into the wall outlet.

6. Power on the UPS device and boot your computer.

7. Install any control/monitoring software that came with your UPS.

Airborne particles and debris

Air quality can impact not just the operation of electronic equipment, but it can also impact the people who work in the same environment. To protect equipment and humans from airborne particles, consider the following tools:

Exam Objective(s): 220-1002 4.5.4, 4.5.5

- Enclosures, with good ventilation, can filter air, remove debris, and return fresh air to a confined space.

- Air filters and masks can help prevent exposure to airborne particles for both humans and equipment.

Compressed air and mechanical blowers are a convenient and effective way to clean accumulated debris from around and inside equipment, such as computer cases. The drawback is that just blowing air around will spread dust and debris and might even send it into sensitive electronics. Consider a vacuum meant specifically for electronics instead. When you do use compressed air, make sure to use breathing filters and clean up the dust afterward.

Exercise: Connecting a UPS

There are many environmental factors that can cause safety issues with either your computers and devices, the health of your employees, or both. A UPS device protects your computer and other electronic equipment from power surges, blackouts, and brownouts.

If you have a UPS that you can connect to a computer system, complete the following steps.

Do This	How & Why
1. Plug the power cords for the computer, display, and any externally powered devices into the UPS.	There are usually two sides. One side continues to provide power temporarily so that you can complete a graceful system shutdown. The other side provides basic surge protection.
2. Plug your network cable into the UPS, then run another network cable from the UPS to your computer's network port.	
3. If you have a POTS phone, you can plug the phone line into the UPS, then run another phone cable to your phone.	If your phone requires power, you can protect it by plugging it into the UPS as well.
4. Run the USB cable from the UPS to a USB port in your computer.	
5. Plug the UPS into the wall outlet.	
6. Power on the UPS device and boot your computer.	
7. Install any control/monitoring software that came with your UPS.	

Safety Data Sheets (SDS)

Safety Data Sheets (SDS) , previously referred to as *Material Safety Data Sheets (MSDS)* , include safety and health information about chemical products, including health risks and storage, disposal recommendations, and procedures for containing a leak or a spill. In the US, OSHA requires that the product manufacturer create and provide these sheets for any chemical product that has the potential to impact or harm people or the environment. Each SDS is in the same user-friendly, 16-section format. OSHA also requires that every employer train their employees in the use of Safety Data Sheets and make the sheets readily available and accessible. OSHA can come in to inspect your workplace and audit your Safety Data Sheets, SDS management system, and employee training process.

CAUTION: By law, an SDS has to be available to all employees at all times. Do not keep your SDS sheets locked up or inaccessible.

Exam Objective(s): 220-1002 4.5.1

Safety data sheets have 16 sections. Any may be brief for some materials, and 12-15 may be omitted entirely.

1. Identifications

2. Hazard(s) identification

3. Composition/Information on ingredients

4. First-Aid Measures

5. Fire-Fighting Measures

6. Accidental Release Measures

7. Handling and Storage

8. Exposure Controls/Personal Protections

9. Physical and Chemical Properties

10. Stability and Reactivity

11. Toxicological Information

12. Ecological Information

13. Disposal Considerations

14. Transport Information

15. Regulatory Information,

16. Other Information - includes when the SDS was last prepared or revised.

SDS or other documentation and labels may include pictograms to warn of specific hazards. If you see one, you should definitely read closer to see what risks it represents.

GHS hazard identification pictograms

Exercise: Examining an SDS document

Having a safety plan in place and educating your employees on their responsibilities in executing and adhering to the plan are critical to keeping your equipment free from damage and your employees unharmed. MSDS documents are required by law for all chemicals in your environment and are a big part of being able to respond to exposure to and spills of these chemicals.

If you have internet access, complete the following steps.

Do This	How & Why
1. In a web browser, navigate to www.hp.com.	
2. Scroll to the bottom of the page.	
3. Under About Us, click **Sustainable impact**.	Many companies place SDS documents along with recycling information or other environmental regulations and policies.

About us

Contact HP
Careers
Investor relations
Sustainable impact
Press center
The Garage

Do This	How & Why

4. At the top of the page, click **Planet > Products and solutions > Safety data sheets**.

HP makes a wide variety of products. In addition to printer supplies, there are SDS downloads for things like laptop batteries, projector lamps, and PC cleaning kits.

5. Click **LaserJet printer supplies**.

6. Click any of the available data sheets and review the information in each of the 16 sections.

Assessment: Environment

1. Humidity above which percentage can cause condensation, potentially destroying electronic equipment?

   - 10-20%

   - 20-25%

   - 25-45%

   - 50-60%

2. Which of the following describes a long-term drop in voltage, typically lasting longer than just a few minutes?

   - Blackout

   - Brownout

   - Power surge

   - Surge suppression

3. To clean accumulated debris from around and inside equipment, such as computer cases, you must use a special vacuum meant specifically for electronics. True or false.

   - True

   - False

4. Your coworker has splashed isopropyl alcohol he is using to clean a computer in his eye. Which section of the isopropyl alcohol SDS would you want to refer to immediately?

   - Section 2: Hazard(s) Identification

   - Section 4: First-Aid Measures

   - Section 8: Exposure Controls

   - Section 11: Toxicological Information

5. You're installing a CPU and CPU fan when you accidently drop the thermal grease container and get some on the floor. What should you do?

   - Call 911.

   - Refer to the SDS for the thermal grease on proper clean-up methods.

   - Report the incident to your immediate supervisor.

   - Wipe it up immediately with a water dampened cloth.

Module C: Professionalism

Part of the job of a support technician is to not just provide competent support, but it also includes acting in a professional manner.

You will learn how to:

- Provide customer support in a professional manner using proper communication techniques.

Demonstrating professionalism

Success as a support technician means not just solving problems successfully but providing good customer service while you do. You can use the following steps as guidelines for providing professional service to your customers.

Exam Objective(s): 220-1002 4.7

1. User proper language.

   - Avoid using technical jargon, acronyms, and slang. Assume your customer doesn't know all the technical terms you do, and explain things in plain language.

   - Speak clearly, with an even tone, and speak loudly enough to be heard.

   - Avoid talking down to the customer or presenting a condescending attitude or tone of voice.

2. Maintain a positive attitude and project confidence.

   - Act like you know what you're doing, even if you might have a doubt about how to proceed.

   - Don't speak negatively about the organization or the products or device's the customer is using.

3. Actively listen and avoid interrupting.

   - Take notes, make eye contact, and use non-verbal cues, such as nodding your head, to ensure the customer know you're listening and taking an interest in what they're saying.

   - Ask questions to help clarify the situation, but let the customer describe the problem fully.

   - Do not interrupt and act like you know what the customer is going to say before they say it.

4. Be culturally sensitive.

   - Know your customer and their basic business and interpersonal traditions and expectations.

   - Address people appropriately. Use professional titles where applicable, and avoid first names if possible.

5. Be on time.

   - Let your customer know you've arrived and are ready to begin work.

   - If you're going to be late, inform the customer as soon as possible and give an updated expected arrival time.

6. Avoid distractions.

   - Avoid personal calls, either on a cell phone or landline. If you must take a phone call, excuse yourself first, and then end the call as quickly as possible.

   - Avoid texting unless it's an urgent business matter. Do not access social media sites while you're working with a customer.

   - Avoid conversations with co-workers while you're working with a customer.

- Avoid or minimize personal interruptions while you're on a job.

7. Display patience and tact when dealing with a difficult customer.

   - Do not argue with a customer or become defensive.

   - Avoid dismissing customer problems. While the problem might not seem like much to you, it's important to the customer. Therefore, it should be important to you.

   - Avoid being judgemental.

   - Ask open-ended questions to clarify customer statements and narrow the scope of the problem. Restate the issue or problem to the customer to verify that you understand it correctly and to show them you're actively engaged in solving their issues.

   - Never disclose your experiences with customer on social media sites, no matter how private you might think your posts are.

8. Set achievable expectations for service activities and their timeline; as the support process continues, regularly communicate your current status with the customer.

   - If possible, offer different options for replacement or repair.

   - Document the work you've done and the services you've provided. Be as detailed as possible.

   - Schedule a follow-up call or email with the customer in the near future to verify that the problem was solved and that they are satisfied with your work.

9. Deal appropriately with confidential and private materials.

   - Do not browse or examine personal or confidential business files unless it is a necessary part of your task. Exceptions may include evidence of policy violations or illegal activities.

   - Do not share the contents of private personal or company materials found in files on a computer, on a desktop workspace or shelves, and in documents on a printer.

   - Keep *personally identifiable information (PII)* confidential and secure, including information such as names and addresses, phone numbers, names of family members or co-workers, and any information that a customer would deem private. Remember that in some settings, the disclosure of private information is prohibited by law.

Exercise: Demonstrating professionalism

Excellent customer service comes from not only computer knowledge, but also the ability to resolve problems and interact with customers in a professional manner using proper communication techniques.

Do This	How & Why
1. Describe negative interactions you've seen between users and customer support professionals. a) What unprofessional behaviors did you witness on behalf of the support professional? b) Did those behaviors upset the customer? c) Did they directly interfere with the support process?	

Do This	How & Why
2. Describe support events you've seen where a support professional was able to effectively help a difficult customer. a) What did the customer say or do to complicate the support process? b) What did the support professional say or do to overcome those difficulties?	
3. With a partner, act out a tech support call. One of you should take the role of a user who has a clearly-defined problem but lacks the knowledge to troubleshoot it, and the other the technician who has to assist the user.	

Assessment: Professionalism

1. Which of the following are appropriate addresses for a customer? Choose all that apply.

   - Buddy
   - Dr. Smith
   - Jimmy
   - Ms. Jenkins

2. An end user has reported a system problem and you're trying to figure out its cause. Which of the following pieces of advice would be a mistake? Choose the best response.

   - Allow the customer to explain the problem fully at first, only asking questions for clarification.
   - Always use detailed technical language when asking for clarifying information.
   - Speak clearly, with an even tone, and loud enough to be heard.
   - While listening to the customer's description, take notes and nod without interrupting.

3. Personally identifiable information includes which of the following?

   - Address
   - Name
   - Names of co-workers
   - Phone number
   - All of the above

Summary: Safety and professionalism

You learned how to:

- Keep yourself, your computer, and the environment safe by following appropriate safety procedures when working on computers and peripheral devices.

- Protect equipment and personnel from hazardous environmental conditions such as temperature, humitity, electrical failures, dust, and hazardous materials.

- Demonstrate proper communication techniques and professionalism.

Appendix A: Glossary

2G - Second Generation Wireless. Early digital cellular networks, used in the 1990s and early 2000s. These networks are the oldest still commonly deployed so 2G devices will still work, but they're obsolete and poorly suited for modern internet access.

3G - Third Generation Wireless technology that includes enhancements over previous iterations (2G), like high-speed transmission, advanced multimedia access, and global roaming.

4G LTE - Fourth Generation Wireless, Long Term Evolution. Wireless technologies being used to transition existing 3G networks to newer, faster standards. 4G networks handle both voice and data using TCP/IP protocols, and data speeds can reach 300Mbps downstream and 75Mbps upstream.

ACL - Access control list. A list attached to a resource, giving permissions, or rules, about exactly who can access it.

ACPI - Advanced Configuration Power Interface. A power-saving feature that allows a computer's operating system to control the amount of power given to each device and to power them down when not in use. Also allows the computer to be "woken up" by an external device such as a keyboard.

ad hoc network - A network composed of individual devices communicating with each other directly. This term implies spontaneous or impromptu construction because these networks often bypass the gatekeeping hardware or central access point such as a router.

address resolution - The process of acquiring a physical address from a machine or virtual address that a network node or computer peripheral has sent.

Administrative Tools - In Windows (Vista and later), a set of tools for managing the computer and its operating system. Found in the Control Panel, it includes Event Viewer, Performance Monitor, System Configuration, and several other components.

ADSL - Asymmetric Digital Subscriber Line. A type of DSL that has a bitrate higher in one direction than the other. More popular than symmetric DSL (SDSL) for consumer connections where download speed is more important than upload speeds.

AES - Advanced Encryption Standard. A strong and widely used encryption standard, supporting 128, 192, and 156-bit key lengths.

AGP - Accelerated Graphics Port. A high-speed port for connecting a video card to your computer.

Originally designed to improve the processing of 3D computer graphics by using its own dedicated bus, AGP ports have been largely replaced by PCIe ports.

ALU - Arithmetic logic unit. One of the two primary components of a CPU. The ALU performs all arithmetic and logic operations.

amplifier probe - One of the two components that comprise a toner probe; the other component is a tone generator. The amplifier probe has a speaker and a metal tip; when the tip comes near the wire it detects the signal from the tone generator and makes a sound.

antivirus/anti-malware - A program that scans your computer system for viruses/malware and removes them if they are found.

APIPA - Automatic private IP addressing.

ARP - Address Resolution Protocol. Used to identify the physical (MAC) address of a given IP address.

artifact - A distortion in an image or sound caused by a limitation or malfunction in a computer system's hardware or software.

aspect ratio - The measurement describing the width and height proportion of an image on screen. Documented as width proportion : height proportion.

attenuation - Any reduction in the strength of a signal.

ATX - Advanced Technology Extended. An industry-wide specification for a desktop computer's motherboard. ATX takes the "Baby AT" motherboard (an earlier industry standard) and rotates the layout of the microprocessor and expansion slots by 90 degrees to allow space for more full-length add-in cards.

authentication - A process that ensures and confirms a user's identity using credentials supplied by the user.

balanced pair - A transmission line consisting of two conductors of the same type, each of which have equal impedances along their lengths and equal impedances to ground and to other circuits.

bare-metal - A type of hypervisor that installs directly onto the hardware of the host machine, serving as its underlying operating system.

BIOS - Basic input/output system.

BitLocker - In cryptography, the result of encryption performed on plaintext using an algorithm, called a cipher. Ciphertext is also known as encrypted or encoded information because it contains a form of the original plaintext that is unreadable by a human or computer.

BitLocker-To-Go - Introduced with Windows 7, a full-disk encryption protection technology for removable storage devices that are connected to one of the USB ports on a computer.

Bluetooth - A wireless communication technology that allows devices to connect over short distances.

BNC connector - Bayonet Neill-Concelman connector. A miniature quick connector used for coaxial cable. It features two bayonet lugs on the female connector; mating is fully achieved with a quarter turn of the coupling nut.

botnet - A network of malware-infected computers that can perform attacks or do other tasks as directed by its controller, without the knowledge of the actual system owners.

bridge - A type of computer network device that provides interconnection with other networks that use the same protocol. Bridge devices work at the data link layer of the OSI model, connecting two different networks together and providing communication between them.

broadband modem - A device that connects cable or DSL Internet service to the computer or network.

broadcast address - A MAC or IPv4 address that designates a packet that should be read by all listening hosts.

brute force attack - A trial-and-error method used to obtain secure information such as a user password or PIN. Automated software is used to generate a large number of consecutive guesses as to the value of the desired data.

buffered DIMM - A type of DIMM that holds data and manages electrical signals before the information passed between the memory chip and the northbridge chip (memory controller) or CPU (if there is no northbridge chip).

burn-in - A display condition in which a fixed image is displayed on screen for an extended period of time, causing phosphor burn in CRTs or pixel deterioration in LCD and plasma units.

bus - A communication system that transfers data between components inside a computer, or between computers. This expression covers all related hardware components (wire, optical fiber, etc.) and software, including communication protocols.

BYOD - Bring your own device. A security policy that allows or even encourages users to employ their own personal devices freely on the network.

CA - Certificate authority. A third-party entity responsible for assignment, verification, and revocation of digital certificates.

cable modem - A device used to connect one or more computers to a cable company's Internet service. The same coaxial cable coming into the house or office also provides TV and VoIP service.

cache - A system component that stores recently used information so that it can be quickly accessed at a later time. Computers incorporate several different types of caching in order to run more efficiently. Common types include browser cache, disk cache, memory cache, and processor cache.

capacitive technology - A touch screen technology that uses the conductive touch of a human finger or a specialized device for input. When a capacitive panel is touched, a small amount of charge is drawn to the point of contact, which becomes a functional capacitor.

carrier lines - Multiplexed trunk lines meant to carry many voice channels at once. Commonly used by telecommunications companies.

carrier wave - A high-frequency electromagnetic wave modulated in amplitude or frequency to convey a signal.

CCMP - Counter Mode with Cipher Block Chaining Message Authentication Code Protocol. An encryption protocol that forms part of the 802.11i standard for wireless local area networks (WLANs), particularly those using WiMax technology.

CDFS - Compact Disc File System. Contains all tracks and boot images extracted from a CD.

CDMA - Code Division Multiple Access. Digital cellular phone technology that does not sub-divide the available bandwidth for several separate calls. Instead, it assigns the entire bandwidth to one call and encodes each call, limiting decoding to the intended receiver.

cellular data - The transmission of data via cellphone. Also called "mobile data" and a separate service from voice calling, cellular data is used for email, web pages, media and app downloads, and software updates.

certificate of destruction - Documentation provided by a media destruction service for legal liability or regulatory compliance.

CFast - CompactFast. Next generation Compact Flash memory card that uses the serial ATA interface and are commonly available with up to 512 GB of storage.

CIDR - Classless Inter-Domain Routing. An expansion of the IP addressing system that allows for a more efficient and appropriate allocation of addresses. Under CIDR, subnetworks of any size can be allocated, just by allowing any mask prefix number. This way, networks can be created to whatever size is needed.

CIFS - A file-sharing protocol that provides an open and cross-platform mechanism for requesting network server files and services. It's based on the enhanced version of Microsoft's SMB protocol.

classful networking - A network addressing architecture used in the Internet from 1981 until the introduction of CIDR in 1993. It divides the address space for IPv4 into five address classes by address range.

client-server - A networking framework in which user systems access centrally managed resources.

cloud bursting - An application deployment model in which an application runs in a private cloud or data center and bursts into a public cloud when the demand for computing capacity spikes.

cloud computing - A service model for network-accessible computing services, which includes on-demand self-service, broad network access, resource pooling, rapid elasticity, and measured service.

CMOS - Stands for "complementary metal-oxide-semiconductor," but means the battery-backed memory that stores BIOS or UEFI settings.

coaxial cable - A transmission line that consists of a tube of electrically conducting material surrounding a central conductor held in place by insulators. Used to transmit telegraph, telephone, television, and Internet signals.

code signing certificate - A type of digital certificate that contains information about the software publisher and the issuing certificate authority, and guarantees that an executable file or script hasn't been altered or corrupted since it was digitally signed.

collision - The situation that occurs when two or more devices attempt to send a signal along the same channel at the same time.

connectivity - A generic term for connecting devices to each other in order to transfer data back and forth. Often refers to network connections, which embraces bridges, routers, switches and gateways as well as backbone networks. May also refer to connecting a home or office to the Internet or connecting a digital camera to a computer or printer.

core - An independent processor embedded on to CPU. It can process a single instruction at a time. Multiple cores allow the CPU to process multiple instructions at once.

counters - Used in Performance Monitor to specify which of your computer's resources you want to monitor, including the processor, memory, page file, TCP/IP connections, and any of the many Windows services that are running at any given time.

CPE - Customer-premises equipment. Communications equipment that resides on the customer's premises (i.e., it is owned or leased by the customer).

CPU - Central Processing Unit. In a computer, the silicon microchip that processes all instructions, whether they be entered through user input or submitted by a computer program.

critical assets - System components that can't be easily replaced, or which will immediately disrupt organizational functions if they're compromised.

critical nodes - Network components that the system needs to function, like essential servers or backbone routers.

crossover cable - A specialized network cable wired as T568A on one end, and T568B on the other. Used to directly join two PCs without a switch between them.

crosstalk - Any phenomenon by which a signal transmitted on one circuit or channel of a transmission system creates an undesired effect in another circuit or channel.

DDNS - Dynamic DNS. A mechanism by which the name server in the DNS is automatically updated with the custom domain name and the ever-changing IP addresses.

DDoS attack - Distributed denial of service. An attack in which multiple compromised computer systems attack a target, such as a server, website or other network resource, and cause a denial of service for users of the targeted resource.

decryption - The process of decoding data that has been encrypted into a secret format.

default gateway - The gateway in a network that a computer will use automatically (by default) to access another network if a specific gateway is not designated for use.

degaussing - The process of using powerful electromagnets to destroy all data on magnetic media like tapes and hard drives, but not optical or flash storage. Some media can be easily reused after degaussing, but others, like most hard drives, require specialized tools to reformat.

demarcation point - (Also called demarc.) The point at which the part of the network legally owned by the consumer is physically connected to that owned by the phone company.

device identifier - The last 64 bits in a typical IPv6 address. Similar to Network ID and Host ID in IPv4.

DHCP - Dynamic Host Configuration Protocol. A client/server protocol that automatically provides an IP host with its IP address and other related configuration information such as the subnet mask and default gateway.

DHCP reservation - Enables routers to remember the MAC address of a specific client, and assign it the same IP address whenever it connects.

dictionary attack - Attackers use automated software to break into a password-protected computer or server or to discover a file encryption/decryption key, by systematically entering every word in a dictionary as the password.

dielectric - A medium or substance that transmits electric force without conduction; an insulator.

digital certificate - An attachment to an electronic message used for security purposes. Commonly used to verify that the sender is who he or she claims to be, and to provide the receiver with the means to encode a reply.

digital signature - A type of digital certificate that allows a software, application, or plug-in publisher to identify themselves and verify the authenticity of their program.

DIMM - Dual inline memory module.

direct thermal printing - A digital printing process that produces a printed image by selectively heating coated thermochromic (thermal) paper when the paper passes over the thermal print head.

disk striping - Also called RAID 0. A storage process that takes the contents of files and spreads them in roughly even parts across the hard drives in the RAID array.

DisplayPort - A connection interface used primarily to transmit video to a display device. It can also transmit digital audio and other forms of data.

distribution frame - A passive device that terminates cables, allowing arbitrary interconnections to be made.

DLP - Data loss prevention software is used to prevent users from accidentally or maliciously sharing particular types of data outside your organization.

DMZ - Demilitarized zone, or perimeter network. A network zone that's under the organization's direct control but separate from, and less trusted than, the internal network.

DNAT - A technique in which multiple public IP addresses are mapped and used with an internal or private IP address.

DNS - Domain Name System. A hierarchical directory service that stores assigned domain names and their corresponding IP addresses.

DOCSIS - Data Over Cable Service Interface Specification.

domain (Windows) - Windows security groups in which users can share networked resources, such as Internet connections, file servers and printers.

domain name - The part of an email or website address on the internet that shows the name of the organization that the address belongs to.

DoS - Denial-of-service. Attacks designed to impair or block legitimate users' ability to use a network resource.

DRAM - Dynamic Random Access Memory.

DRM - Digital rights management. An electronic system that controls what end users may do with the content they have acquired. DRM software prevents users from selling or sharing that content.

DSL - Digital subscriber line. A family of related technologies that carry data as a separate, high-frequency signal over the same physical cables of a voice telephone or ISDN line, without interfering with the telephone service.

dual-channel memory - A DDR, DDR2, or DDR3 chipset on the motherboard providing RAM with two dedicated high-throughput data channels. These channels permit reading from and writing to memory to occur on distinct channels.

DVI - Digital Visual Interface. A digital-based standard designed for use with video projectors and flat-panel displays (LCDs, plasma screens, wide HD televisions). It transmits uncompressed digital video.

dynamic disks - Logical disks that have the ability to utilize multiple hard disks in the computer to provide disk redundancy and mirroring as well as an increase in performance and reliability. Native to Windows OSs and available in Windows Vista, Server 2008, and later OS versions.

ECC - Error correcting code, or error checking and correction. Allows data that is being read or transmitted to be checked for errors and, when necessary, corrected on the fly. Differs from parity-checking in that errors are not only detected but also corrected.

EDGE - Enhanced Data GSM Environment.

EFS - Encrypting File System. Allows encryption of individual drives and folders on any NTFS volume. EFS-encrypted files are unreadable to other users on the same computer.

Email spoofing - A social engineering threat in which the attacker forges an email header so that the email appears to the user as if it originated from a legitimate source. Spammers often use email spoofing to trick users into opening and responding to their emails.

EMI - Electromagnetic interference. Signal noise from electromagnetic sources that interferes with other equipment, especially data cables or wireless transceivers.

eMMC - Embedded multi-media card.

encryption - A security control method that uses mathematical processes to render data unreadable to those without the proper decryption key.

encryption algorithm - A mathematical procedure for performing encryption on data. Information is made into meaningless cipher and requires the use of a key to transform the data back into its original form.

ephemeral port - Also called dynamic port. A temporary communication hub used for IP communications. Created from a set range of port numbers by the IP software and used as an end client's port assignment in direct communication with a well-known port used by a server.

EPROM - Erasable programmable read-only memory.

eSATA - External SATA.

ESD - Electrostatic discharge. The sudden flow of electricity between two electrically charged objects caused by contact, an electrical short, or dielectric breakdown.

Event Viewer - An Administrative Tool used to check your computer's health or troubleshoot problems with the OS or software. "Events" are logged for a variety of situations on a Windows computer, including software installation and errors, operating system errors and updates, and user logons and logoffs.

exceptions - Firewall rules that apply to specific types of traffic.

expansion slot - A hardware interface that enables communication between your PC and expansion devices such as sound cards, network cards, and other connector cards.

ExpressCard - An interface for connecting peripheral devices to a computer, usually a laptop. The ExpressCard standard specifies the design of slots built into the computer and of expansion cards to insert in the slots.

extended partition - A primary partition that has been divided up into logical partitions as a means of creating more partitions than the four that would otherwise be possible.

F connector - A coaxial RF connector commonly used for "over the air" terrestrial television, cable television and universally for satellite television and cable modems.

Faraday Cage - An enclosure used to block electromagnetic fields, as in an antistatic bag.

Fast Ethernet - Also known as 100BASE-TX. A LAN transmission standard that provides a data rate of 100 megabits per second. Workstations with existing 10BASE-T Ethernet cards can be connected to a Fast Ethernet network.

FAT - File allocation table. A table that an OS maintains on a hard disk that provides a map of the clusters (the basic units of logical storage on a hard disk) that a file has been stored in.

FDE - Full drive encryption. A type of hardware-based encryption that encrypts all data on a drive, rendering it unreadable unless the key is entered during system boot or when it's connected.

ferrule - A ceramic, plastic or stainless steel part of a fiber-optic plug that holds the end of the fiber and precisely aligns it to the socket.

fiber coupler - A type of splitter, where multiple fibers on one end are fused to join at a single core.

firewall - A computer system or network component that is designed to block unauthorized access while permitting outward communication.

FireWire - Also known as IEEE 1394. A digital bus with a bandwidth of 400-800 Mbps. It can handle up to 63 units on the same bus, and is hot swappable. First developed by Apple in 1995.

firmware - A software program or set of instructions programmed on a hardware device. Provides the necessary instructions for how the device communicates with the other computer hardware.

fixed wireless - Wireless technology intended for fixed locations like residences or businesses rather than mobile devices. The ISP installs an antenna on customer premises, and attaches it to a wired or wireless LAN.

flashing - The overwriting of existing firmware or data, contained in EEPROM or flash memory modules present in an electronic device, with new data.

form factor - The size, configuration, or physical arrangement of a computing device. Commonly used in describing the size and/or arrangement of a device, computer case or chassis or one of its internal components such as a motherboard.

FQDN - Fully qualified domain name. The complete domain name for a specific computer, or host, on the Internet. Consists of two parts: the hostname and the domain name.

frame - A digital data transmission unit in computer networking and telecommunication. A frame typically includes frame synchronization features consisting of a sequence of bits or symbols that indicate to the receiver, the beginning, and end of the payload data within the stream of symbols or bits it receives.

FTP - File transfer protocol.

FTTB - Fiber to the Building. A type of fiber-optic cable installation where the fiber cable goes to a point on a shared property and the other cabling provides the connection to single homes, offices or other spaces.

FTTH - Fiber to the Home. The installation and use of optical fiber from a central point directly to individual buildings such as residences, apartment buildings and businesses to provide unprecedented high-speed Internet access.

full-duplex - Refers to the transmission of data in two directions simultaneously. For example, a telephone is a full-duplex device because both parties can talk at once.

global routing prefix - The network ID or prefix of the address, used for routing. The first three bits are "001" to indicate a unicast address

GPT - GUID Partition Table. A standard for the layout of the partition table on a physical storage device used in a desktop or server PC, such as a hard disk drive or solid-state drive, using globally unique identifiers (GUID).

GSM - Global System for Mobile.

guest OS - A leading digital cellular system that uses narrowband TDMA, which allows eight simultaneous calls on the same radio frequency.

half-duplex - The transmission of data in just one direction at a time. For example, a walkie-talkie is a half-duplex device because only one party can talk at a time.

HDMI - High-Definition Multimedia Interface. A digital standard used to transfer high-definition video and audio from your computer to a display device. Offers better quality than both the VGA and DVI standards.

heuristic analysis - A method employed by many computer antivirus programs designed to detect previously unknown computer viruses, as well as new variants of viruses already in the "wild."

hexadecimal - A positional numeral system with a base of 16. Uses sixteen distinct symbols, most often 0-9 to represent values zero to nine, and A-F (or a-f) to represent values ten to fifteen.

hibernation - Powering down a computer while retaining its state. Upon hibernation, the computer saves the contents of its RAM to a hard disk or other non-volatile storage.

host ID - The second part of a TCP/IP address that defines the host device (computer, server, printer, etc.). The host ID number is shared with the subnet ID.

host-based firewall - A piece of software running on a single host that can restrict incoming and outgoing network activity for that host only. It can prevent a host from becoming infected and stop infected hosts from spreading malware to other hosts.

HTPC - Home theater PC.

HTTP - Hypertext transfer protocol. The set of rules for transferring files (text, graphic images, sound, video, and other multimedia files) on the web.

HTTPS - HTTP Secure. A protocol used for secure web pages and sites. It includes encryption services.

hub - A simple network device that lets you connect multiple nodes in a star configuration.

hybrid drive - A magnetic hard drive with flash memory chips added to it. These chips act as a buffer for OS and application files, allowing the system to boot up and start applications faster.

hyperthreading - A CPU feature that simulates two logical processors on one physical processor by using registers to overlap two instruction streams.

IDE - Integrated Drive Electronics. Connect hard disk drives and optical drives to the circuitry of the motherboard. Two IDE drives share one data cable and when you install them, you configure one as the master and the other as the slave.

IDS - Intrusion detection systems.

IMAP - Internet Message Access Protocol .Used by clients to receive email from servers; never used to send email.

inheritance factor - An authetication standard based on unique biological user traits, including biometric technologies such as retina, iris, and fingerprint, and facial and voice recognition.

inherited permissions - Permissions that are given to an object because it is a child of a parent object.

IP - Internet Protocol. The communications protocol of the public Internet, many WANs, and most LANs. IP is part of the TCP/IP protocol suite, and the terms "IP network" and "TCP/IP network" are synonymous.

IP address - A unique string of numbers separated by periods that identifies each computer using the Internet Protocol to communicate over a network.

IPS - Intrusion protection system. A system that monitors a network for malicious activities such as security threats or policy violations. Its main function is to identify suspicious activity, log information, attempt to block the activity, and finally to report it.

IPv6 - Internet Protocol version 6. An IP used for carrying data in packets from a source to a destination over various networks. IPv6 is the enhanced version of IPv4 and can support very large numbers of nodes as compared to IPv4. It allows for 2128 possible node, or address, combinations.

IR - Infrared.

ISDN - Integrated Services for Digital Network. A set of communication standards for simultaneous digital transmission of voice, video, data, and other network services over the traditional circuits of the public switched telephone network.

ISO - International Organization for Standardization.

ITU - International Telecommunications Union.

ITX - Information Technology Extended. A family of very small PC motherboards from VIA Technologies.

key - In encryption technology, a random string of bits created explicitly for scrambling and unscrambling data.

KVM switch - Keyboard, video, mouse switch. Allows you to use one keyboard, mouse, and display device for multiple computers.

LAN - Local Area Network.

latency - In networking, how long it takes the network to respond to a request. A high performance network has low latency, and enough throughput to meet the needs of all of its users.

LCD - Liquid Crystal Display.

leases - In a DHCP server system, temporary but renewable assignments of available addresses allocated to clients.

least privilege - A security principle which requires that, in a particular abstraction layer of a computing environment, every module (such as a process, a user, or a program, depending on the subject) must be able to access only the information and resources that are necessary for its legitimate purpose.

LGA layouts - Land grid array layouts. Replace the pins on the bottom of the CPU with gold pads, called lands. In an LGA, the pins are located in the socket instead.

Link Layer - Also known as Network Access Layer or Network Interface. Defines how nodes communicate on local network and adapter level; it corresponds to the NIC on any given node.

link-local address - A network address that is valid only for communications within the network segment (link) or the broadcast domain that the host is connected to. Not guaranteed to be unique beyond a single network segment.

logical network - The information carried by a physical network, and the paths the information follows; in other words, it's the network as seen by the computers that use it.

Lojack - A data protection and theft recovery solution from Absolute Software Corp. that protects your device's data and can locate your lost or stolen device.

loopback address - A special IP number (most commonly 127.0.0.1) that points right back to the local host.

low-level format - A data erasure process that writes zeroes to the entire drive and restores it to its newly installed configuration.

LPAR - Logical partition. The division of a computer's processors, memory, and storage into multiple sets of resources so that each set of resources can be operated independently with its own operating system instance and applications.

MAC address - A unique identifier assigned to network interfaces for communications at the data link layer of a network segment. MAC addresses are used as a network address for most IEEE 802 network technologies, including Ethernet and Wi-Fi.

MAC table - A list of MAC addresses on the network, and which side of the bridge they're on.

Man-in-the-middle attack - A type of electronic eavesdropping where the attacker intercepts a communication between two systems. The attacks allow the attacker to read, insert, and modify information between the two systems in real-time.

mantrap - In physical security, paired doors that only allow one person to pass through at a time.

MBR - Master Boot Record. The information in the first sector of any hard disk or diskette that identifies how and where an OS is located so that it can be loaded into the computer's main storage or random access memory.

MDM - Mobile device management. The administrative area dealing with deploying, securing, monitoring, integrating and managing mobile devices, such as smartphones, tablets and laptops, in the workplace.

Micro-ATX - A motherboard form factor measuring 9.6 inches square or smaller.

millimeter wave band - The 60GHz band used by some new Wi-Fi devices. These frequencies support a very high data rate, but typically don't penetrate walls.

MIME - Multipurpose email extension. A specification for formatting non-ASCII messages so that they can be sent over the Internet.

MIMO - Multiple input, multiple output. A wireless technology that uses multiple antennas to simultaneously transmit and receive separate data streams on the same channel.

Mini-ATX - A motherboard form factor that's a slightly smaller variation of the full ATX, measuring 11.2 inches by 8.2 inches. Typically has fewer buses and memory slots than a full ATX motherboard.

Mini-ITX - A motherboard form factor that measures 6.7 inches square and has a single expansion slot.

Mini-PCIe - A small version of the PCI Express peripheral interface for laptop computers and other portable devices. Using standard PCI Express signaling, Mini-PCIe cards are designed for internal use, plugging directly into the motherboard.

mirroring - Also call RAID 1. A data storage technology that writes identical data to two or more hard drives, giving you a "mirrored" set of drives.

mobile hotspot - A small personal device that creates a small area of Wi-Fi coverage allowing nearby Wi-Fi devices to connect to the Internet.

modem - Modulator-demodulator. An electronic device that allows computers to communicate over telephone wires or cable-TV cable.

motherboard - Container for the electronic circuitry and connectors for the critical components of your computer. All computer devices communicate through the circuitry on the motherboard.

mSATA - Mini-serial ATA. Drive connectors that connect small form-factor (about the size of a business card) hard drives and solid state drives to the motherboard in ultra-portable laptops, netbooks, and tablets.

MSDS - Material Safety Data Sheets. See SDS.

multifactor authentication - A security framework that requires more than one method of authentication from independent categories of credentials to verify the user's identity for a login or other transaction.

multilayer switches - In larger and higher performance networks, switches that are capable of examining frame payloads to understand them on the Internet layer or even higher to the Application layer.

MU-MIMO - Multi-user MIMO. A set of multiple-input and multiple-output technologies for wireless communication, in which a set of users or wireless terminals, each with one or more antennas, communicate with each other.

NAC - Network Access Control. An approach to computer security that attempts to unify endpoint security technology (such as antivirus, host intrusion prevention, and vulnerability assessment), user or system authentication and network security enforcement.

name server - A computer server that implements a network service for providing responses to queries against a directory service. It translates an often humanly meaningful, text-based identifier to a system-internal, often numeric identification or addressing component.

NAT - Network address translation. A method of remapping one IP address space into another by modifying network address information in Internet Protocol (IP) datagram packet headers while they are in transit across a traffic routing device.

NAT Overloading - Also known as Port Address Translation (PAT). A modified form of dynamic NAT where the number of inside local addresses is greater than the number of inside global addresses.

native resolution - The resolution that gives the best image quality on an LCD.

NDP - Neighbor Discovery Protocol. In IPv6, the protocol used to find the physical address corresponding to a local IP address.

nested RAID - RAID levels that combine RAID 0 (data striping) with other RAID techniques.

Netbook - Small, lightweight laptop computers with low processing power and other intentional limitations. They are optimized for surfing the Internet, email, and social networking. The design focus is affordability over fast performance.

Network Access Layer - Also known as Link Layer or Network Interface. Defines how nodes communicate on local network and adapter level; it corresponds to the NIC on any given node.

network discovery - The process through which computers and network devices are able to find each other.

network ID - A portion of the TCP/IP address that is used to identify individuals or devices on a network such as a local area network or the Internet.

Network Interface - Also known as Link Layer or Network Access Layer. Defines how nodes communicate on local network and adapter level; it corresponds to the NIC on any given node.

network prefix - The first 64 bits in a typical IPv6 address.

NFC - Near-field communication. A set of communication protocols that enable two electronic devices, one of which is usually a portable device such as a smartphone, to establish communication by bringing them within 4 cm (1.6 in) of each other.

NFS - Network file system.

NIC - Network interface card. A computer hardware component that connects a computer to a computer network.

NIST - National Institute of Standards and Technology.

northbridge/southbridge chip - A northbridge is one of the two chips in the core logic chipset architecture on a PC motherboard, the other being the southbridge. Unlike the southbridge, northbridge is connected directly to the CPU via the front-side bus and is thus responsible for tasks that require the highest performance.

NTFS - New Technology File System. The file system that the Windows NT operating system uses for storing and retrieving files on a hard disk.

octet - A unit of digital information that consists of eight bits.

OLED - Organic Light Emitting Diode.

ONT - Optical network terminal. Equipment from the telephone company that terminates its optical fibers at the customer's premises. Using electricity from the customer's AC source, the ONT converts the incoming optical signals into electrical signals for telephone, TV and Internet.

overheat shutdown - Occurs when a computer case or central processing unit temperature reaches a critical level at which point the computer will automatically shut down to avoid permanent damage.

packet - A short, fixed-length section of data that is transmitted as a unit in an electronic communications network. Each packet contains the address of its origin and destination, and information that connects it to the related packets being sent.

PAN - Personal area network. A network covering only a very small area, sometimes less than a few meters across. Usually confined to a particular user's devices, a PAN lets you link them all together with unified network protocols and a standard physical interface.

partition - A section of a hard drive that is recognized by the computer and, when formatted, can be used to read and write data.

PAT - Port address translation. An extension to network address translation (NAT) that permits multiple devices on a local area network (LAN) to be mapped to a single public IP address. The goal of PAT is to conserve IP addresses.

patch panel - A device housing a row of modular jacks in front, and a corresponding punch down block in rear. Patch panels make it easier to create and change cross connects with ordinary patch cables, or to connect all of the network's drops to the central hub or switch.

payload - The part of transmitted data that is the actual intended message. It excludes any headers or metadata sent solely to facilitate payload delivery.

PCI - Peripheral Component Interconnect. A local computer bus for attaching hardware devices in a computer. It supports the functions found on a processor bus but in a standardized format that is independent of any particular processor's native bus

PCIe - PCI Express.

PCI-X - PCI Extended.

PCMCIA - Personal Computer Memory Card International Association.

peer-to-peer - A network resource allocation scheme in which each computer negotiates with all the others as an equal.

permission propagation - When changing the permissions of a parent folder, the process of applying the same change to all subfolders.

PGA - Pin grid array. A CPU socket layout in which pins on the underside of the CPU are inserted into the processor sockets.

phablet - A hybrid tablet and smart phone. Slightly larger than a smart phone, it's easier to view and interact with the touch screen, but the device is still small enough to fit in a large pocket or purse

phishing - An attempt to obtain sensitive information such as usernames, passwords, and credit card details (and, indirectly, money), often for malicious reasons, by disguising as a trustworthy entity in an electronic communication.

physical address - Also known as MAC address. A unique identifier assigned to network interfaces for communications at the data link layer of a network segment. MAC addresses are used as a network address for most IEEE 802 network technologies, including Ethernet and Wi-Fi.

piconet - An ad hoc network that links a wireless user group of devices using Bluetooth technology protocols.

PII - Personally identifiable information.

PKI - Public key infrastructure. A set of roles, policies, and procedures needed to create, manage, distribute, use, store, and revoke digital certificates and manage public-key encryption.

plasma - A flat panel screen that uses noble gases and phosphors to create color. An electrical current is applied to the gas, then a tiny bit of plasma (charged gas) illuminates a pixel on the screen.

platform virtualization - The creation and management of virtual machines (VMs). It is performed on a given hardware platform by host software (a control program), which creates a simulated computer environment (a VM) for its guest software.

platters - The circular disk on which magnetic data is stored in a hard disk drive.

plenum cables - Cables with special insulation that has low smoke and low flame characteristics. Plenum cable is mandated to be installed in any "air handling" space.

PnP - Plug and Play. A BIOS firmware feature that enables the computer to discover and configure new hardware, and manage any hardware conflicts that arise when new hardware is added.

PoE - Power over Ethernet. Instead of carrying Ethernet data over power lines, PoE carries electrical power over Ethernet cables.

POP3 - Post Office Protocol version 3. Protocol used by clients to receive email from servers. It is never used to send email. POP3 works best for accounts accessed only on one device, and uses TCP port 110.

port - A connection point or interface between a computer and an external or internal device. Internal ports may connect such devices as hard drives and CD ROM or DVD drives; external ports may connect modems, printers, mice and other devices.

port binding - A process through which a single port on a host can only be used by one application at a time,

port forwarding - Routing inbound traffic to local addresses based on the destination port. For example, all traffic addressed to TCP port 80 can be sent to the company web server, while traffic addressed to ports 20-21 is forwarded to the FTP server.

POS terminal - Point of sale terminal. An electronic device used to process card payments at retail locations.

possession factor - A category of user authentication credentials based on items that the user has with them, typically a hardware device such as a security token or a mobile phone used in conjunction with a software token.

POTS - Plain old telephone service.

PowerShell - A task automation and configuration management framework from Microsoft, consisting of a command-line shell and associated scripting language built on the .NET Framework and .NET Core.

PPP - Point-to-Point Protocol. A data link (layer 2) protocol used to establish a direct connection between two nodes. It is used on everything from dialup connections to SONET leased lines, and can carry IP, IPX, and other high level traffic.

primary partition - A reserved part of a Windows disk that's identified by a drive letter. The C: drive is often one primary partition; however, multiple partitions are created for a user's own organizational purposes or for booting into different operating systems.

private address - An IP network address that cannot be routed over the global internet.

promiscuous mode - And ipconfig mode allowing the interface to read all packets passing through the network segment regardless of where they're addressed.

protocol - A specific set of communication rules.

PS/2 - A six-pin interface used to connect older keyboards and pointing devices to a computer.

PSK - Pre-shared key. A shared secret which was previously shared between the two parties using some secure channel before it needs to be used.

PSTN - Public switched telephone network.

PSU - Power supply unit.

punch down block - A type of electrical connection often used in telephony. It is named because the solid copper wires are "punched down" into short open-ended slots which are a type of insulation-displacement connectors.

PVC - Polyvinyl chloride.

QoS - Quality of Service. Overall connection quality as seen by users of the network, especially as connected to some expected baseline. Generally includes performance, reliability, and availability.

RAID - Redundant array of independent disks. A way of storing the same data in different places on multiple hard disks to protect data in the case of a drive failure.

RAM - Random access memory. A temporary storage space used by the operating system and applications to pass information to the CPU for processing.

RC4 - Rivest Cipher 4.

refresh rate - A measurement of how often a display image is updated per second. It is expressed in hertz (Hz).

registered port - A port that can be used by ordinary user processes or programs on most systems and can be executed by ordinary users. Registered port assignments, numbered 1,024 through 49,151, are generally used with UDP.

Remote Assistance - A Remote Desktop application used for remote technical assistance connections, for example to let you access coworker's system and help directly.

Remote Desktop Connection - A client application that connects you to the desktop of a remote computer, controlling it as though you were physically there.

repeater - A physical network device that cleans and amplifies a signal.

resistive technology - A touch screen technology that uses two layers, a layer of glass and a conductive and resistive metal layer, with an electrical current running between them. The two layers are separated by spacers. When you touch the screen, the pressure on the screen makes the layers touch and there is a change in electrical current in that spot.

resolution - The number of pixels (individual points of light or color) displayed on a screen. Documented as horizontal pixels × vertical pixels.

resource - Anything you might want to access on a network. Resources can be files, connections, devices, or services.

RF - Radio Frequency.

RIR - Regional internet registry. A not-for-profit organization that oversees IP address space and the Autonomous System numbers within a specific geographical region. There are five regional RIRs across the globe.

RJ - Registered jack. A standardized interface used for network cabling, wiring and jack construction. Primary function is to connect different data equipment and telecommunication devices with services normally provided by telephone exchanges or long-distance carriers.

RJ11 - The most recognized of the RJ specification, as it was used in homes for analog voice telephone service. Has a six-position, two-conductor connector (6P2C) and it uses only the center two contacts.

RJ45 - Commonly used for Ethernet over twisted pair networking applications with Category 5 cables. Also applied in telephone systems for high-speed modem applications. Has an eight-position, eight-conductor connector (8P8C), and uses all eight contacts.

ROM - Read-only memory. Computer hardware that stores programs or data that cannot be added to, modified, or deleted.

router - A device that forwards data packets along networks. A router is connected to at least two networks, commonly two LANs or WANs or a LAN and its ISP's network.

routing table - The set of rules and data that the router uses to map its surroundings. On a large network this could be a lot of information, including planning several hops across multiple routers.

SAN - Storage area network. A network that provides access to consolidated, block level data storage. Primarily used to enhance storage devices, such as disk arrays, tape libraries, and optical jukeboxes, accessible to servers so that the devices appear to the operating system as locally attached devices.

sandbox - A type of software testing environment that enables the isolated execution of software or programs for independent evaluation, monitoring or testing. May be known as a test server, development server, or working directory.

SATA - Serial ATA.

SC - Subscriber connector, or standard connector. Square bodied optical connector with a push/pull snap. Commonly two are clipped together in a duplex SC-DC format.

scope - The distance an IPv6 address is relevant across the wider network. The scope of an address can usually be easily told from its network ID.

screen inverter - A small circuit board attached to the display screen on a laptop computers. The inverter takes direct current from the motherboard and converts it into alternating current which is the electrical current used to control the pixels and generate the images on screen.

screen lock - A security feature for computers and mobile devices that helps prevent unauthorized access to the device. Requires a specific action or sequence of actions to be correctly performed by anyone attempting to use a lockscreen-protected device.

SDS - Safety Data Sheets. Documentation that provides safety and health information about chemical products, including health risks and storage, disposal recommendations, and procedures for containing a leak or a spill.

SDSL - Symmetric Digital Subscriber Line. A type of DSL that has the same bit rate in both directions. Compared to Asymmetric DSL (ADSL), SDSL is better for businesses that need to host data but don't need the performance or service guarantees of traditional enterprise connections.

SECC - Single Edge Contact Cartridge.

secure boot - A UEFI feature that verifies an operating system's boot loader is electronically signed by the vendor before it loads. This prevents malware, such as a rootkit, from hijacking your boot process.

SEP - Single Edge Processor.

server - A computer designed to process requests and deliver data to other (client) computers over a local network or the internet. There are a number of categories of servers, including print servers, file servers, network servers and database servers.

SFF - Small form factor.

shadow copy - A Windows technology that allows taking manual or automatic backup copies or snapshots of computer files or volumes, even when they are in use.

shoulder surfing - A security threat in which a person observes a user entering private information in their computer.

SIMM - Single inline memory module. A type of RAM module that has memory chips on one side of the package and supports 32- bit data transfer. SIMMs must be installed in in-line pairs.

Sleep - A power option that saves your work to RAM and powers off your computer. When you choose Sleep, your computer will resume very quickly, almost as if you pressed a Pause button.

smart card - A small plastic card, typically about the size of a credit card, which stores user authentication information.

SMB - Server Message Block.

SMTP - Simple Mail Transfer Protocol.

SNMP - Simple Network Management Protocol.

social engineering - The use of deception to manipulate individuals into divulging confidential or personal information that may be used for fraudulent purposes.

SODIMM - Small outline dual in-line memory module.

SOHO - Small Office/Home Office.

Southbridge chip - See "northbridge/southbridge chip."

spread spectrum - A technique that breaks wireless transmission into a large number of subchannels on nearby frequencies. This way, interference on one frequency won't block everything and the overall bandwidth is much higher.

SSH - Secure Shell. Encrypted replacement for Telnet and FTP. Includes Secure Copy Protocol (SCP) and Secure Shell FTP (SFTP)

SSID - Service set identifier. In a Wi-Fi access point, a string of up to 32 octets that can be used to uniquely identify it to clients.

SSL - Secure Sockets Layer. The standard security technology for establishing an encrypted link between a web server and a browser. This link ensures that all data passed between the web server and browsers remain private and integral.

SSO - Single sign-on. Systems that allow one set of user credentials to give access to a large number of services.

STB - Set-top box.

STP - Shielded twisted-pair.

STU - Set-top unit.

subnet - An identifiably separate part of an organization's network. Typically, a subnet may represent all the machines at one geographic location, in one building, or on the same local area network (LAN).

subnet mask - A 32-bit number that masks an IP address, and divides the IP address into network address and host address. Made by setting network bits to all "1"s and setting host bits to all "0"s.

surface acoustic wave technology - A touch screen technology that uses a glass panel with a receiving and a sending transducer mounted along the sides of the panel. A transducer converts one form of energy to another.

system ports - Ports 0-1023 in the IANA port range list. These are assigned to the most universal and accepted TCP/IP standard applications, or applications the IANA expects to become standards. Also called "well-known ports" and "privileged ports."

system restore - A malware removal tool that saves and restores system files and settings, allowing you to recover from some harmful changes (even those you might accidentally cause in the cleanup process).

tailgating - Also known as piggybacking. Getting into a secure area by tagging along right behind someone who has legitimate access, with or without their knowledge.

TCP - Transmission Control Protocol.

TCP/IP - The language a computer uses to access the Internet. It consists of a suite of protocols designed to establish a network of networks to provide a host with access to the Internet.

TDR - Time domain reflectometer. An electronic instrument that characterizes and locates faults in metallic cables (for example, twisted pair wire or coaxial cable). Can also be used to locate discontinuities in a connector, printed circuit board, or any other electrical path.

terminal adapter - A device that connects a terminal (computer) to the ISDN network. It therefore fulfills a similar function to the ones a modem has on the POTS network, and is therefore sometimes called an ISDN modem.

tethering - The practice of using a mobile device (such as a smartphone) as a modem to connect another device (such as a laptop or another mobile phone) to the Internet. To do so, the phone must have mobile data enabled.

thermal transfer - A printing technology that uses ribbon printer cartridges containing waxy ink. The print head heats the ink on the ribbon and transfers it to the paper.

thin client - A networked computer with few locally stored programs and a heavy dependence on network resources. It may have very limited resources of its own, perhaps operating without auxiliary drives or even software applications. Typically, a thin client is one of many network computers that share computation needs by using the resources of one server.

throughput - The amount of traffic that can pass through a network in a given amount of time.

Thunderbolt - An Apple technology developed to replace FireWire. It combines PCIe and DisplayPort into one serial bus, allowing it to transmit and receive data, video, audio, network data, and power.

TKIP - Temporal Key Integrity Protocol. An encryption protocol included as part of the IEEE 802.11i standard for WLANs. Designed to provide more secure encryption than the notoriously weak WEP, the original WLAN security protocol.

TLS - Transport Layer Security.

toner probe - A connectivity-testing tool that can be used to trace and identify a wire along its entire length.

TPM - Trusted Platform Module. A microchip installed on the motherboard of desktop and portable computers. It stores cryptographic information (such as encryption keys) and communicates with the rest of the system using a hardware bus.

translating bridge - A type of bridge that interconnects two different types of LAN protocols, such as Ethernet and Token Ring.

UDP - User Datagram Protocol. Part of the Internet Protocol suite used by programs running on different computers on a network. Used to send short messages called datagrams. Overall, it is an unreliable, connectionless protocol.

UEFI - Unified Extensible Firmware Interface.

Ultrabook - Thin and light-weight laptops that incorporate the touch-screen feature of a tablet PC.

UPnP - Universal Plug and Play. A set of networking protocols that permits networked devices (such as personal computers, printers, Internet gateways, Wi-Fi access points, and mobile devices) to seamlessly discover each other's presence on the network and establish functional network services for data sharing, communications, and entertainment.

USB - Universal Serial Bus. A common interface that enables communication between devices and a host controller such as a PC. Connects peripheral devices such as digital cameras, mice, keyboards, printers, scanners, media devices, external hard drives, and flash drives.

UTM - Unified threat management. An approach to security management that allows an administrator to monitor and manage a wide variety of security-related applications and infrastructure components through a single management console.

UTP - Unshielded twisted-pair. A popular type of cable that consists of two unshielded wires twisted around each other. Due to its low cost, UTP cabling is used extensively for local-area networks (LANs) and telephone connections.

VGA - Video Graphics Array. An older standard used to connect a display device to your computer. VGA and its associated evolutionary standards, such as SVGA, are analog standards.

virtual desktop - A computer operating system that does not run directly on the endpoint hardware from which a user accesses it. Virtual desktops are accessible through client software installed directly on an endpoint, which presents the desktop to the user and allows them to interact with it.

virtualization - The process of creating a virtual (rather than actual) version of a device or resource, such as a server, storage device, network or even an operating system where the framework divides the resource into one or more execution environments.

VM - Virtual machine. An operating system (OS) or application environment that is installed on software, which imitates dedicated hardware. The end user has the same experience on a virtual machine as they would have on dedicated hardware.

VoIP - Voice over IP. A category of hardware and software that enables people to use the Internet as the transmission medium for telephone calls by sending voice data in packets using IP rather than by traditional circuit transmissions of the PSTN.

VPN - Virtual private network. A network that is constructed using public wires (usually the internet) to connect remote users or regional offices to an organization's private, internal network.

WAN - Wide Area Network. A network that extends over a very large area, with nodes in multiple cities or countries.

WAP - Wireless access point. A hardware device or configured node on a LAN that allows wireless capable devices and wired networks to connect through a wireless standard, including Wi-Fi or Bluetooth.

WEP - Wired Equivalent Privacy. A security protocol, specified in IEEE Wi-Fi standard 802.11b, that 's designed to provide a WLAN with a level of security and privacy comparable to what is usually expected of a wired LAN.

WiMAX - Worldwide Interoperability for Microwave Access.

WinPE - Windows Preinstallation Environment. A "light" version of Windows used for the deployment of PCs, workstations, and servers, or troubleshooting an operating system while it is offline.

WINS - Windows Internet Name Service.

wireless analyzer - A specialized appliance or an app on another mobile device used to verify signal problems.

wireless repeater - A device that takes an existing signal from a wireless router or wireless access point and rebroadcasts it to create a second network.

WLAN - Wireless LAN.

workgroup - A peer-to-peer network using Microsoft software. A workgroup allows all participating and connected systems to access shared resources such as files, system resources and printers.

WPA - Wi-Fi Protected Access. A security standard for users of computing devices equipped with wireless internet connections. It improved upon and replaced the original Wi-Fi security standard, Wired Equivalent Privacy (WEP).

WPS - Wi-Fi Protected Setup. A network security standard to create a secure wireless home network.

zero-day attack - A security threat in which attackers exploit a software vulnerability before the vendor becomes aware of it and can issue a fix or patch.

zombie computer - A computer connected to the Internet that has been compromised by a hacker, computer virus or trojan horse program and can be used to perform malicious tasks under remote direction.

Alphabetical Index